Why Do You Need this New Edition?

If you're wondering why you should buy this new edition of *Progressions with Readings: Paragraph to Essay*, here are 10 good reasons!

① **Essay writing** is now presented in two chapters, one on the writing process and one on the rhetorical modes, with student models, questions for analysis, and writing assignments.

② **A new feature**, "Reading and Writing in Response to Textbooks," presents a brief passage from a current textbook together with a series of questions about usage related to the subject of the chapter and a writing topic asking students to write a response.

③ **All the ESL/ELL** material from the previous edition's appendix has been integrated throughout where appropriate and added to a recast "Tips" feature.

④ **More attention to critical thinking.** A new emphasis on critical thinking informs the approach to the planning, writing, and rewriting stages of the writing process.

⑤ **More useful study skills feature.** The 7e's "Succeeding in College" feature has been retained and updated to help students apply their writing classroom skills beyond the writing classroom and across the curriculum.

⑥ **Updated terminology and refinements in grammar instruction.** Clauses are designated as "independent" and "dependent" rather than "main" and "dependent." Instruction has been added on joining two independent clauses with a semicolon, and other small additions recommended by reviewers improve the grammar instruction.

⑦ **Fresh student and professional writing.** Eleven student paragraphs and essays are new, as are three full-length professional pieces. Altogether, more than one-third of model paragraphs and essays are new.

⑧ **Consolidated "Writing Process Tips."** Steps and bulleted items in the 7e features have been consolidated and condensed. "Writing at the Computer," formerly a separate feature, has been incorporated into the new "Tips" feature, as has instruction for students for whom English is not the first language.

⑨ **Better exercises.** The content of some exercises has been refreshed and strengthened, most regularly with the addition of more academic and cultural content. Collaborative activities have been recast for individual work.

⑩ **MyWritingLab Integration.** MyWritingLab (www.mywritinglab.com) has been integrated throughout the book with a prompt at the end of each chapter to utilize Pearson's dynamic online learning system for additional practice.

Longman
is an imprint of

PEARSON

If practice makes perfect, imagine what *better* practice can do . . .

PEARSON
mywritinglab

MyWritingLab is an online learning system that provides better writing practice through progressive exercises. These exercises move students from literal comprehension to critical application to demonstration of their ability to write properly. With this better practice model, students develop the skills needed to become better writers!

When asked if they agreed with the following statements, here are how students responded:

97%
The MyWritingLab Student-user Satisfaction Level

"MyWritingLab helped me to improve my writing."   **89%**

"MyWritingLab was fairly easy to use."   **90%**

"MyWritingLab helped make me feel more confident about my writing ability."   **83%**

"MyWritingLab helped me to better prepare for my next writing course."   **86%**

"MyWritingLab helped me get a better grade."   **82%**

"I wish I had a program like MyWritingLab in some of my other courses."   **78%**

"I would recommend my instructor continue using MyWritingLab."   **85%**

Student Success Story

"The first few weeks of my English class, my grades were at approximately 78%. Then I was introduced to MyWritingLab. I couldn't believe the increase in my test scores. My test scores had jumped from that low score of 78 all the way up to 100% (and every now and then a 99)."

—Exetta Windfield, *College of the Sequoias* (MyWritingLab student user)

TO PURCHASE AN ACCESS CODE, GO TO
WWW.MYWRITINGLAB.COM

Progressions with Readings

PARAGRAPH TO ESSAY

Eighth Edition

BARBARA FINE CLOUSE

Longman

Boston Columbus Indianapolis New York San Francisco Upper Saddle River
Amsterdam Cape Town Dubai London Madrid Milan Munich Paris Montreal
Toronto Delhi Mexico City Sao Paulo Sydney Hong Kong Seoul Singapore Taipei Tokyo

Acquisitions Editor: Matthew Wright
Development Manager: Mary Ellen Curley
Development Editor: Ann Hofstra Grogg
Senior Supplements Editor: Donna Campion
Marketing Manager: Thomas DeMarco
Production Manager: Eric Jorgensen
Project Coordination, Text Design, and Electronic Page Makeup: Electronic
    Publishing Services Inc., NYC
Cover Design/Manager: Wendy Ann Fredericks
Cover Photo: ©istockphoto.com
Photo Researcher: Linda Sykes
Senior Manufacturing Buyer: Alfred C. Dorsey
Printer and Binder: Edwards Brothers, Inc.
Cover Printer: Demand Production Center

For permission to use copyrighted material, grateful acknowledgment is made to the copyright holders on page 489, which are hereby made part of this copyright page.

Library of Congress Cataloging-in-Publication Data
Clouse, Barbara Fine.
    Progressions with readings : paragraph to essay / Barbara Fine Clouse.—8th ed.
        p. cm.
    Includes index.
    ISBN 978-0-205-66604-1
    1. English language—Rhetoric. 2. English language—Grammar—Problems, exercises, etc.
  3. English language—Paragraphs—Problems, exercises, etc. 4. College readers.
  5. Report writing.   I. Title.
    PE1408.C5355 2009
808'.042—dc22   2009024848

12345678910—EDW—12 11 10 09

Longman
is an imprint of

www.pearsonhighered.com

ISBN-13: 978-0-205-66604-1
ISBN-10: 0-205-66604-3

In loving memory of Faye Thomas Clouse

Contents

PART SIX   From Reading to Writing

Checklists

Tips

Strategies for Learning from Textbooks

Strategies for Succeeding in College

Preface

Through seven editions, *Progressions with Readings* has helped students develop effective writing procedures, write clear sentences, craft strong paragraphs and essays, and revise and edit their own writing. This new edition retains the successful features of past editions and creates an even stronger text with enhanced coverage of the essay and new material that makes the connection between reading and writing, helps students learn critical thinking strategies, integrates cross-curricular content, gives new attention to visual learning, and adds updated, high-interest examples and exercises.

COMPREHENSIVE COVERAGE OF THE WRITING PROCESS

- A thorough discussion of the writing process includes a range of strategies for planning, revising, and editing for students to sample as they discover the ones that work well for them. Many of the strategies are for students who compose at the computer.
- A student work-in-progress illustrates the composing process with extensive annotations.
- Writing process tips help students complete assignments successfully.

COMPLETE COVERAGE OF THE PARAGRAPH AND ESSAY

- In-depth coverage of writing paragraphs and essays is anchored by instruction in the patterns of development.
- A generous number of writing prompts, including topics that call for combining patterns and ones that call for responding to images, offer a variety of writing opportunities.
- Checklists and tips support students and help them write strong paragraphs and essays.
- Material on combining patterns of development, in both paragraphs and essays, emphasizes the versatility of the patterns.
- Marginal notes highlight main points and answer frequently asked student questions.

AN EMPHASIS ON SENTENCE SKILLS AND EDITING

- Explanations of grammar and usage are clear, concise, and accessible.
- Students learn specific strategies for finding and eliminating the most common errors.

- A generous number and variety of exercises offer many opportunities to hone editing skills. Many of the exercises are high-interest, whole and continuous discourse with cultural and academic content.
- Exercises based on textbook excerpts help students recognize the application of their learning across the curriculum.
- A Learning from Textbook feature helps students connect chapter instruction to textbook material they will encounter in other courses.

AN EMPHASIS ON READING AND ACADEMIC SUCCESS

- Two chapters provide important instruction in reading and writing in response to reading.
- Targeted instruction for reading textbooks helps students succeed in all their courses.
- Detailed coverage of active reading helps students in their writing classes and across the curriculum.
- Professional essays appear with study questions, including critical thinking questions, and writing topics.
- Instruction in writing summaries and essay examination answers helps students learn important academic success skills.
- Learning from Textbooks features help students connect chapter instruction to textbook material in other courses.
- Succeeding in College features in every chapter help students apply their learning beyond the writing classroom and develop strategies for success in all their classes.

NEW TO THE EIGHTH EDITION

This new eighth edition of *Progressions with Readings* is an ambitious revision that reflects new teaching approaches and new student interests. It builds on the success of past editions by implementing important research on the connection between reading and writing, on critical thinking strategies, and on integrated cross-curricular content. It gives more attention to visual learning, and it includes updated, high-interest examples and exercises that will better engage students.

- Essay writing is now covered in two chapters for greater instructional range and more practice reading and writing essays. This enhanced coverage adds combining patterns of development to help students use the rhetorical patterns to fulfill their writing purposes.
- A new emphasis on critical thinking helps students bring thoughtful analysis to the planning and writing stages of composition.
- Analysis and response questions that now follow the student essays strengthen the reading–writing connection and help students identify key features of these writings.
- To strengthen further the connection between reading and writing, the last question after each student essay asks students to write a paragraph of personal response or commentary.

- A new Learning from Textbooks feature relates chapter instruction to textbook content across the curriculum. This feature, along with the instruction on reading in Chapter 26, motivates students by helping them connect their learning to other courses.

- The academic content in new exercises further enhances the cross-curricular component of the text.

- Enhanced discussions of key points, including topic sentences, generating supporting details using the journalist's questions, joining independent clauses with a semicolon, and specific word choice offer students clearer, more extensive instruction.

- Updated terminology now defines clauses as "independent" and "dependent" and "lead-in" as "hook."

- English as a second language instruction is now integrated throughout the text so it does not appear marginalized.

- New student and professional writings on current topics freshen the text and increase its appeal, as do new images with accompanying, updated writing assignments.

- Improved writing prompts will engage student interest.

- Many revised exercises include more academic and topical content to broaden their appeal and usefulness.

- The diagnostic self-assessment exercises have been eliminated, and the collaborative activities have been recast as individual exercises for greater flexibility and tighter focus.

- The Sentence Skills Workshop, tightened and renamed "Editing Workshop," has been moved to an appendix.

- To make them more useful, ready references, Tips boxes are shorter and more focused.

- Redesigned graphics and charts strengthen the visual learning component of the text and create a more inviting look.

- A new brief table of contents on the inside front cover can help students find what they need more quickly.

- Links to MyWritingLab connect *Progressions* to this valuable Longman resource.

TEXT-SPECIFIC SUPPLEMENTS

A brand new Instructor's Manual with Answer Key (0-205-66606-X), written by William deDie of Kalamazoo Valley Community College, is now included as a key instructor resource. This completely revised resource includes teaching tips, classroom suggestions, answers to pre/post tests, and much more! Contact your local Pearson sales representative to receive a copy or visit http://www.pearsonhighered.com.

THE PEARSON DEVELOPMENTAL ENGLISH SUPPLEMENTS PACKAGE

Pearson Education is pleased to offer a variety of support materials to help make teaching developmental writing easier for instructors and to help students excel and succeed in their course work. Visit http://www.pearsonhighered.com, contact your local Pearson sales representative, or consult the book's Instructor's Manual for a detailed listing of the various supplements we offer.

ACKNOWLEDGMENTS

I am fortunate, indeed, to be part of a talented team. At Longman, my thanks go to Matthew Wright for overseeing this new edition and for his continued faith in the book. Once again, Ann Hofstra Grogg worked her editorial magic to improve the manuscript in many substantive ways. With Ann's guidance, all things are possible. Her grace, elegant edits, and knowledge continue to astound me.

I gratefully acknowledge the following reviewers, who gave me the gift of their experience, talent, and time: Kathleen Hickey, Dominican College; Terry Clark, Kennedy-King College; Tanya Olson, Vance-Granville Community College; Parvanak Fassihi, Boston University-CELOP; Nancy Davies, Miami Dade College; Virginia Nugent, Miami Dade College, Kendall Campus; Joseph E. Carrithers, Fullerton College; Roberta Moore, Edison College; Elizabeth Smith, Manatee Community College; Brian Spector, Northeastern Illinois University.

Finally, I thank my husband, Denny, for his unstinting support and understanding.

BARBARA FINE CLOUSE

Progressions
with Readings

CHAPTER 1

Planning and Writing

[handwritten note:] To be a successful writer, dunt work too fast and plan all your essays/ papers out.

What do successful writers do? First, let me say what they *don't* do: They don't [work] fast, and they don't produce a finished piece in one sitting. Instead, they [work] over time and in stages. Stage one is **planning,** which is deciding what to say an[d the] best order for ideas. Stage two is **writing,** which is putting ideas down in a preliminary form called a **first draft.** Stage three is **rewriting,** which is improving the draft until it is ready for a reader.

[handwritten note:]
1. planning
2. writing
3. rewriting

The Writing Process

STAGE 1: PLANNING
Decide what you want to say and the best order for saying it.
↓
STAGE 2: WRITING
Write your first draft.
↓
STAGE 3: REWRITING
Make improvements until your draft is reader-ready.

To be a successful writer, you, too, should work in stages. Do not expect your writing to roll off your pen or pop off the keyboard in perfect form. Instead, expect to work and rework a piece, gradually shaping it into a satisfying finished product.

You should also realize that different people favor different writing processes. Some people need to plan more extensively than others. Some writers like to get feedback, but others prefer to work alone. Some writers outline every detail, and some outline only their most important ideas. In truth, the writing process is best described as a variety of processes in the three stages listed in the chart above.

In this chapter, you will learn about the planning and writing stages, and in the next chapter, you will learn about rewriting. In this chapter, you will learn techniques for

- coming up with writing ideas
- arranging your ideas in a suitable order
- writing a first draft

PLANNING YOUR WRITING: GENERATING IDEAS

At first, you may have only a broad **writing subject** in mind—something like *education* or *television*. However, subjects like these take in so much territory that you would need to write a book to cover them. Therefore, your first task may be to find some aspect of your writing subject that you can handle in a reasonable (or the required) length—something like *final examinations* or *reality TV*. That manageable aspect of your writing subject is your **writing topic.**

Sometimes a writer gets lucky and a good writing topic leaps to mind, and all the right ideas spill onto the page in a burst of inspiration. However, such luck is extremely rare, so do not spend too much time staring at a blank page or computer screen. Do not wait for inspiration. Instead, go after the ideas you need with the techniques explained next. Try each one to learn which works the best for you, or use more than one technique. Sometimes combining techniques yields more ideas than using one strategy by itself. Know, however, that at this stage, ideas may be rough. Accept those rough ideas, because you will have time along the way to polish them up.

In addition to using the techniques explained next, keep your writing in mind as you go about your routine activities. Ideas can occur to you while you are walking across campus, washing the car, eating lunch, or taking a shower. Most important, no matter which strategy or strategies you use, give yourself enough time. If you wait until the last minute, you will not have time for ideas to surface.

Listing

When listing, do not evaluate how good your ideas are; write everything that occurs to you.

Listing can supply both writing topics and ideas to develop those topics. To list, spill out every idea that occurs to you without evaluating how good the ideas are. Just record everything you think of. One idea will lead to another until you have columns of useful and not-so-useful thoughts.

Here is a list developed by a student on the broad subject *athletics*:

football	*player salaries*
baseball	*player strikes*
basketball	*what sports mean to boys*
coaching	*betting*
training	*athletic scholarships*
college	*opportunities for women*
professional	*recruiting violations*
when I was cut	*preventing injuries*
* from the basketball team*	
great athletes	*Little League*
* (LeBron James, etc.)*	

Study your list to find a writing topic.

When you run out of ideas, review your list and decide what you want to write about. That's your **writing topic.** The student who wrote the above list decided to write about the time he was cut from the basketball team.

Next, list again—this time to discover ideas you can write about your topic. Here is the student's second list. Notice that he crossed out the ideas he decided not to include, probably because they were not closely enough related to his topic.

went to every practice—played well

really wanted it bad

was sure I made the team

~~*my father wanted it bad too*~~

after school, checked list—didn't see my name

~~*it was like the time I struck out in Little League*~~

cried all the way home

was embarrassed—all my friends made the team

Luis didn't talk to me anymore

~~*Jerrold also didn't make the team*~~

felt like a failure

lost friends because they were always at practice, etc.

felt sorry for myself and stupid

After crossing out ideas, you can determine a suitable order for your ideas and number them to reflect this order. The result is a **scratch outline,** a guide that tells you what ideas will appear in the first draft and what order they will appear in. Here is the student writer's list turned into a scratch outline.

You can turn a list of ideas into a scratch outline.

② *went to every practice—played well*

① *really wanted it bad*

③ *was sure I made the team*

   ~~*my father wanted it bad too*~~

④ *after school, checked list—didn't see my name*

   ~~*it was like the time I struck out in Little League*~~

⑤ *cried all the way home*

⑧ *was embarrassed—all my friends made the team*

⑩ *Luis didn't talk to me anymore*

   ~~*Jerrold also didn't make the team*~~

⑥ *felt like a failure*

⑨ *lost friends because they were always at practice, etc.*

⑦ *felt sorry for myself and stupid*

Practice 1.1

Assume you will write about a person you admire. The subject can be a famous person, a friend, a relative, a teacher, a coach, or anyone you regard highly. To decide whom you will write about, use the space below to list five people you admire for any reason at all.

1. _____

2. _____

3. _____

4. _____

5. _____

Study your list and select the person you want to write about. Using a separate sheet of paper, spend about ten minutes listing to discover the reasons you admire this person. Write three of these reasons in the spaces provided.

1. _____

2. _____

3. _____

Brainstorming

To brainstorm, ask questions.

Brainstorming is asking questions. The answers can help you move from a writing subject to a writing topic, and they can supply ideas to include in your writing.

Some of the following questions will be helpful and some of them will not. Each time you brainstorm, select the appropriate questions and disregard the rest.

Questions for Brainstorming	
▪ Who was involved?	▪ What is (was) the cause? (or effect?)
▪ What happened?	
▪ When did it happen?	▪ How is it made?
▪ Why did it happen?	▪ What are the physical
▪ How did it happen?	characteristics?
▪ How is it done?	▪ Who cares about it?
▪ Why is it important?	▪ How can it be explained?
▪ What can be learned?	▪ What controversies surround it?
▪ What is it like? (or different from?)	▪ What opinion was challenged or changed?
▪ What does it mean?	▪ Why is it right or wrong?

Here are the answers to some brainstorming questions a student wrote about learning that her brother was ill. Notice that the writer used some of the questions but not others.

- **What happened?**
  My brother was diagnosed with bipolar disorder.

- **When did it happen?**
  last year

- **What is it like?**
  It's serious and scary. When he is down, he can be suicidal. When he is up, he can be reckless and out of control with money, but he can also be lots of fun and very creative.

- **What does it mean?**
  He has to take medication and stay in therapy. The family has to watch him for mood swings and intervene if we see them.

- **What is the cause?**
  It's probably genetic and the result of a problem with his body chemistry.

- **What opinion was challenged or changed?**
  I have more understanding of mental illness and more compassion for what the mentally ill and their families go through. I used to think my brother was irresponsible, but now I know he can't help how he acts.

When the writer studied her brainstorming material, she decided to write about what it's like to have a mentally ill family member, using her own experience as an example. Select your topic on the basis of which answers are the most interesting or on the basis of what you have the most information on.

Study your brainstorming to find a writing topic.

Practice 1.2

Assume you will write about a difficult decision you made. (If you cannot think of a decision to write about, try listing on another sheet of paper.) After settling on the decision, brainstorm on a separate page for about fifteen minutes to uncover ideas for the writing. When your brainstorming is complete, study it and decide on a specific writing topic. Write it here:

_____

Now, in the spaces provided, record five ideas that could appear in your writing about a difficult decision.

1. _____

2. _____

3. _____

4. _____

5. _____

Clustering

Clustering helps you see how your ideas relate to each other.

Clustering can help you discover a writing topic *and* see how ideas to develop that topic connect to each other. To cluster, write one idea down in the center of a sheet of paper and circle it:

Around the circled general idea, write related ideas and connect them to the central circle:

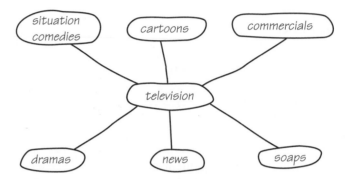

As you think of more ideas, write them down, circle them, and connect them to the ideas they are the most closely related to:

Continue writing, circling, and connecting ideas until you can think of nothing more. Do not censor yourself or evaluate your ideas—just write everything you think of.

Sometimes one clustering gives you enough ideas for a topic and a first draft. If not, study what you have and settle on just a topic for your writing. For example, the writer of the preceding clustering decided to write about television commercials. When you have a topic, cluster again, this time with your topic circled in the middle.

Write a second clustering to discover ideas for developing a topic.

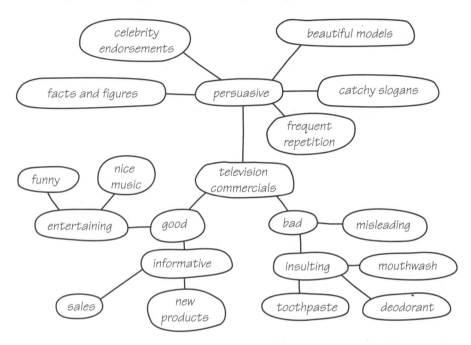

The writer of this second clustering decided to write about the techniques used in television commercials to persuade people to buy products. She used the ideas clustering around the "persuasive" circle in her writing.

Practice 1.3

Assume you have been asked to write about education reform. On a separate sheet, develop a clustering with "education reform" circled in the center. When you discover a topic, write that topic here.

_____

On a separate sheet, write a second clustering, placing your topic in the center. When you can think of nothing more to add to the clustering, record four of the ideas you thought of here.

1. _____

2. _____

3. _____

4. _____

Freewriting

When freewriting, do not stop, do not censor yourself, and do not worry about grammar, spelling, or neatness.

Freewriting is nonstop writing that works like this: For ten to fifteen minutes, write anything and everything that comes to mind. Do not decide whether your ideas are good or bad. Just record everything, even the silly ideas. Also, do not worry about grammar, spelling, or neatness. If you cannot think of anything to write, then write anything, even "I don't know what to write," the alphabet, the names of your family members, or your feelings at the moment. Eventually, more ideas will occur to you and you can record them. Continue this way, without lifting your pen from the page or your fingers from the keyboard.

When time is up, read your freewriting. Most likely you will have one or more usable ideas. These ideas will require shaping, but they can get you started.

The following freewriting was done on the writing subject "a campus issue."

> I'm suppose to write about a campus issue which shouldn't be to hard b/c there's enough of them. Parking, the cost of books, drinking, tuition ect. Which one? Parking Isn't such a serious issue. It doesn't seem worth writing about. Who cares? Drinking is serious. Parents would never believe how much their kids are drinking. Its pretty dangerous actually. Kids passing out, driving, hung over in class, generally trashed. I don't drink so I'm left out a lot. I think banning alcohol on campus is a good idea but most kids would freak out. They'd even transfer. I could also write about the insane cost of books but that's soooooooo boring. I could interview the book store manager and get good ideas though. I don't really care that much b/c I have a scholarship. I really want to write about alcohol I think. It's a big problem, a big issue, even a matter of life and death. There's lots of reasons to ban it. It kills students who binge drink and kids are so trashed half the time they can't really study. Let's see what else? I gotta think of more stuff. She said I could research so I could look up newspaper articles about students who died from drinking. Oh, I know, I could write about how colleges that don't ban drinking are responsible for the deaths.

Notice that the writer recorded a free flow of thought without worrying about grammar, spelling, abbreviations, or any other matter of refinement. Also notice that the writer discovered a topic (banning alcohol on campus) and ideas for developing that topic (students pass out, drive drunk, attend class hung over, can't study, and even die; colleges are responsible for the deaths).

You can write a second freewriting focusing on a topic you discovered in the first freewriting.

Many times, one freewriting will get you started with a topic and a few good ideas. Other times, you will need to do a second freewriting to discover ideas for developing your topic. Your second freewriting will focus on the topic you discovered in your first freewriting. Do not expect polished ideas in your second freewriting. Just look for raw material to shape. If your second freewriting does not unearth enough ideas to get you started, try brainstorming, clustering, or listing. Idea-generation techniques can be combined.

Practice 1.4

Assume you plan to write about ways you have changed in the past three to five years. On a separate paper, freewrite for ten or fifteen minutes to discover four ideas for this writing. Remember, do not stop writing for any reason, do not reject any ideas, and do not worry about grammar, spelling, or neatness. Record your ideas below.

1. _____

_____

2. _____

   _____

3. _____

   _____

4. _____

   _____

Journaling

A journal is not a diary for recording what happened during the day. In a journal, you explore ideas and feelings. Journal writing helps you solve problems, get in touch with feelings, vent anger, consider the significance of events, and discover what you think about issues. A journal can be an excellent source of ideas for writing.

To keep a journal, buy a notebook or start a computer file and write entries every day. Date each entry before you write and then take off—write anything that you are moved to write. Do not get hung up on spelling, handwriting, or grammar. This writing is for you.

Journal entries can be about anything, but here are ten possibilities:

1. Write about something that happened during the day that angered you, surprised you, cheered you, or moved your emotions in some way.

2. Write about a person you admire, love, hate, respect, or do not understand.

3. Write about how school or work is going.

4. Write about your goals.

5. Write about your family relationships.

6. Write about possible solutions to a problem you are having.

7. Write about changes you would like to make.

8. Write about something you recently read or watched on TV.

9. Write about what makes you happy or sad.

10. Write about what is important to you.

Make regular entries in your journal and you will soon have a considerable body of material. When you need ideas for writing, paging through your journal may turn up what you need to get started or keep going. The following sample journal entry shows how keeping a journal can help you think things through and discover topics.

> _October 4, 2009_ I heard a very disturbing news report today. A high school teacher in New York was tortured and killed by a former student who was after the man's PIN number so he could withdraw money from his ATM account. It is not unusual to hear about murder and robbery, but this report has me very upset. The teacher was hugely popular

In your journal, explore how you think and feel. You can also develop a storehouse of ideas for your writing.

FAQ

Q: What if I don't like the ideas I come up with?

A: Try changing your writing topic. If that is not possible, do the best you can with what you have. During writing and rewriting, you may discover an approach that makes your ideas more interesting.

at a tough inner city school. He was known as a kind man who really cared about kids. I heard some of his students interviewed. One student said that every student in the school was robbed as a result of this. Then I watched a film clip of the teacher dancing at the June prom with one of his students.

I've never believed in the death penalty, and I guess I still don't, but my belief is much less strong. The nineteen-year-old who has been arrested is legally an adult. If he is found guilty, I don't think I'd be upset if he were put to death. Loss of this caring teacher, who worked in a school many others wouldn't go near, is terribly sad. Loss of the murderer and torturer and robber doesn't strike me as so bad.

It's scary to find my views shaken like this. I used to know how I felt about capital punishment. Now I'm not so sure. The truth is, I want vengeance, and I don't even know the teacher who was killed. Is vengeance justice?

Working Together: Generating Ideas

Other people can help you when you need ideas.

Working with others can be as simple as asking people what they think about a particular subject or topic. Just say, "I have to write a paper on _____; do you have any ideas?" The response may get you started. Working together can also involve sitting down with one or more people and listing, brainstorming, and clustering.

To list with a group, assign a person to write down what everyone says. Then group members begin saying any and all ideas that occur to them while the recorder gets them down in list form. Listing with others is helpful because one person usually says something that prompts someone else to get an idea.

Brainstorming can also be done with others. Take turns asking questions while the person who needs the ideas answers the questions and records those answers.

To use clustering in a group, assign one group member to do the writing. All group members speak their ideas as they occur to them, and the group decides where on the clustering to connect each idea. Clustering in a group has the same advantage as listing in a group: One person's ideas stimulate the thinking of other people.

PLANNING YOUR WRITING: ESTABLISHING YOUR AUDIENCE AND PURPOSE

Your **purpose** is your reason for writing. Typically, you will write for one or more of these purposes:

to share your feelings or experiences with the reader

to inform the reader of something

to entertain the reader

to persuade the reader to think or act a particular way

Say you are writing about Thanksgiving. If you tell about family celebrations at your grandparents' house, your purpose might be to *share* your experiences with your reader. If you compare modern Thanksgiving celebrations with those of the nineteenth century, your purpose is to *inform.* If you argue that Thanksgiving should be a day of mourning because of our treatment of Native Americans, your purpose is to *persuade.* If you tell an amusing story about the time you made a fool of yourself carving the turkey, your purpose may be both to *share* and to *entertain.* From these examples, you can see that your purpose will influence the nature of your writing. Thus, an essay about Thanksgiving at your grandparents' house will be very different from one comparing Thanksgiving today and in the nineteenth century.

Like purpose, your **audience** (your reader) will affect the nature of your writing. Characteristics of your audience such as age, gender, race, socioeconomic standing, political views, religion, and family background can influence the detail you include. In addition, how much your reader knows about your topic and how much your reader cares about your topic will affect what you do. Say, for example, that you are writing to convince your reader to pass a school tax. If your audience has children, you can discuss improving education. However, if your readers have no children, you may want to mention the improved property values that result from better schools.

To appreciate how audience and purpose affect writing, consider the options for writing about DVD players. Possibilities include:

1. explaining how to program a DVD player (a manufacturer might write this in the owner's manual for the purchaser)

2. convincing someone to purchase a particular brand of DVD player (a store owner might write this in an advertising brochure for a potential customer)

3. writing an entertaining article on the problems of owning a DVD player (a newspaper columnist might write this for the readers of a daily newspaper)

4. explaining how the DVD player has affected family life (a psychologist might write this for the readers of *Family Circle* magazine)

5. explaining how the DVD player affects the movie industry (a studio executive might write this for the readers of an industry trade magazine)

Each of these writings will be different because the audience and purpose are different. The differences will be in the kinds of details, the vocabulary, and the approach. Let's look at each of these elements.

Kinds of Details   Purpose affects details. The piece about how to program a DVD player will include all the steps, but the piece convincing a reader to buy a particular brand will mention only that programming is uncomplicated. Similarly, audience affects details. If the reader of the piece is knowledgeable about electronics, then you may not need to explain where buttons are located, but this information would help a reader who knows nothing about the equipment.

Vocabulary   Your audience will determine the level of vocabulary. For an audience of psychologists, you can use the term *projection,* but for the average parent you may need to say "attributing your own faults to someone else."

Approach   Audience and purpose also affect the approach you take. For example, humor would be appropriate in the piece on the problems of using a DVD player that is meant to entertain the readers of a newspaper. However, humor would be misplaced in the owner's manual that explains how to program the device. This writing needs a serious approach. It might even include illustrations that the entertaining essay would not.

As you plan your writing, you can establish your audience and purpose by asking the questions in the chart on the next page.

FAQ

Q: Why do I have to identify a reader? Isn't my audience my writing teacher?

A: Sometimes your writing teacher will assign an audience, and sometimes you will have to identify an audience on your own. Either way, your instructor can assume the identify of different readers to prepare you for writing outside the classroom.

Your audience and purpose affect the kinds of details, the vocabulary, and the approach.

Questions for Establishing Audience and Purpose
1. Do I want to entertain my reader?
2. Do I want to inform my reader? If so, of what?
3. Do I want to persuade my reader to think or act in a certain way? If so, in what way?
4. Do I want to share my feelings or an experience with my reader? If so, what do I want to share?
5. Who will my reader be?
6. What does my reader already know about my topic?
7. What strong feelings does my reader hold about my topic?
8. How interested will my reader be?
9. Will my reader's age, gender, race, socioeconomic standing, political views, religion, or family background influence the response to my topic?

Practice 1.5

Find two pieces of writing: a newspaper article, a recipe, a magazine article, a business letter, an advertisement, an editorial, an owner's manual, a book or movie review, a textbook chapter, and so on. Analyze each piece and determine the intended audience and purpose and the effect of each on the kind of detail, the amount of detail, the vocabulary, and the approach.

PLANNING YOUR WRITING: ORDERING YOUR IDEAS

An important part of planning is arranging your ideas in an order your readers will find easy to follow. Three common ways to order ideas are **chronological order** (time order), **spatial order** (space order), and **emphatic order** (order of importance).

Chronological Order

For chronological order, arrange events in the order they occurred.

Chronological order is time order, when you arrange events in the order they occurred. You will use chronological order most frequently in story-telling to give details according to what happened first, second, and so forth. You can also use it to explain how to do something, when steps are given in the order they are performed. Details are arranged chronologically in this paragraph:

> The seven ten-year-olds arrived within minutes of each other. I explained that Gregory would be back in a half hour, so they all raced through the downstairs looking for the best hiding places. Julio and Emil hid behind the couch, while Heath and Tod crouched between the end table and wall. Jordan crawled under the dining room table, and Josh scrambled in behind him. Jeffrey found a perfect spot behind the front door. Soon we heard the slam of a car door, and we knew Greg was home. After he walked in the front door, the boys jumped out from their hiding places and yelled, "Surprise!"

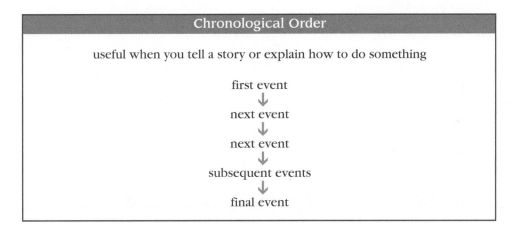

Spatial Order

With a **spatial order,** you arrange details according to their location in a particular area. Spatial order is especially useful when you are describing a place and move through space in some sequence: top to bottom, front to back, near to far, left to right, and so forth. Details in this paragraph are arranged in a spatial order:

For a spatial order, arrange details according to their location.

> When I entered the living room, I was appalled by what I saw. Empty potato chip and pretzel bags littered the coffee table and couch; their contents formed a layer of crumbs on the carpet. The antique crystal lamp on the table next to the couch was resting on its side, and the table itself held at least ten beer cans, all of them squashed in the middle. Beneath the table, the once-beige carpet was stained with a dark splotch that I knew would be permanent. Worst of all was the sight of my teenage son, who had been left in charge. There he was, sprawled across the couch asleep or unconscious—I wasn't sure which.

Spatial Order
useful when you describe something

outside	→	inside
front	→	back
near	→	far
low	→	high
top	→	bottom
left	→	right

Emphatic Order

For **emphatic order,** begin with the least important detail and move to the most important detail. Think of emphatic order as saving the best for last to provide a big finish. Emphatic order is useful when you want to convince your reader of something,

For an emphatic order, begin with your least important point and move to your most important. Also, you can begin with your second most important point and end with your most important.

because the most compelling reasons come at the end for a persuasive final impression. The following paragraph arranges details in an emphatic order:

> For several reasons, voters should pass the school levy when it is placed on the ballot during the August special election. First, the additional funds will allow the senior class to take an annual trip to Washington. More important, passage of the levy means the elementary schools can add more computer instruction to the curriculum. Without this instruction, our students will lag behind others in the country. Finally, if the levy passes, our school system can pay its debts and avoid a state loan that will jeopardize its financial well-being for years to come.

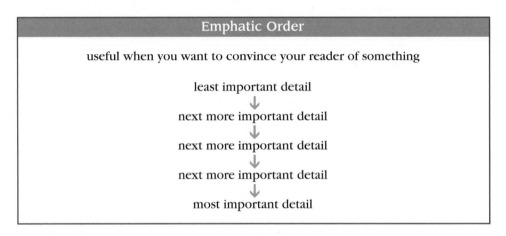

Emphatic Order

useful when you want to convince your reader of something

least important detail
↓
next more important detail
↓
next more important detail
↓
next more important detail
↓
most important detail

Combining Orders

You can use any combination of chronological, spatial, and emphatic orders.

You can use any combination of chronological, spatial, and emphatic orders in the same piece of writing. For example, look back at the paragraph that illustrates chronological order on page 12. Notice that, for the most part, the ideas are arranged according to what happened first, second, third, and so forth. However, notice that a spatial order is also used when the paragraph explains where the children hid (between the end table and the wall, behind the front door, and so forth).

Now look again at the paragraph illustrating spatial order on page 13. For the most part, ideas are arranged according to their location, but some emphatic order is also apparent. You can tell this because the second to the last sentence begins, "Worst of all." This phrase suggests that the most important detail is at the end.

Making a Scratch Outline

FAQ

Q: How do I know what order to use?

A: Your writing topic will often suggest the order of your details. For example, if you are telling a story, you will use chronological order. When you are unsure of the best order, try writing scratch outlines with different arrangements. Then use the one that works the best.

After you have generated enough ideas to get started and you have decided on a chronological, spatial, emphatic, or other suitable order, you can make a **scratch outline,** which is a list of the ideas you will include in your draft, numbered in the order you will write them. A scratch outline is helpful because it guides your draft.

To write a scratch outline, list the ideas you generated that you plan to include in your draft. Then number these ideas in the order you will write them up. Here is an example of a scratch outline, using the ideas from the idea generation list on page 3.

② *went to every practice—played well*

① *really wanted it bad*

(3) was sure I made the team

(4) after school, checked list—didn't see my name

(5) cried all the way home

(8) was embarrassed—all my friends made the team

(10) Luis didn't talk to me anymore

(6) felt like a failure

(9) lost friends because they were always at practice, etc.

(7) felt sorry for myself and stupid

Practice 1.6

1. For each paragraph, indicate whether the order of ideas is chronological, spatial, or emphatic. One paragraph has a combination of orders.

   a. The exasperated mother explained to her son for the fourth time why he could not get a puppy. First, she said, paper training the animal would be too much trouble, especially since no one was home during the day. Then there was the fact that puppies are expensive and the family's budget was too tight to allow for dog food purchases and veterinarian bills. Most important, she said that they live in an apartment and their lease expressly prohibits all pets except birds.

   The ideas are arranged in _chronological, emphatic_ order.

   b. Paper recycling is an interesting process. First, the paper is put into a vat of water with chemicals that remove the ink and turn the paper into soft pulp. This vat is called a *pulper.* From the pulper, the pulp goes to a machine that removes staples, clips, and anything else that is not paper. Next, the pulp is cleaned and mixed with water to form a thick paste that is spread on a metal sheet. There it is heated, dried, and smoothed. When the paste dries, it is crisp, new paper.

   The ideas are arranged in _chronlogical_ order.

   c. When I walked into the hundred-dollar-a-night hotel room, I was outraged by what I saw. Directly in front of me was an unmade bed, its sheets a dingy gray. The wall behind the bed was stained with a brown splotch that looked alarmingly like dried blood. There were no drapes on the window; instead, a tattered blind partially blocked the sun. I turned to check the bathroom to my right. There the situation was just as bad: dirty towels were on the floor; the sink was rust-stained, and the mirror above it was opaque with dust and lint. Furious, I stormed out of the room to find the manager and get a full refund.

   The ideas are arranged in _spatial_ order.

2. Assume that each of the following sentences is the first sentence of a paragraph, the sentence that presents the writer's central idea. In the space provided, indicate whether the order of ideas is likely to be spatial, chronological, emphatic, or some combination of these.

a. Zoning Fifth Avenue to allow the construction of a shopping plaza is a mistake.

The order of ideas is likely to be _____.

b. The kitchen of the model home is the most efficient one I have seen.

The order of ideas is likely to be ____*Spatial*_____.

c. The military should not be responsible for the development of experimental spacecraft.

The order of ideas is likely to be ____*chronological*_____.

d. My first day of college did not go well.

The order of ideas is likely to be ____*chronological*_____.

e. Anyone can learn to change the oil in a car.

The order of ideas is likely to be _____.

3. For each of the writing topics, use the idea-generation technique of your choice to develop at least three ideas. Do this on a separate sheet. Then, in the space provided, write the ideas in the order they are likely to appear in the writing.

a. Topic: Changes I'd Most Like to Make in Myself

First idea _____*my habit*_____

Second idea _____

Third idea _____

The order of my ideas is _____.

The idea-generation technique I used is _____.

b. Topic: A Time When Something Did Not Go as Expected

First idea _____

Second idea _____

Third idea _____

The order of my ideas is _____.

The idea-generation technique I used is _____.

c. Topic: Why the Internet Should (or Should Not) Be Censored

First idea _____*express yourself*_____

Second idea ____*freedom*_____

Third idea _____*get all ideas*_____

The order of my ideas is _____.

The idea-generation technique I used is _____.

CHECKING YOUR PLANNING

After generating ideas, establishing your audience and purpose, and ordering your ideas, stop and think about the results. Here are some questions to help you check your planning to be sure you are ready to write. If your answer to any question is no, adjust or expand on your ideas, returning to your idea generation strategies, if necessary.

Questions for Checking Your Planning

- Does my topic meet the terms of the assignment?
- Is my topic manageable?
- Do all my ideas suit my topic?
- Do my generated ideas suit my audience and purpose?
- Are my ideas arranged in a logical order?
- Do I have enough ideas to begin writing?

WRITING YOUR FIRST DRAFT

After you have checked your planning, you can put your plan into action by writing a **first draft,** which is the earliest version of writing. A first draft is not a finished piece of writing; it is not something you can copy over or type and hand to a reader. Instead, it is a first effort, an early attempt to get your ideas down on the page. It will have problems, perhaps with both content and grammar. For this reason, a first draft is often called a **rough draft.** So forget perfection. No matter how rough your draft is, you should feel encouraged because you have material you can work with.

Because the first draft is supposed to be rough, you can write it from beginning to end in one sitting. Keep your plan in mind by referring often to your list of generated ideas or your scratch outline. Keep pushing forward. If you have trouble starting at the beginning, start in the middle instead. If you still have trouble starting *anywhere,* try writing as if you were speaking to a close friend or writing a letter to a friend. If you get stuck, skip the troublesome part and push on. You can come back to the problems and solve them later. Finally, do not spend much time making changes as you go. You can make changes later, when you revise.

A first draft is your first version of a piece of writing. It is also known as a *rough draft* because it is likely to have problems you will solve later.

Practice 1.7

When you completed number 3a for Practice 1.6, you generated and ordered ideas for a composition about things you would like to change about yourself. Using those ordered ideas as a guide, write a first draft for a paragraph. The first sentence of your draft should be one of these:

The change I'd most like to make in myself is _____.
(You fill in the blank.)

or

The changes I'd most like to make in myself are _____

and _____. (You fill in the blanks.)

Develop your paragraph by explaining why you want to make the change or changes. Remember that the draft is supposed to be rough. (Save your draft, because you will use it in a later activity.)

OBSERVING A STUDENT WRITER AT WORK

In this chapter and the next, you will follow the work of Will, who wrote about the effects of moving frequently when he was a child. In this chapter, you will observe Will's writing process as he generates ideas, establishes his audience and purpose, orders ideas, and writes a first draft. In the next chapter, you will see how Will rewrites his draft to improve it.

Planning: Generating Ideas

You have learned that writers cannot sit around waiting for inspiration. They must go after ideas using one or more idea-generation techniques.

Here is the clustering and brainstorming Will did when he worked to generate ideas. When Will was asked to write about an event or a circumstance that had a significant impact on him, he decided to write about being the son of a career soldier in the army, about being what he calls an "army brat." To come up with a more specific topic, Will wrote the following clustering:

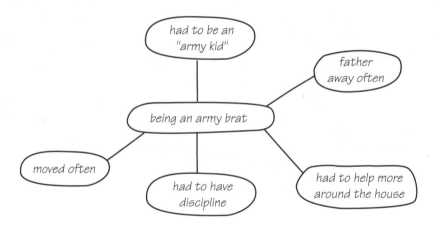

After considering his clustering, Will decided to write about the effects of moving frequently when he was a child. To come up with ideas to develop his topic, he wrote the following brainstorming list.

changed schools a lot

always behind or ahead in class

became self-reliant

lost friends

never felt I belonged

saw a lot of the country

learned to love change (?)

~~started to hate my father but outgrew it~~

Notice that when he reviewed his list, Will crossed out the last item because he decided he did not want to discuss it. Remember, during idea generation, you can add and delete ideas at any point. Also notice that Will placed a question mark next to a point he was not sure he wanted to discuss. Adding, deleting, and questioning all indicate thoughtful planning.

Planning: Establishing Audience and Purpose

To establish the audience and purpose for his writing, Will answered many of the questions on page 12. He decided that his audience would be his best friend, Tony. He characterized Tony as someone who knew that Will's father was in the army, but who did not realize how seriously Will was affected by the frequent moving around. He considered Tony to be a reader who would be interested in what he had to say. Answering the questions on page 12 also helped Will establish his purpose as informing Tony about an important part of his life so that his friend would understand him better. Checking the compatibility of audience and purpose and identifying the characteristics of the reader are part of careful planning.

Planning: Ordering Ideas

To develop a scratch outline that would guide his drafting, Will numbered the ideas in his brainstorming list in the order he would write them up. Notice that in the process of doing this, he thought of another idea, which he added to the list (tell about Mike).

1. changed schools a lot
2. always behind or ahead in class
5. became self-reliant
4. lost friends (tell about Mike)
3. never felt I belonged
7. saw a lot of the country
6. learned to love change (?)

Writing the First Draft

You learned that a first draft is usually rough and has grammatical errors because it is a first effort. The following is Will's first, rough draft. Although it has problems, it is a strong first effort. When you read it, you may notice that Will departs from his idea-generation material and scratch outline a bit. He did so because he kept thinking about his ideas as he wrote. He also kept his audience and his purpose in mind, and he arranged his details in a logical, chronological order. New ideas occurred to him as he wrote, and he used them.

One fact of my life rises above all others. My father is in the army. I spent my childhood moving from place to place. I lived from one end of the country to the other. I lived in New England, Alaska, and about seven states in between. This lifestyle has had a definite impact on me.

While travelling all over the country might sound exciting to you, it does have drawbacks. For one thing, I had to change schools every couple of years, which was really hard for me because I never knew how I would compare to the rest of the students academically. I also worried about fitting in and whether I would be treated like an outsider.

While the first few weeks in a new place were hard, the last ones were even worse because I had to say goodbye to friends who I know I would probably never see them again. This was the case when I had to leave my best friend, Mike. I met him my very first day of school in a brand new town. Mike was the only one who instantly made contact with me. We became inseperable from that moment on. Mike was like a brother to me, leaving him left a hole that no one has been able to fill. I'm not really sure why Mike and I somehow lost touch with each other, but I sure wish I knew where he was now because I would write him and try to renew our friendship.

Although there have been these disadvantages, my life as an army brat has had its good points too. I know much more about the United States and its people than the average person, I have seen more different kinds of people than anyone else I know except my father. I have become more self-reliant, I also learned how to cope with the loss of friends and how to make new friends fast. You can't move as many times as I have and be shy.

Long ago I decided I would never force my kids to move as often as I did, however, I notice that if I live in a place more than a few years I get restless. There is so much out there to see, I feel like I have only just begun to see it.

WRITING ASSIGNMENT

When the "little light" of inspiration did not go off in his head, the character in this comic strip responded by raiding the refrigerator. As you learned in this chapter, writers are blessed with inspiration on occasion, but more often, they have to go after their ideas.

Tell about a time you were inspired to do something, such as write an essay, compose a song, paint a picture, redecorate a room, take some kind of social action, or act in some other way. Describe the moment of inspiration and the activity that followed. As an alternative, tell about a time you were *not* inspired when you needed an idea, or a time you were stuck when you wanted or needed to take action. Describe the situation and your response to it.

Copyright © Shoe-New Business MacNelly. Distributed by King Features Syndicate.

Tips

PLANNING AND WRITING

- Use e-mail to discuss your writing subject or topic with others and get ideas.
- At the computer, use the cut and paste commands to arrange your idea-generation material into a scratch outline.
- If you have trouble writing even though you have generated ideas and arranged them in order, try speaking your draft into a recording device. Then play it back and transcribe.
- Don't be a perfectionist. Remember that a draft is supposed to be rough and that you can improve it later.
- **If English is not your first language,** tap into your rich cultural background. Consider your experiences in your birth country and how they have shaped your experience in the United States. Think about cultural similarities and differences. You have a cultural vantage point that can make your writing fascinating.

SUCCEEDING IN COLLEGE

Use Idea-Generation Techniques as Learning Strategies

Much of what you learn in this book can help you succeed in your other classes. For example, the strategies for generating ideas are also excellent learning strategies that you can use in many of your other courses.

- *Listing* can help you learn lecture and textbook material. After studying a portion of your lecture notes or textbook, stop, look away from the material, and list all the important points that you can think of. Then look back at the material to determine whether you omitted anything. If so, add it to the list in a contrasting color and study the list. Writing this way helps imprint the learning.

- *Brainstorming* is an excellent way to prepare for a test with a study partner. Each of you should draft questions about the material. Then trade questions and answer them. Discuss your answers, and identify where your information is sketchy or incorrect to target what you should study.

- *Clustering* can also help you learn material and see the relationships among ideas. Write and circle a major point you are studying and then add all the points you can think of that are related to the circled point. Check your text and lecture notes for omissions and add them in a contrasting color.

- *Journaling* improves comprehension and retention. Keep a separate notebook for each subject, and in each one record your reactions to reading assignments and lectures. Note how you can use the material, how it relates to your experience and learning in other classes, whether you agree or disagree with it, and any questions you have.

Write about It

Like writing, studying is a process. How do you currently study textbook material and lecture notes? Explain the process you follow, whether or not you are satisfied with the results of that process, and why. In the future, will you include listing, brainstorming, clustering, or journaling into your study process? Why or why not?

For more practice with planning and writing, go to www.mywritinglab.com.

CHAPTER 2

Rewriting

A first draft is often called a *rough draft* for good reason: It has many problems and requires considerable improvement before it is ready for a reader. Rewriting a first draft to improve it involves *revising, editing,* and *proofreading.* During **revising,** you improve the content, organization, and wording of your draft. During **editing,** you correct grammar and usage mistakes. Finally, during **proofreading,** you make a final check to correct mistakes after copying or typing your writing into its final form.

Rewriting
STEP 1: REVISING Improve content, organization, and wording. ↓ **STEP 2: EDITING** Correct grammar and usage mistakes. ↓ **STEP 3: PROOFREADING** Correct copying or typing mistakes.

REWRITING: REVISING YOUR FIRST DRAFT

When you revise, make changes in your draft to improve it. This revision process is important and often time-consuming.

During revising, consider content, organization, and wording from your reader's viewpoint. Do not worry about grammar and usage.

Revising is the most important aspect of any writing process, and for that reason, it is the most time-consuming part. Revising requires you to make a concentrated effort to see the draft from the reader's perspective and make substantial changes to improve content, organization, and wording. During revising, you do not attend to grammar and usage errors, such as misspellings, misplaced commas, and subject-verb agreement. Does that surprise you? Many writers mistakenly think that revising is merely a matter of reading over the draft and fixing a few misspellings or adding commas. Hold off on these corrections for now. Take care of them during editing.

When you revise, try to think like your reader. Ask yourself the questions in the chart that follows because the answers help determine what changes you should make in the content, organization, and wording of your draft. Those changes can be made directly on the draft, and they can involve scratching out, drawing arrows, and writing in margins. Revision is a messy process, but the mess actually indicates that you are revising thoughtfully and thoroughly.

Questions for Revising

TO CONSIDER CONTENT

1. Do I need to add details to explain or prove a point to my reader?

2. Do I need to delete details that are not related to my topic?

3. Is there anything my reader might not understand?

4. Are my details well-suited to my audience and purpose?

TO CONSIDER ORGANIZATION

1. Are all my details arranged in a logical order that my reader can follow?

2. Will my reader understand how my ideas relate to each other?

TO CONSIDER WORDING

1. Do I need to improve any word choice for clarity and an appealing style?

2. Do I need to improve the flow of my sentences so my style appeals to my reader?

Part Two of this book explains ways to improve content, organization, and wording.

Get a Different Perspective

You know what you meant to say. *You* agree with the points you are making. *You* understand how your ideas relate to each other. But the question is, will your reader understand these things? To assess that, you need to read your draft the way your reader will, and that means you need to view your draft from a different perspective. These strategies can help:

- Take a break for a day. This time-out helps restore your objectivity so you can view your draft like your reader and see its problems.

- If you wrote your draft by hand, type it before revising. You will get a new perspective because your work will resemble printed matter. You will be amazed at the number of problems you notice when your work is no longer in your own handwriting.

- Evaluate your draft from the perspective of a different sense, and read your draft out loud—or have someone read it to you. You may hear problems that you overlooked in writing.

- Work in stages. You may not be able to deal with all aspects of content, organization, and wording at the same time. Try attending to each separately. Or you might want to make the easy changes first and then make the harder ones.

Get Reader Response

Other readers can give you information about the strengths and weaknesses of your draft, information you can factor into your revision decisions. Try using this procedure. Give each of your readers a copy of your draft, along with a copy of the Reader Response Sheet on page 25. Before doing so, however, review the following suggestions.

FAQ
Q: How do I find a good reader?

A: Use readers who know the qualities of effective writing. Good choices include writing center tutors, classmates, and students who have already taken writing courses. Avoid friends and relatives who will not be honest because they fear hurting your feelings.

Suggestions for Reader Response

IF YOU ARE THE WRITER SEEKING INFORMATION

1. Give your readers a legible draft; recopy, retype, or reprint it if necessary.

2. If you want information not covered by the questions on the response sheet, write out additional questions.

3. Get the opinions of at least two readers. (Make copies of your draft so each reader is evaluating an unmarked copy of your writing.)

4. Do not automatically accept the responses. Instead, weigh them carefully and make thoughtful decisions about which responses to accept and which to reject.

5. If your readers disagree or if you are unsure if a response is reliable, ask your instructor for advice.

IF YOU ARE THE READER EVALUATING A DRAFT

1. Read the entire draft before writing any comments.

2. Explain why you react as you do. Rather than say, "Sentence 4 is unclear," say, "Sentence 4 is unclear because I don't understand why you believe more men should become elementary education majors."

3. Give specific suggestions for revision. Rather than say, "Add more detail," say, "Add more detail about why you were so angry when you did not make the team so I understand what caused the emotion." In other words, suggest a revision strategy.

You can also visit your campus writing center to find sensitive readers who will read and react to your draft. Writing center tutors will not "fix" your draft for you, but they will give you the benefit of reader reaction.

READER RESPONSE SHEET

Writer's Name _Silvana Al-Barwair_

Reader's Name _Phuong Tran_

1. What do you like best about the draft? Be specific.

    be specific

2. Do all the details clearly relate to the writing topic? Place parentheses around unrelated details.

3. Underline any unclear points. What can be done to clarify?

4. Place brackets around any points that need more explanation. What detail should be added?

5. Are ideas arranged in an easy-to-follow order? If not, what changes should be made?

    Yes, they are.

6. Place an ! next to any particularly effective word choice; circle any ineffective word choice.

7. Does the draft hold your interest? Explain why or why not.

    Yes, it does. Because it explains about the big university and I would like to transfer here too.

simecolon ;

Practice 2.1

Reread the Questions for Revising on page 23 and then proceed with this practice exercise.

1. Reread the draft you wrote for Practice 1.7. As you do, place a check mark beside anything you wish to revise. (Remember, do not be concerned with grammar and usage at this point.)

   a. Did you notice problems with the draft you did not notice when you wrote it?

   _____

   If you did, you have seen how setting your work aside can help you become more objective.

   b. How many check marks did you place? _____

2. Take a few minutes to type and print your draft; then reread it. On the typed copy, place a square beside anything you would like to change. (Do not be concerned with grammar and usage at this point.)

   a. Did you notice problems on the typed copy you did not notice before?

   _____

   If you did, you have seen how typing and printing a draft can help a writer.

   b. How many squares did you place? _____

3. Read your draft out loud very slowly. Each time you hear a problem you did not notice before, place an *X* by the problem.

   a. Did you hear any problems you did not notice before?

   _____

   If you did, you have seen how reading a draft aloud can help a writer.

   b. Did reading your draft out loud give you a fresh slant on your work?

   _____

4. Go over your draft again and answer these questions:

   a. Do you need to eliminate points that are not related to your topic?

   _____

   b. Do you need to add details so a point is well explained or proven?

   _____

   c. Do you need to make changes to make a point clear?

   _____

    d. Do you need to make changes to improve word choice?

_____

    e. Do you need to improve the flow of your writing because it sounds choppy?

_____

(Save your draft because you will need it for a later activity.)

Practice 2.2

Photocopy the Reader Response Sheet on page 25 and trade drafts with a classmate. Each of you should fill out a response sheet and then answer the following question:
    What did you learn about your draft as a result of getting reader response?

_____

_____

REWRITING: EDITING YOUR DRAFT

During revising, you may write several drafts before you are satisfied with your content, organization, and wording. Then, you can turn your attention to editing—finding and correcting any mistakes in grammar, punctuation, capitalization, and spelling. Careful editing is important because mistakes can distract a reader and create confusion.

    When you edit, ask the questions in the chart that follows. The chapter numbers in parentheses direct you to the relevant sections of this book.

Edit to find and correct errors in grammar and usage that detract from the effectiveness of your writing.

Questions for Editing
1. Have I written any sentence fragments? (Chapter 17)
2. Have I written any run-on sentences or commas splices? (Chapter 18)
3. Have I made any errors with verb forms? (Chapter 21)
4. Have I made any inappropriate tense shifts? (Chapter 21)
5. Do all my subjects and verbs agree? (Chapter 21)
6. Do all my pronouns and antecedents agree? (Chapter 22)
7. Do I have any faulty pronoun reference? (Chapter 22)
8. Have I avoided person shifts? (Chapter 22)

(continued on next page)

9. Have I avoided dangling and misplaced modifiers? (Chapter 23)

10. Have I used comparative and superlative forms correctly? (Chapter 23)

11. Have I capitalized correctly? (Chapter 24)

12. Have I punctuated correctly? (Chapter 24)

13. Do I have any spelling errors? (Chapter 25)

Parts Four and Five of this book explain various editing issues.

Get a Fresh Perspective

Has a reader noticed an error in your writing that you cannot believe you did not catch and correct yourself? You probably overlooked the mistake because by the time you were ready to edit, you had spent a considerable amount of time planning, writing, and revising your draft. As a result, you were so close to your work that you saw what you *meant* to write rather than what you actually *did* write. The following strategies can help you look at your draft with fresh eyes, so you are less likely to overlook mistakes.

- Take a break for a day to refresh yourself. This time-out will help you see your writing more clearly so you are more likely to notice mistakes.

- Read your draft out loud—or have someone read it to you—to take advantage of a different sense. You may hear problems that you overlooked visually. Be sure that you read exactly what is on the page, not what you meant to write.

- Read backward, from the last sentence to the first. Reading from the end to the beginning will help you see your work from a different vantage point, making it easier to spot errors.

- Work slowly. Place a ruler under the line you are editing and don't move it until you have studied everything in that line. Or use a pen or pencil to point to each word and punctuation mark. Linger a second over every item, and force yourself to pay attention.

Learn the Rules

Learn the grammar rules in this book, because you cannot edit with confidence if you do not know them. Pay particular attention to the errors your instructor marks on your papers, so you can make a special effort to learn the rules for correcting those mistakes. (The Personal Editing Profile on the inside back cover can help you keep track of your pattern of errors.) If you need help learning and applying the rules, visit your campus writing center.

FAQ

Q: Can a writing center tutor help me edit?

A: Writing center tutors will happily respond to specific questions. They will also explain grammar and usage points, such as how to find and correct fragments and when to use commas. They will *not* read over your writing to find and correct your errors—that is *your* job.

Practice 2.3

1. Review the Questions for Editing on pages 27–28. Which of these concerns have you had trouble with in the past? _____

2. Look again at the list of questions. Is there anything in that list you have never heard of before? Is there anything that you do not know the meaning of? If so, what?

_____

_____

3. What chapters of this text cover the concerns you noted in your answer to number 1?

_____

_____

4. When you completed Practice 2.1, Exercise 2, you typed a copy of a draft. Using a pen to point to each word and punctuation mark in that draft, edit very slowly, looking for errors in grammar and usage. Be sure to read what you actually wrote—not what you *meant* to write. Make corrections directly on the page, referring to Parts Four and Five of this book as necessary.

   How many errors did you find? _____

_____

5. Check the draft one separate time for each kind of mistake you have a habit of making. Place a ruler under each line as you go. If you are unsure how to correct any errors that you find, consult Parts Four and Five.

   How many errors did you find? _____

_____

6. What pages of Parts Four and Five do you think you should study first?

   _____ What pages do you think you should study second?

_____

REWRITING: PROOFREADING YOUR FINAL COPY

After careful editing, copy or type your composition into its final form. Before submitting your work to your reader, however, run a final check for copying or typing errors. This final check is **proofreading.**

Before you proofread, leave your writing for a few hours to refresh yourself and increase your chances of noticing mistakes. Then proofread very slowly, pointing to each word and punctuation mark. If you move too quickly, you will overlook errors. If you do find mistakes, ink in minor corrections neatly, if your instructor permits. A page with many corrections should be recopied in the interest of neatness. Of course, if you are using a computer, you can easily type corrections and print out a fresh page.

Proofread your final copy to check for careless errors made while recopying or typing.

OBSERVING A STUDENT WRITER AT WORK

In Chapter 1, you followed the planning and drafting done by Will, who wrote about the effects of moving frequently as a child. (To review that material, turn to page 18.) In this chapter, you will follow Will's rewriting processes.

Rewriting: Considering Reader Response

Will's teacher read his first draft and gave him the following written response to consider when he revised. First, reread Will's draft on pages 19–20. Then read his teacher's response and consider whether you reacted similarly to the draft.

Will,

Your topic interests me because I have always wondered how people are affected by frequent moves in childhood. However, I need some more details to better understand the impact on you. In paragraph 2, tell me more about fitting in academically and socially. I would also like to know more about your friendship with Mike. I can tell he was important to you. Perhaps you could say more about how you met and the nature of your friendship. This information could replace the detail about losing touch with Mike, since that strays a bit from your focus. I like that you give the advantages as well as the disadvantages of moving often, but I could use more detail to better appreciate the positive aspects. Your last paragraph makes an excellent conclusion. It really helps me appreciate the restlessness you feel.

1. Are any of the instructor's reactions to Will's draft the same as your reactions? Which ones?

   _____

   _____

   _____

2. Do you disagree with any of the instructor's reactions? Which ones? Why do you disagree?

   _____

   _____

   _____

3. Do you have any reactions to Will's draft that are not noted in the instructor's comments? What are they?

   _____

   _____

   _____

Rewriting: Revising the First Draft

Using his teacher's responses and his own ideas as a guide, Will revised to produce the following second draft. The changes are noted in the margin. Notice that Will focused on details rather than grammar when he revised.

One fact of my life rises above all others. My father is in the army. I spent my childhood moving from place to place. I lived from one end of the country to the other, I lived in New England, Alaska, and about seven states in between. This lifestyle has had a definite impact on me.

While travelling all over the country might sound exciting to you, it does have drawbacks. For one thing, I had to change schools every couple of years, which was really hard for me because I never knew how I would compare to the rest of the students academically. Sometimes I was ahead of the class and sometimes I needed tutoring to catch up. I also worried about fitting in and whether I would be treated like an outsider because my clothes were not right or I had an accent or I did not know the local slang.

(A) Sentence added to explain not fitting in academically.

(B) Words added to explain not fitting in socially.

While the first few weeks in a new place were hard, the last ones were even worse because I had to say goodbye to friends who I know I would probably never see them again. This was the case when I had to leave my best friend, Mike. I met him my very first day of school in a brand new town. I walked into biology class in front of twenty-five strangers, feeling that familiar fear and awkwardness as I made my way over to my new lab partner. Mike looked up from his frog and immediately made a wisecrack that made me laugh. As soon as school was over, we would meet in the woods behind his house and go exploring. We spent Saturdays biking around town, then we spent evenings at each other's houses. Mike was like a brother to me, leaving him left a hole that no one has been able to fill.

(C) Detail added on relationship with Mike.

(D) Irrelevant material omitted.

Although there have been disadvantages, my life as an Army brat has its good points too. I know much more about the United States and its people than the average person, I have seen more different kinds of people than anyone else I know except my father. I have fished alongside New England fishermen, and watched loggers in Washington and shrimpers in South Carolina. I have lived in an old farmhouse in the Midwest and in an old mill town in Ohio. I have played with kids whos houses line the shore of the Mississippi and kids who live in high rise apartments. Most importantly, I have become more self-reliant, I also learned to cope with the loss of friends and how to make new friends fast. You can't move as many times as I have and be shy.

(E) Sentences added to tell about people he met.

(F) Transition added.

Long ago I decided I would never force my kids to move as often as I did, however, I notice that if I live in a place more than a few years I get restless, almost as if I am ready to move on. There is so much out there to see, I feel like I have only just begun to see it.

(G) Explanatory words added.

To understand the kinds of changes made, answer these questions.

1. What do you think of the details Will added?

   _____

   _____

2. Do you think Will needs to add any additional details? Explain.

   _____

   _____

   _____

3. What does revision G contribute to the essay?

   _____

   _____

4. Did Will solve the problem of irrelevant detail? Explain.

   _____

   _____

   _____

5. Did Will make any ineffective revisions? Explain.

   _____

   _____

   _____

Here is the teacher's response to Will's second draft.

Will,
   You did an excellent job of adding explanatory detail; your new material about meeting different people is particularly helpful and well written. I would still like to know more about your relationship with Mike and your efforts to fit in socially. Those points seem important. When you revise, read your first paragraph out loud to hear the choppiness. You should be able to smooth that out. When you edit, look for comma splices.

Revising, Editing, and Proofreading the Draft

On the basis of his instructor's reactions to his second draft, Will did additional revising. Then he edited to eliminate errors in grammar and usage. The result was Will's final draft, which appears here.

On the Move Ⓐ

Ⓑ Because my father is in the army, I have spent most of my life moving from place to place. I have lived from one end of the country to the other, from New England to Alaska and about seven states in between. This lifestyle has had a definite impact on me.

Ⓒ While traveling all over the country might sound exciting to you, it does have drawbacks. For one thing, I had to change schools every couple of years, which was really hard for me because I never knew how I would compare to the rest of the students academically. Sometimes I was ahead of the class and sometimes I needed tutoring to catch up. I also worried about fitting in and whether I would be treated like an outsider because my clothes were not right or I had an accent or I did not know the local slang. Ⓓ If I spoke too much, I could unintentionally say the wrong thing because I did not know the local customs. If I said too little for fear of offending, I was considered shy or conceited. As a result, I could never relax and feel like one of the gang.

While the first few weeks in a new place were hard, the last ones were even worse because I had to say goodbye to friends Ⓔ I knew I would never see again. This was the case when I had to leave my best friend, Mike. I met him my very first day of school in a brand new town. I walked into biology class in front of twenty-five strangers, feeling that familiar fear and awkwardness as I made my way over to my new lab partner. Ⓕ Mike looked up from the frog he was dissecting and in a corny accent said, "Velcome, Igor—care for some lunch?" as he dangled the mutilated frog in front of my face. We were inseparable from that moment on. As soon as school was over, we would meet in the woods behind his house and go exploring. We spent Saturdays biking around town. Ⓖ Then we spent evenings at each other's houses. Mike was like a brother to me, Ⓗ and leaving him left a hole that no one has been able to fill.

Ⓘ Although there were these disadvantages, my life as an army brat had its good points too. I know much more about the United States and its people than the average person. Ⓙ I have seen more different kinds of people than anyone else I know except my father. I have fished alongside New England fishermen, and watched loggers in Washington and shrimpers in South Carolina. I have lived in an old farmhouse in the Midwest and in an old mill town in Ohio. I have played

Ⓐ Title added.

Ⓑ Introduction revised to eliminate choppiness.

Ⓒ Spelling corrected.

Ⓓ Detail added to further explain problems fitting in.

Ⓔ Sentence structure revised and tense corrected.

Ⓕ Mike's wisecrack given.

Ⓖ Comma splice eliminated.

Ⓗ Comma splice eliminated.

Ⓘ Tenses corrected.

Ⓙ Comma splice eliminated.

Ⓚ Spelling corrected.

Ⓛ Comma splice eliminated.

with kids whose houses line the shore of the Mississippi and kids who live in high rise apartments. Most importantly, I have become more self-reliant. I also learned to cope with the loss of friends and how to make new friends fast. You can't move as many times as I have and be shy.

Ⓜ Comma splice eliminated.

Long ago I decided I would never force my kids to move as often as I did. However, I notice that if I live in a place more than a few years I get restless, almost as if I am ready to move on. There is so much out there to see, and I feel that I have only just begun to see it.

Ⓝ Comma splice eliminated.

WRITING ASSIGNMENT

In Chapter 1, you planned a paragraph about a time you were (or were not) inspired to do something. Your assignment now is to rewrite that paragraph, edit it, and proofread it.

If you rewrite with a pen or pencil, your draft may end up looking messy, filled with cross outs, arrows, and writing above the lines and in the margins. Such messiness is normal. Even the founders of our country had messy drafts, as the reproduction of an early revision of the Declaration of Independence (on the next page) illustrates. If you revise at the computer, your screen and pages will look neater, but you will still make just as many changes.

Tips

REWRITING

- Work in stages. Don't think you can revise and edit and proofread in one sitting. Time-outs help you see your work anew, so you are better able to evaluate and improve it.
- If you wrote your draft by hand, type it before revising. You might be amazed at how many problems you notice when your writing is in a printed format.
- Read your draft aloud or have someone read it to you. You may hear problems that you overlooked in writing.
- If you're using a computer, feel free to revise on the screen, but also print out your drafts and revise on the hard copy as well. Working on a printout is good for editing, too.
- Use your computer's thesaurus (dictionary of words with similar meanings) when you cannot think of the right word. Just be sure you understand a word's shades of meaning before using it.
- Use your computer's grammar and spell checkers with caution, as they are not foolproof. For example, the spell checker cannot distinguish between soundalikes, such as *there* and *their*.
- Use your computer's search function to locate your personal trouble spots, such as the difference between *accept* and *except*.
- Trust your instincts. If something seems "off," it is probably wrong. If you can't identify the error and its correction, check with a writing center tutor or your instructor.
- **If English is not your first language,** ask a native English speaker to read your draft. Tutors in your campus writing center or English language lab make excellent readers.

+ Dr. Franklin

"abolishing our most ~~important~~ valuable Laws

for taking away our charters & altering fundamentally the forms of our governments;

for suspending our own legislatures & declaring themselves invested with power to legislate for us in all cases whatsoever.

he has abdicated government here, [withdrawing his governors, & declaring us out of his allegiance & protection;]

he has plundered our seas, ravaged our coasts, burnt our towns & destroyed the lives of our people;

he is at this time transporting large armies of foreign mercenaries to compleat the works of death, desolation & tyranny already begun with circumstances of cruelty & perfidy unworthy the head of a civilized nation:

he has endeavoured to bring on the inhabitants of our frontiers the merciless Indian savages, whose known rule of warfare is an undistinguished destruction of all ages, sexes, & conditions [of existence.]

[he has incited treasonable insurrections of our fellow ~~citizens~~, with the allurements of forfeiture & confiscation of our property.

he has waged cruel war against human nature itself, violating it's most sacred rights of life & liberty in the persons of a distant people who never offended him, captivating & carrying them into slavery in another hemisphere, or to incur miserable death in their transportation thither. this piratical warfare, the opprobrium of infidel powers, is the warfare of the Christian king of Great Britain. determined to keep open a market where MEN should be bought & sold he has prostituted his negative for suppressing every legislative attempt to prohibit or to restrain this execrable commerce; and that this assemblage of horrors might want no fact of distinguished die, he is now exciting those very people to rise in arms among us, and to purchase that liberty of which he has deprived them, by murdering the people upon whom he also obtruded them: thus paying off former crimes committed against the liberties of one people, with crimes which he urges them to commit against the lives of another.]

+ Dr. Franklin

in every stage of these oppressions we have petitioned for redress in the most humble terms; our repeated petitions have been answered only by repeated injuries. a prince whose character is thus marked by every act which may define a tyrant, is unfit to be the ruler of a people who mean to be free. future ages will scarce believe that the hardiness of one man, as ventured within the short compass of twelve years only, to lay a foundation so broad & undisguised, for tyranny over a people fostered & fixed in principles of freedom.]

SUCCEEDING IN COLLEGE

Achieve Your Academic Goals

Just as following specific procedures can help you write paragraphs and essays, following specific procedures can help you achieve your goals in college.

Some of your goals will be **short-term goals** because you want to achieve them in the coming days. Examples of short-term goals are

- Learn to use the library online catalog.

- Make an appointment with my academic advisor.

- Finish my biology lab report by the end of the week.

Some of your goals will be **long-term goals** because you expect to achieve them further into the future, in the coming weeks, months, and years. Examples of long-term goals are

- Raise my overall grade average one full point.

- Decide on my major by the end of the school year.

- Complete my history paper in three weeks.

List Your Goals

Writing a list of your short-term and long-term goals helps you identify your goals, make them specific, and commit to them. Posting your list of goals in a conspicuous place will also help you. It is easy to become caught up in the routine events and inevitable distractions of the day and lose sight of your goals if you do not have a written reminder of them. Furthermore, if you are inclined to procrastinate, a written list may help keep you moving forward.

Develop a Plan

Write a specific plan for achieving each goal. For example, if your goal is to decide on a major by the end of the school year, you might develop this plan:

- Go through the catalog and check mark every major that interests me.

- Read the requirements for each major I have marked.

- Read the course descriptions for classes in each major.

- Talk to a faculty member about each major and learn about job opportunities.

- Talk to students in each major to learn what they think.

Identify Helpful Campus Resources

Your school has many support services to help students, such as a writing center, a study skills center, a reading lab, a math lab, a financial aid office, a counseling center, and an international student center. Use your college online catalog to identify these resources and then visit the offices that can help you achieve your goals.

Write about It

Like writing, identifying and achieving your academic goals is a process. What are your academic goals? List three short-term and three long-term goals. Then write out a plan for achieving each of these goals. Do you think your written plan will help you succeed in college? Explain.

For more practice with rewriting, go to www.mywritinglab.com.

CHAPTER 3
Paragraph Basics

A **paragraph** is a group of sentences developing one central point. Sometimes a paragraph stands alone as a brief composition, and sometimes it is combined with other paragraphs in longer writings. You will frequently write stand-alone paragraphs for brief essay examination answers and homework responses, for short business memos, for some personal and professional e-mail, and for brief thank you and condolence notes.

THE PARTS OF A PARAGRAPH

Most paragraphs have two parts:

- the sentence that presents the central point of the writing—this is the **topic sentence**

- the sentences that explain or prove that central point—these are the **supporting details**

In addition, some paragraphs have a **closing,** a sentence or two to tie things up in a satisfying way.

As you read the following sample paragraph, decide which sentence presents the central point. That is the *topic sentence*. Also decide which sentences explain or prove the central point. They are the *supporting details*. Finally, determine whether there is a *closing* to end the paragraph in a satisfying way.

> The two main parts of a paragraph are the topic sentence and the supporting details. A closing may also appear.

A Lounge for Women over Thirty

[1]Because so many women in their thirties, forties, and fifties are returning to school, our university should set up a special lounge area for these students. [2]Women in this age group are often uncomfortable in the student union because they are surrounded by students no older than twenty-two or so. [3]They are not interested in the upcoming rock concert or fraternity party, so often they find they have little to discuss with their younger counterparts. [4]A special lounge would provide a meeting place for the older women. [5]It would be a place they could go knowing they would find others who share the same interests and concerns. [6]Also, this lounge would be a place these students could come together to help each other with their unique problems, the ones they face as a result of returning to school after a long absence. [7]It would also provide a place for group study. [8]Finally,

> The topic sentence presents the central point of the paragraph, and the supporting details develop the central point.

because many returning to school after an absence need some brushing up, the lounge could be a place for tutoring activities. [9]If the university provided this facility, this important group of students would feel more comfortable as they pursued their degrees.

1. Which sentence presents the central point of the paragraph? That is, which sentence is the topic sentence?

   _____

2. Most of the sentences after the topic sentence are the

   _____.

3. The last sentence is the_____.

If you identified the first sentence of the paragraph as the topic sentence, you were correct. This sentence provides the central point of the paragraph (the university should provide a lounge for female students over thirty). The remaining sentences (except the last) are the supporting details (they develop the central point). The last sentence is the closing (it ties the paragraph up in a satisfying way).

The Structure of a Paragraph

The Topic Sentence gives the central point
↓
The Supporting Details explain or prove the central point
↓
The Closing finishes the paragraph in a satisfying way

Practice 3.1

Each group of sentences could be part of a paragraph. One sentence could be a topic sentence, and the others could be part of the supporting details. Write *TS* if the sentence could be a topic sentence and *SD* if it could be part of the supporting details.

Example
   _SD_   He humiliates players by yelling at them in front of fans.
   _TS_   My nephew's baseball coach should be fired.
   _SD_   The coach allows pitchers to give up too many runs before he pulls them out.

1. _SD_ Long lines at check-in counters, security scanners, and gates are common.
   _SD_   Passengers are uncertain about what they can put in their carry-on luggage.
   _TS_   New security measures at airports have changed the nature of air travel.
   _SD_   More people are having their luggage opened and searched.

2. _____ Giant toads may weigh three pounds and grow to twelve inches.

   _____ Giant toads have glands that secrete a poison strong enough to kill a dog.

   _____ The number of giant toads in Florida is increasing.

   _T. S_ If you go to Florida, watch out for the giant toads.

3. _T. S_ People can learn to manage their stress.

   _____ Regular exercise helps control stress.

   _____ Focusing on successes rather than defeats keeps stress in check.

   _____ Talking things out with a sympathetic friend relieves stressful feelings.

4. _____ The eleven-month school year saves school districts money.

   _____ More school systems should adopt the eleven-month school year.

   _____ The eleven-month school year keeps students from forgetting important concepts over a long summer recess.

   _T. S_ The eleven-month school year makes efficient use of staff and facilities.

5. _____ Saline is injected into the blood vessel.

   _____ The procedure is quick, taking only a few moments.

   _T. S_ If you have spider veins in the legs, sclerotherapy can help you.

   _____ Sclerotherapy involves only minor discomfort in most cases.

THE TOPIC SENTENCE

You should usually begin your paragraphs with a **topic sentence** to present the central point of your paragraph. When readers see that topic sentence, they do not have to wonder; they *know* what your paragraph is about. Here, for example, is the first sentence of "A Lounge for Women over Thirty," on page 37.

> Because so many women in their thirties, forties, and fifties are returning to school, our university should set up a special lounge area for these students.

As soon as you read this opening sentence, you understand exactly what the paragraph will be about. That is, you know the paragraph's central point.

A topic sentence usually has two parts: One part gives your topic, and one part gives your assertion about the topic. Your assertion is how you feel about the topic or why it is important.

A topic sentence includes your topic and assertion about the topic.

> your topic + your assertion about the topic = your topic sentence

Here are some examples. The topic is underlined once, and the assertion about the topic is underlined twice.

1. Property taxes are *an ineffective way to finance public education*.

2. Many people *do not know how to relax*.

3. *I greatly admire* my Aunt Hattie.

4. Changing my major from engineering to computer science *proved to be a smart move*.

5. Warrick Inn's *best feature is its country charm*.

Practice 3.2

For each topic sentence, underline once the words that present the topic and underline twice the words that present the assertion about the topic.

Example

If you plan to purchase a new car, *proceed cautiously*.

1. Considering its size and location, the house is overpriced.

2. The aging shopping mall is exceptionally dreary.

3. Pornography on the Internet should not be regulated.

4. Being an only child is a lonely existence.

5. If you ask me, nurses are the most underappreciated healthcare providers.

6. The auto company's bankruptcy will have serious consequences throughout the economy.

7. Psychologists understand that birth order significantly affects personality.

8. Carlos Morales is the most qualified candidate for student government.

9. After the party, the living room looked like a war zone.

10. The effects of depression can be devastating.

The Qualities of Effective Topic Sentences

You have learned that your topic sentences should include your topic and your assertion about that topic. In addition, remember these points.

1. **Avoid statements of fact.** A topic sentence that states a fact leaves you with nothing to say in the supporting detail. Consider these factual statements:

   I wake up every morning at 6:30.

   Education is very important.

   Soap operas are on in the daytime.

   These statements of fact offer no room for the writer's assertion. What can you say after noting that you wake up at 6:30? Who does not agree that education is important? How can you develop a whole paragraph about the fact that daytime TV includes soap operas?

   Statements of fact can be rewritten to be more effective by including the writer's assertion:

   I highly recommend waking up early each day.

   To attract better teachers, we must pay higher salaries.

   The number of daytime soap operas should be reduced.

2. **Avoid very broad topic sentences.** They are impossible to treat adequately in a single paragraph. Consider these statements:

> The terrorist attacks of September 11, 2001, affected our country profoundly.
>
> Our educational system must be revamped.

The topics introduced in these sentences cannot be managed in one paragraph. They require treatment in essays made up of several paragraphs.

3. **Avoid vague words.** Words such as *nice, interesting, great, good,* and *bad* do not give your reader a clear sense of your assertion.

vague:	Being a camp counselor last summer was great.
clearer:	Being a camp counselor last summer helped me decide to become a teacher.
vague:	Playing in piano recitals was awful.
clearer:	Playing in piano recitals made me feel self-conscious.

4. **Avoid formal announcements.** Topic sentences like these can be boring:

> This paragraph will discuss how to interview for a job.
>
> I plan to explain why this university should offer a major in hotel management.
>
> The following sentences will describe my first day of college.

Topic sentences like these are more appealing:

> Remember two points when you interview for a job.
>
> A major in hotel management is needed at this university.
>
> My first day of college was hectic.

5. **Avoid using a pronoun to refer to something in the title.** If your title is "The Need for Campaign Finance Reform," avoid a topic sentence like this: "It is needed for a variety of reasons." Instead, write this: "Campaign finance reform is needed for a variety of reasons."

6. **Place the topic sentence first.** The topic sentence can actually appear anywhere in the paragraph. However, placing it first is convenient. You can try other placements as you become a more experienced writer.

> Avoid topic sentences that are statements of fact or too broad. Also, avoid the formal announcement, vague language, and reference to the title.

Practice 3.3

If the topic sentence is acceptable, write *OK* in the blank; if it is too broad, write *broad* in the blank; if it is a statement of fact, write *fact* in the blank; if the language is vague, write *vague* in the blank; if the sentence is a formal announcement, write *announcement* in the blank.

Example

> _____announcement_____ The following paragraph will explain how to use the principles of feng shui to improve the quality of your life.

1. _____ The time I spent working as a hospital orderly was great.

2. _____ I attended the Browns–Dolphins football game.

3. _____ Living in a dorm is miserable.

4. _____ The most pressing problems facing us today are world hunger and overpopulation.

5. _____ I will explain here why I believe grading on the curve is unfair.

6. _____ Children need lots of attention.

7. _____ Professor Wu's group dynamics class is interesting.

8. _____ My paragraph will describe the campus commons at sundown.

9. _____ Two tricks will help a dieter maintain willpower.

10. _____ *OK* _____ The Cameron triplets are very different: Jud is an optimist; Jake is a pessimist; Judy is apathetic.

Practice 3.4

Pick three of the unacceptable topic sentences from Practice 3.3 and rewrite them to make them acceptable. Use a separate sheet.

Practice 3.5

If the statement includes both the topic and assertion, write *OK* in the blank; if the topic is missing, write *topic;* if the assertion is missing, write *assertion.*

Example

____topic____ It was so unexpected I was not sure what to do.

1. _____ In my senior year, a championship basketball game taught me the true meaning of sportsmanship.
2. _____ Job-sharing has benefits for an employer.
3. _____ I began my student teaching in a seventh-grade study hall.
4. _____ It was very depressing to be there.
5. _____ The governor's tax bill will be voted on in November.

Practice 3.6

Select two of the unacceptable topic sentences in Practice 3.5 and rewrite them on a separate sheet to make them acceptable.

Practice 3.7

For each subject given, write an acceptable topic sentence. Remember to include both a topic and your assertion. Also, remember the qualities of an effective topic sentence. The first one is done as an example. (If you are stuck for ideas, try listing, brainstorming, clustering, or freewriting.)

Example

pets   *My calico cat, Call, has an annoying habit.* _____

1. your favorite holiday   _____

2. a childhood memory   _____

3. a favorite teacher   _____

4. your first day of college   _____

5. television   _____

Practice 3.8

For each list of supporting details, write an acceptable topic sentence. Avoid broad topic sentences, statements of fact, vague language, and formal announcements.

1. topic sentence _____

_____

   a. Check local fashions and be sure your child dresses to conform to them.

   b. Ask the new teacher to assign a friendly classmate as a lunch or gym partner.

   c. Instruct your child to strike up conversations and not just wait for others to introduce themselves first.

   d. After a week, have your child invite one of his or her new classmates over after school.

2. topic sentence _____

_____

   a. I wanted to study criminal justice.

   b. I was offered a scholarship to play football.

   c. I wanted to move away from home.

   d. My girlfriend was attending college.

3. topic sentence _____

_____

    a. The walls were covered with grease stains.

    b. Pieces of cereal, cat food, and dried food covered the floor.

    c. Dried jelly and other, unidentified matter were caked on the refrigerator door.

    d. The smell of rotting garbage filled the air.

4. topic sentence _____

_____

    a. Running improves cardiovascular fitness.

    b. It helps manage stress.

    c. It helps maintain desired weight.

    d. It can be competitive or noncompetitive, as the runner prefers.

5. topic sentence _____

_____

    a. Professor Rios involves students in class discussions.

    b. She gives extra help to those who need it.

    c. She never criticizes anyone who makes an error.

    d. She gives fascinating lectures.

Planning, Writing, and Rewriting Your Topic Sentence

Study your idea-generation material to decide on your topic and your assertion for your topic sentence. Say, for example, that when you brainstormed, you came up with this list of ideas for a paragraph about modern communication:

Cell phones are everywhere.

They are annoying in restaurants and other public places.

They can be lifesavers in emergencies.

They help people stay in touch.

They can play music.

They can take pictures.

They can save money on long-distance calls.

They can be easily damaged.

They are not always reliable.

Computers help people connect with e-mail.

Instant messaging is more common than telephoning for teenagers.

Sometimes e-mail creates misunderstandings.

It can get lost in cyberspace.

This list reveals that your topic can be either cell phones or computers. You must decide which topic to use. Say you decide on cell phones. The list shows that one possible assertion about the topic is that cell phones can be a positive thing, and another possible assertion is that they can be a problem. To plan a topic sentence, you must decide which assertion to use. Say that you decide to write about cell phones as a positive thing.

topic: cell phones

assertion: they are a positive thing

To write the first draft of your topic sentence, be sure to include both the topic and the assertion about your topic that you settled on during planning. For example, you might include this topic sentence in your first draft about cell phones:

Cell phones are a good thing.

To revise your topic sentence with a critical eye, rework it to make sure it has all the qualities of an effective topic sentence. Thus, when you revise "Cell phones are a good thing," you may end up with this topic sentence:

Although people complain about cell phones, they are a convenience we would not want to live without.

THE SUPPORTING DETAILS

You cannot expect your reader to believe what you say in your topic sentence just because you write it in a paragraph. You must *demonstrate* that your topic sentence is true, and that is where your *supporting details* come in. **Supporting details** explain or prove your topic sentence. They are all the facts and opinions you present to show why you have your particular assertion about your topic. Turn back to pages 37–38 and reread "A Lounge for Women over Thirty." Notice that the first sentence presents the writer's topic and assertion. The university should set up a lounge for female students over thirty. Thoughtful readers will not believe that the university should set up the lounge just because the writer says it should; thoughtful readers require evidence. That evidence comes in the supporting details after the topic sentence, supporting details which explain why the university should set up the lounge.

To explain or prove the topic sentence, supporting details must be *adequate, specific,* and *relevant.* They must also have *coherence.* These characteristics are explained next.

Supporting details develop the topic sentence by explaining why you have your assertion about the topic. Supporting details should be adequate, specific, and relevant. They should also have coherence.

Adequate Supporting Detail

When a paragraph has **adequate supporting detail,** it has enough facts and opinions to explain or prove the topic sentence.

Read and think about this paragraph:

> My high school biology teacher changed my life. He saw I was heading for trouble and straightened me out. He also helped me improve my grades so I could play basketball. In fact, he even helped me get into college. I will always be grateful to Mr. Friedman for being there when I needed help the most.

Supporting details must be adequate; the writer must supply enough information so that the reader understands why the writer has his or her assertion.

The paragraph begins with an effective topic sentence that includes both topic and assertion. The topic is the biology teacher, and the assertion is that he changed the writer's life. However, the supporting details are not adequate. Too few points are made to demonstrate that the topic sentence idea is true. The reader still needs information. How did the teacher straighten the writer out? How did he help the writer improve his grades? How did he help the writer get into college?

Now read and think about this revised paragraph:

> My high school biology teacher changed my life. He saw I was heading for trouble and called me in after school one day. He explained that he cared what happened to me and wanted to help if he could. When I told him how depressed I was, he arranged counseling at the local mental health center. He also helped me improve my grades by showing me how to take notes and study efficiently. As a result, I regained my basketball eligibility. In fact, Mr. Friedman even helped me get into college by talking to admissions counselors on my behalf. I will always be grateful to Mr. Friedman for being there when I needed help the most.

You probably feel more satisfied after reading the revised version because necessary details have been added. The supporting details in the paragraph are now *adequate*.

FAQ

Q: Where do my supporting details come from?

A: As you generate ideas for supporting details, consider what you have experienced, observed, learned in the classroom, read in the newspapers, and heard on the television and radio.

Practice 3.9

After each topic sentence, list three supporting details that could be written to prove or explain the topic sentence. Use the idea generation techniques if necessary.

Example

My sixteenth birthday was the best ever.

I was given a surprise party.

My sister bought me a leather coat.

My parents took me out to dinner.

1. Daltonde Department Store's end-of-year sale was chaotic.

_____

_____

_____

2. Advertising creates unrealistic expectations in people.

_____

_____

_____

3. We would be better off if we threw out our television sets.

_____

_____

_____

4. I will always remember the time I collided with a truck.

_____

_____

_____

5. Laricia's is an excellent restaurant.

_____

_____

_____

Specific Supporting Detail

Specific detail helps your reader form a clear, detailed understanding of your meaning. The opposite of specific detail is a **general statement,** which gives your reader only a vague sense of your meaning. The following examples show the difference between general and specific:

general statement: The car went down the street.

specific detail: The 1962 Impala sedan rattled down Oak Street, dragging its tailpipe.

You probably formed a clearer picture in your mind when you read the sentence with specific detail. Also, you probably found the specific detail more satisfying than the general statement. Because specific detail is more satisfying and helps the reader form a clearer mental picture, strive for specific supporting details.

Use Specific Words   One way to provide specific detail is to use specific words. **Specific words** are more exact than general words, so they help your reader form a clear mental picture. Study the following lists of specific and general words to appreciate the difference between the two.

Specific details help ensure adequate detail.

Use specific words to help your supporting details be specific enough.

General Words	Specific Words
dog	collie
song	"Home on the Range"
book	*The DaVinci Code*
music	jazz
run	sprint _= very fast_
said	shouted
take	grab

Now consider these two sentences to appreciate the difference specific words can make.

1. The young child was on the floor.
2. Ten-year-old Miro was sprawled across the living room floor.

Sentence 2 is more interesting because it creates a clearer mental picture. This clearer mental picture comes from replacing the general words *young, child,* and *was on* with the more specific *ten-year-old, Miro,* and *sprawled across.* Also, the words *living room* are added to identify where Miro was.

To be sure your words are specific, choose specific nouns and verbs; also, use modifiers.

FAQ
Q: What if I have trouble think-ing of specific words?

A: Use a dictionary or the-saurus, but use words from these sources appropriately. *Gnaw* is more specific than *chew,* but it also means some-thing a bit different.

specific nouns:	Nouns are words for people, places, ideas, emotions, and items. Instead of general nouns like *movie, car,* and *restaurant,* choose specific nouns like *Hairspray, Camaro,* and *IHOP.*
specific verbs:	Verbs are words that show action. Instead of general verbs like *went, spoke,* and *looked,* choose specific verbs like *raced, shouted,* and *glanced.*
specific modifiers:	Modifiers describe nouns and verbs. You can use modi-fiers to make your detail more specific. Add the modi-fier *pounding* to describe the noun *rain,* and you get the specific *pounding rain.* Add the modifier *carefully* to the verb *stepped,* and you get the specific *stepped carefully.* Be sure your modifiers are specific. Rather than the general "sang *badly,*" choose the more specific "sang *off-key*"; rather than the general "*nice* house," choose the more specific "*roomy* house."

Practice 3.10

Next to each general noun or verb, write a more specific alternative.

Examples

shoes _penny loafers_   walk _stroll, skip_

1. drink _soft drink_   3. college course _Math_

2. hit _strike, smack,_   4. looking _watching, observing,_
home run   _spying_
slap, punch, attack

5. house _home condo,_ (*apartment*)   7. flower _rose, tulip_

6. said _told, yell_   8. took _steel, drop, grab, borrow_

Use one or more specific modifiers with each noun and verb.

Examples

the sweater _the pink angora sweater_

study _study diligently_

1. the commercial _beer commercial, miller_

2. drive _reckless, careful_

3. the rose _expensive_

4. barking _____

5. the kitten _____

6. sang _classical singer_

7. the apartment _comfortable_

8. sleep _my dog sleeps all day_

Practice 3.12

Rewrite each sentence by using a more specific alternative for each underlined word and by following the directions in parentheses.

Example

The <u>dog went</u> down <u>the street</u>. (Add a specific modifier after the substitute for *went*.)
The German shepherd dashed excitedly down Laurel Avenue.

1. <u>The man</u> left <u>his tools</u> on the floor. (Add a specific modifier before *floor*.)

Ly left his stuff on the floor.

_____

_____

2. <u>Several items of clothing</u> were scattered across the floor in Ralph's bedroom. (Add a specific modifier before *bedroom*.)

hands and gloves were scattered

_____

3. <u>A number of things</u> were good bargains at the garage sale. (Add a specific modifier before *garage sale*.) _____

A lot of trunks _____

_____

4. Jan decided to buy <u>the car</u> that Stavros was selling, even though it <u>had so much wrong with it</u>. (Add a specific modifier either before or after *decided*.)

_____ *honda* ^{blue} *2000, corola.   the brake*

put on Toyota _____

_____

5. The scouts <u>went away</u> from the campsite because it smelled <u>bad</u>. (Add a specific modifier before *scouts*.) _____

_____

_____

Practice 3.13

Rewrite the sentences to make them more specific. Change general nouns, verbs, and modifiers to specific ones, and add specific modifiers where you wish.

Example

A variety of people were at the convention. <u>Executives, laborers, students, and parents</u>

<u>attended the third annual ham radio convention in Morgantown.</u>

1. Rhoda and I worked hard in the yard. *Rhoda* _____

_____

_____

2. The dish I ordered at the restaurant tasted terrible. _____

The tackle I ordered from the res is terrible

_____

3. The baby cried in the middle of the night. _____

The sick one year old baby cried ——— at 12

_____

4. The smell in Jim's apartment was awful. *The smell of food in Jim's* _____

_____

5. The view from the window was very nice. *The Mountain Fuji from the window was very nice*

6. The heat made me miserable. *The heat in the city made me miserable.*

7. The teacher helped the girl feel good. *The teacher helped the girl do her homework*

8. The dog made so much noise that he kept me awake all night. _____
The dog Crakle barking too much noise that he kept me _____

Follow General Statements with Specific Statements Another way to make your supporting details specific is to follow general statements with specific ones. Here is a paragraph with general statements that are *not* followed by specific ones.

> Much of what circulates on the Internet is untrue. People assume that the stories they read in the Internet are true, so they pass them along in e-mails. However, often the stories are hoaxes. Some stories have been circulating for years, but people still believe them, regardless of how preposterous the stories are. Particularly persistent are false stories about making money or receiving gifts by forwarding e-mail. If the Internet proves anything, it's that people will fall for any ridiculous story.

The detail in this paragraph is not adequate—there is not enough of it, so you probably come away feeling unsatisfied. To make the detail adequate, follow each general statement with one or more specific ones, as in the following revision. (The specific statements are underlined to make studying the paragraph easier.)

> Much of what circulates on the Internet is untrue. People assume that the stories they read in the Internet are true, so they pass them along in e-mails. However,

FAQ

Q: Why do I have to follow general statements with specific ones? Can't I just state a point and move on?

A: Thoughtful readers do not believe what they read without proof. Your specific statements provide that proof.

often the stories are hoaxes. <u>One false story making the rounds these days says that we can end the funding of terrorists if we all stop buying gasoline on the same day.</u> Some stories have been circulating for years, but people still believe them, regardless of how preposterous the stories are. <u>Consider the story that says students get 220 points on the SAT if they spell their names correctly. That falsehood has been around since I was a high school sophomore. Or consider the ridiculous tale that a girl's jaw swelled because she ate cockroach eggs when she was licking envelopes.</u> Particularly persistent are false stories about making money or receiving gifts by forwarding e-mail. <u>Different versions of these hoaxes say you can get cash from Microsoft, shoes from Nike, clothes from the Gap, and computers from IBM. One even states that you can receive a trip to Disney World just by forwarding e-mail.</u> If the Internet proves anything, it's that people will fall for any ridiculous story.

Practice 3.14

Follow each general statement with a specific statement that helps prove the general statement.

Example

Six-year-old Leo and five-year-old Juanita were not getting along.

They refused to share their toys and spent the afternoon arguing about everything from the best cartoon show to what game to play.

1. Suddenly the weather turned threatening. *The weather is getting worse because of a terrible storm.*

2. Some television commercials insult the viewer's intelligence.

   The TV commercials which

3. The cost of textbooks is outrageous.

   The Chemistry textbook is most expensive

4. Dr. Stone is a dedicated teacher.

   Dr. Stone is a great teacher she helps her student to do the homework

5. Professional athletes are not always good role models. _Tiger Wood_

athletes _____

_____

Practice 3.15

Write three specific points that could be made after each of the following general statements.

Example

The students in third-period history class were out of control.

The students in the back were talking loudly among themselves.

Two boys were roaming around the room.

When the teacher called for order, the students talked back to him.

1. Wanda treats people badly.

   show unrespect

   insult

   punch

2. Driving with Chuyen is a frightening experience.

   speed

   drive to fast

   drunk driver

3. To succeed in college, students need effective study habits.

   Make a schedule

   Learn how to take note

   attendence in the class

4. Babysitting the Carlson twins aged me ten years.

   cry all night

   tentrumph

   fight

5. The gale-force winds caused extensive damage to the coastal town.

_____

_____

_____

Practice 3.16

The following paragraphs lack specific details because general statements are not followed by specific ones. On a separate sheet, revise these paragraphs by following general statements with specific ones.

1. Don't Eat at Joe's

Joe's Eatery on Third Avenue is the worst restaurant in town. When I was there last Tuesday, I was appalled by the condition of the dining room. Also, the service could not have been worse. When my food finally arrived, I had to send it back because it was poorly prepared. Things at Joe's are so bad that I would not be surprised if the place went out of business soon.

2. How to Protect Your Health in College

College students should be conscious of how to take care of their health. First, they should choose carefully what they eat in the dining hall. Also, they should schedule a regular exercise session. Equally important is building in some recreation time because too much work will lead to stress. Finally, students should know what to do in the event they do become ill on campus.

Relevant Supporting Detail

> Supporting details must be relevant. This means they must be clearly related to the topic and assertion presented in the topic sentence.

Relevant detail means that the supporting details are directly related to the topic and assertion presented in the topic sentence. If your details stray from the topic and assertion, you have a **relevance problem** (sometimes called a problem with **unity**).

The following paragraph has two relevance problems. As you read it, look for the supporting details that are not directly related to the topic sentence.

The Left-Handed Advantage

Left-handed people have the advantage in baseball and tennis. For one thing, left-handed batters are in a better position to run to first base. Left-handed first basemen also have an edge. At first base, players often field balls hit to the right side of the infield. Of course, left-handed basemen wear their gloves on their right hands, so they can catch balls without moving around, the way right-handed players have to. Unfortunately, the left-handed third baseman does not enjoy the same advantage. In tennis, too, a left-handed player is fortunate. A right-handed player generally has little experience playing a lefty, but a lefty has considerable experience playing a righty. Thus, right-handed players will be more confused playing left-handed players than left-handed players will be playing right-handed players. This fact alone helps explain the large number of left-handed tennis champions. Outside of sports, lefties still face problems with door handles and radio knobs meant to be used with the right hand, with right-handed scissors, and with writing from left to right. Still, in sports, the left-handed athlete has an advantage.

You probably noticed two relevance problems. The sentence that says the third baseman does not have an advantage is not relevant because it does not relate to the topic sentence idea, that left-handed people *do* have an advantage. Also, the sentence about the problems lefties have outside of tennis and baseball with handles, knobs, scissors, and writing is not relevant because it does not discuss the advantage in tennis and baseball.

To revise, eliminate supporting details that are not relevant to your topic sentence, or alter the details to make them relevant.

Practice 3.17

In the following paragraphs, draw a line through the details that are not relevant.

1. Although it may have seemed so at the time, the 2000 election between Al Gore and George Bush was not the closest, most controversial U.S. presidential election. That distinction belongs to the election between Republican Rutherford B. Hayes and Democrat Samuel J. Tilden in 1876. Tilden won the popular vote by a very small margin—4,284,020 to 4,036,572. But Florida, South Carolina, and Louisiana sent in disputed returns, and one electoral vote in Oregon was disputed. Both Republicans and Democrats charged election fraud. Congress established a fifteen-member electoral commission to decide the matter. Because the Republicans had a majority in Congress, they had a majority on the commission, and every disputed vote was awarded to Hayes, who then won the presidency by a single electoral vote. Although they were not controversial decisions, both of Bill Clinton's elections were achieved without a majority vote. He had 43 percent in 1992 and 49 percent in 1996. Clearly, the U.S. system of government is resilient enough to survive election disputes.

2. My friend Hank is a remarkable person. Although he was abused by his parents until he was sixteen and placed in a foster home, Hank is a kind, gentle guy. Studies show that abused children often become abusive adults, but Hank is different. He is a Big Brother to a fatherless child and treats this boy with love and compassion. He also works summers as a swim instructor at a local day camp, where he is a favorite among all the campers. He plans to major in math. Hank underwent three years of therapy to work through the problems that his parents caused. Clearly he has beaten the odds because he shows no signs of becoming abusive the way his parents were.

Logical Order

In Chapter 1, you learned about the importance of arranging your ideas in a logical order, that is, in an order your readers can follow easily. You also learned about three common logical orders for ideas: chronological, spatial, and emphatic. If you need to review that material, return to pages 12–14.

Transitions and Repetition for Coherence

Readers need adequate, relevant details arranged in a logical order to help them understand and believe the topic sentence. In addition, readers need to understand how ideas relate to each other, and they need the connections to be smooth and graceful. When you connect ideas smoothly and show how your ideas relate to each other, you achieve **coherence.** Two strategies help you achieve coherence: using transitions and repeating key words and ideas.

Transitions are words or phrases that help your reader understand the order of your ideas and signal their relationship to each other. In addition, transitions help your sentences flow smoothly. Here is an example:

> The health commissioner told the board of health that asbestos had to be removed from three schools. *Also,* he told the board that asbestos may be a problem in two libraries.

The transition *Also* signals that the idea in the second sentence functions in addition to the idea in the first sentence. The transition also helps the first sentence flow smoothly into the second. To appreciate this, read the sentences without the transition and notice that they are harder to follow:

> The health commissioner told the board of health that asbestos had to be removed from three schools. He told the board that asbestos may be a problem in two libraries.

Following is a chart that gives you many commonly used transitions.

Transitions
TO SIGNAL ADDITION   also, and, and then, in addition, too, the next, furthermore, further, moreover, equally important, another, first, second, third

> If the school levy does not pass, some teachers will be laid off. *Furthermore,* band and choir will be eliminated.

TO SIGNAL ILLUSTRATION   for example, for instance, an illustration of this is, to illustrate

> Chuck became very irritable when he quit smoking. *For example,* when James asked to borrow his chemistry notes, Chuck yelled at him and called him irresponsible.

TO SIGNAL EMPHATIC ORDER   more important, most important, most of all, best of all, of greatest importance, least of all, even better, the best (worst) case (example, instance, time)

> Mayor DeSalvo has been working hard to bring new industry to our area. *More important,* she has devised a plan to restore confidence in local government.

TO SIGNAL SPATIAL (SPACE) ORDER   near, nearby, far, alongside, next to, in front of, to the rear, above, below, over, across, under, around, beyond, beneath, behind, on one side, to the left

> The high school is centrally located, and *directly behind* it is the football stadium.

TO SIGNAL CAUSE AND EFFECT so, therefore, since, if . . . then, thus, as a result, because, hence, consequently

> Only five hundred students bought tickets to the spring concert. *As a result*, the concert had to be canceled.

TO SIGNAL CONTRAST (DIFFERENCES) but, yet, still, however, in contrast, on the other hand, nevertheless

> Nigel sprained his knee in practice; *however*, he plans to be in shape for Saturday's game.

TO SIGNAL COMPARISON (SIMILARITIES) similarly, likewise, in the same way, in like manner

> Most of today's movies are unsuitable for young viewers. *Similarly*, many television shows are not appropriate for children.

TO SIGNAL PURPOSE for this reason, for this purpose, in order to

> Theresa hopes to make the women's basketball team. *For this reason*, she is training very hard.

TO SIGNAL CHRONOLOGICAL (TIME) ORDER now, then, later, soon, suddenly, next, afterward, earlier, at the same time, meanwhile, often

> I bought a used car. *Then* I had it checked over by a reliable mechanic.

TO SIGNAL EMPHASIS indeed, in fact, truly, certainly, to be sure, surely, without a doubt, undoubtedly, of course

> Our basketball team has the best record in our division. *Undoubtedly*, we will win a spot in a postseason tournament.

TO SIGNAL SUMMARY OR CLARIFICATION in conclusion, in summary, to sum up, in other words, in brief, that is, all in all

> I cannot support a candidate who is opposed to women's rights. *In other words*, I will not vote for Nathaniel Q. Wisherwaite.

TO SIGNAL CONCEDING A POINT although, even though, while it is true, granted

> *Although* the temperature is rising quickly, I am still going skiing this weekend.

A second way to achieve coherence is to repeat key words or ideas. Here is an example with a key word repeated:

> The doctor put Dov on a special <u>diet. This diet</u> required him to restrict his intake of fats and proteins.

The second sentence repeats the word *diet*, which appears in the first sentence. This repetition helps the reader understand the relationship of the ideas in the two sentences, and it helps the first sentence flow smoothly into the second.

Now here is an example with a key idea repeated:

> The senior class raised five thousand dollars for homeless people. <u>Such an effort</u> should not go unnoticed.

In this example, the second sentence opens with *Such an effort*. These words repeat the key idea of the first sentence: that the class raised five thousand dollars for homeless people. Repeating the key idea shows how the ideas in the two sentences relate to each other; it also helps the first sentence flow smoothly into the second.

Practice 3.18

Fill in the blanks with a transitional word or phrase from the chart beginning on page 56.

Example

Douglas is the biggest practical joker I know. <u>For example,</u> last week he glued Dana's shoes together.

1. I refuse to speak to Alonzo unless he learns to control his temper.

    <u>Also</u> I refuse to be in the same room with him.

2. Diana was not expecting to be transferred to Houston.

    <u>Therefore</u> she needs some time to adjust to the idea.

3. The novelty shop in the mall rarely advertises. <u>Therefore</u>

    _____ not many people realize what unusual items are sold there.

4. Television shapes our thinking more than we realize.

    <u>Furthermore</u> it can influence our emotions.

5. First I will make myself the most valuable employee I can be.

    <u>Then</u> I will ask my boss for a raise.
    Next, Therefore

Practice 3.19

Fill in the blanks with suitable coherence devices. Use the words and phrases from the chart beginning on page 56 and repetition of key words and ideas.

The idea that the number 13 is unlucky is a superstition. [1]_____, it is probably the most widely held superstition there is. In one way or another, it is observed all over the world. [2]_____ hotels everywhere do not have a thirteenth floor. [3]_____, their rooms are not numbered with 13. Many people will not have 13 guests at the dinner table. Strangely, there is no single explanation for the superstition. [4]_____ has many different stories behind it. [5]_____, some experts say that 13 was unpopular from the time when people learned to count. By using their ten fingers and two feet as a unit, people came up with the number 12. [6]_____ 13 became unlucky because it was unknown and frightening—beyond 12. In religious circles, the 13 superstition is traced to the Last Supper. In attendance were Jesus and the twelve disciples—13 in all. Others trace the superstition to the story of the Valhalla banquet in Norse mythology, to which twelve gods were invited. [7]_____, Loki, the Spirit of Strife and Mischief, intruded to make 13. [8]_____ Balder, the favorite of the gods, was killed. [9]_____ 13 is generally regarded as unlucky, the number was considered lucky by the ancient Chinese and Egyptians.

Practice 3.20

1. Write two sentences that describe the location of some of the things in your writing classroom. Begin the second sentence with a transition that signals a spatial order.

2. Write two sentences about what you did this morning. Begin the second sentence with a transition that signals chronological order.

3. Write two sentences that tell why foreign languages should (or should not) be taught in high school. Begin the second sentence with a transition that signals emphatic order.

4. Write two sentences about the stress of being a college student. Use repetition to achieve coherence between the sentences.

THE CLOSING

Many times you need a final sentence to bring your paragraph to a satisfying finish. This sentence is the **closing.**

An appropriate closing often occurs to you. However, if you are unsure how to handle your closing, write a sentence that refers to the topic and/or assertion presented in your topic sentence. For example, look at the closing of "The Left-Handed Advantage" on page 55. Notice that this final sentence mentions the left-handed athlete, a reference to the topic noted in the topic sentence (left-handed people). Also notice that the closing mentions that left-handed people have an advantage in sports, a reference to the assertion in the topic sentence (having an advantage in baseball and tennis).

Another way to handle the closing is to answer the question "So what?" about your topic sentence. The final sentence of "A Lounge for Women over Thirty" on page 38 takes this approach.

> The closing gives a paragraph a satisfying finish. This closing can refer to the topic or assertion presented in the topic sentence. It can also answer the question "So what?"

Practice 3.21

The following paragraph lacks a closing. Add a closing sentence that provides a satisfying finish. Use any approach you like, including the ones explained above.

Wildlife habitat destruction occurs in many ways. First, habitats are ruined when large areas are taken over for agricultural, residential, and industrial purposes. Some animals, like the mountain lion, have had their environments destroyed with the clearing of forests. Another factor leading to habitat destruction is pollution. Chemicals are released into the air and water, spoiling streams, rivers, and land environments. Finally, habitats are destroyed when people bring non-native plants and animals into an area. The non-native plant or animal may interfere with the careful balance of the native ecosystem.

_____

_____

_____

PLANNING, WRITING, AND REWRITING YOUR PARAGRAPH

When you plan your writing, use idea-generation techniques. As you write, express your ideas the best way you can. When you revise, pay careful attention to adequate detail, specific detail, relevant detail, and coherence. Check to be sure that your detail is adequate and that you have backed up all your general statements with specific ones, so your reader will believe that your topic sentence is true. Then check your details against the topic and assertion in your topic sentence to be sure you do not have any relevance problems. Add transitions to achieve coherence. Use this checklist to help you.

Checklist for a Paragraph

- [ ] 1. My topic sentence includes both my topic and my assertion.
- [ ] 2. My topic sentence has the qualities of an effective topic sentence explained on pages 40-41.
- [ ] 3. My supporting details adequately explain or prove my topic sentence.
- [ ] 4. General statements are backed up by specific details expressed in specific words.
- [ ] 5. All my supporting details are relevant to my topic sentence.
- [ ] 6. Supporting details are arranged in a logical order.
- [ ] 7. Where needed, transitions and repetition are used for coherence.
- [ ] 8. The last sentence ends the paragraph in a satisfying way.
- [ ] 9. I have edited carefully (more than once) to find and correct mistakes.
- [ ] 10. I have proofread carefully after copying or typing the paragraph into its final form.

WRITING ASSIGNMENT

Write a paragraph that explains *one* influence a person has had on you. Perhaps a teacher helped you to learn to love reading or a coach helped you gain confidence. Maybe a neighbor taught you how to play guitar. Or maybe a sibling or friend—like the boys in the picture on page 61—taught you about sharing. Before you begin, read the sample student paragraph that follows for an idea of what such a paragraph can be like.

Megen

Because of a nine-year-old named Megen, I decided to major in physical therapy. I met Megen last quarter, when I worked as an orderly at St. Joseph's Hospital. She was only nine, but she had experienced more pain in those nine years than most people experience in a full lifetime. Megen was paralyzed, but she never used that as an excuse to stop trying. Each day I would wheel Megen down for her grueling physical therapy sessions. I would watch and encourage her as she worked through exercises that brought beads of sweat to her forehead and upper lip. Sometimes the pain was so great she cried, but she never stopped working as long as there was the slightest chance it would help. More than anything, Megen wanted to go to school and play with the other nine-year-olds, and she was willing to work as hard as she could for her dream. But it wasn't to be, for Megen died October 19th. I will never forget Megen's courage, for it showed me what I wanted to do with the rest of my life. It showed me that I wanted to be a physical therapist and help others strive for their dreams.

Tips

COMPOSING YOUR PARAGRAPH

- Freewrite about people who have affected your fears, ambitions, successes, failures, talents, or career plans—go all the way back to your childhood if you like.
- Answering these questions can also help you generate ideas:

  How important was the influence? How long lasting was the influence? Why?

  How did you know the person?   Is the influence positive or negative?

  How did the influence occur?   When did the influence occur?

- Begin with a topic sentence that names the person and the influence.
- If you need help with your topic sentence, fill in the blanks in this sentence:

  Because of _____, I _____.

  Put the person's name in the first blank and the influence in the second to get something like this: Because of Uncle Harry, I am no longer afraid of heights.

- Underline every general statement. Is each one followed by one or more specific statements?
- Use the checklist on page 60.
- Give your draft to someone with good judgment about writing and ask that person to complete the Reader Response Sheet on page 25.
- Read your draft aloud. If you hear an abrupt shift or a gap, you may need a transition or repetition at that spot.
- **If English is not your first language,** try to avoid thinking in your native language and translating into English. Instead, both think and write in English.

SUCCEEDING IN COLLEGE

Write Paragraphs across the Curriculum

You will often write paragraph responses to homework assignments and to examination questions in your other classes. You may even write paragraph-length e-mails to your classroom instructors or to your advisor.

When you write these school-related paragraphs, follow the structure explained in this chapter. Begin with a topic sentence that has both a topic and assertion. For homework and examination questions, you will want that topic and assertion to reflect the question you are being asked. Follow the topic sentence with supporting details that are adequate, specific, and relevant. Be sure your details have coherence, and finish with a satisfying closing. Here, for example, is a one-paragraph response to a question on a psychology examination. The parts are labeled as a study aid.

Exam Question: Explain what *shaping* is and tell why it is important.

Shaping is a gradual teaching process that works by rewarding behavior that comes closer and closer to a desired behavior. At first, any behavior that is even remotely close to a desired behavior is rewarded. In the next step, behavior a little bit closer than the previous behavior is rewarded. As the process continues, only behavior that is increasingly closer to the desired behavior is rewarded until finally only the desired behavior is rewarded. Shaping is an important teaching tool because it helps both people and animals learn complicated behaviors that they might otherwise have trouble learning. For example, an animal trainer would use shaping to teach a dog to walk on its back legs. The trainer might first reward the dog for standing on the back legs for a second and then for successively longer periods. Next, the trainer might reward the dog for taking a single step and then reward the dog for taking increasingly more steps. A common expression that represents the principle of shaping is "You have to crawl before you walk."

Topic sentence reflects question.

Supporting details are adequate, specific, and relevant.

Note the transitions for coherence.

When you write your paragraph responses in your other classes, you can follow the procedures you have learned so far in this book. In particular, try listing the ideas you want to include in the paragraph. Then number those ideas in the order you want to write them. Developing a scratch outline like this can be particularly helpful when you are taking an exam and must write both quickly and completely.

Write about It

Discuss the writing you do in one or more of your other classes. You might consider these questions: What kinds of writing have you been asked to do in your other classes? How much did that writing affect your final grade? Were you able to complete the writing tasks successfully? Why or why not? What have you learned so far in this book that you can apply to writing in your other classes?

For more practice with paragraph basics, go to www.mywritinglab.com.

CHAPTER 4
Narration

Narration is story-telling.

Narration is story-telling. You tell, hear, and read stories often. When you explain to your roommate what happened on your date last night, you tell a story. When your friend writes to you about the minor car accident she was in, you read a story. When you listen to a classmate tell what happened during the third quarter of the football game, you hear a story.

A SAMPLE NARRATIVE PARAGRAPH

Read the following narrative paragraph, written by a student.

Able-bodied but Addle-brained

[1]I became very angry the day I saw an able-bodied woman get out of a car she had just parked in a handicapped space. [2]Last Thursday I had just gotten out of my car in K-mart's parking lot when a woman in a beat-up Ford swerved into a spot clearly marked for handicapped parking. [3]She emerged with three children, all under six, and headed for the entrance. [4]If she had a handicap, I saw no sign of it. [5]I caught up with her and said, "Excuse me, but you parked in a handicapped spot." [6]She just looked at me as if I had beamed down from Mars, and then she said that she was handicapped because she had three kids. [7]That made me furious. [8]I yelled at her that if she considered her children handicaps, she should be investigated. [9]Then I told her that I would report her to store security and ask that her car be towed. [10]When I told the security police officer what happened, he said there was nothing he could do because she had not broken a law. [11]I was so angry at the insensitive woman that I stormed out of the store without doing my shopping. [12]If you ask me, any able-bodied person who parks in a handicapped space should have to spend a week in a wheelchair. [13]I guarantee the person would be more careful about parking after that.

THE TOPIC SENTENCE

In the topic sentence for your narrative paragraph, the topic is the event to be narrated, and the assertion is how you feel about the event. Look again at the topic sentence of "Able-bodied but Addle-brained":

I became very angry the day I saw an able-bodied woman get out of a car she had just parked in a handicapped space.

topic (event narrated): the day the able-bodied woman parked in a handicapped space

assertion (how writer feels about the event): angry

Mention the event and how you feel about the event or why it is important in your topic sentence.

One way to express your assertion is to mention why the story is important, like this:

On a cold, rainy April afternoon of my senior year in high school, an unexpected encounter led me to my career path.

topic (event narrated): an unexpected encounter

assertion (why the event is important): led to the writer's career path

Practice 4.1

The sentences that follow could be topic sentences for narrative paragraphs. Underline the topic (the event to be narrated) once and the writer's assertion opinion about the topic (how the writer feels about the event or why the event is important) twice.

Example

The day my dog was killed I learned the importance of leash laws.

1. My most frightening experience occurred on a Boy Scout hike.
   weather; raining

2. My family witnessed a surprising act of courage when our town flooded after Hurricane Ophelia.
   they said a baby / a dog on the beach

3. The need for gun education was made apparent by the recent accidental shooting of a three-year-old.

4. Mayor Fuentes's block watch program had an unanticipated effect on one neighborhood.

5. When my little sister choked on a piece of steak, I learned the importance of mastering the Heimlich maneuver.

6. One of my happiest moments occurred when Dad taught me how to fish.
   my dad

7. I felt like a hero when the Rayen Tigers won the City Series basketball championship.

8. My first day as a college student was stressful.

9. Getting my ham radio license was the high point of my year.

10. Finding five hundred dollars did not bring me good luck.

Practice 4.2

Write a topic sentence for a narrative paragraph about each of the subjects given.

Example

a first experience   My first summer job was a nightmare. _____

1. a childhood memory _____

_____

2. a school experience _____

_____

3. a time spent with a friend _____

_____

4. a holiday celebration _____

_____

5. a time when you were disappointed (or pleasantly surprised)

_____

_____

        ■

SUPPORTING DETAILS

Supporting details for a narrative paragraph often answer the following questions, known as the **journalists' questions.**

Supporting details answer most or all of the journalists' questions.

```
                    THE JOURNALISTS' QUESTIONS

  ■ Who was involved?        ■ Where did it happen?

  ■ What happened?           ■ Why did it happen?

  ■ When did it happen?      ■ How did it happen?
```

If the answers to some of the journalists' questions are not important to your narration, you do not have to include them. Similarly, if some answers are more important than others, you can emphasize those more. For example, if you are telling about the time you lost your wallet, you may say more about how the event happened than when it happened.

Notice that the answers to most—but not all—of the journalists' questions make up the supporting details for "Able-bodied but Addle-brained":

• **Who** was involved?
  the writer and a woman

• **What** happened?
  The writer became angry and had a confrontation with a woman who parked in a handicapped space.

• **When** did it happen?
  last Thursday

• **Where** did it happen?
  K-mart's parking lot

- **Why** did it happen?
  The woman was insensitive.

- **How** did it happen?
  This question is not answered. (A narrative paragraph sometimes answers most, but not all, of the questions.)

Order and Transitions

Arrange the supporting details for your narrative paragraph in chronological order.

Supporting details in a narrative paragraph are arranged in a **chronological** (time) **order.** This means the details are arranged in the order they occurred, so what happened first is written first, what happened second is written second, and so forth. (Chronological order is also discussed on page 12.) Reread "Able-bodied but Addle-brained" and notice the chronological order.

Transitions can help your reader identify the order of your ideas. The transitions in the following chart signal chronological order. They will probably be very useful, but the other transitions in the chart on pages 56–57 may also help you achieve coherence.

Transitions for Narration
TO SIGNAL CHRONOLOGICAL (TIME) ORDER now, then, later, soon, suddenly, next, afterward, earlier, at the same time, meanwhile, often
I explained to Kim why I was upset. *Afterward*, she apologized.

Practice 4.3

We have all had our embarrassing moments. Pick one of yours and assume you will write a paragraph narrating what happened. To develop supporting details, on a separate sheet answer the journalists' questions.

Practice 4.4

To practice arranging details in chronological order, list on a separate sheet the first ten things you did today in the order they occurred.

Writing Dialogue

When words a person spoke are important to the story, you can reproduce them. For example, "Able-bodied but Addle-brained" includes this dialogue:

I caught up with her and said, "Excuse me, but you parked in a handicapped spot."

When you reproduce exact spoken or written words, use quotation marks according to the guidelines explained on pages 394–396. When you just mention that something was said, do not use quotation marks, as this example from "Able-bodied but Addle-brained" illustrates:

I yelled at her that if she considered her children handicaps, she should be investigated.

Using Specific Words

In Chapter 3, you learned about using specific nouns, verbs, and modifiers. Specific words can help bring your narration to life. Consider, for example, the energy in the following sentence from "Able-bodied but Addle-brained." (The specific words are underlined as a study aid.)

> <u>Last Thursday,</u> I had just gotten out of my car in <u>K-mart's</u> parking lot when a woman in a <u>beat-up Ford swerved</u> into a spot clearly marked for handicapped parking.

Now consider how much less interesting the sentence is without specific words:

> The other day I had just gotten out of my car in a store parking lot when a woman in a car pulled into a spot clearly marked for handicapped parking.

THE CLOSING

You can end a narrative paragraph any way that provides a satisfying finish. One approach is to state or restate the importance of the event or how you feel about the event. Consider again "Able-bodied but Addle-brained." The first closing below mentions the importance of the event, and the second closing, which is the one that appears in the paragraph, mentions how the writer feels about the event.

closing states the importance of event:	This woman's insensitive behavior shows that we must work to increase sensitivity to the needs of the disabled.
closing restates how the writer feels about the event:	If you ask me, any able-bodied person who parks in a handicapped space should have to spend a week in a wheelchair. I guarantee the person would be more careful about parking after that.

The Structure of a Narrative Paragraph

The Topic Sentence
states the event
mentions your feeling about the event or its importance
↓
The Supporting Details
answer the journalists' questions
may include dialogue
are expressed in specific words
↓
The Closing
may state or restate your feeling about the event or its importance

---

PLANNING, WRITING, AND REWRITING NARRATION

To plan your narrative paragraph, think about your audience and purpose when you decide which journalists' questions to emphasize. Say you are telling about the time you broke your leg playing high school basketball. If you are telling the story to convince referees to call more fouls to avoid injuries, then you will emphasize who was involved (the referees) and how the accident happened (they did not call the game closely enough).

During writing, don't worry too much about writing dialogue and choosing specific words. Just write your draft the best way you can. During revising, however, look for sentences where dialogue and specific language will help you energize the narration for your particular reader. Use this checklist to help you.

✓ **Checklist for a Narrative Paragraph**

- ☐ 1. My topic sentence includes both the event and my assertion about the event.
- ☐ 2. My topic sentence has the qualities of an effective topic sentence explained on pages 40–41.
- ☐ 3. All the appropriate journalists' questions are answered.
- ☐ 4. Every sentence is relevant because it advances the story or explains my assertion.
- ☐ 5. If appropriate, I have used dialogue, and I have punctuated it correctly.
- ☐ 6. Specific words enliven the narration.
- ☐ 7. Supporting details are arranged in chronological order.
- ☐ 8. Where needed, transitions and repetition are used for coherence.
- ☐ 9. The last sentence ends the paragraph in a satisfying way.
- ☐ 10. I have edited carefully (more than once) to find and correct mistakes.
- ☐ 11. I have proofread carefully after copying or typing the paragraph into its final form.

Practice 4.5

Read the following narrative paragraph and answer the questions after it.

A Preventable Tragedy

¹A devastating apartment fire last week that caused the deaths of three children underscores the need to check smoke detectors regularly. ²The mother was asleep upstairs with her five-year-old when the smoke and heat awakened her. ³ She screamed frantically to the children downstairs to get out of the house, but she was trapped upstairs by the smoke. ⁴She broke a second-story window and in desperation lowered the five-year-old as far as she could before she dropped her, shouting "Someone, please catch my baby!" ⁵The hysterical child landed on the sidewalk in a broken heap with multiple breaks and a head injury. ⁶Then the mother jumped from the window after dropping the child, and she, too, broke

bones. [7]The three children downstairs never made it out. [8]According to fire-fighters, the house had two smoke detectors, but neither one was working.

FAQ
Q: How can I make my story more interesting?

A: You can create interest by describing people and scenes.

1. What is the topic sentence? The writer's topic? The assertion?

2. What do you think the writer's audience and purpose are?

3. Which of the journalists' questions are answered? Which ones are emphasized? Why are they emphasized?

4. Cite three examples of specific word choice. What do the specific words contribute to the narration?

5. Sentence 4 includes dialogue. What does it contribute to the paragraph?

6. Are all the supporting details relevant? Explain.

7. Cite two examples of transitions to signal chronological order.

8. Does the author bring the paragraph to a satisfying close? If so, how? If not, what is the problem?

WRITING ASSIGNMENTS

For your narrative paragraph, you have a choice of assignments. The topic sentences you drafted for Practice 4.2 may be helpful.

1. Tell a story about a first experience, the first time you did something.

2. Tell a childhood memory.

3. Narrate a school experience.

4. Tell about a time you spent with a friend.

5. Tell a story about a holiday celebration.

6. Tell a story about a time you were disappointed (or pleasantly surprised).

7. **Combine Narration and Description.** Narrate a childhood memory. Describe a person or scene to make the narration vivid. For example, if your memory is about a time you took a trip with your grandfather, you might mention that "his bony fingers, joints swollen with arthritis, gripped the steering wheel." One of the topic sentences your drafted for Practice 4.2 may help you. In addition, see Chapter 5 on how to write descriptive detail.

8. **Respond to an Image.** In a paragraph, tell the story of what happens immediately after the man's toupee is blown off his head. As an alternative, tell about an embarrassing moment you experienced. If you write about an embarrassing moment, the supporting detail you developed for Practice 4.3 may be helpful.

Tips

COMPOSING YOUR NARRATIVE PARAGRAPH

- Write a scratch outline by listing everything that happened in the order it occurred.
- Answer all the journalists' questions in as much detail as you can, and then decide which answers you will include, keeping your audience and purpose in mind.
- If you need help with your topic sentence, fill in the blanks in this sentence:

  I will never forget the time _____, because _____.

  Put the event you are narrating in the first blank and the reason the event is memorable in the second to get something like this: I will never forget the time I lost my temper with Sara, because I learned I have a problem with anger management.
- As you rewrite, ask yourself what people involved in the events had to say. Should any of that dialogue be included?
- Underline the general words and substitute more specific alternatives as appropriate.
- Use the checklist on page 68.
- **If English is not your first language,** remember that although in some cultures, speaking about yourself is considered impolite, in the United States, you can write about yourself and use *I* without appearing rude. So feel free to write narrations about you and your experiences (see also the Tip in Chapter 1 on page 21).

SUCCEEDING IN COLLEGE

Use Narration across the Curriculum

Narration is an important part of writing in your other classes. For example, on a history midterm, you might be asked to narrate the events that led to the Confederate defeat at Gettysburg. For a social work internship, you might be asked to write a case study that is a narrative account of the interaction you have with a client.

When you write narration in your other classes, you might combine it with other patterns you will learn in this book. For example, in a paper for an American history class, you might narrate the events that led up to the Great Depression *and* explain the effects of the Great Depression on banks, using *cause and effect analysis,* which is explained in Chapter 10.

When you write narration in your other classes, you will often emphasize the significance of the story. For example, in addition to telling the events that led to the Confederate defeat at Gettysburg, you may also note why that battle was so important.

Learn the Conventions and Expectations for Writing in Your Other Classes

Different academic disciplines have different conventions, and different teachers may have different expectations. For example, some instructors may require you to format your papers a particular way. In some disciplines, you should not use *I,* but in others it is acceptable to refer to yourself. If your instructor has not discussed the conventions and expectations for your writing, ask what they are so you are fully informed.

Write about It

Interview three instructors from three different academic disciplines and ask them to describe the conventions and expectations for student writing in their classes. Write what you have learned to share with other students in your writing class.

For more practice with narrative paragraphs, go to www.mywritinglab.com.

CHAPTER 5

Description

A descriptive paragraph gives your reader a mental picture of a person, object, or scene.

When you write description, you choose words and details to create a mental picture for your reader of a person, object, or scene. Description is important in writing you encounter every day. For example, your biology text may describe the appearance of a cell, and an online catalog may describe the features of the clothing it is selling.

A SAMPLE DESCRIPTIVE PARAGRAPH

The following descriptive paragraph was written by a student. As you read it, notice how carefully words and details were chosen to paint a clear mental picture.

Grandma's Thanksgiving Table

[1]My grandmother's Thanksgiving table was always so inviting. [2]Silver polished to a gleam was meticulously aligned on either side of bone china plates that had traveled with Grandma from Russia. [3]The crystal goblets, standing as straight and tall as sentinels, sparkled in the last rays of the sun streaming through the dining room window. [4]In the precise center of the table, orange and yellow mums were arranged around slender tapers. [5]Just before we all sat down, the candles were lit, and the flaming tips would bend and flicker; those seated close to the candles could feel their warmth. [6]Once the candles were lit, we sat down to give thanks, with the warm aroma of cinnamon, the sweetness of vanilla, and the delicate scent of apple filling the room. [7]The goblets were clinked with each toast of thanks, their ping reverberating and lingering for several seconds. [8]In that time, I realized that the care Grandma took with her Thanksgiving table reflected the love she had for her family.

THE TOPIC SENTENCE

In the topic sentence for your descriptive paragraph, your topic is what you describe, and your assertion is your dominant impression. A **dominant impression** is a prominent reaction you to what you are describing. Look again at the topic sentence for "Grandma's Thanksgiving Table":

My grandmother's Thanksgiving table was always so inviting.

topic (what is described):	the writer's grandmother's Thanksgiving table
assertion (the dominant impression):	inviting

Be sure your topic is narrow enough for treatment in one paragraph. You would have a difficult time describing your whole house in a single paragraph, but you could describe your bedroom.

Also be sure to express your dominant impression in specific language. Avoid words like *nice, bad, great,* and *awful,* and use more specific alternatives like *peaceful, hectic, exciting,* and *run-down.*

> Mention what you are describing and your dominant impression in your topic sentence.

Practice 5.1

Write a topic sentence for each of the subjects given. Include what you are describing and your dominant impression. Be sure your topic is narrow enough and that your dominant impression is expressed in specific language.

> Your topic should be narrow enough to be treated in one paragraph. Your dominant impression should be expressed in specific language.

Example

a campus cafeteria at noon   *At noon, the cafeteria in Beeman Hall is hectic.*

1. your bedroom   My bedroom is messy / warm blanket too small comfortable pillow.

2. a particular outdoor area on campus _____

3. a kitchen after a five-year-old has made breakfast *is getting dirty now* The dessert was not clean / broken plate

4. a favorite restaurant   Noodle Soup / the services, the location, the asmosphere

5. your writing classroom _____

SUPPORTING DETAILS

Your descriptive details should be sensory details.

The supporting details for a descriptive paragraph are sensory details. **Sensory details** appeal to one of the five senses (sight, sound, smell, taste, and touch). Most of the details in "Grandma's Thanksgiving Table" appeal to sight, but some details appeal to sound ("their ping reverberating and lingering for several seconds"), some details appeal to smell ("warm aroma of cinnamon, the sweetness of vanilla, and the delicate scent of apple"), and one detail appeals to touch ("feel their warmth").

In a descriptive paragraph, use specific nouns, verbs, and modifiers.

For sensory details that create a vivid mental picture, use specific words. The writer of "Grandma's Thanksgiving Table" chose specific nouns, verbs, and modifiers like these:

sparkled in the last rays of the sun	goblets were clinked
slender tapers	flaming tips would bend and flicker

Now is a good time to review the discussion of specific word choice on pages 47–48.

Practice 5.2

Write one description that could be used as supporting detail for each topic sentence. Be sure your words are specific. Also, try to appeal to a different sense in each sentence.

Example

Dan's old car is ready for the junk yard. *The tailpipe, eaten away by rust, hangs so low it almost scrapes the ground.*

1. The children's playroom is a disaster area. _____

   _____

   _____

2. The mall on Christmas Eve was festive. *christmas tree*

   Santa Clause _____

   _____

3. Eleni's backyard is beautifully landscaped. _____

   _____

   _____

4. The atmosphere of the Paris Café is romantic. _warm feeling,_
music / wine

5. My grandmother's attic is spooky. _scary_ _spider well_

■

Order and Transitions

A spatial arrangement often works well for descriptive details. With a spatial arrangement, you move from front to back, from top to bottom, from inside to outside, from left to right, or in some other ordered way across space. To help your reader identify the spatial arrangement, use the transitions in the following chart to signal spatial order. In addition, the other transitions in the chart on pages 56–57 can help you achieve coherence.

Use transitions that signal spatial order.

Transitions for Description
TO SIGNAL SPATIAL (SPACE) ORDER near, nearby, far, alongside, next to, in front of, to the rear, above, below, over, across, under, around, beyond, beneath, behind, on one side, to the left
Inside the train station, thousands of commuters scurried to reach their destinations. *Outside,* however, the scene was surprisingly tranquil.

The writer of "Grandma's Thanksgiving Table" used this transition to signal spatial order in sentence 4:

In the precise center of the table

The writer also uses a number of transitions to signal time order (see page 12):

Just before we all sat down
Once the candles were lit
In that time, I realized

THE CLOSING

You can end your descriptive paragraph any way that provides a satisfying finish. One approach is to answer the question, "Why does my description matter?" The writer of "Grandma's Thanksgiving Table" uses this approach. The last sentence explains that the description of the Thanksgiving table matters because the table reflects the grandmother's love:

> In that time, I realized that the care Grandma took with her Thanksgiving table reflected the love she had for her family.

The Structure of a Descriptive Paragraph

The Topic Sentence
states what you will describe
indicates your dominant impression
↓
The Supporting Details
appeal to the senses
paint a mental picture
are expressed in specific words
↓
The Closing
may state the significance of the description

PLANNING, WRITING, AND REWRITING DESCRIPTION

To plan, evaluate the ideas you generate and choose details that strongly convey your dominant impression. Thus, if you want to convey that the office where you work is dreary, you can mention the dust on the file cabinets, but not the bright sun streaming through the window.

During writing, don't worry about getting your descriptions just right. Get them down the best way you can, knowing that you can rewrite during revising.

During revising, you will likely rewrite sensory language multiple times, gradually improving your descriptions. For example, say your draft includes this sentence: "The room smelled bad." When you evaluate that sentence, you might decide to make the description more vivid. You might revise it to "The pool room smelled like cigar smoke." To be even more vivid, you might revise a third time to "The paneled pool room smelled like a six-month accumulation of cigar smoke."

Before giving your descriptive paragraph to your reader, use this checklist to help you.

✔ Checklist for a Descriptive Paragraph

☐ 1. My topic sentence includes what I will describe and my dominant impression.

☐ 2. My topic is narrow enough for one paragraph.

☐ 3. My dominant impression is expressed in specific language.

☐ 4. All my details relate to what I am describing and my dominant impression.

☐ 5. My supporting details include sensory details and specific nouns, verbs, and modifiers.

☐ 6. Supporting details are arranged in a spatial or other logical order.

☐ 7. Where needed, transitions and repetition are used for coherence.

☐ 8. The last sentence ends the paragraph in a satisfying way.

☐ 9. I have edited carefully (more than once) to find and correct mistakes.

☐ 10. I have proofread carefully after copying or typing the paragraph into its final form.

Practice 5.3

The following descriptive paragraph was written by a student. Notice the specific words and the details that appeal to the senses. Answer the questions after the paragraph to check your understanding.

A View of Winter

[1]The view from the window over my kitchen sink revealed the harsh winter we were enduring. [2]Acres of yellowed field grass lay matted on the frozen ground. [3]Trees that once stood majestically in the field were now stripped of their colorful foliage. [4]Their naked limbs were straining under the pressure of the winter wind. [5]Row after row of dried corn stubs stood erect, in silent testimony to the tall, productive plants they had once been. [6]To the right, a gray, weather-beaten doghouse lay on its side, unable to protect its Irish setter any longer. [7]Behind the useless doghouse, a child's swing, tossed by the wind, creaked a lonely tune. [8]Overhead, gray, heavy clouds hovered close to the earth like a shroud covering the lifeless scene. [9]Then suddenly, a gust of wind parted a cloud, and the sun's warmth caressed my face to remind me to take hope. [10]Spring would eventually arrive.

1. What is the topic sentence? According to the topic sentence, what will be described, and what is the dominant impression?

2. What senses does the writer appeal to? Give an example of a description that appeals to each of these senses.

3. Give five examples of specific word choice.

4. Give three examples of transitions to signal spatial order.

5. Are all the supporting details relevant? Explain.

6. Does the paragraph have an effective closing? Explain.

FAQ

Q: Can I have too much sensory detail?

A: Too much sensory detail can overwhelm your reader. Balance highly descriptive sentences with less descriptive ones.

WRITING ASSIGNMENTS

For your descriptive paragraph, you have a choice of assignments.

Write an essay

1. Use one of the topic sentences you wrote for Practice 5.1.

2. Describe a place you go when you want to be alone.

3. Describe your favorite nightspot.

4. Describe a place you find unpleasant.

5. Describe the place where you like to study.

6. Describe a scene at a sporting event or other public gathering.

7. **Combine Description and Cause-and-Effect Analysis.** Describe a place that is very important to you and explain why that place is important. When you explain why the place is important, you will be using cause-and-effect analysis, which is explained in Chapter 10.

8. **Respond to an Image.** Assume you work for a travel agency and are preparing a travel brochure. Write a paragraph describing the scene in the photo. Your goal is to describe the place in a way that will make readers of the brochure want to visit it. Remember to include a topic sentence that conveys a dominant impression.

Tips

COMPOSING YOUR DESCRIPTIVE PARAGRAPH

- Describe a place you can visit, as generating ideas from firsthand sensory impressions may be easier than working from memory.
- If you have trouble drafting, write five sentences that convey your dominant impression, each one related to a different sense. If one sense is not relevant to your topic sentence, then write two sentences for another sense.
- If you need help finding specific words, use a dictionary or thesaurus. However, be sure you understand the connotations (implied or suggested meanings) of any words you draw from these sources.
- You will likely use a number of modifiers in your paragraph. See Chapter 23 if you need help using these words correctly.
- **If English is not your first language,** remember that in English, the form of adjectives remains the same, whether the nouns they describe are singular or plural.

  yes: The *red* sneakers were under Silas's bed.

  no: The *reds* sneakers were under Silas's bed.

SUCCEEDING IN COLLEGE

Use Description across the Curriculum

You may be surprised at how often you use description in your other classes. In an art history class, you may be asked to describe the distinguishing features of a Renaissance painting. In an advertising class, you may need to describe magazine advertisements to point out their persuasive strategies, or in a biology class, you may need to describe something you view under a microscope.

Make a Schedule

Writing tasks you have for your other classes will be more manageable if you make a schedule. Some of your writing assignments will require longer papers, and most certainly you will need to complete those assignments at the same time you complete other course requirements. A schedule will keep you organized and allow you to break large tasks down into manageable chunks. For example, if your history paper on the rise of labor unions is due in two weeks, you can schedule your work something like this:

- Monday—Review relevant chapters in textbook.
- Tuesday and Wednesday—Find and read three articles in the library.
- Thursday—Generate ideas.
- Friday and Saturday—Outline and write a rough draft.
- Sunday—Let draft cool.

(continued on next page)

SUCCEEDING IN COLLEGE (continued)

- Monday—Revise draft.

- Tuesday—Ask three classmates to read and react to the revision.

- Wednesday and Thursday—Revise again.

- Friday—Let draft cool.

- Saturday—Revise and edit final draft.

- Sunday—Proofread.

Write about It

The next time you have a writing assignment, in this class or another, make a schedule for it. After you complete the writing assignment, write a paragraph that explains whether or not you found the schedule helpful and why.

For more practice with descriptive paragraphs, go to www.mywritinglab.com.

CHAPTER 6
Illustration

Writers and speakers often use examples to make their points clear. Consider this conversation between Bob and Julio:

An illustration paragraph has examples for supporting details.

Bob: The food in this cafeteria stinks.

Julio: What do you mean?

Bob: The meat is always rubbery, the mashed potatoes are cold, and the Jell-O is warm.

To explain what he meant, Bob gave examples: rubbery meat, cold potatoes, and warm Jell-O. Another name for an example is an **illustration.** A paragraph with supporting details made up of examples is an **illustration paragraph.**

A SAMPLE ILLUSTRATION PARAGRAPH

The following illustration paragraph was written by a student.

With My Head in the Clouds

[1]As someone who is 6 feet 9 inches tall, I speak with authority when I say that the world is not set up for tall people. [2]For example, everything that is supposed to be high is too low. [3]Not long ago I was home for dinner with my parents. [4]As I stood up from the table to go into the kitchen, I slammed my head into the chandelier, causing the lights to sway wildly and my head to throb annoyingly for hours. [5]Each time I enter a room, I must duck to avoid hitting my head on a door frame. [6]Beds are also not made with the very tall in mind. [7]I do not fit in a standard size bed, so I have to sleep diagonally across a double bed to keep my feet from dangling off the end. [8]Cars are an even bigger problem. [9]I have to recline my seat and push it back to keep my head from scraping the ceiling. [10]Because this is so uncomfortable and a little bit dangerous, I often drive with the sunroof open so I can keep the seat in a proper position. [11]Of course, there is still the problem of getting into the car. [12]I will smash my head if I forget to fold myself over like an envelope. [13]Most people think that height has its advantages, but on most days, I do not see them.

THE TOPIC SENTENCE

Your topic sentence gives a general statement that will be supported with examples.

The topic sentence for your illustration paragraph is the general statement that will be explained or proven with examples. It includes both a topic and your assertion about the topic. Consider this topic sentence from "With My Head in the Clouds":

As someone who is 6 feet 9 inches tall, I speak with authority when I say that the world is not set up for tall people.

topic: tall people
assertion: The world is not set up for them.

The examples that follow the topic sentence show (illustrate) that the world is not geared for tall people.

Practice 6.1

Write a topic sentence that could be developed with examples for each of the subjects given. Be sure to include a topic and assertion.

Example

surprise parties   *Surprise parties rarely go as planned.* _____

_____

1. taking tests in school _____

_____

2. first impressions _____

_____

3. waiting in a doctor's office _____

_____

4. reality television _____

_____

5. fast food restaurants _____

_____

SUPPORTING DETAILS

The supporting details for your illustration paragraph are examples that explain or prove your topic sentence. Look again at "With My Head in the Clouds." This topic sentence idea will be explained or proven with examples:

> . . . the world is not set up for tall people.

The supporting details include these examples:

> Everything that is supposed to be high is too low.
> Beds are too small.
> Cars are too small.

Notice, however, that the writer does more than *give* examples—he *explains* them.

Example	Explanation
Everything that is supposed to be high is too low.	hit head on chandelier; must duck entering a room
Beds are too small.	must sleep diagonally
Cars are an even bigger problem.	must recline and push back seat; drives with sunroof open; must fold himself to get into the car

"With My Head in the Clouds" also shows that details that explain an example can be descriptive details. Here is an example:

> I slammed my head into the chandelier, causing the lights to sway wildly and my head to throb annoyingly for hours.

As the paragraph demonstrates, specific nouns, verbs, and modifiers contribute to adequate detail:

For adequate detail, use enough examples, and explain your examples.

> I *slammed* my head . . .
> I have to sleep *diagonally* across a *double bed* to keep my feet from *dangling* off the end.
> I will *smash* my head if I forget to *fold myself over like an envelope*.

To have adequate detail, use enough examples to explain or prove your topic sentence. In one paragraph, three examples can be enough. If they are highly detailed, two examples may be enough.

Order and Transitions

Placing your examples in emphatic order is often effective because you save your strongest example for last. (See pages 13–14 on emphatic order.) The examples in "With My Head in the Clouds" are in emphatic order. The clue to this is that the last set of examples is introduced with the words "an even bigger problem." If your examples occurred in a particular time order, you can arrange them in chronological order (discussed on pages 12–13).

You can arrange examples in an emphatic or chronological order.

When you write an illustration paragraph the transitions in the chart below will help you achieve coherence. In particular, three kinds of transitions may be helpful: transitions that signal illustration, transitions that signal addition, and transitions that signal emphatic order. In addition, use transitions to signal chronological order if your examples occurred in a particular time sequence.

Transitions for Illustration

TO SIGNAL ADDITION also, and, and then, in addition, too, the next, furthermore, further, moreover, equally important, another, first, second, third

> The children hid from the babysitter at bedtime. *Another example* of their bad behavior occurred when they hid her car keys.

TO SIGNAL ILLUSTRATION for example, for instance, an illustration of this, to illustrate

> Juan's math teacher is too easy. *For instance*, she has not assigned homework for at least a month.

TO SIGNAL EMPHATIC ORDER more important, most important, most of all, best of all, of greatest importance, least of all, even better, the best (worst) case (example, instance, time)

> Louise is often thoughtless. *One of the worst cases* of her thoughtlessness occurred when she did not pick up her six-year-old sister at school because she wanted to finish watching her soap opera.

TO SIGNAL CHRONOLOGICAL (TIME) ORDER now, then, later, soon, suddenly, next, afterward, earlier, at the same time, meanwhile, often

> Carlo is unusually generous. *First*, he gave a large donation to the food bank. *Then*, he invited a homeless family to Thanksgiving dinner.

Practice 6.2

Under each topic sentence, list three examples that can be used for supporting details.

Example

Ms. Lyons did more work than the average fifth-grade teacher.

She took her class camping to collect leaf specimens.

She visited a sick student at home to tutor her.

She skips lunch to grade papers.

1. Stress is a part of a college student's life.

_____

_____

_____

2. Living alone can be difficult.

_____

_____

_____

3. Elderly people can be dangerous drivers.

_____

_____

_____

4. Parents sometimes take children where they do not belong.

_____

_____

_____

5. Advertisements cause people to want products they do not need.

_____

_____

_____

Practice 6.3

Reread "With My Head in the Clouds" on page 81. Notice that most of the examples are introduced with a transition. On a separate sheet, list the transitions that introduce examples and tell what each one signals.

THE CLOSING

Any approach that brings your illustration paragraph to a satisfying finish is acceptable. One approach is to refer to the topic and assertion in your topic sentence. Another way is to mention an idea related to your topic sentence. Finally, you can close by both referring to the topic sentence and mentioning a related idea, the way the writer of "With My Head in the Clouds" does. Here are examples using the topic sentence from "With My Head in the Clouds":

topic sentence: As someone who is 6 feet 9 inches tall, I
                                         speak with authority when I say that the
                                         world is not set up for tall people.

closing that refers to topic sentence:	Frequent problems like these demonstrate that the world is not a comfortable place for tall people.
closing that mentions a related idea:	Ironically, people think height has advantages, but they do not realize the daily struggles it creates.
closing refers to the topic sentence and mentions a related idea:	Most people think that height has its advantages, but on most days, I do not see them.

The Structure of an Illustration Paragraph

The Topic Sentence
states what will be explained or proven
↓
The Supporting Details
are examples
include details that explain the examples
↓
The Closing
may refer to the topic sentence
may mention a related idea

PLANNING, WRITING, AND REWRITING ILLUSTRATION

To plan an illustration paragraph, think about your audience and purpose when you decide what examples to include. Say, for example, that you want to illustrate that bullies are not just in the school yard; they are also in the workplace. If you want to inform your human resources manager that bullying goes on in your office, choose examples from your workplace, not an example you read about in the paper.

Continue to think about your audience as you write. How much explanation of your examples is your reader is likely to need in order for you to achieve your writing purpose?

During revision, evaluate whether your example would be more effective if you added descriptive details or made your words more specific. The following checklist can help.

✓ Checklist for an Illustration Paragraph

☐ 1. My topic sentence includes both a topic and an assertion.

☐ 2. My topic sentence has the qualities of an effective topic sentence explained on pages 40–41.

☐ 3. I have enough examples in enough detail to explain or prove my topic sentence.

☐ 4. Each example is explained with specific information.

☐ 5. Where appropriate, I have used specific nouns, verbs, and modifiers.

☐ 6. All my details are related to my topic and assertion.

☐ 7. My examples are arranged in chronological, emphatic, or other logical order.

☐ 8. Where needed, transitions and repetition are used for coherence.

☐ 9. The last sentence ends the paragraph in a satisfying way.

☐ 10. I have edited carefully (more than once) to find and correct mistakes.

☐ 11. I have proofread carefully after copying or typing the paragraph into its final form.

Practice 6.4

Read the illustration paragraph that follows and then answer the questions to test your understanding.

Commitment and College

^{1}As a first-year college student with a full course load and a work-study job, I speak with authority when I say that college is a full-time commitment. ^{2}For example, my Elementary Statistics course requires constant commitment. ^{3}My instructor gives homework every night and a quiz every week. ^{4}Since each concept we learn builds on the next, I could be in deep trouble if I miss a class or do not ask my instructor for help when I get stuck. ^{5}If I do not stay on top of my assignments and learn the concepts for this course, I could fall behind and have a hard time catching up. ^{6}I am also enrolled in General Psychology, which requires me to read as many as fifty textbook pages before each class meeting. ^{7}Pop quizzes are a frequent occurrence in this class, so finishing the required reading before class is a must. ^{8}In addition, this course requires additional commitment, because students must participate in research projects at the college by serving as subjects in psychological experiments. ^{9}Currently, I am participating in what is called a "deception study." ^{10}That is, I am not allowed to know the purpose of the study until it is over so that my behavior is not influenced by prior knowledge. ^{11}All I know is that I have to sit in a room twice a week for an hour per session and talk with other students about the stresses of college life while observers take notes on our discussions. ^{12}Finally, my work-study job at the college's Core Curriculum office requires me to work ten hours each week. ^{13}In this job, I make photocopies for the various Core Curriculum courses, I help students decide which courses to sign up for, and I facilitate events like last month's guest lecture on astronomy. ^{14}With all of these responsibilities, I realize more and more how much of a commitment college really is.

1. What is the topic sentence of "Commitment and College"? What is the writer's topic and assertion?

2. How many examples does the writer give?

3. Which of the examples are explained?

4. List the transitions that introduce examples and explanations and tell what they signal.

5. Does the paragraph come to a satisfying closing? Explain.

WRITING ASSIGNMENTS

You have a choice of assignments for an illustration paragraph.

1. Use a version of one of the topic sentences from Practice 6.1.

2. Use a version of one of the topic sentences from Practice 6.2. If you like, you can use some or all of the examples you generated for that exercise.

3. Use examples to illustrate that high school did (or did not) prepare you for college.

4. Use examples to illustrate that things are not always what they seem.

5. Use examples to show that little white lies are helpful (or harmful).

6. Use examples to show that cell phones are a nuisance (or a convenience).

7. **Combine Illustration and Description.** Use examples to illustrate one personality trait of someone you know. For example, you can illustrate that a friend is generous, that a coworker is ambitious, that a neighbor is lazy, that a relative is optimistic, and so on. Try to make the illustrations more vivid by including some description. For example, if you illustrate that a friend is generous with an example of the time she lent you her heirloom earrings, you can describe the earrings or the friend's smile when she handed them to you.

8. **Respond to an Image.** People buy cars for many reasons. Sometimes we choose cars because they help us project a particular image. For example, what kind of image do people who buy the car in this advertisement project? Use examples to illustrate the fact that certain products help us to project certain images. For ideas, browse through magazines and look at the advertisements.

Tips

COMPOSING YOUR ILLUSTRATION PARAGRAPH

■ If you need help coming up with examples, answer these questions:

- What have I observed that can be an example?
- What have I experienced that can be an example?
- What have I read or seen on television that can be an example?
- What have I learned in the classroom that can be an example?

■ Place each example at the top of a column, and underneath, list ideas for developing it. Then number the columns in the order you want to write them up in your draft. Now you have a scratch outline.

■ As you write your first draft, you may think of additional examples. Don't hesitate to use them.

■ Give your draft to two reliable readers. Ask them to answer these questions:

- Do I have enough of the right kind of examples?
- Is each example sufficiently detailed?
- Should I add any description?

■ If you open a sentence with "For example" or "For instance," follow each phrase with a comma.

■ **If English is not your first language,** play the radio or television while you cook or clean. Listen regularly, and you will internalize much about English sentence structure, vocabulary, and grammar that will transfer to your writing.

FAQ

Q: Why can't I make up examples?

A: Real examples are easier to write about because they are authentic and specific.

SUCCEEDING IN COLLEGE

Use Illustration across the Curriculum

Because examples are so important for clarifying points, you will use illustration often in all of your college writing. For example, in a research paper about alternative schools for an education class, you could cite examples of successful and unsuccessful charter schools. A midterm exam in a business class might ask you to explain and illustrate three kinds of management techniques, and an examination in a literature class might ask you to define and give examples of *irony*.

Notice Examples during Note-taking and Highlighting

When your instructor says, "for example," "for instance," or "such as," you know one or more clarifying examples will follow. If you are confident that you understand the concept being illustrated, you do not need to take detailed notes on the examples; instead, jot down a key word or two that will remind you of the example when you review your notes. If a long example is given, listen carefully and summarize that example more briefly.

If you like to highlight your textbooks as a study aid, look for examples. If an example seems particularly important for some reason, or if you need the example to help you understand or remember the point being illustrated, then highlight it. Otherwise, you do not need to highlight examples. If a long example seems important, consider summarizing it in the margin rather than highlighting long paragraphs.

(continued on next page)

Keep in mind that examination questions may call upon you to give examples of important concepts, so even if you do not highlight them or include them in your lecture notes, you should be prepared to supply examples as supporting detail.

Write about It

Select a textbook chapter for another course you are taking or have taken. Read the chapter and count the number of examples. Then write a paragraph explaining how the examples help you understand the important material in the chapter.

For more practice with illustration paragraphs, go to www.mywritinglab.com.

CHAPTER 7
Process Analysis

A **process analysis** explains how something is made, how something is done, or how something works. Some process analyses explain procedures readers will never perform. For example, a biology textbook explains how plants turn carbon dioxide into oxygen, a pamphlet available to bank customers explains how mortgage loan rates are determined, and a magazine article explains how the Internet works. Other process analyses explain procedures readers can or might perform. For example, a recipe explains how to make burritos, instructions packaged with a toy tell how to assemble it, and a fitness magazine explains how to get a good workout in thirty minutes a day.

A process analysis explains how something is made or done, or how something works.

A SAMPLE PROCESS ANALYSIS

This process analysis is a revision of a piece written by a student.

Making Money with a Garage Sale

[1]If you plan it right, you can make a great deal of money from a garage sale. [2]First, you must gather all the salable items collecting dust in your basement and attic. [3]Do not include anything badly broken, but keep everything else. [4]The items you think are the most worthless may be the first to sell. [5]Toys and tools are hot sellers, but clothes (unless they are children's) probably will not sell very well. [6]Next—and this is very important—clean this junk up. [7]Dirty items will not sell, but you will be surprised at the weird stuff that goes if it is clean. [8]Once your items are clean, display them properly, so get lots of tables, even if you have to rent them. [9]Arrange everything attractively, trying to keep housewares together, toys together, and so forth. [10]Now for the most important part, pricing. [11]I have just three words of advice: cheap! cheap! cheap! [12]Remember, this trash has been in your basement collecting spider eggs for the past five years, so do not get greedy. [13]Price it to move because the last thing you want to do is drag this stuff back in the house because it did not sell. [14]If you really want a great sale, advertise. [15]Put signs up and place an ad in the classifieds. [16]Finally, pamper your customers by providing grocery bags for carrying those marvelous purchases home in, and by serving coffee—for twenty-five cents a cup, of course. [17]Follow this advice, and you can turn your unwanted items into extra cash.

THE TOPIC SENTENCE

Mention the process that will be explained and why the reader should understand the process in your topic sentence.

The topic sentence for a process analysis includes the topic and your assertion about the topic. The topic is the process. The assertion can explain why understanding the process is important. Look again at the topic sentence of "Making Money with a Garage Sale":

If you plan it right, you can make a great deal of money from a garage sale.

topic (process to be explained):   how to have a garage sale

assertion (why understanding the process   Money can be made.
is important):

Practice 7.1

For each topic sentence, tell the process to be explained and why understanding the process is important.

Example

If you want to keep your sanity, select your classes the way I do.

Process   *selecting classes (selecting the way the author does)*

Why understanding the process is important *to keep sanity*

1. To get the best value for your money, shop carefully for a used car.

   Process   *how to buy used car*

   Why understanding the process is important *to get value*

2. In order to survive, every babysitter should know how to handle children who act like monsters.

   Process   *how to handle children*

   Why understanding the process is important *to survive*

3. To move up the corporate ladder, you must learn how to network.

   Process   *how to* *connect w/people*

   Why understanding the process is important _____

4. College students must learn how to relax so the pressures of studying do not overwhelm them.

   Process   *how to relax*

   Why understanding the process is important *not stress out*

5. To have a successful garden, you must plan carefully.

Process _how to have a success garden_

Why understanding the process is important _plant carefully_

SUPPORTING DETAILS

The supporting details for your process analysis are the steps in the process. Look back at "Making Money with a Garage Sale" to see that the supporting details are everything a person must do—all the steps a person must perform—in order to have a profitable garage sale.

If the reason for a step is not obvious, you can explain why it is performed. For example, in "Making Money with a Garage Sale," sentence 7 explains the importance of cleaning items: "Dirty items will not sell." Explaining why a step is performed can emphasize its importance, especially if you fear your reader might skip it or perform it hastily.

If the proper way to perform a step is not clear, you should explain. Notice that sentences 8 and 9 explain how to display items properly: Use lots of tables, arrange things attractively, and keep similar things together. Finally, if it will help your reader avoid a mistake, you can explain what *not* to do, which the writer does in sentence 3: "Do not include anything badly broken. . . ."

> Supporting details for a process analysis are the steps performed. Sometimes you must also explain *why* to perform a step, *how* to perform a step, or what *not* to do.

Order and Transitions

Since the steps in a process are usually given in the order they are performed, supporting details for a process analysis are most often arranged in a chronological (time) order. To signal that order, use the transitions in the following chart. In addition, the transitions on pages 56–57 may also be useful.

> The supporting details are usually arranged in chronological order.

Transitions for Process Analysis
TO SIGNAL CHRONOLOGICAL (TIME) ORDER now, then, later, soon, suddenly, next, afterward, earlier, at the same time, meanwhile, often
Unpack the carton and make sure no parts are missing. *Next*, read through the directions from start to finish to be sure you understand them.

Notice that in "Making Money with a Garage Sale," the writer uses several transitions to signal chronological order.

First, you must gather . . .

Next—and this is very important . . .

Now for the most important part . . .

Finally, pamper your customers.

FAQ

Q: Some steps are obvious. Should I leave them out?

A: You can omit steps your reader will certainly know to perform. In a recipe, for example, you need not say to plug in the mixer.

*how to be
a terrible server*

Practice 7.2

Pick three of the following processes. On a separate sheet, list the steps performed in each.

1. checking a book out of your campus library

2. picking an advisor

3. registering for classes

4. buying a used car

5. planning a party

6. failing an exam (be humorous)

7. Christmas shopping at the last minute

8. editing

9. interviewing for a job

10. using a search engine

THE CLOSING

If your topic sentence already states the importance of the process, your closing can restate that idea, the way the writer of "Making Money with a Garage Sale" does:

topic sentence states the importance of the process:	If you plan it right, you can make a great deal of money from a garage sale.
closing restates:	Follow this advice, and you can turn your unwanted items into extra cash.

The Structure of a Process Analysis Paragraph

The Topic Sentence
gives the process that will be explained
may indicate why understanding the process is important
↓
The Supporting Details
give the steps in the process
may explain how to perform the steps
may mention what *not* to do
↓
The Closing
may state or restate the importance of the process

PLANNING, WRITING, AND REWRITING PROCESS ANALYSIS

As you plan, think about your audience when you decide whether to explain how to perform certain steps. For example, in a recipe for children that calls for egg whites, you may need to explain how to separate an egg. Experienced cooks, however, would not need this explanation.

As you write, remember that transitions are vital to helping readers understand or perform a process. If you are using chronological order, transitions such as *first, next,* and *finally* are important. If you are explaining why or how to perform a step, transitions such as *for this reason* and *in order to* are helpful.

As you revise, try to picture someone doing the process for the first time. Are all the steps and necessary information included?

Before giving your process analysis to your reader, use the following checklist.

✓ Checklist for a Process Analysis Paragraph

☐ 1. My topic sentence mentions the process and why understanding the process is important.

☐ 2. I have included every important step in the process.

☐ 3. Where necessary, I have explained why or how to perform steps.

☐ 4. Where necessary, I have explained what *not* to do.

☐ 5. Supporting details are arranged in a chronological or other logical order.

☐ 6. Where needed, transitions and repetition provide coherence.

☐ 7. All supporting details are relevant to my topic sentence.

☐ 8. The last sentence states or restates the importance of the process.

☐ 9. I have edited carefully (more than once) to find and correct mistakes.

☐10. I have proofread carefully after copying or typing the paragraph into its final form.

Practice 7.3

Study the following paragraph written by a student and answer the questions.

Dress for the Job You Want

¹No matter how qualified you are for a job, you will not make a good impression if you don't dress appropriately. ²If you follow these simple steps, you will look just right. ³First, find out what is appropriate for the job you want. ⁴Dress codes vary widely in different jobs, different industries, and different companies, so do some research. ⁵Ask the person who sets up your interview what employees in the position you are interviewing for usually wear. ⁶Are skirts required for women or ties for men? ⁷If so, that's how you should dress for the interview. ⁸If employees wear a uniform, try to mimic it by donning similar attire, say a blue shirt with a button-down collar and a pair of khakis or

a yellow polo shirt. [9]Your goal is to show how well you would fit in to the company by looking like an employee. [10]Little things count, so pay close attention to small details by making sure your shirt is tucked in, your tie is tied straight, your shirt and pants are pressed, and your shoes are polished. [11]Even if appropriate attire for the job you want is jeans and a T-shirt, they should be plain, neat, and clean. [12]No logos, labels, or insignia of any kind should be visible. [13]Because the business world is a conservative one, tattoos should be covered; tongue, eyebrow, or other unusual, visible body jewelry should be removed. [14]For the same reason, hairstyles should be conservative, and makeup should be minimal. [15]Finally, be prepared. [16]Bring a change of clothes just in case you spill something on your shirt or rip your hem on your way to the interview. [17]Follow these simple rules, and when you walk into the interview, you'll feel confident that you are making an excellent first impression.

1. What is the topic sentence? (*Hint*: It is not just the first sentence.) What is the topic? The assertion?

2. Which sentences explain how to perform a step?

3. Which sentences explain why to perform a step?

4. Which sentences explain what *not* to do?

5. The details are not arranged in chronological order. Why?

6. Does the paragraph have a satisfying closing? Explain.

WRITING ASSIGNMENTS

For your process analysis, you have a choice of assignments.

1. Use one of the processes in Practice 7.2. For three of these, you have already listed steps performed.

2. Use one of the topic sentences in Practice 7.1.

3. Pick something you do well and explain that process.

4. Explain how to relax.

5. Explain how to choose a great birthday gift.

6. Explain how to apologize.

7. **Combine Process and Illustration.** Explain how to deal with bad behavior or rudeness in a movie theater or checkout line without behaving badly or being rude yourself. Include examples of the kinds of bad behavior or rudeness you are dealing with (such as seat kicking) and show how the steps in the process can deal with the behavior, something like this:

   When you confront people behaving badly, try not to be confrontational. For example, if someone sitting behind you is kicking your seat, do not turn around and flash a dirty look. Instead, smile and say, "I'm sure you don't realize it, but you are kicking my seat."

8. **Respond to an Image.** The following diagram, taken from a psychology textbook, depicts a process that takes place in the endocrine system of a person's body. (The

endocrine system involves glands and the hormones they secrete.) In a paragraph, explain the process depicted in the diagram. You can begin this way: "First, the brain signals the hypothalamus to release a hormone that. . . ." After writing the paragraph, think about which version is easier for students to understand, the diagram or the paragraph.

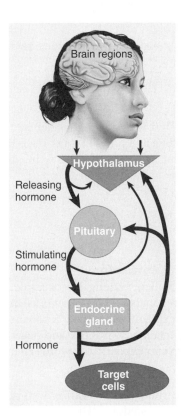

Tips

COMPOSING YOUR PROCESS ANALYSIS PARAGRAPH

- Pick a process you have performed successfully or that you understand well, so you are sure of all the steps.
- To discover an audience, ask yourself who does not understand the process well or who would benefit from learning about the process.
- If you have trouble beginning, fill in the first blank in the following sentence with the process and the second with why the process is important.

  Knowing how to _____ is important because _____.

  You will get something like "Knowing how to perform CPR is important because CPR can be a life-saver." Then use that sentence or a version of it as your topic sentence.

- If your reader is likely to do something wrong, explain how to perform a step and/or what not to do.

(continued on next page)

FAQ
Q: How can I be sure I included all the important steps?

A: Give your process analysis to a reader you trust and ask that person to perform the process. If he or she cannot perform it successfully, revise. If the process analysis is not meant to be performed, ask whether your reader understands the process completely.

Tips for Composing Your Process Analysis Paragraph (continued)

■ If you have addressed your reader directly using *you* (as is done in "Making Money with a Garage Sale"), edit to be sure you have not shifted between *you* and a noun or other pronouns, such as *he, she, him,* or *her.* (See the explanation of person shift in Chapter 22.)

> no: *You* should clean items for a garage sale because *people* can't sell dirty items.
>
> yes: *You* should clean items for a garage sale because *you* can't sell dirty items.

■ **If English is not your first language,** consider writing about a process unique to your culture, such as a particular marriage ritual, holiday celebration, or native food preparation. That way, you will write about a process you know well *and* you will educate an American reader.

SUCCEEDING IN COLLEGE

Use Process Analysis across the Curriculum

Process analysis is important in college writing. For example, in a paper for an economics class, you might have to explain how a market economy works. In a homework assignment for a nursing class, you might have to explain how to take a patient's blood pressure. For a psychology exam, you might have to explain how positive and negative reinforcement work, and for a linguistics exam, you might have to explain how words change meaning.

Assess Your Learning Style

Like the writing process, the learning process varies from person to person so that individuals must discover their own best procedures. The procedures that work best for you will depend upon your learning style.

- **Visual learners** do best when they *see* what they are learning. They prefer to watch videos and see demonstrations. Thus, a visual learner would rather study a diagram than listen to a lecture.

- **Auditory learners** do best when they *hear* what they are learning. They prefer to read out loud, listen to CDs, and hear explanations. Thus, an auditory learner would rather listen to a lecture than read a textbook.

- **Tactile learners** do best when they have their hands on something or when they are doing something. They prefer to work at the computer, build a model, or create a chart. Thus, a tactile learner would rather use flash cards than read or hear a lecture.

You can visit your campus learning lab or counseling center and complete a simple questionnaire to find out what kind of learner you are and to discover a learning process that works best for you.

Write about It

In a paragraph, explain what kind of learner you think you are: visual, auditory, or tactile. Also explain why you think you are that kind of learner.

For more practice with process analysis paragraphs, go to www.mywritinglab.com.

CHAPTER 8
Definition

You know that dictionary definitions explain the meanings of words. In this chapter you will learn to write a different kind of **definition,** one that goes beyond the dictionary meaning to explain your opinion about the term, the significance of the term, or your personal meaning of a term. For example, you can look up *electoral college* in the dictionary and read a definition of what it is, but in a definition paragraph, you do more than tell what it is; you might explain how it affects the way candidates campaign. Similarly, if you wrote a paragraph definition of *stress,* you might define stress from a college student's point of view.

A definition explains the significance of a term, your opinion about the term, or your personal meaning of the term.

A SAMPLE DEFINITION PARAGRAPH

The following definition paragraph was written by a student.

The Crazed Coupon Clipper

[1]The crazed coupon clipper is a fanatic. [2]Fired up at the prospect of saving a few quarters, this species accumulates hundreds, even thousands, of cents-off coupons. [3]Strangely though, it does not even matter if the clipper can use the products the coupons are good for. [4]My father has been a crazed clipper for years. [5]His coupon envelope marked "pets" is so fat with coupons for dog biscuits, cat food, and flea collars you would think we had dozens of cats and dogs running around. [6]The funny thing is, we have not owned a dog, cat, or any other four-legged animal since I was born. [7]While the clipper may appear to be organized (having coupons arranged alphabetically in labeled envelopes), do not be fooled—every crazed clipper has grocery bags, shoe boxes, and crates hidden at the back of the closet with unfiled, largely expired coupons jammed in. [8]The clipper is harmless for the most part; however, the species can be dangerous when turned loose in a market that offers double-coupon savings. [9]Stay out of these places, for dozens of crazed clippers will be there with glazed eyes and fistsful of coupons. [10]So ecstatic are they at the prospect of doubling their savings that they race their carts frantically about, snatching products in a savings frenzy. [11]More than once, normal shoppers have been run over by clippers crazed by the thought of saving twice as much. [12]So beware! [13]If ever you open your newspaper only to find rectangular holes where the news used to be, you no doubt have a crazed coupon clipper under your roof.

THE TOPIC SENTENCE

The topic sentence includes the term being defined and a main characteristic of the term in your topic sentence.

The topic sentence for your definition paragraph includes the term being defined (this is your topic) and a main characteristic of what is being defined (this is your assertion about the topic). Take another look at the topic sentence of "The Crazed Coupon Clipper":

> The crazed coupon clipper is a fanatic.

topic (term to be defined):   coupon clipper
assertion (main characteristic):   He or she is a fanatic.

Practice 8.1

Write topic sentences for paragraphs defining each of the terms given. Be sure to mention a main characteristic of what you are defining.

Example

Optimism *Optimism is the ability to think positively even when things look the worst.*

1. the couch potato _____

   _____

2. exam anxiety _____

   _____

3. courage _____

   _____

4. a jerk _____

   _____

5. a good sport _____

   _____

SUPPORTING DETAILS

Your supporting details develop the characteristic of the term being defined.

Your supporting details may include description and examples.

Your supporting details explain the characteristic of the term that you mention in the topic sentence. Description can be helpful with this explanation. Notice, for example, that "The Crazed Coupon Clipper" includes description to show what clippers are like in a store that offers double coupon savings:

> . . . they race their carts frantically about, snatching products in a savings frenzy.

Examples can also help explain the characteristic. Look back at sentences 3–6 of "The Crazed Coupon Clipper" and notice that the writer's father illustrates that the clipper clips coupons for products that are not used.

If your audience has a misconception about the term, you can explain what something is *not*. For example, when defining *patriotism*, you can explain that patriotism is *not* a blind love of every aspect of a country. After this explanation, you can go on to explain what patriotism *is*: loving a country while disliking its faults and trying to correct them. Look back at sentence 7 of "The Crazed Coupon Clipper," and notice that the writer explains that the clipper is not organized.

Try not to write a definition that sounds as if it really came from a dictionary. For example, if you are defining *freedom*, avoid saying "Freedom is the state of being at liberty or free of confinement." The definition should be in your own words and in your personal writing style. Also, avoid stating the obvious. For example, if you are defining *situation comedy*, do not say that it is a kind of television program.

Your supporting details may mention what something is not.

Do not write a definition that sounds like it came from a dictionary, and do not state the obvious.

Order and Transitions

You can arrange your supporting details in emphatic order by giving the characteristics of your term from the least significant to the most significant. To achieve coherence, use the transitions in the chart on pages 56–57. In particular, you may want to use transitions to signal emphatic order. If you include examples, you can use transitions that signal illustration, and if you explain what your term is *not*, you may need a transition of contrast.

Transitions for Definition

TO SIGNAL EMPHATIC ORDER more important, most important, most of all, best of all, of greatest importance, least of all, even better, the best (worst) case (example, instance, time)

> Fear of public speaking can affect a person's ability to perform well in school and on the job. *More important*, it can undermine a person's self-confidence.

TO SIGNAL ILLUSTRATION for example, for instance, an illustration of this is, to illustrate

> A football fanatic is completely obsessed. *For example*, my brother, a classic football fanatic, was found listening to the Baltimore Colts during his wedding reception.

TO SIGNAL CONTRAST (DIFFERENCES) but, yet, still, however, in contrast, on the other hand, nevertheless

> Some people think that depression is a mood a person can "snap out of." *However*, without medication, a person can be helpless to overcome it.

Practice 8.2

Assume you are writing a definition paragraph with this topic sentence:

Writer's block is the curse of the writing student.

FAQ

Q: Can I include a dictionary definition?

A: Readers can go to the dictionary if they want to; you should give them something they cannot get there: your own thoughts on what the term means.

1. List three ideas that could be used for supporting details. (If you are stuck for ideas, try brainstorming, clustering, or freewriting.)

   _____

   _____

   _____

2. List an example that could be used to develop one of the ideas you wrote for number 1. _____

   _____

3. List three details that could be included in a description of a student with writer's block. _____

   _____

   _____

4. Mention something that writer's block is *not*. _____

   _____

THE CLOSING

Any approach that provides a satisfying finish is appropriate. One approach is to refer to your topic sentence. Here is an example using the closing from "The Crazed Coupon Clipper":

topic sentence:	The crazed coupon clipper is a fanatic.
closing that refers to the topic sentence:	If ever you open your newspaper only to find rectangular holes where the news used to be, you no doubt have a crazed coupon clipper under your roof.

Another way is to explain the importance of the term being defined, especially if that was not done elsewhere in your paragraph. Here is an example that could close "The Crazed Coupon Clipper":

closing that explains the importance of the term:	Some may go overboard, but in today's difficult economy, coupon clippers can save a family a great deal of money.

The Structure of a Definition Paragraph

The Topic Sentence
states the term
gives a main characteristic of the term
↓
The Supporting Details
explain the characteristic
may include description and examples
may state what the term is *not*
↓
The Closing
may refer to the topic sentence
may explain the importance of the term

PLANNING, WRITING, AND REWRITING DEFINITION

To generate ideas, think carefully about your writing purpose and try to discover details that will help you fulfill that purpose. Are you defining *high school coach* because you want to increase your readers' appreciation of this person? Then you might want to mention the coach's dedication to young people rather than his love of sports.

Continue to think about your purpose as you write. To increase your audience's appreciation of a high school coach, you might have planned to note the long hours the coach puts in. As you write, you may also decide to state specifically what those hours are, because this clarifying information helps you achieve your purpose.

As you revise, keep your focus on your purpose. Evaluate whether adding description, examples, or an explanation of what your term is *not* will help you achieve that purpose with your particular audience.

The following checklist can help you write your definition paragraph.

✓ Checklist for a Definition Paragraph

☐ 1. My topic sentence mentions the term to be defined and a main characteristic of the term.

☐ 2. I have enough supporting details to explain the characteristic.

☐ 3. I have included description and examples where these would help explain the characteristic.

☐ 4. I have avoided a dictionary style and stating the obvious.

☐ 5. Where necessary to dispel a misconception, I have explained what the term is *not*.

☐ 6. Supporting details are arranged in emphatic or another logical order.

☐ 7. Where needed, transitions and repetition provide coherence.

(continued on next page)

☐ 8. All supporting details are relevant to my topic sentence.

☐ 9. The last sentence ends the paragraph in a satisfying way.

☐ 10. I have edited carefully (more than once) to find and correct mistakes.

☐ 11. I have proofread carefully after copying or typing the paragraph into its final form.

Practice 8.3

The following definition paragraph was written by a student. Read it and answer the questions that follow.

Christmas Spirit

[1]Christmas spirit is a joyous feeling that results from the anticipation of a wondrous celebration. [2]It is a feeling of excitement people get as they walk through the mall and realize Christmas carols are filtering through the speaker system. [3]It is the tingle they get when their eyes catch the snow and tinsel shimmering in store windows draped in red and green. [4]When they step outside and feel the brisk, cold wind brush their faces, Christmas spirit is the hope for a white December 25, the hope for the beauty of quarter-sized snowflakes floating down to blanket a frozen earth. [5]Christmas spirit is the joy of helping people. [6]It is Mr. Jones shoveling the walk of an elderly neighbor, or Mrs. Smith distributing loaves of her Christmas bread to shelters and halfway houses, or children collecting toys for the poor. [7]No, Christmas spirit has not been commercialized, as some say. [8]It is the special excitement people feel as they look forward to the one day of the year devoted exclusively to peace and love.

1. What is the topic sentence of "Christmas Spirit"? According to the topic sentence, what term will be defined, and what is the main characteristic of the term?

2. Which two sentences provide description?

3. Which sentence provides examples?

4. Give three examples of specific word choice.

5. Where does the writer explain what Christmas spirit is *not*?

6. Has the writer avoided a dictionary style? Has the writer avoided stating the obvious?

7. Are the supporting details adequate? Explain.

8. Are all the details relevant? Explain.

9. Does the paragraph have a satisfying closing? Explain.

WRITING ASSIGNMENTS

For your definition paragraph, you have a choice of assignments.

1. Define one of the terms in Practice 8.1. If you choose one of these, you already have a draft of a topic sentence.

2. Define *writer's block*. You may be able to use some of the ideas you developed for Practice 8.2.

3. Define *college student*.

4. Define *friendship*.

5. Define *good teacher*.

6. Define *tacky*.

7. **Combine Definition and Illustration.** Define *peer pressure*. Use several examples to help your reader understand the term. For instance, if you say that peer pressure exists in the workplace, cite one or more examples to demonstrate, something like this:

> People think of peer pressure as something only young people experience, but adults in the workplace experience it as well. Any time one coworker makes another coworker feel forced to do something, such as contribute to the office football pool or gossip about the boss, that's peer pressure.

8. **Respond to an Image.** The Dilbert cartoon below humorously depicts an ineffective boss. In a paragraph, write a definition of an effective boss or an effective leader. For ideas, you can think about the positive traits the boss in the cartoon is *not* demonstrating.

© 2004 DILBERT: © Scott Adams/Dist. by United Features Syndicate.

Tips

COMPOSING YOUR DEFINITION PARAGRAPH
- Think of three words that best describe your term. One of these can be the main characteristic (your assertion).
- To generate ideas, answer these questions:
  - What can I describe?
  - What examples can I give?
  - What is the term like? What is it different from?
  - What misconceptions exist about the term?

(continued on next page)

FAQ
Q: What if I can't think of a term to define?

A: Think about the roles you play and define one: student, daughter, father, softball coach, lifeguard, runner, and so on.

Tips for Composing Your Definition Paragraph (continued)

- As you write, express the characteristic in specific language. Rather than "Jealousy is terrible," write "Jealousy can destroy most relationships." Rather than "A good teacher is great," write "A good teacher makes students excited about learning."
- In revising, look for opportunities to add specific nouns, verbs, and modifiers that will create a vivid impression.
- Avoid using a term in its own definition. If you are defining *external drive,* do not say, "An external drive is a drive that. . . ." Instead, say, "An external drive is a device that. . . ."
- **If English is not your first language,** you may check a thesaurus often, looking for just the right words. But be aware that words often have both a *denotation* (dictionary meaning) and a *connotation* (implied or suggested meaning). Because some connotations are positive and some are negative, you should understand a new word's connotation before using it. For example, the denotation of *lanky* is "tall and thin." However, the connotation suggests "ungraceful" as well. Thus, you might describe a runway model as tall and thin, but a fast-growing teenager as lanky. (You can check a word in a dictionary to discover any positive and negative connotations.)

SUCCEEDING IN COLLEGE

Use Definition across the Curriculum

Every course you can take require writing definition. For example, in a homework assignment for a criminal justice class, you might have to define *reasonable force* or *civil disobedience.* In a literature class quiz, you might have to define *symbolism* or *stream of consciousness.* In a midterm for a labor studies class, you might have to define *mutual gains bargaining.* In a paper for a media course, you might have to define *pornography.*

Learn Specialized Definitions in Your Courses

Every subject has its own specialized vocabulary, and you must learn the definitions of the important terms. Often the important terms will appear in boldface type in your textbooks. Other times, your instructor will mention and define important terms in class lectures. To learn these terms, these procedures may be helpful.

- Define terms in your own words. If you have any questions, check for a glossary in your textbook or ask a question in class.

- Make flashcards. Place the term on one side and the definition on the other. Study the cards alone and with a study partner.

- Highlight important definitions in your textbooks and review them often. Use the terms in class discussions, so you become comfortable with them.

- Learn to identify similar word parts. For example, in biology class, you might find it easier to remember that *renin* is an enzyme released by the kidneys if you know that the word *renal* refers to the kidneys.

Write about It

Select a specialized term from another course, and in a paragraph, define it so that someone who is not taking that class can understand it and why it is important.

For more practice with definition paragraphs, go to www.mywritinglab.com.

CHAPTER 9

Comparison and Contrast

A paragraph that **compares** shows how two things are similar; a paragraph that **contrasts** shows how two things are different; a paragraph that **compares and contrasts** shows both similarities and differences. Comparison and contrast are important because they help us decide which of two people or items is better. For example, by comparing and contrasting two political candidates, we can decide whom to vote for. By comparing and contrasting two cars, we can decide which to buy. Comparison and contrast also help us better understand the items compared and contrasted. For example, by comparing and contrasting the workings of the human brain and a computer, we can better understand the operation of both.

> A comparison shows similarities; a contrast shows differences; a comparison and contrast shows both similarities and differences.

SAMPLE COMPARISON AND CONTRAST PARAGRAPHS

The following paragraphs were written by students.

Different Worlds

[1]A stark contrast exists between the small town where I grew up and the big city where I live now. [2]I grew up in a small Midwest town with minimal amenities but with a strong sense of community. [3]When I was growing up, my town had one local market where my family shopped on Sundays, but shopping in that store was a delightful social event. [4]Friends and neighbors were there, and we all took extra time to chat with one another in the aisles about last week's events, the upcoming week's goings-on, and everyone's family and health. [5]Because our town had so few people, my high school graduating class totaled a whopping ninety students. [6]Our school was so small that our cafeteria also functioned as a gym and performance hall. [7]Despite the small size of our town, people drove everywhere, and the instant I turned sixteen I got my license to join the car culture. [8]I cruised around town with my friends for fun, and I enjoyed the convenience of running all my errands in one outing. [9]In contrast to the small-town life of my childhood, my college life in the big city offers many amenities but with urban anonymity. [10]On my block alone, students and professionals swarm in and out of two convenience stores and a supermarket in a high-rise, but people hardly look one another in the eye, let alone say hello. [11]The number of people in my first-year college biology lecture (almost 300) is about the total number in my hometown

high school. [12]My college just built a new sports and entertainment complex that boasts a full gym, lap pool, and 800-seat theater. [13]Although I loved driving in my hometown, I have learned that a car in the city is more trouble than it is worth because of traffic and expensive parking, so I neither cruise around town nor run errands easily. [14]Instead, my roommate and I take the bus from our dorm to class, and for fun we either take the subway downtown or walk ten blocks to our favorite pub. [15]After sampling both small-town life and big-city life, I am convinced that the sense of community and interaction in a small town affords a better quality of life. [16]Having lots of amenities does not compensate for lack of human intimacy.

Identical But Different

[1]My twin sister, Loretta, and I look very much alike, but we have very different personalities. [2]Because we look so much alike, Loretta and I are frequently mistaken for each other by teachers and those who do not know us well. [3]We both wear our curly, auburn hair to the shoulder. [4]Similarly, we both are just over five feet, and weigh about the same. [5]Our facial features mimic each other, although I think Loretta is prettier, and she thinks that I am, so I guess it is a toss-up. [6]From our earliest days, we became accustomed to responding to "Hey Twin" because people cannot tell us apart. [7]On the other hand, our personalities have always been different. [8]As children, Loretta liked beautiful Barbie Dolls in sophisticated, feminine outfits, and I preferred rugged G. I. Joes in full battle gear. [9]Loretta would always want my G. I. Joes to be boyfriends for her Barbie Dolls. [10]Of course, I would never consent to such a thing. [11]Another difference was apparent in school, where Loretta was the more serious student. [12]When we had class together, she would be listening attentively to the teacher. [13]However, I was busy passing notes and planning the night to come. [14]Predictably, Loretta's grades were always excellent, and mine were rather ho-hum. [15]As an adult, my twin is quiet and conservative and always seems to do the right thing. [16]In contrast, I am outgoing and adventurous—and always in trouble. [17]Thus, although Loretta and I may look identical, inwardly we are very different people.

THE TOPIC SENTENCE

The topic sentence includes your topic (the subjects to be compared and/or contrasted) and assertion about the topic (the point of comparison and/or contrast).

The topic sentence for comparison and contrast includes your topic and your assertion about your topic. The topic is the subjects to be compared, contrasted, or both compared and contrasted. The assertion is the point of comparison and/or contrast the paragraph will make. Take another look at the topic sentence for "Different Worlds":

A stark contrast exists between the small town where I grew up and the big city where I live now.

topic: where the writer grew up and where the writer lives now

assertion (point of contrast):   A stark contrast exists between them.

Now look at the topic sentence of "Identical But Different":

My twin sister, Loretta, and I look very much alike, but we have very different personalities.

topic: the author and her twin sister

assertion (the point of   They look alike but have different personalities.
comparison and contrast):

Write a topic sentence for the following subjects. Be sure to state the subjects and the point of comparison and/or contrast.

Example

two friends   <u>My friend Jeremy is always optimistic, but Phyllis constantly expects</u>

<u>the worst.</u>

1. two teachers   <u>My teacher Smith is very dedicated, but John are the worst</u>

2. two television comedies _____

_____

3. two ways of studying _____

_____

4. two birthday celebrations _____

_____

5. high school and college _____

_____

SUPPORTING DETAILS

When you compare, your supporting details show the ways your subjects are alike. When you contrast, your supporting details show the ways your subjects are different. When you both compare and contrast, your supporting details show the similarities and the differences.

Each of your points of comparison and contrast is a general statement that most often needs to be backed up by a specific statement. (See pages 47–48 for more on following general statements with specific statements.) The specific statements can be explanation, illustration, or description. In "Identical But Different," for example, this description helps explain the first similarity between the twins, that they look alike:

> We both wear our curly, auburn hair to the shoulder. We both are just over five feet, and weigh about the same.

Supporting details state and explain the points of comparison and contrast.

In "Different Worlds," these examples help explain the first contrast, that the small town had minimal amenities but a sense of community, whereas the big city has many amenities but little sense of community:

example from the small town:	only one market and people who shopped there knew each other and socialized
example from big city:	on one block alone, two convenience stores and a supermarket, but people did not say hello

Practice 9.2

For each topic sentence you wrote for Practice 9.1, write a sentence or two that gives one point of comparison or contrast, whichever is appropriate to the topic sentence. Then note something you can say to explain, illustrate, or describe the point of comparison or contrast. Complete this practice on a separate sheet.

Example topic sentence: My friend Jeremy is always optimistic, but Phyllis constantly expects the worst.

Sentence with point of contrast: Jeremy always assumes he will do well on tests, whereas Phyllis always expects to fail.

Explanation, illustration, or description: Before the history final, Jeremy was confident enough to take a nap. Phyllis was so sure she would fail that she threw up.

Order and Transitions

Use a subject-by-subject pattern to discuss first one subject and then the other. Discuss the same points for both subjects.

Your supporting details can be ordered two ways: *subject-by-subject* or *point-by-point*. In a **subject-by-subject pattern,** you write everything about your first subject and then go on to write everything about your second subject. "Different Worlds" follows this pattern. First the writer says everything about the small town where she grew up, and then the writer says everything about the big city where she lives now. An outline of this paragraph using a subject-by-subject pattern looks like this:

I. The small town where I grew up
   A. Amenities and sense of community
   B. Size of school
   C. Use of car

II. The big city where I live now
   A. Amenities and sense of community
   B. Size of school
   C. Use of car

Notice that the writer discusses the same points (amenities and sense of community, size of school, and use of car) for both subjects. You, too, should discuss the same points for both subjects.

The ideas in the contrast part of "Identical But Different" are ordered in a **point-by-point pattern.** A point is made about one subject and then it is made about the second subject. Another point is made about the first subject and then it is made about the second, and so on. Here is an outline of the contrast portion of that paragraph:

Use a point-by-point pattern to alternate between subjects. The points discussed for one subject should also be discussed for the other.

   I. As children
      A. Loretta
      B. Author

   II. In school
      A. Loretta
      B. Author

   III. As adults
      A. Loretta
      B. Author

Notice that with the point-by-point pattern, too, the writer treats the same points about both subjects.

If you want to discuss both similarities and differences, you can do what the writer of "Identical But Different" does. You can briefly mention the similarities and then go on to explain the differences using a point-by-point pattern.

To compare and contrast, first mention the similarities and then explain the differences using a point-by-point pattern.

The following transitions can help you achieve coherence, as can the ones in the chart on pages 56–57.

Transitions for Comparison and Contrast

TO SIGNAL COMPARISON similarly, likewise, in the same way, in like manner

   A college football coach must have years of experience before he becomes a head coach. *Similarly,* a professional football coach is an assistant coach for a long time before taking on the top spot.

TO SIGNAL CONTRAST but, yet, still, however, in contrast, on the other hand, nevertheless

   I thought motherhood would be nothing but bliss. *However,* I soon learned it is a trying time.

THE CLOSING

You can use any approach that provides a satisfying finish for your comparison and contrast paragraph. Referring to your topic sentence is often effective. The writer of "Identical But Different" uses this approach.

| topic sentence: | My twin sister, Loretta, and I look very much alike, but we have very different personalities. |
| closing that refers to the topic sentence: | Thus, although Loretta and I may look identical, inwardly we are very different people. |

Another approach is to draw a conclusion from your comparison or contrast, as the writer of "Different Worlds" does.

| topic sentence: | A stark contrast exists between the small town where I grew up and the big city where I live now. |
| closing that draws a conclusion: | After sampling both small-town life and big-city life, I am convinced that the sense of community and interaction in a small town affords a better quality of life. Having lots of amenities does not compensate for lack of human intimacy. |

The Structure of a Comparison or Contrast Paragraph

The Topic Sentence
gives the subjects to be compared or contrasted
states the point of comparison or contrast to be made
↓
The Supporting Details
explain the comparisons or contrasts
may include explanation, illustration, or description
↓
The Closing
may refer to the topic sentence
may explain the conclusion drawn from the comparison or contrast

---

Practice 9.3

There are three transitions of contrast and one of comparison in "Identical But Different" on page 108. There are three transitions of contrast in "Different Worlds" on page 107. On a separate sheet, write the sentences that contain these transitions.

PLANNING, WRITING, AND REWRITING COMPARISON AND CONTRAST

Be sure your audience and purpose work well together. Do you want to convince your reader that one presidential candidate is better than the other? Then a reader who is undecided about who to vote for is probably a better audience than someone who has made up his or her mind.

During drafting, take note of your general statements of comparison or contrast. Do they need specific follow up statements of explanation, description, or illustration, in order for you to achieve your purpose with your particular reader? If so, but you can't think of what to say, underline them and push on. You can develop follow-up statements when you revise.

When revising, study your draft from your reader's point of view. Add any explanation, description, or illustration you think your reader will need. Have you used a subject-by-subject or a point-by-point pattern? Will your reader be able to follow your points with that pattern, or should you revise using the other pattern?

The checklist that follows can help you write your comparison and contrast paragraph.

✓ Checklist for a Comparison and Contrast Paragraph

- ☐ 1. My topic sentence mentions the subjects to be compared and/or contrasted and the point of comparison or contrast.

- ☐ 2. Where necessary, general statements of comparison or contrast are followed by specific explanation, illustration, or description.

- ☐ 3. I have mentioned the same points for both subjects.

- ☐ 4. Details are arranged in a subject-by-subject or a point-by-point pattern.

- ☐ 5. Every sentence is relevant to the topic sentence.

- ☐ 6. Where needed, transitions (especially of comparison and contrast) and repetition provide coherence.

- ☐ 7. All supporting details are relevant to my topic sentence.

- ☐ 8. The last sentence ends the paragraph in a satisfying way.

- ☐ 9. I have edited carefully (more than once) to find and correct mistakes.

- ☐ 10. I have proofread carefully after copying or typing the paragraph into its final form.

Practice 9.4

The following paragraphs were written by students. Read them and answer the questions.

Let's Hear It for Tradition

[1]The Christmas gatherings we used to have at my grandparents' house were much better than the celebrations I now have at my house. [2]It used to be that all the aunts, uncles, and cousins gathered for a festive reunion. [3]Now the gathering is just my husband, my children, and me. [4]In the past, every family brought a tasty dish, so no one had too much work to do. [5]Now I spend days knocking myself out making turkey with all the trimmings. [6]My aunts used to bake scrumptious cobblers and pies to go with all the traditional holiday cookies. [7]Somehow my children's iced trees and stars do not compare, although they are special in their own right. [8]At my grandparents' there was a ritual for opening gifts that

took the whole afternoon. [9]Everyone took turns opening one gift at a time. [10]This stretched out the excitement and allowed everyone a chance to ooh and aah. [11]In contrast, my children rip into their gifts in record time without savoring anything. [12]There was conversation and laughter at my grandparents'. [13]Everyone tried to catch up on what had happened since the last gathering. [14]Now, however, we talk about what we talk about any other day. [15]I miss the old gatherings. [16]However, Grandma and Grandpa and most of the aunts and uncles are gone, and the rest of us are too scattered around the country to have many gatherings.

College Is Not What I Expected

[1]Now that I have been a college student for half a year, I can say that college is not what I thought it would be. [2]After being accepted at YSU, I thought about all the fun I would have living away from home. [3]I figured I would meet a lot of new people and do a lot of new things. [4]I never had much trouble with my high school classes, so I did not think college work would be too tough. [5]After being here a short time, I knew I was wrong. [6]I have not had much fun yet. [7]Most of the nightlife centers around bars, and I am not much of a drinker. [8]I have been to a few parties, but everyone seems to know everyone else, and no one knows me. [9]I usually stand around with my roommate, and usually we go home early without meeting anyone. [10]Most of the time I cannot go out anyway because I have to study so much. [11]The homework keeps me up late at night, and still it is a struggle to get Cs. [12]Everyone tells me I need more time to adjust to college life, so maybe things will look up for me soon, and college will be more like I expected it to be.

1. The supporting details for "Let's Hear It for Tradition" are arranged in a point-by-point pattern. To understand this pattern better, complete the following outline of the paragraph.

    I. Number of people
      A. In the past
      B. Now

   II. Food preparation
      A.
      B.

  III. Opening gifts
      A.
      B.

  IV.
      A.
      B.

2. The supporting details for "College Is Not What I Expected" are arranged in a subject-by-subject pattern. To understand this pattern better, complete the following outline.

    I. What college was expected to be
      A. Fun
      B. Meeting people
      C.

II. What college really is
   A.
   B.
   C.

Practice 9.5

Reread "Let's Hear It for Tradition" and "College Is Not What I Expected" in Practice 9.4 and then answer the following questions.

1. What is the topic sentence for each paragraph? What does each topic sentence mention as the topic and the assertion about the topic? Do the topic sentences indicate the writer will compare, contrast, or do both?

2. In each paragraph, are the points discussed for one subject also discussed for the other?

3. For each paragraph, cite a point that is explained with examples or description.

4. In "Let's Hear It for Tradition," what transitions signal contrast?

5. Does either paragraph have a problem with adequate or relevant detail? Explain.

6. Does each paragraph have a satisfying closing? Explain.

WRITING ASSIGNMENTS

You have a choice of assignments for a comparison and contrast paragraph.

1. Use one of the topic sentences you wrote for Practice 9.1.

2. Contrast two of the same type of television programs, such as two situation comedies, two crime dramas, or two reality shows.

3. Compare and contrast—or just contrast—the way something is with the way you thought it would be.

4. Compare and contrast—or just contrast—the techniques of two athletes who play the same sport or two musicians who play the same instrument.

5. Contrast two print or television advertisements for the same kind of product, such as toothpaste, automobiles, life insurance, or soft drinks.

6. Compare and contrast—or just contrast—two people you admire.

7. **Combine Comparison and Contrast and Process Analysis.** Contrast two processes, such as eliminating sugar from your diet, avoiding distractions when studying, or avoiding procrastination. Use a subject-by-subject pattern for organization, so you can explain one process and then explain the other process.

8. **Respond to an Image.** In the next cartoon, Cupid contrasts his new computer mouse with his old bow and arrow. Contrast a way to do something with a computer and without one, such as shop online and at the mall, send e-mail and snail mail, or watch DVDs on your computer and on television. Is one way preferable to the other?

© 2008 David Coverly.

Tips

COMPOSING YOUR COMPARISON AND CONTRAST PARAGRAPH

- List every comparison and/or contrast you can think of without evaluating the worth of your ideas. Then go back and circle the ones you want to use.
- If you are unsure how to order your ideas, outline twice, once with a point-by-point pattern and once with a subject-by-subject pattern. Which pattern works better?
- For writing comparison and contrast, outlining first is very helpful, so select your pattern and refine your outline before you begin to write.
- In revising, if you used a subject-by-subject pattern, check for a transition in which you move from one subject to the next. If you used a point-by-point pattern, evaluate whether you need a transition each time you move from one point to another.
- When you compare and contrast, you often use the *-er, -est, more,* and *most* forms of adjectives and adverbs, forms such as *harder, clearest, more convenient,* and *most awkward.* If you are unsure about how to use these forms, check Chapter 23 when you edit.
- **If English is not your first language,** consider comparing and contrasting some aspect of your native culture with that same aspect in the United States—the study habits of students in the two cultures, the attitudes toward the elderly or death, the dating habits, marriage customs, or social etiquette.

SUCCEEDING IN COLLEGE

Use Comparison and Contrast across the Curriculum

Comparison and contrast is important in college writing, often because it helps students understand one subject in terms of another. For example, an exam in an art appreciation class might require you to compare and contrast the styles of two Renaissance painters. A research paper in an economics class might involve comparing and contrasting socialism and capitalism, whereas a report in a history class might require you to compare and contrast the foreign policies of two presidents.

Make Good Decisions

As a college student, you have many important decisions to make, such as what to major in, which material to study first, whether to take a part-time job, whether to join the basketball team, whether to transfer schools, and whether to move out of the residence hall and into an apartment. When those decisions are difficult to make, comparison and contrast can help. If you have only two choices—such as whether to attend school part time or full time—try listing the advantages and disadvantages of each option so you can compare and contrast them. If that does not help you decide, give each advantage and disadvantage a point value from 1–5. Use 5 for the most compelling points and 1 for the least compelling. Then add up the values for the advantages and for the disadvantages and let the totals help you decide.

Here are some other tips for making sound decisions:

- Compare your choices to your long-term goals, and try to choose the options that help you realize those goals.

- Use your resources. Are there people on campus who can advise you, perhaps people in the counseling center, housing office, admissions office, or financial aid office? Are there any friends or relatives with good judgment who can advise you?

- Take your time, but not too much. If you wait awhile, the right decision may reveal itself. However, if a reasonable amount of time passes and you are still unsure, make the best decision you can and move on.

- Write about the decision. Freewriting or writing in your journal about your decision may help you find clarity.

Write about It

Select a decision you made in the not-too-distant past. Then write a paragraph that explains what the decision was, what you did to make the decision, and what you think of the decision-making strategy you used.

For more practice with comparison and contrast paragraphs, go to www. mywritinglab.com.

CHAPTER 10
Cause-and-Effect Analysis

A cause-and-effect analysis explains why something happens or the results of an event.

Cause-and-effect analysis explains why something happens (the causes) or what its results are (the effects). People need to understand why events occur and what their effects are so that they can better understand their world. For example, to analyze cause, a biology textbook can explain why leaves turn color in autumn, or a magazine article may explain why women live longer than men. To analyze effects, a newspaper editorial may predict the results of passing a tax bill, or a medical journal may explain the results of using a particular medication.

SAMPLE CAUSE-AND-EFFECT PARAGRAPHS

Each of the following cause-and-effect analyses was written by a student. The first paragraph explains causes, and the second explains effects.

Fitness and the Media

[1]The media are causing people to feel dissatisfied with their bodies. [2]At any time of the day or night, a half dozen aerobics or weight training programs are on television. [3]The people on these shows do not have normal bodies—they have super bodies. [4]Normal channel-surfing folks see these people and instantly feel inadequate. [5]Commercials and infomercials are no better. [6]They are loaded with beautiful bodies selling treadmills and other exercise paraphernalia, exercise videos, and health spa memberships. [7]One look at these people and a perfectly healthy, reasonably fit person feels hopelessly out of shape. [8]Leafing through a magazine does not bring any relief, either. [9]The pages are filled with ads for Slimfast and articles about how to cut fat. [10]Of course, all are illustrated by bodies with 0% body fat, so the reader, no matter how fit and trim, feels like a whale. [11]It is time the media bombardment stopped because it is causing people with perfectly fine bodies to feel dissatisfied with themselves.

Wolves, Elk, and Cottonwood Trees in Yellowstone

[1]About fifteen years ago, wolves, which had disappeared from Yellowstone National Park because of hunting, were reintroduced to the park, with several beneficial consequences. [2]Within ten years after the wolves' return, the number of elk in the

Lamar River valley region of the park decreased by 40 percent. ³The decline benefited the region, and it was a major reason that scientists had placed the wolves in this very area. ⁴Without predators, the number of elk had became too large for the area's plants to support. ⁵Simply stated, the elk had eaten all the available plants and might soon begin starving to death. ⁶However, scientists also noticed that all along the river valley, there were suddenly hundreds of young cottonwood trees, where before there were only a few large trees and tiny seedlings. ⁷With fewer elk to graze on the young trees, the cottonwood groves along the river began to reappear. ⁸Young willows and many types of berry-producing shrubs began to come back along the river as well. ⁹Where there are shrubs and berries, there are insects and the birds that eat them. ¹⁰Therefore, many types of birds began nesting in the area. ¹¹The shrubs growing along the river-banks slowed the current, allowing fish to live in the river. ¹²The fish attracted even more birds and many types of small mammals. ¹³All in all, the changes caused by the rein-troduction of wolves led to a series of beneficial changes in Yellowstone.

THE TOPIC SENTENCE

The topic sentence for your cause-and-effect analysis includes your topic and your assertion about the topic. It can also indicate whether you plan to explain causes or effects. Look again at the topic sentence for "Fitness and the Media":

> The media are causing people to feel dissatisfied with their bodies.

topic:	the media
assertion:	They cause people to feel dissatisfied with their bodies.
word indicating causes will be discussed:	causing

The topic sentence mentions the topic and assertion. It can also suggest whether causes or effects will be explained.

Now look at the topic sentence for "Wolves, Elk, and Cottonwood Trees in Yellowstone":

> About fifteen years ago, wolves, which had disappeared from Yellowstone National Park because of hunting, were reintroduced to the park, with several ben-eficial consequences.

topic:	the reintroduction of wolves in Yellowstone Park
assertion:	It had beneficial consequences.
word indicating that effects will be discussed:	consequences

Practice 10.1

For each of the following subjects, write a topic sentence for a cause-and-effect analysis. Then indicate whether the paragraph will explain *causes* or *effects*. The first one is done as an example.

Example

computers   *Rather than help students work efficiently, computers can cause students*

to procrastinate.—causes

1. losing a job _____

_____

2. exam anxiety _____

_____

3. moving to a new city _____

_____

4. working while attending school _____

_____

5. cell phones _____

_____

■

SUPPORTING DETAILS

Think of each statement of cause or effect as a general statement that should be followed by one or more specific statements. The specific statements can be explanation, examples, description, or narration.

Each time you mention a cause or an effect, think of that sentence as a general statement that must be followed by one or more specific statements (see pages 47–48 for a discussion of following general statements with specific ones). The specific statements can be explanation, illustration, description, or narration. For example, look again at "Fitness and the Media." The first cause is given in sentence 2 in the general statement "At any time of the day or night, a half dozen aerobics or weight training programs are on television." This is followed by a specific explanation that the people on these shows have such super bodies that they make others feel inadequate.

Sometimes, causes and effects form a causal chain. A **causal chain** occurs when a cause leads to an effect, and that effect itself becomes a cause, which leads to an effect, and so on. For example, the box on page 121 illustrates a causal chain from sentences 2–10 of "Wolves, Elk, and Cottonwood Trees in Yellowstone."

Make causal chains clear.

If the causes and effects you are writing about form a causal chain, you should arrange your supporting details so that chain is evident.

You should also remember that an earlier event is not necessarily the cause of a later event. For example, if a university builds new residence halls and then experiences an enrollment increase, you may be tempted to assume that the residence halls *caused* the increase. However, other factors may be the cause: a new recruitment campaign, a tuition decrease, or an increased unemployment rate.

Do not assume that an earlier event caused a later event, and remember that an event may have more than one cause or effect.

Finally, remember that most events have more than one cause or effect. You need to consider all possibilities. The enrollment increase may actually be the result of the new residence halls, the recruitment campaign, the tuition decrease, *and* the unemployment rate.

CAUSAL CHAIN

cause: introducing wolves in Yellowstone
↓
effect: elk population reduced
↓
cause: elk population reduced
↓
effect: cottonwood and shrubs become more abundant, providing food
for birds and insects
↓
cause: cottonwood and shrubs become more abundant, providing food
for birds and insects
↓
effect: bird and insect population increase

Practice 10.2

After each topic sentence, write one cause or one effect (whichever is appropriate) in a general statement. Then note a specific point that could be made after the general statement.

Example

Our football team is doing poorly for three reasons.

general statement: Many of our starters are inexperienced freshmen.

specific point: Nichols, the quarterback; Sanders, the end; and Zanders and Michaelson

in the backfield are all first-year players.

1. Jan is failing history, and no one is surprised.

general statement: _____

_____

specific point: _____

_____

2. Teenagers begin smoking for a number of reasons.

general statement: _____

_____

specific point: _____

_____

3. Owning a pet can be beneficial.

general statement: _____

_____

specific point: _____

_____

4. Exam anxiety can be disastrous.

general statement: _____

_____

specific point: _____

_____

5. People often get into trouble as a result of peer pressure.

general statement: _____

_____

specific point: _____

_____

Order and Transitions

Often you will arrange your cause-and-effect details in emphatic order by moving from your least significant causes or effects to your most significant ones. In that case, you will use transitions to signal that order, like this:

> *A more surprising reason* for the loss of jobs in the area is . . .
> *The most damaging* effect of providing businesses with tax incentives is . . .

If your causes or effects occur in a particular time sequence, you will use chronological order and transitions to signal that order, like this example from sentence 2 of "Wolves, Elk, and Cottonwood Trees in Yellowstone":

> *Within ten years* after the wolves' return, the number of elk in the Lamar River valley region of the park decreased by 40 percent.

Finally, the transitions that signal cause and effect and those that signal addition will often help you achieve coherence, as these examples from "Wolves, Elk, and Cottonwood Trees in Yellowstone" illustrate:

Young willows and many types of berry-producing shrubs began to come back along the river *as well. Therefore,* many types of birds began nesting in the area.

Use the transitions on pages 56–57 to achieve coherence. In particular, the transitions in the following chart can help you signal emphatic order, chronological order, cause and effect, and addition.

Transitions for Cause-and-Effect Analysis

TO SIGNAL EMPHATIC ORDER more important, most important, most of all, best of all, of greatest importance, least of all, even better, the best (worst) case (example, instance, time)

> Because of the hurricane, tourists stayed away from the coastal town. *Of greater importance* is the fact that beach erosion is a serious threat to most of the oceanfront homes.

TO SIGNAL CHRONOLOGICAL (TIME) ORDER now, then, later, soon, suddenly, next, afterward, earlier, at the same time, meanwhile, often

> *At first,* regular exercise increased my energy. *Later,* it improved my self-image.

TO SIGNAL CAUSE AND EFFECT so, therefore, since, if . . . then, thus, as a result, because, hence, consequently

> Movies are becoming increasingly violent. *As a result,* parents should pay careful attention to what their children are viewing.

TO SIGNAL ADDITION also, and, and then, in addition, too, the next, furthermore, further, moreover, equally important, another, first, second, third

> The tax levy failed because senior citizens, who are often on a fixed income, did not support it. *In addition,* many supporters did not go to the polls because of the snowstorm.

THE CLOSING

You can close a cause-and-effect paragraph any way that provides a satisfying finish. One approach is to refer to the topic sentence and also mention a related idea. Here is an example using the closing from "Fitness and the Media":

topic sentence:	The media are causing people to feel dissatisfied with their bodies.
closing that refers to the topic sentence and mentions a related idea:	It is time the media bombardment stopped because it is causing people with perfectly fine bodies to feel dissatisfied with themselves.

In this example, reference to the topic sentence is made with the restatement that the media are causing people with fine bodies to feel dissatisfied; the new, related idea is that the bombardment must stop.

Another way to close is to restate the topic and assertion. Here is an example using the closing from "Wolves, Elk, and Cottonwood Trees in Yellowstone":

topic sentence:	About fifteen years ago, wolves, which had disappeared from Yellowstone National Park because of hunting, were reintroduced to the park, with several beneficial consequences.
closing that restates the topic and assertion:	All in all, the changes caused by the reintroduction of wolves led to series of beneficial changes in Yellowstone.

The Structure of a Cause-and-Effect Paragraph

The Topic Sentence
states the topic and the assertion
may indicate whether causes or effects will be explained
↓
The Supporting Details
state each cause or effect
explain each cause or effect
↓
The Closing
may refer to the topic sentence
may mention a related idea

PLANNING, WRITING, AND REWRITING A CAUSE-AND-EFFECT ANALYSIS

As you generate ideas, think about why you want to explain causes or effects. For example, perhaps you want to explain the effects of using plastic water bottles. If your goal is to convince your reader to stop using the bottles, then you can focus on the negative effects the bottles have on the environment rather than on their convenience.

As you draft, notice your general statements. If some of them need specific follow-up statements, but you can't think of what to say, underline them and push on. You can develop follow-up statements when you revise.

As you revise, continue to think about why you want to explain causes or effects so you can better assess whether adding explanation, illustration, description, or narration will help you achieve your purpose with your particular reader.

The checklist that follows can help you with your paragraph.

Checklist for a Cause-and-Effect Paragraph

☐ 1. My topic sentence mentions my topic, my assertion, and, perhaps, whether I am explaining causes or effects.

☐ 2. General statements of cause or effect are followed by specific explanation, illustration, description, or narration.

☐ 3. If appropriate, I have made causal chains evident.

☐ 4. I have not assumed that an earlier event caused a later one.

☐ 5. I have considered that an event likely has multiple causes or effects.

☐ 6. Supporting details are arranged in emphatic, chronological, or other logical order.

☐ 7. Where needed, transitions and repetition provide coherence.

☐ 8. All supporting details are relevant to my topic sentence.

☐ 9. The last sentence ends the paragraph in a satisfying way.

☐ 10. I have edited carefully (more than once) to find and correct mistakes.

☐ 11. I have proofread carefully after copying or typing the paragraph into its final form.

Practice 10.3

The following two cause-and-effect analyses were written by students. Read them and answer the questions that follow.

Why Children Grow Up Too Fast

[1]The reasons children become sexually active at an early age are clear. [2]For one thing, there is a great deal of peer pressure for sexual experimentation. [3]I know one fourteen-year-old who ran around with sixteen- and seventeen-year-olds. [4]The older kids made it clear that to be accepted, the fourteen-year-old would have to demonstrate her maturity by sleeping with a particular seventeen-year-old. [5]Parents are also a contributing factor. [6]Parents are now more open with their sexual displays and speech. [7]They tell dirty jokes in front of children and tease about sex in front of them. [8]Parents are also more lenient. [9]They are letting their children wear makeup, date, and wear mature fashions at a younger age, all of which lead to growing up faster. [10]Finally, the greater sexual explicitness of rock lyrics has caused children to mature faster. [11]These lyrics teach kids that sex is expected and virginity is outdated. [12]Thus, it is no surprise that today's youth are engaging in sex at an early age.

A Blessing in Disguise

[1]Getting laid off from Edison Corporation after twenty-five years proved to be a blessing in disguise. [2]At first, I was devastated because Edison was my life. [3]The company was not only my livelihood but also my social network and my safety net. [4]All my friends were there. [5]I got my health insurance through my job, and a large portion of my self-esteem resulted from my position as a manager. [6]I was proud of doing a good job and knowing that people looked up to me. [7]However, I began to feel better when I learned that I would get almost two years' severance pay and health insurance coverage. [8]Those

benefits presented an amazing opportunity. [9]Now I could go to college. [10]I had time, I had enough money, and I had freedom. [11]My son was now out on his own and did not need my financial support. [12]I could live frugally and make the money last until I graduated. [13]As I write this, I am two years away from graduating with a double major in studio art and education. [14]As I look forward eagerly to the next chapter in my life—a career as an art teacher—I think gratefully of Edison. [15]The company gave me many blessings, but the greatest one was to lay me off.

1. Which paragraph explains causes and which explains effects?

2. What is the topic sentence for each paragraph? What is the topic and what is the assertion? Which words mention whether causes or effects will be explained?

3. In "Why Children Grow Up Too Fast," which sentences are statements of cause? In "A Blessing in Disguise," which sentences are statements of effect?

4. In "Why Children Grow Up Too Fast," one general statement is followed by an example. What is that example? In "A Blessing in Disguise," which general statements are followed by explanation?

5. Are there any problems with adequate or relevant detail? Explain.

6. Do the paragraphs have satisfying closings? Explain.

WRITING ASSIGNMENTS

You have a choice of assignments for your cause-and-effect analysis.

1. Use one of the topic sentences your wrote for Practice 10.1.

2. Explain what would happen if _____ (you fill in the blank). For example, you can explain what would happen if no one told white lies, if there were no required courses, if public schools were in session twelve months a year, and so on.

3. Explain how attending college has affected you.

4. Explain the causes of cheating among college students.

5. Explain the causes or effects of a bad habit that you have, such as smoking.

6. Explain how the way we dress affects how people perceive us.

7. **Combine Cause-and-Effect Analysis and Description.** In a few sentences, describe a situation that creates stress, such as a traffic jam, waiting in a long line, a person talking loudly on a cell phone in a public place, or oversleeping. Use specific nouns, verbs, and modifiers to create your description. Then use cause-and-effect analysis to explain one or more effects of this stress.

8. **Respond to an Image.** College and professional sports teams often have mascots like the one in the picture on page 127. In a paragraph, explain the effects of a sports mascot on a sports team and/or on fans of the team.

Tips

COMPOSING YOUR CAUSE-AND-EFFECT ANALYSIS PARAGRAPH

■ List every cause or effect you can think of without evaluating the worth of your ideas.

■ Ask "why?" after every cause and "then what?" after every effect. The answers will help you uncover more causes and effects, and, perhaps, a causal chain.

■ List the causes and effects you will discuss and number the ideas in the order you will discuss them to create a scratch outline. Use this outline to guide your draft.

■ In revising, underline every general statement of cause or effect. Is each followed by specific explanation, illustration, description, or narration?

■ If you have used the words *effect* or *affect*, be sure you understand the difference. *Effect* is a noun meaning "result," and *affect* is a verb meaning "to influence."

> A side *effect* of the medication is drowsiness.

> The dreary days *affect* my mood.

(continued on next page)

FAQ

Q: What if there are too many causes or effects to explain in one paragraph?

A: Limit yourself to the most important ones. You can explain that a tuition increase will cause some full-time students to drop out, others to attend part time, and a subsequent layoff of teachers. You do not have to discuss the anger students will feel.

Tips for Composing Your Cause-and-Effect (continued)

■ **If English is not your first language,** use your computer's spelling and grammar checkers to help you find and correct mistakes, but be sure you understand the nature of every flagged error, what the correction should be, and why. In short, learn the rules to become a more confident editor. (For help with the rules, visit your campus writing center or English language lab.)

SUCCEEDING IN COLLEGE

Use Cause-and-Effect Analysis across the Curriculum

You will use cause-and-effect analysis often in your college writing. In a history research paper, for example, you might have to explain the causes or effects of important events or developments, such as the Industrial Revolution. For an examination in a real estate class, you might need to explain the effects of the prime interest rate on the housing market. For a paper in an educational psychology class, you might have to explain the causes of violence in schools, and for a business administration homework assignment, you might need to explain the effects of the Internet on interstate commerce.

Manage Stress

For college students, the causes of stress are many, and the effects can be serious. Stress can make you feel anxious, it can interfere with your academic performance, and in the extreme, it can harm your health. Still, there are ways to manage that stress, so it does not get the best of you.

- Maintain good physical and mental health. Eat wisely, sleep well, and exercise regularly. Keep balance in your life by scheduling time with friends.

- Identify the source of your stress and deal with the cause. For example, if you fear taking tests, go to the study skills center and learn how to manage test taking situations. If you are you short of money, visit the financial aid office to learn about scholarships and part-time work.

- Practice relaxation techniques. Your campus may offer regular yoga or meditation classes at the recreation center. They can be effective ways to cope with stress.

- Stay in control by staying on top of your assignments and attending classes, so you do not fall behind. Write to-do lists (see page 36) that represent realistic goals.

- Accept what you cannot change. If you have a miserable class schedule, but it is too late to add and drop classes, then know that you can try for a better schedule next term. If your roommate makes you crazy, but you are stuck with that person for the year, then practice patience.

- See a counselor, if necessary. If you are having trouble dealing with stress, see a campus counselor and tackle the problem head on.

SUCCEEDING IN COLLEGE (continued)

Write about It

In a paragraph, explain the biggest cause of stress in your life. Explain why this factor is a source of stress and mention the offices on campus with services that can help you deal with that stress. (You might also visit these offices to get some assistance.)

For more practice with cause-and-effect paragraphs, go to www.mywritinglab.com.

CHAPTER 11
Classification

Classification places items in groups according to a specific principle. For example, medical personnel in a hospital emergency room classify patients according to how seriously ill or injured they are, so they can determine who to treat first, second, and so on. The principle of classification in this case is the degree of sickness and injury. Similarly, a human resources manager may classify job applicants according to how experienced they are in order to determine which ones to interview. In this case, kind and amount of experience are the principles of classification. Often, items can be classified more than one way—according to more than one principle. For example, colleges can be classified according to their size, according to their location, according to their course offerings, or according to their cost.

Classification is important because it helps us sort and group things. To appreciate its importance, think of how hard it would be to find a book in the library without a classification system.

A SAMPLE CLASSIFICATION PARAGRAPH

The following classification paragraph was written by a student.

Different Kinds of Shoppers

[1]After working at K-mart for over a year, I have come to know well the four different kinds of shoppers. [2]The first shopper is the browser. [3]Browsers have endless amounts of time to waste. [4]Nonchalantly, they wander around my department picking up every item that catches their eye. [5]Unfortunately, browsers never put things back in the right place, so I have to straighten stock when they leave. [6]The browsers are also a pain because they want to look at every item locked in the showcase. [7]Of course, after all this, the browsers leave without buying a thing. [8]The dependent shoppers are also annoying. [9]They have to be shown where everything is, including the items in front of their noses. [10]Dependent shoppers never bother to look for anything. [11]They walk through the front door, find a clerk, and ask him or her to get a dozen items. [12]The hit-and-run shoppers are much easier to deal with. [13]They are always frantic and rushed. [14]They will buy anything, regardless of price, if they can get it fast. [15]Price does not matter. [16]One recent hit-and-runner raced in, asked breathlessly if

he could pay for a stereo by check, picked out the first one he saw, and bought two of them. [17]He wrote a check for over four hundred dollars as if it were $1.98 and raced out. [18]Independent shoppers are the easiest to deal with. [19]They want no part of sales clerks except for ringing up the sales. [20]Independent shoppers find what they want on their own, put things back in the right places, and never ask questions. [21]As far as I am concerned, this world needs more independent shoppers.

THE TOPIC SENTENCE

The topic sentence for you classification paragraph states your topic and your assertion. Your assertion is the words that let your reader know that you are placing items in groups. Look again at the topic sentence for "Different Kinds of Shoppers":

> After working at K-mart for over a year, I have come to know well the four different kinds of shoppers.

topic:	shoppers
assertion (indicates that items will be placed in groups):	There are four different kinds.

The topic sentence mention: the topic. It can also indicate that items will be placed in groups, the principle of classification, or the groupings.

Most items can be classified more than one way. For example, you can classify cars according to their impact on the environment, their fuel efficiency, their cost, or their model (sedan, sports car, sports utility vehicle, and so on). When items can be classified more than one way, the criterion you use for your groupings is the **principle of classification.** In addition to noting the topic and assertion in your topic sentence, you can also state the principle of classification, like this:

> After working at K-mart for over a year, I have come to know that shoppers vary according to how much trouble they cause the sales clerk.

topic:	shoppers
assertion (indicates that items will be placed in groups):	The kinds vary.
principle of classification:	how much trouble is caused for the sales clerk

Finally, the assertion portion of the topic sentence can state the grouping you will discuss, like this:

> After working at K-mart for over a year, I realize that people who shop can be browsers, dependent shoppers, hit-and-runners, or independent shoppers.

topic:	shoppers
assertion (the groupings):	browsers, dependent shoppers, hit-and-runners, or independent shoppers

Practice 11.1

The sentences below could be topic sentences for classification paragraphs. For each, do the following:

a. Underline the topic once.

b. If there are words to indicate that items will be placed in groups, underline them twice.

c. If there are words that state the principle of classification, bracket them.

d. If there are words that indicate the groupings, place them in parentheses.

Examples

Three chief types of <u>babysitters</u> can be identified by most mothers of small children.

<u>Automobiles</u> can be (high-performance cars, luxury cars, or family cars).

Most <u>horror movies</u> *can be classified* according to [how they scare people].

1. An athlete soon learns of the several kinds of coaches.

2. Four categories of <u>employers</u> exist in the workplace.

3. Four methods of studying for an exam are practiced by college students.

4. If you have eaten in as many restaurants as I have, you know that most <u>table servers</u> can be classified as attentive, uninterested, or rude.

5. With so many brands and models to choose from, buying a <u>computer</u> can be confusing unless you look at which types give you the best value for the dollar.

SUPPORTING DETAILS

Place items in groups according to a single principle of classification.

Place items in groups according to *only one* principle of classification. For example, you may group shoppers according to how hard they are to deal with (like the writer of "Different Kinds of Shoppers") or according to age or according to how carefully they shop. However, you cannot mix the groupings. You cannot discuss the careful shopper, the careless shopper, and the teenage shopper, for you would be using two principles of classification.

The sentence that mentions a particular group is a general statement that must be followed by specific statements that describe the group.

When you develop your supporting details, think of each sentence that presents a particular group as a general statement that must be followed by specific statements. For example, look again at "Different Kinds of Shoppers." Each of the following sentences presents a group. (The group is underlined as a study aid.)

The first shopper is the <u>browser.</u>
The <u>dependent shoppers</u> are also annoying.
The <u>hit-and-run shoppers</u> are much easier to deal with.
<u>Independent shoppers</u> are the easiest to deal with.

After each general statement that presents a group, specific statements explain what the members of the group are like. For example, the following details are given to explain what browsers are like:

- They have time to waste.

- They wander around picking up items.

- They don't put the items back.

- They want to look at every item in the showcase.

- They don't buy anything.

Practice 11.2

Write a principle of classification, groups that fit the principle, and items that belong in each group.

Example

kinds of group exercise classes

principle of classification *degree of difficulty*

group 1 *gentle*

group 2 *moderate*

group 3 *extreme*

items in group 1 *yoga, toning classes*

items in group 2 *low-impact aerobics, spinning*

items in group 3 *boot camp, high-impact aerobics*

1. kinds of teachers

   principle of classification the way they teach

   group 1 math teacher

   group 2 bio teacher

   group 3 His teacher

   people in group 1 _____

   people in group 2 _____

   people in group 3 _____

2. kinds of restaurants

   principle of classification country good

   group 1 French food

   group 2 Chinese food

   group 3 Mexican food

   items in group 1 _____

   items in group 2 orange chicken

   items in group 3 burito

3. kinds of friends

principle of classification _closer how long you known the friend_

group 1 _a kid_

group 2 _a highschool_

group 3 _college_

people in group 1 _____

people in group 2 _____

people in group 3 _____

Practice 11.3

After each topic sentence, state a principle of classification and list three classification groups.

Example

I have attended three kinds of dinner parties.

principle of classification _degree of formality_

group 1 _formal_

group 2 _semiformal_

group 3 _casual_

1. Bosses fall into one of three groups.

principle of classification _____

group 1 _strick_

group 2 _layback_

group 3 _bully_

2. It is possible to identify three kinds of birthday celebrations.

principle of classification _age_

group 1 _16 years_

group 2 _15_

group 3 _21 years old_

3. A sales clerk is usually one of three types.

principle of classification ___helpfullness___

group 1 _____

group 2 ___give advice___

group 3 ___carry product___

4. Radio stations can be classified according to the audiences they appeal to.

principle of classification ___talk show   music___

group 1 ___107___

group 2 ___98.___

group 3 _____

5. A person can have one of three kinds of neighbors.

principle of classification _____

group 1 ___friendly___

group 2 ___helpful___

group 3 ___noise___

Order and Transitions

Sometimes the order of your groupings does not matter. Other times, you will arrange your groups in emphatic order. For example, if you classify ways teachers grade, you can classify from the easiest to the hardest graders. Sometimes you can arrange your groups in a chronological order. For example, if you classify ways to discipline children, you can move from techniques for preschool children, to those for elementary school children, and on to techniques for high school children.

To help you achieve coherence, transitions that signal emphatic order, chronological order, and addition may be helpful. Consult the following chart and the one on pages 56–57.

Transitions for Classification

TO SIGNAL EMPHATIC ORDER more important, most important, most of all, best of all, of greatest importance, least of all, even better, the best (worst) case (example, instance, time)

Students like teachers who allow them to assign their own grades. *The most popular* teachers are still those who grade on the curve.

(continued on next page)

TO SIGNAL CHRONOLOGICAL (TIME) ORDER now, then, later, soon, suddenly, next, afterward, earlier, at the same time, meanwhile, often

> Isolating preschool children is an effective disciplinary technique. *As soon as* they reach elementary school, children respond better when valued possessions and privileges are withheld.

TO SIGNAL ADDITION also, and, and then, in addition, too, the next, furthermore, further, moreover, equally important, another, first, second, third

> Horror movies that frighten with graphic blood and gore are popular among adolescents. *Another* kind of horror movie is one that frightens with suspense rather than graphic violence.

THE CLOSING

Any approach that creates a satisfying finish makes an acceptable closing. One approach frequently used with classification is mentioning an idea closely related to your topic sentence, the way the writer of "Different Kinds of Shoppers" does:

topic sentence:	After working at K-mart for over a year, I have come to know well the four different kinds of shoppers.
closing that mentions a closely related idea:	As far as I am concerned, this world needs more independent shoppers.

Another useful approach is to explain the value of your classification, like this:

closing that mentions the value of the classification:	Anyone who works in retail sales needs to understand the different kinds of shoppers.

The Structure of a Classification Paragraph

The Topic Sentence
mentions the topic
indicates that items will be grouped
may give the principle of classification
may give the groupings

The Supporting Details
group items according to one principle of classification
explain or describe the members of each group

↓

Closing
may mention a related idea
may mention the value of the classification

PLANNING, WRITING, AND REWRITING CLASSIFICATION

During planning, make sure you have at least three groupings. If you have only two, you are really writing comparison and contrast. Also, think carefully about your audience so you classify for a purpose that will matter to your reader.

As you draft, remember to introduce each grouping with a sentence that mentions the group, so your reader knows when you have moved from one group to another. During revising, check coherence when you move from one grouping to the next. Will your reader need a transition or repetition to move smoothly from one group to the next?

This checklist can help you write your classification paragraph.

✓ Checklist for a Classification Paragraph

☐ 1. My topic sentence mentions my topic; my assertion mentions that items will be placed in groups, the principle of classification, or the groupings.

☐ 2. My topic sentence has the qualities of an effective topic sentence explained on pages 40–41.

☐ 3. I have classified according to a single principle.

☐ 4. Each grouping is introduced with a general statement.

☐ 5. The general statements introducing each group are followed by specific statements about the groups.

☐ 6. Every sentence is relevant to the topic sentence.

☐ 7. Supporting details are arranged in a logical order.

☐ 8. Where needed, transitions and repetition are used for coherence.

☐ 9. The last sentence ends the paragraph in a satisfying way.

☐ 10. I have edited carefully (more than once) to find and correct mistakes.

☐ 11. I have proofread carefully after copying or typing the paragraph into its final form.

Practice 11.4

Study this classification paragraph and then answer the questions that follow.

Kinds of Note-takers

[1]In the past year of college, I have observed three kinds of note-takers in lecture halls. [2]The first is the speedwriter. [3]Speedwriters never reflect on what their professors are saying. [4]They don't distinguish main points from secondary ones, generalizations from examples, or important facts from brief digressions. [5]Instead, they madly copy every word the professor utters, assuming each is equally important. [6]By the end of an hour these students are exhausted, and their hands are cramped. [7]Speedwriters have a difficult time studying their notes because they must sort through reams of paper and

figure out what is important. [8]The second kind of note-taker, the memory whiz, is at the other extreme. [9]Memory whizzes have an exaggerated faith in their ability to remember. [10]They write down one or two points and assume those ideas will remind them of everything else spoken. [11]They are relaxed when class is over, but studying their notes is futile because they have so little information. [12]Memory whizzes end up borrowing someone else's notes, so they can fill in the gaps. [13]The best note-taker is the informal outliner. [14]Informal outliners listen attentively for main points, write them down, and give them a number. [15]Below each numbered main point, they list any examples, explanatory points, or definitions the professor mentioned, using abbreviations, phrases, and personal shorthand. [16]The informal outliner rarely has too much or too little information written down, so studying the notes is productive. [17]If you have trouble taking notes, try informal outlining, and if that technique does not work for you, visit the study skills center to hone your skills.

1. What is the topic sentence? What is the topic? Which words mention that items will be placed in groups?

2. What is the principle of classification?

3. What general statements mention the groups?

4. Is there enough specific information after the general statements? Explain.

5. Does the paragraph have a satisfying closing? Explain.

WRITING ASSIGNMENTS

For your classification paragraph, you have your choice of assignments.

1. Use one of the topics and principles of classification in Practice 11.2.

2. Use one of the topic sentences in Practice 11.3. You may want to use the groups and principle of classification you developed when you completed this exercise.

3. Classify types of scary movies. *annomedic, comedy*

4. Classify types of people in a theater audience. *noisy, talker, kicker*

5. Classify sources of frustration.

6. Classify kinds of women's or men's magazines.

7. **Combine Classification and Cause-and-Effect Analysis.** Classify the different kinds of lies according to how serious the effects of those lies are. When you give each grouping, use cause-and-effect analysis to specify the effects of the lies in the group.

8. **Respond to an Image.** Using this photo for inspiration if you like, classify kinds of sports fans or spectators. You may find it easier to limit yourself to fans or spectators for one sport, such as football, baseball, or Little League.

Tips

COMPOSING YOUR CLASSIFICATION PARAGRAPH

- To decide on a principle of classification, list every principle you can think of. For example, if you are classifying restaurants, you could list these principles:

food	service	patrons
atmosphere	price	location

  Study your list and decide on the principle you will use.

- On a sheet of paper or on your computer, make one column for each of your groups. For example, to classify restaurants by food, you might have one column for fast food, one for homestyle cooking, and one for gourmet food. In each column, list the characteristics for the items in that grouping. Use your sheet with columns to guide your draft.

- If you have trouble beginning, write a topic sentence that states your topic and your groupings.

- As you revise, underline each sentence that presents a grouping. Then read the sentences that follow each of these sentences. Do you have enough explanation for each grouping?

(continued on next page)

Tips for Composing Your Classification Paragraph (continued)

■ As you study your draft, be sure all your details relate to your principle of classification.

■ **If English is not your first language,** do not worry about getting all the idioms, sentence structure, and vocabulary correct. Remember, even native English speakers make mistakes when they draft. Instead, express yourself in English the best way you can, knowing that during revising and editing you can make corrections—with the help of a writing center or English language lab tutor, if you like.

FAQ

Q: Do I have to include every grouping in my classification?

A: Yes. If you have too many groupings to treat in one paragraph, you should use a different topic.

SUCCEEDING IN COLLEGE

Use Classification across the Curriculum

Classification is common in college writing. In a paper for an advertising class, you might classify kinds of radio advertisements, and for a communications class exam, you might classify kinds of hate speech. An assignment for a sociology class might require you to classify kinds of nuclear families, and one in a political science class might require you to classify ways to organize city governments.

Overcome Procrastination

Procrastination is putting off until later tasks you should be doing now. Occasional procrastination is not a serious problem, but if you habitually wait until the last minute to begin assignments, or if you often delay studying for exams until the night before the test, then something is wrong, and you should address the issue in the following ways.

• **Understand your pattern of procrastination.** Are you avoiding some tasks but not others? Ask yourself why you are avoiding these tasks and devise a solution. If you habitually avoid studying for exams, for example, you may need more efficient study skills. Visit your campus learning center for suggestions.

• **Create a realistic, balanced schedule of tasks.** Schedule a reasonable mix of work and play for yourself. And if possible, schedule the work before the play. A Saturday filled with nothing but schoolwork will be oppressive and invite procrastination. But a Saturday that includes three hours of studying followed by intramural sports will likely work better.

• **Break tasks down into steps.** If a task is so large it intimidates you, break it down into a series of smaller tasks, and reward yourself after you complete each step. For example, if you must study a hundred pages for an exam, study ten at a time and treat yourself to a break after each ten pages.

• **Get a study partner.** If you make a commitment to work with someone at regularly scheduled times, you are less likely to procrastinate.

Write about It

In a paragraph, tell about the last time you procrastinated. What did you put off? Why? What were the consequences? Is procrastination normally a problem for you?

For more practice with classification paragraphs, go to www.mywritinglab.com.

CHAPTER 12
Argument

Argument, which aims to convince a reader to think or act a particular way, is everywhere. Magazine advertisements try to convince you to buy toothpaste, cleaning products, and life insurance; newspaper editorials try to convince you that tax reform is a good idea; campaign literature tries to persuade you to vote for particular candidates; letters from credit card companies try to persuade you to use their services; e-mail from a friend may try to persuade you to cut class and go to a movie. How successful these arguments are—that is, whether or not you are convinced—will largely depend on how effectively the argument is written. In this chapter, you will learn about writing effective argument paragraphs.

An argument paragraph aims to convince a reader to think or act a certain way.

A SAMPLE ARGUMENT PARAGRAPH

The following argument paragraph was written by a student.

Wear a Helmet

¹Every state should pass a law requiring motorcyclists to wear helmets. ²First of all, helmets provide increased visibility. ³Motorcycles are sometimes hard to see, but the glare from a helmet can help solve this problem. ⁴Many times I have seen the flash of a helmet before I have seen the motorcycle itself. ⁵Because automobile drivers are not conditioned to look for motorcyclists, anything that increases the cyclist's visibility will improve safety. ⁶The main reason for requiring helmets is decreasing the number of deaths. ⁷As proof of this, I offer a friend of mine who swerved to miss a car that pulled out in front of him. ⁸As a result, my friend hit a ditch at sixty miles per hour. ⁹He had several broken bones and some horrendous bruises, but because he was wearing a helmet, he did not sustain a head injury that could have killed him. ¹⁰Another friend of mine was married only three months when a car pulled out in front of his Harley. ¹¹Wearing no helmet, he hit the car at thirty miles per hour. ¹²He flew off the bike and hit his head on the curb. ¹³After a week in a coma, he died. ¹⁴If he had worn a helmet, he might have lived. ¹⁵Because helmets increase visibility and provide protection, all motorcyclists should be required by law to wear them.

THE TOPIC SENTENCE

Include a debatable issue and your position on the issue in your topic sentence.

The topic sentence for an argument paragraph includes your topic and your assertion about the topic. The topic should be an issue that people disagree about—that is, it should be something debatable. The assertion should express your position on that debatable issue. Look again at the topic sentence of "Wear a Helmet":

> Every state should pass a law requiring motorcyclists to wear helmets.

| topic (debatable issue): | whether states should require motorcyclists to wear helmets |
| assertion (writer's position on the debatable issue): | All states should pass laws requiring the helmets. |

Debatable issues—that is, issues suitable as topics for an argument paragraph because people disagree about them—are *never* statements of fact. A **fact** is something that can be proven or that has already been proven. For example, it is a fact that many college students have credit cards. Thus, you cannot write an argument paragraph with the topic sentence "Many college students have credit cards." You can, however, use this topic sentence because the issue is debatable:

> Colleges should require all first-year students to take a course in debt management.

Statements of fact and matters of personal taste do not make suitable topics for argument.

Suitable topics for an argument essay should not be matters of personal taste. You cannot argue that country living is better than city living, or that dogs make better pets than cats, because these issues are matters of personal preference.

> *Practice 12.1*

1. On a separate sheet, write the debatable topic and the writer's position on it for each topic sentence.

example:	Jan Mineo is the best candidate for governor.
debatable topic:	the best candidate for governor
position:	Mineo is the best candidate.

  a. The federal government should not subsidize galleries that display pornographic art.

  b. State property taxes are a poor way to finance public education.

  c. Students should have a say in the hiring and firing of teachers.

  d. Laws should be passed requiring the recycling of aluminum cans.

  e. Deregulation of the airline industry has caused more problems than it has solved.

2. For each of the following, write a topic sentence for an argument paragraph.

Example

placing warnings on compact discs with sexually explicit lyrics <u>Putting warnings on</u>

<u>CDs with sexually explicit lyrics is a misguided effort to protect young people.</u>

    a. 21 as the legal drinking age

<u>Should age 21 be a limit drinking alcohol)</u>

_____

    b. having to pass an exam to get a high school diploma

_____

_____

    c. mandatory drug testing for high school athletes

_____

_____

    d. the sale of handguns

_____

_____

    e. single-sex schools

_____

_____

SUPPORTING DETAILS

    Supporting details include the reasons for your position on the debatable topic. However, since your purpose is to convince your reader to think or act a particular way, you want those reasons to be persuasive. To accomplish that goal, back up your reasons with specific information, called **evidence.**

    Your evidence can be presented in one or more of the patterns you have already learned: narration, description, illustration, process analysis, definition, comparison and contrast, cause-and-effect analysis, and classification. For example, look at the way the writer of "Wear a Helmet" supports the reason he gives in sentence 2:

    First of all, helmets provide increased visibility.

The supporting details are the reasons for your position and the evidence that shows the reasons are true. Evidence can be written in any of the patterns explained in this book.

The writer backs up increased visibility as a reason in sentences 3, 4, and 5 with evidence that combines explanation, illustration, and cause-and-effect analysis:

explanation of problem and solution:	Motorcycles are sometimes hard to see, but the glare from a helmet can help solve this problem.
illustration of solution working:	Many times I have seen the flash of a helmet before I have seen the motorcycle itself.
cause of problem and effect of solution:	Because automobile drivers are not conditioned to look for motorcyclists, anything that increases the cyclist's visibility will improve safety.

Now look at the writer's second reason for requiring helmets, given in sentence 6:

The main reason for requiring helmets is decreasing the number of deaths.

This reason is backed up with evidence in sentences 7 through 13 that combines illustration, cause-and-effect analysis, and comparison-contrast:

example (sentences 6–9)	the friend who swerved to miss a car that pulled out in front of him
example (sentences 10–13)	the friend hit by the car who died
cause-and-effect analysis:	the first friend lived because he wore a helmet; the second friend died because he did not wear a helmet
comparison-and-contrast:	the contrast in the fates of the two friends

FAQ
Q: Should I explain both sides of the issue I am arguing?

A: No. You can mention one or two reasons against your position and go on to say something that makes those reasons less powerful or compelling, but do not give all the reasons on both sides of an issue. Present a case for just one side.

In addition to giving reasons and evidence, your supporting details can include cause-and-effect analysis to indicate the consequences of adopting or not adopting your position, like this:

effect if the position is adopted:	If states require motorcyclists to wear helmets, fewer motorcyclists will die or sustain brain damage.
effect if position is not adopted:	Without mandatory helmet laws, we are risking the lives of motorcyclists unnecessarily.

You can note what would happen if your position were or were not adopted.

Another way to support your topic sentence and convince your reader is to mention one or more of the most compelling reasons *against* your position and then say something to make those opposition points less powerful, like this:

Some people say that helmet laws infringe on personal freedom. In fact, they are no more a threat to freedom than seat belt laws.

Avoid name-calling and expressions like "most people believe."

Finally, avoid these two strategies. The first is name-calling. Saying things like, "Only the uninformed believe" or "As any fool knows" will insult your reader who may not "believe" or "know." You can attack ideas, but do not attack people. Second, avoid generalized expressions like "most people believe" unless you are certain that they are true.

Order and Transitions

Your supporting details will often be in emphatic order, so they gradually build up to the most convincing reason, which appears last. To signal that emphatic order, you can use the transitions in the following chart. If you mention a reason against your position and then say something to make the point less powerful, you may want to use a transition that signals conceding a point, like this:

Details are often arranged in emphatic order.

> *While it is true* that students in the United States are falling behind in math and science, proficiency tests will not solve that problem.

Transitions for conceding a point are also given in the chart below. In addition, the transitions on pages 56–57 can help you achieve coherence.

Transitions for Argument

TO SIGNAL EMPHATIC ORDER more important, most important, most of all, best of all, of greatest importance, least of all, even better, the best (worst) case (example, instance, time)

> The university should revise the core curriculum because it does not reflect twenty-first century priorities. *Even more important* is the fact many students are transferring to other schools to take a more contemporary curriculum.

TO SIGNAL CONCEDING A POINT although, even though, while it is true, granted

> *Even though* hybrid cars are more expensive than their gasoline-driven counterparts, the money saved on gasoline makes up for the higher sticker price.

Practice 12.2

List three reasons to support each topic sentence.

Example

Little League baseball places too much pressure on young children.

   a. The pressure to win teaches the wrong values.

   b. The pressure not to let teammates down causes stress.

   c. The pressure not to let parents down affects self-esteem.

1. Beer and wine commercials should (or should not) be banned.

   a. _____

b. _____

c. _____

2. Workplaces with more than seventy-five employees should (or should not) have a day-care center. *should have*

    a. *cost less* _____

    b. *less rest* _____

    c. _____

3. Parents should (or should not) help select the textbooks used in public schools.

    a. *Should not have* _____

    b. *don't know the system.* _____

    c. _____

4. Alcohol should (or should not) be banned on college campuses.

    a. *Should not be banned* _____

    b. *for study* _____

    c. *too dangerous* _____

5. An eleven-month school year is (or is not) a good idea.

    a. *not a good idea* _____

    b. _____

    c. _____

Practice 12.3

1. Pick one of the following topic sentences and give one reason for the position stated in that topic sentence.

    a. Rather than require certain courses, colleges should allow students to take whatever courses they want.

    b. Requiring college students to take certain courses is an educationally sound idea.

    c. After age sixty-five, drivers should have to pass a driving test every year.

    d. After age sixty-five, drivers should not have to pass a driving test every year.

    e. Final examinations should be abolished. *eliminate*

    f. Final examinations should not be abolished.

reason: _____

_____

2. List two pieces of evidence to back up the reason you wrote for number 1.

evidence: _____

_____

_____

evidence: _____

_____

_____

Practice 12.4

Complete the following on a separate sheet:

1. Select one of the topic sentences from Practice 12.2 and write a sentence or two that mentions a reason against the position and says something to make that opposition point less powerful.

2. Select one of the topic sentences from Practice 12.2 and write a sentence or two that mentions what would happen if the position were adopted. Then write a sentence or two that mentions what would happen if the position were *not* adopted.

THE CLOSING

Any approach that gives your argumentation paragraph a satisfying finish is acceptable. One approach is to restate the reasons for your position, the way the writer of "Wear a Helmet" does.

topic sentence:	Every state should pass a law requiring motorcyclists to wear helmets.
closing restates the two reasons explained in the paragraph:	Because helmets increase visibility and provide protection, all motorcyclists should be required by law to wear them.

Another approach is call your readers to action. Here is an alternate closing to "Wear a Helmet" that illustrates this approach:

closing with a call to action:	Before anyone else dies unnecessarily, write your senators and representatives and urge them to support helmet laws.

The Structure of an Argument Paragraph

The Topic Sentence
mentions a debatable issue
gives your position on the issue
↓
The Supporting Details
give the reasons for your position
back up the reasons with evidence
↓
The Closing
may restate your reasons
may call readers to action

PLANNING, WRITING, AND REWRITING ARGUMENT

As you plan, be sure your audience and purpose work well together. For example, it is unlikely you can convince a member of the National Rifle Association to support a law banning hand guns. Perhaps you should adjust that purpose to lessening that reader's objection to the law; or perhaps you should find a different audience, such as shop owners or the average reader of a city newspaper.

As you write, consider how likely it is that your reasons will be convincing to your reader. If you think some of your details fall short of your persuasive goal, underline them for later consideration, but do not interrupt your drafting momentum to revise.

As you revise, study your draft from your reader's point of view. Consider how convincing your reasons and evidence are, and how likely they are to convince your reader to agree with your topic sentence. Add and delete reasons and evidence as necessary.

The checklist that follows can help you with your argument paragraph.

✓ Checklist for an Argument Paragraph

☐ 1. My topic sentence states a debatable issue and mentions my position on that issue.

☐ 2. My supporting details include reasons for my position and evidence to back up those reasons.

☐ 3. Reasons and evidence are aimed at convincing my reader to think or act a particular way.

☐ 4. If it would help convince my reader, I have mentioned important reasons against my position and made them less compelling.

☐ 5. If it would help convince my reader, I have noted what would happen if my position were or were not adopted.

☐ 6. I have avoided name-calling and generalized expressions such as "most people believe."

☐ 7. Supporting details are arranged in emphatic or other logical order.

☐ 8. Where needed, transitions and repetition are used for coherence.

☐ 9. The last sentence ends the paragraph in a satisfying way, perhaps by restating my position or calling the reader to action.

☐ 10. I have edited carefully (more than once) to find and correct mistakes.

☐ 11. I have proofread carefully after copying or typing the paragraph into its final form.

Practice 12.5

The following argument paragraph was written by a student. Read it and answer the questions.

No Degree Required

[1]We should discontinue the requirement in this state that people must earn teaching degrees before they can teach in public schools. [2]The requirement that a person have a teaching degree from a four-year college means that talented, knowledgeable people, people who would be terrific teachers, cannot give what they have to offer—just because they have not taken a handful of teaching courses. [3]Consider an accountant who loves children and has a way of inspiring them. [4]He or she cannot teach arithmetic without earning a teaching degree even though that person already has the knowledge and talent to be a fine teacher. [5]Or what about a former U.S. senator who loves children and knows the government inside out? [6]That person cannot teach social studies without going back to school to earn a teaching degree. [7]In both cases and countless more like them, people who could educate and inspire young people are prevented from doing so. [8]Of course, we can't let just anyone with knowledge of a subject into the classroom. [9]We must be sure the person has the other qualities necessary to teach. [10]We should set up training programs to teach prospective teachers about classroom management, and we should have tests to judge the knowledge and talent of people who want to teach. [11]Then we should require a year of probation to weed out those who are not suitable. [12]Deans of colleges of education all over the country are likely to cry out that only accredited schools can train teachers, but that point of view is self-serving. [13]After all, our current method of requiring teaching degrees has done little to assure quality education.

1. What is the topic sentence of "No Degree Required"? What is the writer's debatable issue? What is the writer's position on the issue?

2. Write the sentences that state the reasons for the writer's position.

3. The evidence to prove the first reason is which of the following:

    a. narration

    b. example

    c. narration and example

4. What reason against the writer's position is given? How does the writer attempt to make that reason less powerful? Does the writer succeed in making the reason less powerful? Explain.

5. Does the paragraph have a satisfying closing? Explain.

WRITING ASSIGNMENTS

For your argument paragraph, you have your choice of assignments.

1. Use one of the topic sentences you wrote in response to number 2 of Practice 12.1.

2. Use one of the topic sentences from Practice 12.2. You may want to use some or all of the reasons you developed when you completed this exercise.

3. Write a paragraph to persuade someone who graduated from your high school to attend your college.

4. Write a paragraph arguing that Internet chat rooms are harmful (or helpful).

5. Argue for or against using torture to interrogate suspected terrorists.

6. Argue for or against requiring high school students in public schools to wear uniforms.

7. **Combine Argument and Cause-and-Effect Analysis.** Write a paragraph to convince the appropriate campus administrator that a specific change is needed at your college, such as a change in registration procedures, course requirements, parking facilities, or residence hall rules. Use cause-and-effect analysis to give the effects the change would have.

8. **Respond to an Image.** Print advertisements are a form of argument because they try to convince readers to think or act in a particular way. Most commonly, they try to convince us to think positively about a product and buy it as a result. Study the following advertisement and write an explanation of its persuasive strategies. Consider the following questions:

    • Who is the intended audience?

    • How does the picture work to persuade that audience?

    • How do the words work to persuade that audience?

    • How does the ad try to overcome the health risks associated with smoking?

    • Do you think the ad achieves its purpose with its intended audience?

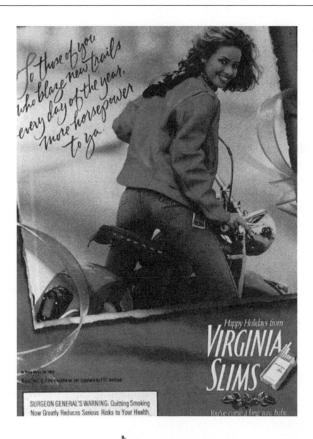

To those of you who blaze new trails, every day of the year, more horsepower to ya.

Happy Holidays from

VIRGINIA SLIMS

SURGEON GENERAL'S WARNING: Quitting Smoking Now Greatly Reduces Serious Risks to Your Health.

Tips

COMPOSING YOUR ARGUMENT PARAGRAPH

- Be sure to choose a debatable issue that you know something about. If you need help finding a topic, review your campus and local newspapers for controversial (debatable) issues.
- List every reason you can think of to support your position. Next to each reason, note a piece of evidence you can use for backup support.
- Number your list of reasons in emphatic order.
- As you write, begin with a topic sentence that states the debatable issue and your position on the issue.
- During revising, underline each of your reasons. Is each followed by evidence? If not, consider whether you should add details.
- What is the most compelling point against your position? Should you state that point and make it less compelling?
- Ask someone with good judgment about writing to read your paragraph and judge whether it is convincing.
- **If English is not your first language,** be aware that in some cultures, arguing for a position is considered impolite, but in the United States, it is not. Do not think you need to explain both sides of an issue. Present a case for just one side.

Use Argument across the Curriculum

Argument is an important part of college writing because it requires you to do more than recall information: It requires you to analyze, evaluate, and draw conclusions. In other words, argument is a real test of your understanding of material and how carefully you have reflected on it. Thus, in an education class, you might be asked to argue for or against proficiency examinations. In a labor studies class, you may be asked to argue for or against unions for public employees. In a literature class, you might have to state and then defend your interpretation of a poem.

Learn How to Resolve Conflict

From time to time, you may experience a conflict with a classmate, roommate, or instructor. You can resolve that conflict gracefully using some of what you learned about writing argument.

- Consider what would happen if your position were not adopted. Maybe you will realize that nothing much would change, so you might as well drop the matter. If you received a B– and believe you deserve a B, the disagreement with your instructor may not be worth pursuing because your overall average is not affected.

- Identify areas of agreement. You may discover that you have common ground that you can use to forge a solution. For example, say that you and your roommate disagree about how often to clean your room, but you agree that you both need to study hard to keep your scholarships. You might discuss the fact that studying in a neat, clean room is easier than studying in a messy, dirty one.

- Try to see the other person's point of view, and you might find a good solution. For example, say that you are annoyed because a classmate is not completing her parts of a group assignment. When you look at it from her point of view, you may realize that she did not get to choose her tasks the way other group members did because she joined the group late. The solution may be to ask her if she would prefer to do a different task.

- Talk over the disagreement respectfully. Explain how you see the disagreement and offer a solution. Then let the other person talk, and listen respectfully without interruption. Above all, avoid name-calling. It will only create anger and lessen the chances of resolving the conflict.

Write about It

Write about a recent conflict you had with someone. What was the conflict about? Did you resolve it? How? If you had the chance, would you have handled the conflict differently? If so, how?

For more practice with argument paragraphs, go to www.mywritinglab.com.

CHAPTER 13
Writing an Essay

In college, you will often write **essays,** which are compositions made of several paragraphs. Because an essay has several paragraphs, it allows you to develop a topic in more detail than you can in a single paragraph. When you write research papers, book reviews, reports, summaries, and other papers in your classes, you will use the essay form so you can treat your topic in the appropriate depth.

An essay is a composition made of several paragraphs.

THE PARTS OF AN ESSAY

An essay has three parts: the introduction, the supporting paragraphs, and the conclusion.

Each part serves an important purpose. The **introduction** presents the writer's central point and stimulates the reader's interest in that point. The **supporting paragraphs** provide details to prove or explain the central point. The **conclusion** brings the essay to a satisfying finish.

The parts of an essay are:
1. the introduction
2. the supporting paragraphs
3. the conclusion.

THE PARTS OF AN ESSAY

The Introduction
states the central point
stimulates the reader's interest in the central point
↓
The First Supporting Paragraph
provides details to help explain or prove the central point
↓
The Second Supporting Paragraph
provides more details to help explain or prove the central point
↓
The Third Supporting Paragraph
provides more details to help explain or prove the central point
↓
The Conclusion
closes the essay in a satisfying way

The following essay was written by a student. It appears here to illustrate the parts of an essay: the introduction, the supporting paragraphs, and the conclusion. Each of these parts is labeled and explained in the margin.

Runner's High

Paragraph 1

Introduction: The first four sentences create interest. The last sentence gives the central point: Runner's high is a special feeling.

[1]Some people run religiously (five or six times a week); some run periodically (five or six times a month); and some run whenever they feel an urge to be physically fit (once a year). What makes these people run? What inner drive makes them go out onto the lonely road, with their iPods strapped to their arms and their large sticks to beat off attacking dogs? Do they like the feel of Ben-Gay rubbed all over their tired, aching bodies? No, these people run to experience that special feeling known as runner's high.

Paragraph 2

This paragraph explains the central point by describing what runner's high feel like.

[2]The high is difficult to explain to nonrunners, but put simply it feels like getting an A on a final exam you were sure you failed. The high takes you by surprise. Just when you feel you are about to see your dinner come out through your nose, the high picks you up and gives you incentive to keep going. The high is similar to a painkiller in the way it suppresses the pain in your joints. It also relaxes your tense muscles. In some instances, it even replenishes your energy, which makes you go farther and faster.

Paragraph 3

Supporting Paragraph: This paragraph explains the central point by discussing when a runner feels the high.

[3]Some runners feel this high when they begin running, while others feel the rush as soon as they are finished. The most common time to feel the high, though, is about halfway into the run when the adrenaline is pumping. When a runner feels the high can be deciding factor in a race. A runner who peaks too early and experiences the high too soon will more than likely "hit the invisible wall," lose momentum, and lose the race.

Paragraph 4

Supporting Paragraph: This paragraph explains the central point by noting how long runner's high lasts and what happens when it goes.

[4]If the high lasted longer than its normal few seconds (or even minutes in distance races), then the track world would have an incredible number of outstanding runners. However, all good things end, and a runner's high disappears just as suddenly as it comes. As soon as the runner's high disappears, the runner loses the sense of well-being and must dig deep to ignore aching limbs, throbbing chest, and weariness in order to finish the race. The high now is just a memory.

Paragraph 5

Conclusion: This paragraph brings the essay to a satisfying close.

[5]Many people wonder why runners make themselves suffer so much just to achieve a few moments of bliss. Unfortunately, there is no way to explain this to someone who has never experienced runner's high.

Comparing Paragraph and Essay Parts

You may have noticed these similarities between paragraph and essay parts:

- Both the paragraph and the essay have a sentence that states a central point.

- Both the paragraph and the essay have parts that explain or prove that central point (the supporting details in a paragraph and the supporting paragraphs in an essay).

- Both the paragraph and the essay have a part that brings the writing to satisfying finish (the closing sentence in a paragraph and the conclusion in an essay).

A COMPARISON OF PARAGRAPH AND ESSAY PARTS AND FUNCTIONS

Paragraph Part		Function		Essay Part
topic sentence	→	presents writer's central point	←	introduction
supporting details	→	explain or prove writer's central point	←	supporting paragraphs
closing	→	brings writing to satisfying close	←	conclusion

Practice 13.1

Following is a paragraph that first appeared on page 149, along with a revision expanded to an essay. Read both versions and answer the questions that follow them.

The Paragraph Version

No Degree Required

[1]We should discontinue the requirement in this state that people must earn teaching degrees before they can teach in public schools. [2]The requirement that a person have a teaching degree from a four-year college means that talented, knowledgeable people, people who would be terrific teachers, cannot give what they have to offer—just because they have not taken a handful of teaching courses. [3]Consider an accountant who loves children and has a way of inspiring them. [4]He or she cannot teach arithmetic without earning a teaching degree even though that person already has the knowledge and talent to be a fine teacher. [5]Or what about a former U.S. senator who loves children and knows the government inside out? [6]That person cannot teach social studies without going back to school to earn a teaching degree. [7]In both cases and countless more like them, people who could educate and inspire young people are prevented from doing so. [8]Of course, we can't let just anyone with knowledge of a subject into the classroom. [9]We must be sure the person has the other qualities necessary to teach. [10]We should set up training programs to teach prospective teachers about classroom management, and we should have tests to judge the knowledge and talent of people who want to teach. [11]Then we should require a year of probation to weed out those who are not suitable. [12]Deans of colleges of education all over the country are likely to cry out that only accredited schools can train teachers, but that point of view is self-serving. [13]After all, our current method of requiring teaching degrees has done little to assure quality education.

The Essay Version

No Degree Required

[1]Education in the United States is in trouble. That statement won't surprise anyone because we hear it all the time. What is surprising is that we don't seem to be doing much about the problem. Well, one suggestion can improve the quality of education in the United States, and it won't even cost a lot of money. We should discontinue the requirement in this state that people must earn teaching degrees before they can teach in public schools.

[2]The requirement that a person have a teaching degree from a four-year college means that talented, knowledgeable people, people who would be terrific teachers, cannot give what they have to offer—just because they have not taken a handful of teaching courses. Consider an accountant who loves children and has a way of inspiring them. He or she cannot teach arithmetic without earning a teaching degree, even though that person already has the knowledge and talent to be a fine teacher. Or what about a former U.S. senator who loves children and knows the government inside out? That person cannot teach social studies without going back to school to earn a teaching degree. In both cases and countless more like them, people who could educate and inspire young people are prevented from doing so. This fact is particularly disturbing when you consider that the accountant and senator probably know more about math and government than some people with teaching degrees who are currently teaching math and social studies.

[3]Of course, we can't let just anyone with knowledge of a subject into the classroom; we must be sure the person has the other qualities necessary to teach. We should set up training programs to teach prospective teachers about classroom management, and we should have tests to judge the knowledge and talent of people who want to teach. Then we should require a year of probation to weed out those who are not suitable. Deans of colleges of education all over the country are likely to cry out that only accredited schools can train teachers, but that point of view is self-serving. After all, our current method of requiring teaching degrees has done little to assure quality education.

[4]An important benefit of this plan is that it taps an important source of potentially gifted teachers: retired people. These days, people are retiring younger, and they are looking for productive second careers. Teaching could be that career. Men and women with lifetimes of valuable experience and knowledge have much to share with young people. They should be able to teach without spending time and money to go back to school themselves to take courses that may not even make them better teachers. Furthermore, these people are, in many cases, financially secure because their children are grown and gone, their mortgages are paid off, and their expenses are fewer. Thus, they are likely to be more satisfied with the meager salaries that teachers often make. Hiring retirees to teach means we can spend less on teacher salaries, a real saving to financially troubled school districts.

[5]With American education in trouble, we need creative solutions that do not cost more than school districts can afford. Hiring talented people without teaching degrees to educate our children can be one such solution.

1. In the paragraph, place parentheses around the sentence that states the central point.

2. In the essay, place parentheses around the sentence that states the central point.

3. In the paragraph, underline the first idea to explain or prove the central point.

4. In the essay, underline the first idea to explain or prove the central point.

5. In the paragraph, underline the second and third ideas to explain or prove the central point.

6. In the essay, underline the second and third ideas to explain or prove the central point.

7. The essay has a sentence that gives a fourth point to explain or prove the central point, but the paragraph does not. Put a wavy line (~) under that point in the essay.

8. Put brackets ([ ]) around the closing of the paragraph and the conclusion of the essay.

THE INTRODUCTION

The introduction, which opens your essay, has two purposes:

1. The introduction mentions the central point of your essay. The statement of the central point is the **thesis.**

2. The introduction stimulates your reader's interest in the central point. The material that stimulates interest is the **hook.**

The two parts of your introduction are the thesis and the hook.

The Thesis

The **thesis** is the sentence or two in your introduction that states the central point of the essay. Like the topic sentence of a one-paragraph composition, the thesis gives your topic and your assertion about the topic. Look again at the thesis of "No Degree Required" to see the parts of a thesis:

Your thesis states the essay's central point.

thesis:	We should discontinue the requirement in this state that people must earn teaching degrees before they can teach in public schools.
topic:	the requirement that people must earn teaching degrees before they can teach in public schools
assertion:	We should discontinue it.

Here is another example:

thesis:	Situation comedies portray American families in a negative light.
topic:	situation comedies
assertion:	They portray American families in a negative light.

You can also write an effective thesis by stating your topic, your assertion, and the main points you will make in your supporting paragraphs. Here is an example:

Your thesis includes your topic and assertion about the topic. It can also state the main points you will cover.

thesis:	I love my brothers, but living with them is difficult because they eat all the food, they expect me to be their maid, and they treat me like a child.
topic:	living with my brothers
assertion:	It is difficult.
main points to be made in supporting paragraphs:	The brothers eat all the food, they want me to be their maid, and they treat me like a child.

Here is another example:

thesis:	College students should study a foreign language because knowing a second language increases job opportunities, and it creates an important cultural perspective.
topic:	studying a foreign language
assertion:	College students should do it.
main points to be made in supporting paragraphs:	It increases job opportunites; it creates an important cultural perspective.

Practice 13.2

For each thesis, underline once the words that state the topic, and underline twice the words that state the assertion. If the thesis also indicates the main points to be covered, place those words in brackets.

Example

> <u>Animals</u> <u>should not be</u> <u>used to test cosmetics</u> because [the testing is cruel to animals, and it is unnecessary.]

1. The summers I spent at Lake Erie as a child were always a time of discovery.

2. Despite what our state senator claims, tax cuts are not the best way to stimulate the economy.

3. Because doing so would increase the amount of instructional time, make more efficient use of resources, and keep young people out of trouble, the school year should be extended to ten months.

4. Although they cost the same, these two cars are very different.

5. Most magazine advertisements cause both males and females to have negative self-images.

The Qualities of an Effective Thesis

To write an effective thesis, you must understand the following points.

1. **Avoid statements of fact.** A thesis that merely states a fact that everyone agrees about will leave you with nothing to say in your essay.

statement of fact:	Many people enjoy watching game shows.
acceptable revision:	Game shows are popular because they entertain people and make them feel smart.

   The statement of fact is an unacceptable thesis because it gives the writer nothing more to say. The revision is acceptable because it allows the writer to explain two reasons that game shows are popular.

2. **Avoid very broad statements.** An essay allows you to discuss more ideas than you can discuss in a one-paragraph composition, but there are still limits to how much territory you can cover.

| too broad: | Computers have changed the way we live. |
| acceptable revision: | Computers have changed the way students communicate. |

Computers have affected so many aspects of life for so many people that to discuss them all would take a book. However, in a single essay you can reasonably limit yourself to one group of people (students) and one aspect of life (communication).

3. **Avoid expressing your assertion in vague words.** Vague words, such as *good, bad, nice, great, awesome,* and *interesting* do not give your readers a clear enough understanding of your assertion.

| vague: | Google is an awesome search engine. |
| acceptable revision: | Google is an efficient search engine for researchers who know how to use it. |

The thesis with *awesome* as an assertion merely gives the reader a vague sense that Google is good. However, the second thesis gives reader a specific understanding of the assertion: Google is efficient for researchers who know how to use it.

4. **Avoid formal announcements.** A formal announcement can seem abrupt, so many readers consider it poor style.

| formal announcement: | This thesis will explain why people should buy hybrid cars. |
| acceptable revision: | Hybrid cars will protect our environment and reduce our dependence on foreign oil. |

In many science and social science classrooms, the formal announcement is acceptable. If you are unsure whether you can use it, check with your instructor.

5. **Avoid referring to the title as if it were part of the introduction.** The title is an independent entity, not the first sentence of your introduction.

| part of the introduction: | [The title of the essay is "The Benefits of Yoga"] It helps manage stress and create a positive outlook. |
| acceptable revision: | Yoga helps manage stress and create a positive outlook. |

Practice 13.3

If the thesis is acceptable, write OK on the blank. If it is unacceptable, indicate the problem on the blank by writing one of the following: *fact, broad, vague, announcement.* On a separate sheet, rewrite the unacceptable thesis statements to make them acceptable.

<u>broad</u>   example: The United States should revise its economic policy.

                     revision: The United States should place tariffs on imported steel.

_____ 1. No one should drive a car when drunk.

_____ 2. Public education would improve if students were required to wear uniforms.

_____ 3. Trying juvenile offenders as adults—even for violent crimes—is a bad idea.

_____ 4. Some people oppose stem cell research on moral grounds.

_____ 5. Until we can eliminate unjust convictions, we should abolish the death penalty.

_____ 6. As the next paragraphs will illustrate, HBO's original programming includes excessive violence.

_____ 7. Modern technology has improved our lives in many ways.

_____ 8. Recycling is easier than many people realize.

Practice 13.4

For each topic given, write a thesis for an essay. Include a topic and your assertion. Also, be sure to meet the requirements for an effective thesis.

Example

an annoying relative   My cousin Lee is very stubborn. _____

_____

1. the best way to relax (Mention two or three points that will be developed in supporting paragraphs.) _____

_____

2. the rewards of college life _____

_____

3. the frustrations of college life _____

_____

4. television (or magazine) advertisements _____

_____

5. writing classes _____

_____

■

The Hook

Your hook should create interest in your essay.

The **hook** stimulates interest in your essay. Remember the last time you started reading something and put it aside because the opening did not engage your interest? You do not want your reader to put your essay aside or push through it feeling bored. To stimulate interest in your essay, you can draw on a number of strategies, illustrated in the following examples. (The thesis is underlined as a study aid.)

1. **Give background information.** Tell your reader something he or she should know to understand the importance of your thesis or some of the detail in your essay.

> On the first day of classes, students who applied for guaranteed student loans were inconvenienced by a lack of funds. <u>Clearly, the loans should be distributed in advance.</u>

The writer's thesis is that guaranteed student loan funds should be distributed in advance. The first sentence is the hook, which provides the background fact that students did not have their loans on the first day of school.

2. **Tell a story.** A brief story can create interest in your essay and help prove your thesis.

> When I was nine, I woke up in the middle of the night to the sounds of yelling. Terrified, I went to the top of the stairs and discovered my parents were screaming at each other. I sat there, confused, shaken, and unable to move. Then the horrible thing happened. I watched my father throw a vase at my mother. It missed her and shattered against the wall. <u>However, from that moment on, I knew that married people should not stay married "for the sake of the children."</u>

The thesis is that people should not stay married because they think divorce will hurt the children. To create interest in this point and help prove its truth, the writer tells a story from her childhood.

3. **Ask a question that relates to your thesis.** Be sure the question is one your reader will find interesting, not something like, "Don't you just hate parking decks?"

> Do you change from a nice, polite, helpful, caring individual into a monster when you park in one of the campus parking decks? <u>If so, you are not alone, because parking in these structures brings out the worst in everybody.</u>

The question in the hook relates to the writer's thesis: Parking in the campus decks brings out the worst in people.

4. **Describe a person or a scene.** Be sure the description relates to your essay. Do not describe the weather, for example, if it is not important to events in your narration.

> My legs were shaky and weak. My whole body trembled, and my heart pounded violently in my throat. My palms were wet. The smell of chlorine sickened my stomach as the screams of children having fun and the hum of murmuring adults surrounded me. <u>I knew I had to jump if I was ever going to overcome my fear of water.</u>

5. **Use a quotation.** Select something likely to interest your reader.

> In "School Is Bad for Children," John Holt says that "any kid in class who, for whatever reason, would rather not be there not only doesn't learn anything himself but makes it a great deal tougher for anyone else." Holt is right. <u>I believe we should abolish compulsory school attendance.</u>

The writer's thesis is that we should abolish compulsory attendance. The quotation in the hook is original, not overused, such as "Don't count your chickens before they hatch."

SUPPORTING PARAGRAPHS

Supporting paragraphs explain or prove your thesis. In "No Degree Required," for example, the supporting paragraphs (paragraphs 2, 3, and 4) work to prove the thesis assertion that earning a teaching degree should not be required to teach in public schools.

Supporting paragraphs have the same two parts you learned when you studied the one-paragraph composition:

> Your supporting paragraphs explain or prove your thesis.
>
> Your supporting paragraph should have a topic sentence and supporting details.

1. The **topic sentence** gives the central idea of the paragraph.

2. The **supporting details** develop that central idea.

To illustrate the parts of a supporting paragraph, here is paragraph 3 of "No Degree Required." Remember, the thesis of the essay is "We should discontinue the requirement in this state that people must earn teaching degrees before they can teach in public schools.

> The first sentence is the topic sentence. It presents the central idea of the paragraph.
>
> All the other sentences in the paragraph are supporting details. They develop the central idea given in the topic sentence.
>
> Together, the topic sentence and supporting details help explain or prove the thesis.

³Of course, we can't let just anyone with knowledge of a subject into the classroom; we must be sure the person has the other qualities necessary to teach. We should set up training programs to teach prospective teachers about classroom management, and we should have tests to judge the knowledge and talent of people who want to teach. Then we should require a year of probation to weed out those who are not suitable. Deans of colleges of education all over the country are likely to cry out that only accredited schools can train teachers, but that point of view is self-serving. After all, our current method of requiring teaching degrees has done little to assure quality education.

The Topic Sentence

The topic of a supporting paragraph states one idea that will help explain or prove the thesis. That idea is the central point of the paragraph.

Study these topic sentences from the supporting paragraphs of "No Degree Required" to notice that each one gives the central point of the supporting paragraph. In each case, the central point is an idea that helps explain or prove the thesis (that people should not be required to have teaching degrees in order to teach in public schools).

> Each topic sentence states an idea to explain or prove the thesis.

topic sentence:	The requirement that a person have a teaching degree from a four-year college means that talented, knowledgeable people, people who would be terrific teachers, cannot give what they have to offer—just because they have not taken a handful of teaching courses.
topic sentence:	Of course, we can't let just anyone with knowledge of a subject into the classroom; we must be sure the person has the other qualities necessary to teach.
topic sentence:	An important benefit of this plan is that it taps an important source of potentially gifted teachers: retired people.

Supporting Details

As you know from studying the one-paragraph composition, supporting details explain or prove the topic sentence. To do that, the supporting details must be adequate, specific, and relevant. These are all characteristics you learned earlier when you studied paragraphs, and they are included in the following chart.

Characteristics of Supporting Details

FOR ADEQUATE SUPPORTING DETAILS
- Provide enough facts and opinions to explain or prove the topic sentence of that paragraph.
- Provide enough adequately detailed paragraphs to explain or prove your thesis.

If you need to review adequate details, return to pages 45–46.

FOR SPECIFIC SUPPORTING DETAILS
- Use specific nouns, verbs, and modifiers.
- Follow general statements with specific statements.

If you need to review specific detail, return to pages 47–48.

FOR RELEVANT SUPPORTING DETAILS
- Be sure that the topic sentence of each supporting paragraph is directly related to the thesis.
- Be sure that all the supporting details are directly related to the topic sentence of the paragraph.

If you need to review relevant detail, return to pages 54–55.

Logical Order

In Chapter 1, you learned the importance of arranging your details in a logical, easy-to-follow order. You also learned these three common ways to arrange details:

- chronological order (in the order events occurred)

- spatial order (according to location in a particular area)

- emphatic order (in order of importance)

If you need to review the importance of logical order and the ways to order details logically, return now to pages 12–14, because you must arrange your essay details logically.

Coherence

In Chapter 3, you learned how to connect ideas using transitions and repetition of key words and ideas. When you write an essay, you should use transitions and repetition to connect ideas within each paragraph. In addition, you should use these same coherence devices in your topic sentences when you need to achieve coherence from one paragraph to the next. To illustrate this point, study these excerpts from "No Degree Required":

end of paragraph 1:	We should discontinue the requirement in this state that people must earn teaching degrees before they can teach in public schools.
beginning of paragraph 2:	The requirement that a person have a teaching degree . . .
coherence device:	repetition of word *requirement*

end of paragraph 2:	. . . the accountant and senator probably know more about math and government than some people with teaching degrees who are currently teaching math and social studies.
beginning of paragraph 3:	Of course, we can't just let anyone with knowledge of a sub-ject into the classroom. . . .
coherence device:	*Of course* is a transition of emphasis.

Using the Patterns of Development

When you studied paragraph writing, you learned of the different kinds of para-graphs: narration, description, illustration, process analysis, definition, comparison and contrast, cause-and-effect analysis, classification, and argument. These different ways to develop paragraphs are called the **patterns of development.**

When you write your essays, you will draw on these patterns of development. Some-times you will write an essay that uses just one of these patterns, and sometimes you will combine two or more of these patterns in a single essay. When you combine pat-terns, the most-used pattern is the **primary pattern of development,** and the lesser-used pattern or patterns are the **secondary patterns of development.**

For an example of how to combine patterns of development in a single essay, reread "Runner's High" on page 154. The primary pattern of development is definition because most of the essay explains what *runner's high* is. However, description and cause-and-effect analysis appear as secondary patterns:

- Paragraph 2 *describes* what runner's high feels like.

- Paragraph 3 explains the *effect* of experiencing runner's high too early in a race.

- Paragraph 4 explains the possible *effect* of runner's high lasting longer than it usu-ally does. It also explains the effect of a high coming to an end.

Practice 13.5

Pick two thesis statements you wrote when you completed Practice 13.4. For each of these thesis statements, write two topic sentences that could be in supporting paragraphs.

Example

Thesis: My cousin Lee is very stubborn.

Topic sentence: Once Lee refused to go to the prom because he wasn't chosen for the prom committee.

Topic sentence: Lee will never apologize to anyone for anything, even when he knows he is wrong.

1. Thesis: _____

_____

Topic sentence: _____

_____

Topic sentence: _____

_____

2. Thesis: _____

_____

Topic sentence: _____

_____

Topic sentence: _____

_____

FAQ

Q: How many supporting paragraphs should an essay have?

A: The number of supporting paragraphs varies from essay to essay, depending on how many aspects of the thesis you want to discuss. However, you should discuss at least two aspects in two supporting paragraphs. If you have only one point, which is developed in one supporting paragraph, you are better off writing a one-paragraph composition.

Practice 13.6

The following are thesis statements and topic sentences for three essays. Write three supporting details on a separate sheet to develop each topic sentence. (If you need help with ideas, try the idea-generation techniques.)

Example

Thesis: Babysitting is not an easy way to make money.

Topic sentence: The children can be difficult to care for.

Supporting detail: Marco refused to eat supper.

Supporting detail: Carlotta wasn't toilet-trained.

Supporting detail: Ed hit his brother.

Topic sentence: The parents can be just as hard to deal with.

Supporting detail: The Calloways returned at 3 a.m.

Supporting detail: The Chus did not pay.

Supporting detail: The Kellys didn't tell me where they were going.

1. Thesis: People often change when they get behind the wheel of a car.

   Topic sentence: Normally calm people become enraged.

   Topic sentence: Also, normally cautious people become reckless.

2. Thesis: Two kinds of sales clerks work in the mall.

Topic sentence: The first kind of clerk ignores me.

Topic sentence: The second kind of clerk smothers me with attention.

3. Thesis: In my study skills class, I learned how to study.

Topic sentence: Preparations before sitting down to study are important.

Topic sentence: Students should follow a specific procedure once they sit down to study.

Practice 13.7

Answer the questions by referring to "Runner's High" on page 154 and "No Degree Required" on page 156.

1. How does the writer of "Runner's High" achieve coherence from paragraph 1 to paragraph 2?

_____

2. How does the writer of "No Degree Required" achieve coherence from paragraph 3 to paragraph 4?

_____

3. In "No Degree Required," the primary pattern of development is argument. What two secondary patterns of development help develop paragraph 2? What secondary pattern helps develop paragraph 3?

_____

_____

THE CONCLUSION

Your conclusion brings your essay to a satisfying finish.

The **conclusion** is the paragraph that brings your essay to a satisfying finish. Some approaches to the conclusion are illustrated here.

1. **Refer to the topic or assertion presented in your thesis.** Following is an example for an essay with this thesis: Student loans should be distributed before the term begins.

   Students count on their loan money to pay for tuition, books, and other college-related expenses. Therefore, to avoid problems for students, the loans should be given out before classes begin.

2. **Summarize the main points of your essay.** Following is an example for an essay with this thesis: We should abolish compulsory school attendance.

> Compulsory attendance serves no purpose because when students are required to attend against their will, they disrupt the classroom and distract the teacher's attention. Students who do not want to be in school will not learn anyway, so we should let them leave and enter the workforce or the military, where they can contribute to society and earn their way in the world.

3. **Introduce an idea closely related to your thesis or the main points of your essay.** Following is an example for an essay with this thesis: I knew I had to jump in the pool if I was ever going to overcome my fear of water.

> Now that I have overcome my fear of water, I feel better about myself. I realize that I can face whatever obstacles are in my path by using the same courage I used to jump in the pool.

4. **Combine approaches.** Following is an example for an essay with this thesis: People should not stay married "for the sake of the children." The conclusion combines a reference to the thesis and a summary of main points.

> More often than not, staying married for the sake of the children is a mistake. The spouses' resentment and anger grow until the children are affected by the tension. Ultimately, the children are better off living with one parent in an atmosphere of harmony than with two parents in an atmosphere of discord.

FAQ

Q: Why don't the professional essays in the book always have the organization explained in this chapter?

A: Professional writers often follow the organization explained here, but they often depart from it as well. As you become more experienced, you, too, may want to try different strategies. If so, consult with your instructor.

Practice 13.8

The following student essay lacks a conclusion. On a separate sheet write a suitable conclusion.

Braces at Twenty-One

[1]I was seventeen and without a care in the world when my mother woke me at 9:00 a.m. for my dental appointment. After the dentist finished checking my teeth, he informed me that I had no cavities, but I needed braces. The news came as a total shock because I thought only children got braces. I have had them for four years now, and I can truly say that having braces at the age of twenty-one creates serious problems.

[2]Because the braces make me look younger than I really am, people never believe I am twenty-one and in college. Once when I met a friend's father, he wanted to know what high school I went to. When I go to the local bars, the person carding twists my ID every possible way, sure that it is a fake and I am too young to drink. When I am out with friends, people always think I am the kid brother who is tagging along. All of this makes me feel very self-conscious.

[3]The braces also affect my social life. I am afraid girls do not want to go out with someone who wears braces, so I hesitate to ask for dates. If I do manage to get a date, I am in the embarrassing situation of excusing myself after I eat so I can go get the food out of my braces. Kissing is not the fun it should be, either, because when my lips are pressed against the metal, they get sore.

[4]Worst of all, the braces are painful. By the age of seventeen, a person has adult teeth that are pretty well set. When the dentist tightens my braces, all the teeth in my mouth hurt because they are difficult to move. I am unable to eat anything harder than Jell-O for a week. The tightening of my braces also gives me headaches from my upper jaw to the top of my skull. The insides of my lips become raw, and it is difficult to talk. It seems that as soon as the pain passes, it is time to go back to the dentist to get my braces tightened again.

ESSAY STRUCTURE

The chart on page 153 gives you the parts of an essay. Now that you have a more detailed understanding of essay structure, study the following chart for a more detailed description of essay structure.

THE STRUCTURE OF AN ESSAY

The Introduction
states the central point in a thesis
stimulates the reader's interest in the central point with a hook
↓
The First Supporting Paragraph
includes a topic sentence that presents an idea to explain or prove the thesis
includes adequate, specific, relevant supporting details to help explain
or prove the topic sentence
↓
The Second Supporting Paragraph
includes a topic sentence that presents the next idea to explain or prove the thesis
includes adequate, specific, relevant supporting details to help explain
or prove the topic sentence
↓
The Third Supporting Paragraph
includes a topic sentence that presents the next idea to explain or prove the thesis
includes adequate, specific, relevant supporting details to help explain
or prove the topic sentence
↓
The Conclusion
closes the essay in a satisfying way

The essay structure in the chart is not the only suitable one, but it is very serviceable. To use it effectively in your own writing, you can use the outline form on page 169 to plot your first draft.

PLANNING, WRITING, AND REWRITING AN ESSAY

As you plan your essay, be sure your thesis meets the terms of your writing assignment. If you have been asked to identify a problem on campus and suggest a solution, do not write that everything on campus is perfect as it is. As you consider the strategy

Paragraph 1: Introduction

Approach to hook _____

_____

Early version of thesis _____

_____

Paragraph 2: Supporting paragraph

Topic sentence idea _____

_____

Supporting details _____

_____

Paragraph 3: Supporting paragraph

Topic sentence idea _____

_____

Supporting details _____

_____

Paragraph 4: Supporting paragraph

Topic sentence idea _____

_____

Supporting details _____

_____

Paragraph 5: Conclusion

Approach to conclusion _____

_____

FAQ

Q: Where do I get the ideas for my supporting paragraphs?

A: The idea-generation techniques explained in Chapter I can help you discover ideas to explain and prove your thesis.

for your essay's hook, keep your audience and purpose in mind. If you aim to convince your school's academic counsel to abolish final exams, your hook should not relate a humorous story about the time you partied late, slept through the alarm, and missed your chemistry final. Also, consider how much your reader already knows about your topic to decide whether background information would be helpful or whether you should explain why your topic is important. As you consider stratetegies for your conclusion, consider your supporting details. If you make three easily remembered points, your reader will not need a summary; however, if you have many complicated ideas, your reader may appreciate a summary.

As you write, think about whether you are including specific details. If you are not, make a note in the margin to attend to specific details when you revise. If you sense that you have *no* specific details, that you are moving from one general statement to another, stop and take a look at your thesis. Is it too broad; that is, are you trying to cover too much territory? If so, narrow your thesis, and you may find it easier to be specific.

As you rewrite, assess your draft from your reader's perspective to determine whether you have done all you can to achieve your writing purpose. The tips in Chapter 2 on page 34 can help you, as can the following checklist.

✓ Checklist for an Essay

☐ 1. My thesis states both my topic and my assertion.

☐ 2. My thesis has the qualities of an effective thesis explained on pages 158–159.

☐ 3. I have written a hook aimed at creating interest in my essay.

☐ 4. Each supporting paragraph has a topic sentence that presents the paragraph's central point, which is relevant to the thesis.

☐ 5. Supporting details, which include one or more of the patterns of development, are adequate, specific, and relevant to the topic sentence.

☐ 6. Supporting paragraphs and supporting details are arranged in a logical order.

☐ 7. Where needed, transitions and repetition are used to achieve coherence within paragraphs and between paragraphs.

☐ 8. My concluding paragraph ends the essay in a satisfying way.

☐ 9. I have edited carefully (more than once) to find and correct mistakes.

☐ 10. I have proofread carefully after copying or typing the essay into its final form.

Practice 13.9

The following essay was written by a student. Read it and answer the questions that follow.

The Binge Drinker

[1]During my first week on campus, I joined other first-year students in an orientation program that warned us about binge drinking. According to the

brochure handed out at orientation, a binge drinker is a man who consumes five or more drinks in a row on a single occasion or a woman who consumes four or more drinks in a row. The study defined a single drink as 12 ounces of beer, 8 ounces of malt liquor, 5 ounces of wine, or $1\frac{1}{2}$ ounces of 80-proof distilled spirits (whiskey, etc.). This definition might be technically accurate, but it won't prompt most students who are binge drinkers to recognize themselves as such. They are not likely to count their drinks or measure their alcohol content. Therefore, a more useful definition of binge drinker is needed.

[2]A binge drinker drinks to get drunk. It doesn't matter whether it takes one drink or six, whether the drinks contain $1\frac{1}{2}$ ounces of distilled spirits or half an ounce. *What* a person drinks is less significant than *why* a person drinks. The binge drinker is partying, intent on drinking until he or she loses the ability to speak clearly, think rationally, and—at times—remain conscious. Getting drunk is the binge drinker's idea of having a good time. The binge drinker is also characterized by the speed with which he or she drinks. Binge drinkers often engage in drinking games that allow them to get drunk in as little as a half hour.

[3]Students who binge drink are just like people who binge on a gallon of ice cream or max out their credit cards on clothes they will never wear: Bingeing is a way of getting so lost in a behavior that the binger forgets about confronting and solving real problems. Thus, the binge drinker is someone who has trouble confronting problems head-on and instead drinks to escape reality and avoid problems.

[4]Some people think that to be a binge drinker a person must drink excessively several times a week. A person who drinks that often is probably an alcoholic. A person who drinks just to get drunk is a binge drinker each time he or she drinks for that purpose. Thus, an individual can be a binge drinker on one occasion but not on another, when only one drink is consumed.

[5]Finally, binge drinkers can be defined by their rationalizations for binge drinking. Some students believe that binge drinking is the only way to blow off the stress of earning grades, keeping up with work, and finding enough financial aid. Binge drinkers also tell themselves that their excessive drinking is merely a form of socialization, something that brings them closer to their pals or teammates.

[6]Instead of using a definition of binge drinking that focuses on the number and size of drinks consumed, campus health educators should craft their definition based on the reasons people drink. Shifting the focus would also shift campus health services resources to helping these students find more healthy and productive ways to cope with stress and to socialize.

1. What is the thesis of "The Binge Drinker?" What is the writer's topic? The writer's assertion?

2. What strategy does the writer use for the hook?

3. What is the topic sentence of each supporting paragraph? (*Hint:* The topic sentences are not all in the same place in the paragraphs.) What does each topic sentence present as the central idea of the paragraph?

4. Do you think any of the supporting paragraphs need additional supporting details? Explain.

5. Cite three examples of specific details (using specific words and following general statements with specific ones).

6. What is the primary pattern of development? What secondary pattern appears in paragraph 2? In paragraph 4?

7. How does the writer achieve coherence between paragraphs 1 and 2? Between paragraphs 4 and 5?

8. What strategy does the writer used for the conclusion?

WRITING ASSIGNMENTS

For your essay, you have a choice of assignments.

1. Use one of the thesis statements you wrote for Practice 13.4. Check your responses to Practice 13.5 for possible topic sentences.

2. Write an essay that argues the assertion opposite the one given in "No Degree Required" (page 156).

3. The writer of "Binge Drinking" (pages 170–171) points out a problem that exists on many college campuses. Select this problem or another one that exists on your campus. Explain the problem and suggest a solution.

4. The eighteenth-century Scottish philosopher David Hume said, "Custom, then, is the great guide to human life." Explain what Hume means and show that he is or is not correct.

5. Explain the appeal of something on television, such as MTV, reality shows, talk shows, or soap operas.

6. Select your own writing topic. Just be sure to get your instructor's approval for your selection.

7. **Combine Description and Cause-and-Effect Analysis.** Describe a popular fashion or fad and explain why that fashion or fad is popular.

8. **Respond to an Image.** Assume that the alien pictured on page 173, who is Sark from Planet Grzink, has managed to land in your town and remain undetected for a year. During that time, Sark has been observing Earthlings in your town and sending regular reports on various aspects of Earth culture and behavior back to the mother ship. Write one of Sark's reports. Be sure to pick a focus, such as some aspect of education, sports and recreation, work life, or human communication, habits, or interaction. Feel free to be humorous or satirical.

Tips

COMPOSING YOUR ESSAY

- Photocopy the outline form on page 169 and use it to outline your essay. If you have trouble filling in parts of the outline, return to idea-generation.
- If you have trouble writing your hook, just begin with your thesis. After completing the rest of your draft, you may find it easier to write the hook.
- If you have trouble writing your conclusion, keep it brief. Try writing two sentences that explain the importance of your topic and assertion.
- As part of your revising, ask two people to read your introduction and tell you whether it creates interest in your essay. If it does not, revise as necessary.
- Check each of your topic sentences against your thesis. Is the relevance for each one clear?
- Underline your general statements. Are they followed by specific ones?
- **If English is not your first language,** you might need to move back and forth between English and your first language for something as long as an essay. When you have enough ideas to move into outlining and drafting, switch to English exclusively. Just be careful of literal translations of idea-generation material in your first language, because they may not yield idiomatic English.

SUCCEEDING IN COLLEGE

Be a Successful Note-taker

To become a better note-taker, read the assignment before the lecture, so the terminology and ideas are familiar to you. Then you can write about them without pausing to wonder what your instructor is saying. Use abbreviations to maintain speed and do not worry about neatness. Rewrite your notes after class, while the lecture is fresh in your mind, while your abbreviations still make sense, and while you can still decipher your handwriting. Rewriting helps "set" ideas so you remember them.

When you rewrite your notes, you can use a version of the outline form, like this:

Subject of lecture _____

_____

Main point _____

_____

Supporting details _____

_____

Main point _____

_____

Supporting details _____

_____

If your note-taking skills need improvement, visit your campus study skills center to learn about the different kinds of note-taking techniques.

Write about It

Learn about two different strategies for taking notes by visiting your campus study skills center, checking out a study skills book from the library, or purchasing a study skills book in your campus bookstore. Explain what you learned that can help you take better notes. As an alternative, compare and contrast your current note-taking process with one you learned about.

For more practice with essays, go to www.mywritinglab.com.

CHAPTER 14
Kinds of Essays

In earlier chapters, you learned about the patterns of development: narration, description, illustration, process analysis, definition, comparison and contrast, cause-and-effect analysis, classification, and argument. Sometimes you will write an entire essay using just one of these patterns. Other times, you will combine two or more of these patterns in a single essay. In this chapter, you will see examples of both single-pattern essays and multiple-pattern essays. Read them carefully, and to enhance your understanding, answer the questions that follow each one.

NARRATION

Narration is story-telling. The chief features of narration are given in the following chart. For more information, review Chapter 4. To review essay structure, see Chapter 13.

Features of Narration
■ Tells a story and notes how you feel about the event or why it is important.
■ May include a thesis that states what the event is (the topic) and your feeling about it or why it is important (the assertion)
■ Answers some or all of the journalist's questions
■ May include dialogue
■ May include specific descriptions of people and scene
■ Uses chronological order and transitions that signal that time order

Student Essay

The following student essay is developed primarily with narration. However, there are elements of description and cause-and-effect analysis as well.

A Deadly Afternoon

[1]Many of my friends are anxious because they have no idea what they want to do with their lives. They have tried a number of majors, but, so far, they have not

discovered anything they feel passionate about, and they worry that they will never find something they can get excited about doing. I am fortunate that I do not have their concern because I discovered what I wanted to do even before I came to college. On a rainy and miserable afternoon of my senior year in high school, on May 19 to be exact, a dramatic incident showed me what I wanted to do with my life.

[2]I was walking to my seventh period class when I noticed a disturbance in the hallway. I could see that Tom had Collette pinned against the wall, causing her to tremble violently. Collette had broken up with Tom just a few days earlier, and everyone was waiting for trouble because Tom had a history of violence and most sensible people were afraid of him. If I had stopped to think, I probably would have run for help, but instead I acted reflexively. I grabbed Tom's arm and shouted, "Let her go!" He squinted at me like he was having trouble focusing, and at that moment I became afraid. Then, suddenly he stormed away muttering, "I'll make you sorry, both of you." At that point, the principal showed up, so I told her what I knew and walked away.

[3]I was shaken up, so before going to class, I stepped into the bathroom to splash water on my face. I was startled to see that Tom was there. At first I was scared. Tom had a short fuse and was likely to use his fists. I fully expected him to lash out at me for my interference in the hallway. Then I noticed the blood spreading across his shirt and the knife on the floor. At that instant, Tom sagged to the floor. His skin had a blue cast, and the blood covered his chest. I ran to the door and screamed for help. Instantly, the principal and three teachers arrived. They frantically tried to stop Tom's wound from bleeding. After what seemed like hours, the paramedics arrived. They did what they could, but Tom did not make it. He was pronounced dead at the hospital. Everyone knew Tom was violent, but no one expected him to turn that violence on himself.

[4]Eventually, it came out that Tom was an abused child who equated love and violence. His life had been an extremely difficult one of poverty and deprivation, as well as abuse. There were some pretty good reasons for his antisocial behavior, and if any of us had bothered to look more closely, we would have seen them.

[5]Tom's death made me realize how troubled people can be. I decided at that point to major in psychology and become a school counselor to help troubled kids like Tom.

Responding to a Reading

1. What strategy does the writer use for the hook? Does the hook engage your interest? Why or why not?

2. What is the thesis of the essay? What is the topic? The assertion?

3. Which of the journalist's questions does the essay answer? Which ones are emphasized the most? Why?

4. Paragraph 4 includes cause-and-effect analysis (an explanation of why an event occurred and/or the results of an event). What does that cause-and-effect analysis add to the essay? What other element of cause-and-effect analysis is part of the essay?

5. Cite two examples of description in the essay. What purpose does the description serve?

6. For what purpose do you think the writer wrote "A Deadly Afternoon"? Does the essay achieve that purpose? Explain.

7. **Writing Assignment.** Write a paragraph expressing your reaction to the essay. You might focus on a thought or feeling prompted by something in the essay, or indicate whether you liked or did not like some aspect of it, and why.

DESCRIPTION

Description uses words to create mental pictures. The chief features of description are given in the following chart. For more information, review Chapter 5. To review essay structure, see Chapter 13.

Features of Description
■ Focuses on a dominant impression (one prominent reaction to what you are describing)
■ Includes a thesis that states what is being described (the topic) and the dominant impression (the assertion)
■ Includes sensory details (details that appeal to sight, sound, taste, smell, and touch)
■ Includes specific words to paint a mental picture
■ May use a spatial order and transitions that signal that order

Student Essay

The following student essay describes a place important to the author. As you read, ask yourself if the description is vivid enough to help you understand why.

My Place of Solitude

¹Whenever I need to be alone, I go to Cherry Flat, a little-known area in the mountains of Sequoia National Forest. It is a peaceful, isolated, rustic place.

²To get to Cherry Flat, I have to ascend Sugarloaf Mountain. The road resembles a snake. The turns are so sharp I cannot resist the temptation to take a quick peek back to make sure the rear end of my car made it around with me. A little-used turnoff at the summit leads down a deeply rutted, muddy lane to Cherry Flat.

³Cherry Flat is a primitive campground. There is only a small, unpainted, rough wood hut with a half-moon cut into the door. The only place to pitch a tent is on one of the four flat spots carved out of the sloping hillside.

⁴Any hardship I encounter because of the lack of conveniences is made up by the spectacular scenery. Majestic mountains surround the camp. Redwood Mountain stands to the north; Burnt Point is to the east, and Big Baldy, its granite dome glistening, is to the west. The Kaweak River at the bottom of the gorge resembles a silvery ribbon. My eyes are slowly pulled upward following the march of tall pines to the crest of Redwood Mountain where the azure sky begins.

⁵After setting up camp, I hike down the mountain and explore along the river. The trail is a mile long and drops one thousand feet in elevation on its way to the bottom. Halfway, I stop for a sip of clear, cool spring water that is trickling down the face of a rock ledge. Down a steep section and around a bend, the path leads past Disappearing Creek. In a small pool are brilliantly colored rainbow trout. The fish, when they sense my presence, dart away to hide. Lying on a smooth, warm boulder beside the swift running river, I like to watch the billowy clouds float by. The trail ends by a small waterfall. Water spills over the edge and falls twenty feet into a deep pool below. Ripples radiate outward and lap gently on the shore.

⁶As the light grows dim and the clouds glow orange and pink, the sun inches its way behind a mountaintop. I relax and enjoy a cold drink back at camp—a fitting end to a peaceful day.

400 words

Responding to a Reading

1. What is the thesis of "My Place of Solitude"? What does that thesis state as the topic and the dominant impression? Should the writer have included a hook along with the thesis? Explain.

2. Cite four examples of effective descriptive language. What makes the description effective? What senses does the writer appeal to?

3. In what order does the writer arrange details? Why is that order used?

4. Are the details in the essay adequate and relevant? Explain.

5. What do the topic sentences state as the focus of each supporting paragraph?

6. For what purpose do you think the writer wrote "My Place of Solitude"? Does the essay achieve that purpose? Why or why not?

7. **Writing Assignment.** Write a paragraph expressing your reaction to the essay. You might focus on a thought or feeling prompted by something in the essay, or indicate whether you liked or did not like some aspect of it, and why.

ILLUSTRATION

Illustration uses examples to develop a thesis. The chief features of illustration are given in this chart. For more information, review Chapter 6. To review essay structure, see Chapter 13.

Features of Illustration
■ Includes a thesis that gives a general statement to be supported by examples
■ Must have enough adequately detailed examples to explain or prove a general statement given in the thesis
■ Can include description or other patterns to develop the examples
■ Can include explanation to develop the examples
■ May use emphatic or chronological order and transitions that signal that order, as well as transitions of addition and illustration

Student Essay

The following student essay uses examples to explain and prove the thesis. Notice that that the writer uses cause-and-effect analysis as a secondary pattern.

One Step Forward and Two Steps Back

[1]Americans love technology. Every time some new time-saving or labor-saving device hits the market, we rush out to buy it. Price is no object. If it is new and more advanced, we want it. Americans are proud of our technological advancements, but technology often comes with a price.

[2]Consider cell phones, for example. They give us mobility, but they rob us of privacy. No matter where we are, and no matter what we are doing, someone can reach us. The cell phone is so seductive, we refuse to disconnect even briefly. In restaurants, cell phones ring, people answer, and meals are disrupted both for the person taking the call and all those around that person who are forced to listen to the

conversation. On vacation, we take our phone on the beach and chat away instead of enjoying the sand and surf. In the car, out on a walk, even (and this astounds me) in public restrooms, cell phones are ringing, chirping, and playing pop songs—and we are answering. When we do answer, there is little certainty that we can hear or be heard. These phones snap, crackle, and pop more than most breakfast cereals. If you use your phone for business, that unreliability can be a real problem.

[3]The Internet is another example. It offers limitless access to information, entertainment, gaming, and general silliness, but it enslaves us. Users are so glued to their screens downloading music, watching YouTube, shopping, bidding on eBay, playing poker, instant messaging, Googling, blogging, tweeting, and surfing that they no longer have a life away from their computers. Sadly, avid computer users find e-mail and chat rooms an acceptable substitute for face-to-face communication. Once on the information highway, some people become so obsessed that they never find the off ramp.

[4]Then there are digital video recorders (DVRs). This technology allows us to record multiple television programs to watch later, call up movies and other programming on demand, and fast forward through commercials. As a result, people are watching significantly more television. Instead of picking one program to watch in any given time slot, we can now watch one and record two to catch later, and then select an on-demand movie after that. To watch that much television is a real time commitment, and since there are still only twenty-four hours in a day, DVR addicts don't get out in the world very much.

[5]It is commonly believed that everything has its price, and technological devices are no different. They may make life easier, but they are not without their problems.

Responding to a Reading

1. The thesis gives the general statement that the examples will explain or prove. What is that general statement in the essay?

2. What examples explain or prove the general statement given in the thesis? Are there enough examples in enough detail? Explain.

3. How does the writer develop the examples—with explanation and/or with one or more of the patterns of development?

4. What transition opens paragraph 2? Paragraph 3? Paragraph 4?

5. How does the writer use cause-and-effect analysis as a secondary pattern of development?

6. For what purpose do you think the writer wrote "One Step Forward and Two Steps Back"? How does the conclusion help the writer achieve that purpose?

7. **Writing Assignment.** Write a paragraph expressing your reaction to the essay. You might focus on a thought or feeling prompted by something in the essay, or indicate whether you liked or did not like some aspect of it, and why.

PROCESS ANALYSIS

Process analysis explains how something is made, how something is done, or how something works. The chief features of process analysis are given in the following chart. For more information, review Chapter 7. To review essay structure, see Chapter 13.

> ### Features of Process Analysis
>
> - Includes a thesis that mentions the process (the topic) and why understanding the process is important (the assertion)
> - Explains the steps in the process
> - May explain what is *not* done, how to perform a step, or why to perform a step
> - May use a chronological order and transitions that signal that order

Student Essay

The following essay, an example of process analysis, is an expansion of the paragraph on page 91. It uses examples to explain and prove the thesis. Notice that that the writer uses cause-and-effect analysis as a secondary pattern.

Making Money with a Garage Sale

¹Have you noticed how many garage sales there are every spring, summer, and fall? Do you assume people must be crazy to flock to these things just to buy other people's junk? Maybe they are crazy, but people do love to buy other people's used stuff, and if you plan it right, you too can make a great deal of money from a garage sale.

²First, you must gather all the saleable items collecting dust in your basement and attic. Do not include anything badly broken, but keep everything else. The items you think are the most worthless may be the first to sell. Remember that Buddha statue with the clock in the belly that you would not be caught dead having in your living room? That will sell. So will the velvet painting of Elvis, the pink lawn flamingoes, and all those trashy trip souvenirs. Toys and tools are hot sellers, but clothes (unless they are children's) probably will not sell very well.

³Next—and this is very important—clean this junk up. Dirty items will not sell, but you will be surprised at the weird stuff that goes if it is clean. Two days before the sale, take an afternoon, a bottle of Fantastik spray cleaner, and some paper towels and get the years of dust and grime wiped away. Be careful, though. Once this stuff is clean, you may be tempted to keep it. This would be a big mistake. Not only will you not make a profit, but you will be stuck with your own junk again.

⁴Once your items are clean, display them properly. Get lots of tables, even if you have to rent them. Arrange everything attractively, trying to keep housewares together, toys together, and so forth. Do not crowd the items, and put large objects to the rear of the table so you do not hide the smaller things from the discriminating eyes of eager bargain hunters.

⁵The most important part is pricing. I have just three words of advice: cheap! cheap! cheap! Also, be prepared to bargain. Shoppers will often ask if you will take less than you are asking, and your answer should always be yes. Remember, this trash has been in your basement collecting spider eggs for the past five years, so do not get greedy. Price it to move because the last thing you want to do is drag this stuff back in the house because it did not sell. Also, write the price of each item on a white sticker placed on the object.

⁶If you really want a great sale, advertise. Put signs up on telephone poles and trees, directing people to the sale, and place an ad in the classifieds.

⁷Finally, pamper your customers. Provide grocery bags for carrying those marvelous purchases home in, and serve coffee—for twenty-five cents a cup, of course. If the day is hot, lemonade or iced tea at a reasonable price is always a hit.

[8]Follow these steps, and you can pocket a significant amount of money. I once made two hundred dollars with a garage sale and got my basement cleaned out for good measure.

Responding to a Reading

1. What is the thesis of "Making Money with a Garage Sale"? What does the thesis give as the topic and the assertion?

2. Where does the writer indicate why understanding the process is important? (*Hint*: This information appears twice.)

3. Which paragraphs include information about what *not* to do? Which paragraphs include information about how to perform a step? Which paragraphs include information about why to perform a step? Why does the writer include each of these pieces of information?

4. Two orders are used to arrange the details in "Making Money with a Garage Sale." What are those orders? What transitions signal those orders?

5. What approach does the writer take to the hook in the introduction? Is the hook a good one? Explain.

6. What approach does the writer take to the conclusion? Is the conclusion effective? Explain.

7. **Writing Assignment.** Write a paragraph expressing your reaction to the essay. You might focus on a thought or feeling prompted by something in the essay, or indicate whether you liked or did not like some aspect of it, and why.

DEFINITION

Definition explains the significance of a term, your opinion about a term, or your personal meaning of a term. The chief features of definition are given in the following chart. For more information, review Chapter 8. To review essay structure, see Chapter 13.

Features of Definition
■ Includes a thesis that mentions the term being defined and a main characteristic of the term ■ May include description, illustration, or other patterns of development ■ May explain what the term is *not* ■ Should not be written in a dictionary style ■ May use emphatic order and transitions that signal that order

Student Essay

The following essay, which is developed primarily with definition, also includes process analysis as a secondary pattern.

Online Identity

[1]I am now one of several million registered users on MySpace.com. To use MySpace, I had to create an online profile. An online profile is a brief biography crafted to interest other users of MySpace enough that they will want to become "my friends."

[2]An online profile is like a billboard advertising the essence of an individual, particularly the person's chief characteristics and interests. With the "Profile Edit" section of MySpace, users can construct their profiles by posting various kinds of personal information in numerous categories. For example, the categories "Name" and "Basic Info" allow users to give key details, including date of birth, place of residence, and purpose for using MySpace (choices include "Dating," "Serious Relationships," "Friends," or "Networking"). Other categories allow users to flesh out their profiles. "Interests & Personality" and "Background & Lifestyle" give users the chance to tell as much or as little about themselves and their interests as they want. For instance, users can write about their hobbies or favorite music, movies, television shows, and books. If a user does not want to provide certain information, simply adding a <Z> in the text box for a given category will remove that category from the online profile. Finally, users can customize their online profiles by adding images, songs, and video clips that illustrate aspects of the online identity.

[3]An online identity is not a complete picture of a person. The customization options in MySpace allow users to tailor their profile so that it depicts any image or persona they like. A profile does not cover everything about a person, because most MySpace users do not want to read that much. Instead, the online profile focuses on the personality aspects, characteristics, or interests that users want to advertise about themselves, perhaps to attract other "friends" with similar interests or to get a job. For example, my roommate uses MySpace only to advertise his background and skills as a drummer, in the hopes that other musicians will notice him and hire him for their gigs. On the other hand, I use MySpace to display the comic books that I write and illustrate. I want my online profile to get comics fans interested in me so that they will read my comics and check back often for updates.

[4]Of course, all good advertising needs a hook to grab people's attention, and the online profile is no different. In an online profile, the hook is the "Headline." The best headlines are short, catchy, and unique, not long, unfocused, or clichéd. For example, streaming across the top of my profile, my headline reads "Comics Illustrator Extraordinaire." To really grab attention, users can apply different colors, fonts, and layout design to the headline for visual impact. When done well, the headline can take more time and thought than other parts of the online profile.

[5]Altogether, the various sections of the online profile define a user's identity to the online world. For this reason, creating a focused and interesting online profile is essential to attracting other MySpace users, whether for personal or professional reasons. My biggest challenge has been to craft an online profile that will first attract comics fans to my biography, and then direct them toward my online "Album," which contains my best comic strips. Like all MySpace users, I want to draw people in so that, hopefully, they are inspired to read on.

Responding to a Reading

1. What does the essay define, and what characteristic of the term does the definition focus on? Where is that information given?

2. Which paragraph includes process analysis? What purpose does that process analysis serve?

3. Which paragraph explains what the term is *not*? What purpose does that information serve?

4. Which paragraphs include examples? Why do these examples appear?

5. For what purpose do you think the writer wrote "Online Identity?" Who do you think the intended audience is?

6. Do you think the essay achieves its purpose with its intended audience? Why or why not?

7. **Writing Assignment.** Write a paragraph expressing your reaction to the essay. You might focus on a thought or feeling prompted by something in the essay, or indicate whether you liked or did not like some aspect of it, and why.

COMPARISON AND CONTRAST

Comparison explains the similarities between two subjects or items; **contrast** explains the differences between two subjects or items; **comparison and contrast** explains both similarities and differences. The main features of comparison and contrast are given in the following chart. For more information, review Chapter 9. To review essay structure, see Chapter 13.

Features of Comparison and Contrast

- Gives subjects or items compared and/or contrasted in thesis
- States points of comparison and contrast in topic sentences
- Includes a thesis that mentions the two subjects (the topic) and whether they will be compared, contrasted, or both (the assertion)
- Backs up statements of comparison and contrast with specific supporting details
- May include explanation, illustration, or description in supporting details
- May use a subject-by-subject or point-by-point order for details
- Includes transitions to signal comparison and contrast

Student Essay

In the following comparison and contrast essay, which is an expansion of the paragraph on page 108, the student author explains that she and her twin are different, despite their physical similarities. Notice that the writer includes definition, description, and illustration in her supporting details.

Identical But Different

¹There are two kinds of twins, fraternal and identical. Fraternal, or dizygotic twins, are the product of two fertilized ova. Identical twins develop from a single fertilized ovum. I am an identical twin. My twin sister Loretta is older by six minutes. During our infancy, my twin and I were so identical that our baby bracelets were left on for quite a while after we were released from the hospital. Her bracelet identified her as Baby A; I was known as Baby B. Although physically we are still similar, my twin sister and I have very different personalities.

²Loretta and I still look alike, so we are frequently mistaken for each other by teachers and those who do not know us well. We both wear our curly, auburn hair to the shoulder. We both are just over five feet, and I weigh only two pounds more than my twin. Our facial features mimic each other, although I have been told there is more of a sparkle in my eyes than in Loretta's. This, of course, angers my twin. I think Loretta

is prettier, but she thinks I am, so I guess it is a toss-up. From our earliest days, we became accustomed to responding to "Hey Twin" because people cannot tell us apart.

³When we were young, my twin and I realized that our interests were different. We would often play dolls together. Loretta had beautiful Barbie Dolls with sophisticated, feminine outfits. I had rugged G.I. Joes in full battle gear. Loretta would always want my G.I. Joes to be boyfriends for her Barbie Dolls. Of course, I would never consent to such a thing. Once Loretta was particularly persistent; she wanted Barbie and Joe to marry. I got angry and made one of my G.I. Joes drive through the little house we had constructed from old cardboard boxes and trample over her Barbies. Then I ran outside to play in the dirt pile behind our house, leaving Loretta crying in the midst of the destruction.

⁴Another difference was apparent in school, where Loretta was the more serious student. When we had class together, she would be listening attentively to the teacher, while I was busy passing notes and planning the night to come. After dinner, Loretta would faithfully retreat to our bedroom to read and do her homework. I would race outside to throw a Frisbee, play basketball, or do anything that was not homework. Needless to say, Loretta's grades were excellent, and mine were rather ho-hum.

⁵Even now, the difference in our personalities is obvious. My twin is quiet and conservative. She always does the right thing. I'm outgoing and adventurous—and always in trouble. A good example of this difference occurred during spring break in Florida, Loretta and I met some guys on the beach, and they invited us to a party. Loretta declined and begged me not to go. She said we hardly knew them and that they were rowdy. She was afraid we would get into trouble. I went anyway. Guess which twin was arrested two hours later for disorderly conduct?

⁶Thus, Loretta and I may look identical, but inwardly we are very different people.

Responding to a Reading

1. What is the thesis of "Identical But Different"? What does the thesis give as the subjects to be compared and/or contrasted? What does it give as the assertion?

2. Which paragraph or paragraphs compare? Which paragraph or paragraphs contrast?

3. The topic sentences give the points of comparison and contrast. What are those topic sentences?

4. Which paragraph includes definition, and which includes description? Which two paragraphs include illustration? How do these patterns help the writer support her thesis?

5. Are the details arranged in a subject-by-subject pattern or in a point-by-point pattern?

6. How does the writer achieve coherence from paragraph 1 to paragraph 2? From paragraph 2 to paragraph 3? From paragraph 3 to paragraph 4? From paragraph 4 to paragraph 5?

7. **Writing Assignment.** Write a paragraph expressing your reaction to the essay. You might focus on a thought or feeling prompted by something in the essay, or indicate whether you liked or did not like some aspect of it, and why.

CAUSE-AND-EFFECT ANALYSIS

Cause-and-effect analysis explains why something happens (the causes) and/or the results of an event (the effects). The chief features of cause-and-effect analysis are given in the following chart. For more information, review Chapter 10. To review essay structure, see Chapter 13.

Features of Cause-and-Effect Analysis

- Gives the topic and the assertion in the thesis
- May also indicate in the thesis whether causes, effects, or both will be discussed
- Backs up general statements of cause or effect, which can be given in topic sentences, with specific supporting details
- May include explanation, illustration, description, or narration in supporting details
- May make causal chains evident
- Does not assume that earlier events caused later ones, and recognizes that an event can have more than one cause or effect
- May arrange details in emphatic, chronological, or other order
- May include transitions to signal chronological order, cause-and-effect, or addition

Student Essay

In the following cause-and-effect analysis, the student author explains the effects of giving up cigarettes.

What Happened When I Quit Smoking

¹People who have never smoked do not understand how difficult it is to kick the habit. They think quitting is a relatively simple matter of throwing the cigarettes away and never lighting up again. However, these people are wrong. When I quit smoking two years ago, I was miserable.

²First of all, I gained fifteen pounds. As a result, I looked terrible, and I was like a sausage in a casing when I wore my clothes. Every morning it was a struggle to find something to put on that did not cut off my circulation. When I looked in the mirror, I was depressed by my appearance and self-conscious about how terrible I looked. I tried not to eat, but I had to do something if I was not going to smoke, and eating was the only alternative because it kept my hands and mouth busy.

³Even worse, I was so irritable no one could stand to be near me. I snapped at people and picked fights with my best friend. I knew I was being unreasonable, but I could not help myself. Once I screamed at my girlfriend and called her a nag when she reminded me to go buy my mother a birthday present. I did not mean it, but she spent the rest of the night in tears.

⁴For the first month, I was actually hallucinating. I would turn suddenly, thinking I heard a sound, or jump up startled, feeling like something clammy had touched me. Once in a movie theatre, I jumped a foot out of my seat because I thought I felt someone put a hand on my shoulder.

⁵Even in my sleep there was no relief. I would wake up in a cold sweat several times a night after dreaming about smoking a Winston. Then I would lie in bed and shake, unable to get back to sleep because the craving was so bad. I would feel depressed because the pleasure I felt from smoking in my dream was not real.

⁶It has been two years since I have had a cigarette, and I am in much better shape now, but I still have some weight to lose, and in social situations, I still get a little jumpy. Believe me, people who think it is easy to quit smoking have never been through what I have gone through.

Responding to a Reading

1. What is the thesis of "What Happened When I Quit Smoking"? What does the thesis give as the topic and the assertion?

2. What is the first indication that the essay will discuss effects?

3. Each general statement of an effect is stated in a topic sentence. What are the topic sentences, and what effects do they give?

4. Which paragraphs include description, and which include illustration? What purpose do the description and illustration serve?

5. What transitions appear in paragraph 2? What do these transitions signal? What transition opens paragraph 3, and what does this transition signal?

6. What approach does the author take to the hook in the introduction? What approach does the author take to the conclusion? Are the hook and the conclusion effective? Explain.

7. **Writing Assignment.** Write a paragraph expressing your reaction to the essay. You might focus on a thought or feeling prompted by something in the essay, or indicate whether you liked or did not like some aspect of it, and why.

CLASSIFICATION

Classification groups items according to a specific principle. The chief features of classification are given in the following chart. For more information, review Chapter 11. To review essay structure, see Chapter 13.

Features of Classification

- Places items in groups according to one principle of classification
- Mentions in the thesis the items under consideration (the topic) and that the items will be placed in groups (the assertion)
- May also indicate the principle of classification in the thesis
- Mentions each group in a topic sentence that is followed by specific supporting details to describe the group
- May arrange details in emphatic, chronological, or other order
- Includes transitions for coherence

Student Essay

In the following classification essay, the student author explains ways to store data. The writer also explains the advantages and disadvantages of each method. Try to determine why.

Different Ways to Save Files

[1]A friend recently told me that no computer file really exists unless it is saved in more than one place. He should know, since he lost his final sociology paper (and other files as well) when his hard drive crashed last spring. As a first-year college student, I learned pretty quickly the importance of backing up my work. I use four primary data storage tools, depending on what kind of work I am saving and for what purpose.

[2]The first storage tool is the recordable CD and DVD. This is a handy and cheap way to save entire folders of files, or large files, in a short amount of time. Of course, a CD or DVD writer as well as CD- or DVD-writing software are required to use this method, but most new computers now bundle these features automatically. At the end of every semester, I am now accustomed to saving (or "burning") my course files to recordable CDs. Sometimes, like for my interactive animation class, my course files are so big that I need to use a larger-capacity recordable DVD in order to save everything to one disc. The major drawback to recordable CDs and DVDs is usually not a concern for me: They can only be burned once, so once data has been saved to disc, it cannot be edited and resaved to the same disc.

[3]The second storage tool overcomes the limitations of the first. Rewritable CDs and DVDs allow the user to save and resave work to the same disc. Usually more costly than recordable CDs and DVDs, rewritable discs offer even more convenience (but at a higher price) to quickly save, transport, edit, and resave files. Like recordable discs, rewritable discs offer an easy way to save lots of files, large or small, in one place. However, I have sometimes found that rewritable discs are less dependable, and buggier, than recordable discs. For example, some of the files from my Web publishing class that I saved to rewritable discs would not open when I tried to access them, so I ended up storing my files in another way.

[4]I save work for my Web publishing class on a password-protected Web site that is hosted by the college for students to store their work online. This type of data storage allows me to access my files at any time from any computer with Internet access. In addition, each student can save up to ten gigabytes of data online—far more space than is available on CD or DVD. The only major inconvenience that I can see to this type of data storage involves editing work: In order to edit a file, I have to download it from the site, edit it, and then re-upload it to the site. Editing a file that is stored online always depends on having a reliable Internet connection.

[5]The fourth storage device is the most convenient and versatile. I take my USB flash drives with me everywhere I go. These handy devices are small and easy to carry in a pocket or attached to a key ring. USB flash drives can save different amounts of data. Usually, the higher-capacity drives are also more expensive. Still, a mid-capacity drive is a relatively cheap way to have on-the-go data backup. No matter where I am, I can insert my drive into any computer's USB port to view, edit, and re-save my files. These portable drives act like extra, mini computer hard drives. However, since they are so small, flash drives are easy to misplace or lose. For this reason, I always use my flash drives as a way to backup work saved to my computer and elsewhere, like recordable CDs or the college Web site, not as my only method for saving work.

[6]All college students know the importance of having saved work available and accessible at all times. With the different data storage tools at our fingertips, blaming the dog for lost work is no longer an option.

Responding to a Reading

1. What is the thesis of "Different Ways to Save Files"? What does the thesis give as the topic? What words indicate that items will be placed in groups?

2. What is the principle of classification? Where is that principle given?

3. Which sentences mention each group? (*Hint:* Sometimes two sentences together mention a group.)

4. Who do you think the writer's intended audience is? What is the intended purpose?

5. The author mentions the advantages and disadvantages of each group. Why?

6. What approach does the author take to the hook in the introduction? What approach does the author take to the conclusion? Are the hook and the conclusion effective? Explain.

7. **Writing Assignment.** Write a paragraph expressing your reaction to the essay. You might focus on a thought or feeling prompted by something in the essay, or indicate whether you liked or did not like some aspect of it, and why.

ARGUMENT

Argument aims to convince a reader to think or act a particular way. The chief features of argument are given in the following chart. For more information, review Chapter 12. To review essay structure, see Chapter 13.

Features of Argument
■ Has a thesis that gives a debatable issue (the topic) and your position on that issue (the assertion)
■ Supports thesis with reasons and evidence to back up the reasons
■ May include any one or more of the patterns of development
■ May mention reasons against the assertion and make those reasons less compelling
■ May mention what would happen if the assertion were adopted or were not adopted
■ May conclude with a call to action
■ Does not argue matters of taste or statements of fact, does not engage in name-calling, and does not include generalized expressions such as "most people believe"
■ Usually arranges details in emphatic order and includes transitions to signal that order

Student Essay

As you read the following essay, ask yourself how convincing the argument is.

Let's Pay College Athletes

[1]College athletics is big business. A great deal of money is at stake, so colleges are under pressure to recruit the best players. To do so, they offer full and partial scholarships, hoping to lure players to their schools. However, rather than offer scholarships, colleges should pay the players a salary.

[2]Athletes attending school on scholarships have a difficult time. To keep their scholarships, they must carry full-time loads. Because their sport demands so much of their time, they often find that they do not have enough time to study. As a result, their grades suffer. However, if athletes were paid, they could attend part-time and perform better academically without being stretched so thin.

[3]Some people say that without athletic scholarships many students could not afford to attend school, but this is not true. Paid athletes would simply use their salary to pay for tuition and books. Some athletes may even decide to save their salary and wait to attend school until they are finished playing ball. They could thus attend during the off-season or when their athletic careers are over, when they can really focus on their studies.

⁴Paying college athletes would also eliminate the people who are in college but who will never graduate. Some scholarship athletes were recruited to play ball, but they really are not college material. Paid athletes would not have to take classes, and we would be left with qualified students in the classroom, not athletes who are marking time for four years or trying to get a shot at the pros. Furthermore, the seats these athletes now occupy could go to academically qualified students who do want to graduate.

⁵If we paid athletes, colleges would benefit financially. Attendance would be up at games because the level of play would be high. Also, tuition could be collected from the students who take the athletes' places in classrooms.

⁶Awarding athletic scholarships is an old tradition. However, not all traditions stand the test of time. Now we should reconsider how we recruit athletes. Why not just pay them and let them decide if they want to use the money to attend college? Everyone would benefit.

Responding to a Reading

1. What is the thesis of "Let's Pay College Athletes"? What is the debatable issue? What is the writer's position on that issue?

2. What reasons does the writer include to support the thesis?

3. Are the reasons backed up with enough evidence?

4. What reason is given against the writer's assertion? How does the writer make that reason less compelling?

5. Why is the financial reason for the writer's assertion given in the last supporting paragraph?

6. What is the writer's intended purpose and who is the intended audience? Do you think the essay achieves that purpose with that audience? Why or why not?

7. **Writing Assignment.** Write a paragraph expressing your reaction to the essay. You might focus on a thought or feeling prompted by something in the essay, or indicate whether you liked or did not like some aspect of it, and why.

COMBINING PATTERNS

Narration, description, illustration, process analysis, definition, comparison and contrast, cause-and-effect analysis, classification, and argument are patterns of development that you have learned and that have been illustrated in this chapter. You can use these patterns in any combination to support your thesis and help you achieve your writing purpose. For example, "A Deadly Afternoon" on pages 175–176 is a narration that also includes cause-and-effect analysis. "Online Identity" on pages 181–182 is primarily definition, but it includes process analysis as well. For more information, on combining patterns and to review essay structure, see Chapter 13.

Features of an Essay That Combines Patterns

■ Has a thesis with a topic and assertion
■ Includes multiple patterns to explain or prove the thesis
■ Usually includes one primary pattern and one or more secondary patterns
■ Includes supporting details characteristic of the patterns used
■ Orders details and uses transitions according to what is appropriate for the patterns used

Student Essay

Toward a Safer Campus

[1]With recent shootings at Virginia Tech and Northern Illinois University, campus violence is a very real and very pressing concern among college officials. To help ensure the physical safety of students, faculty, and staff, most colleges and universities have implemented three kinds of security measures.

[2]First, academic institutions use various notification systems to alert people on campus to potential safety threats. For example, my college recently launched an e-mail and text-messaging alert system to distribute instant notifications of campus-wide safety concerns. My friend who attends a nearby college told me that administrators at his school use Voice over Internet Protocol (VoIP) phones to send both audio- and text-message alerts throughout campus. My college also recently installed outdoor sirens on both ends of campus to alert people about emergencies.

[3]Of course, the effectiveness of campus notification systems depends on the second security measure: a force of trained, vigilant guards who patrol campus. These security guards usually undergo training both on and off campus to learn to spot signs of trouble and intervene effectively. If necessary, they activate the campus-wide alert system. On campuses that have armed police forces, the personnel take additional training in use and safety of firearms. At one time, security and police forces maintained a low profile, preferring to blend into the campus scene. The thinking then was that a campus with visible police or security personnel was off-putting because it made students feel that they were in an unsafe environment. Now, however, we know that no place is completely safe. As a result, police and security forces strive for maximum visibility in order to be a deterrent. On my campus, for example, several times throughout the day and especially after my evening classes, I see security personnel in vehicles with flashing yellow lights patrolling the campus.

[4]A third campus security measure involves campus auxiliary services aimed at protecting students. One such service offered on many campuses is a shuttle bus that runs late into the night, helping students get safely back to their dorms after evening classes or late visits to the library. In addition, many schools have campus escorts who work around the clock to accompany students to their destinations. Most campuses also have strategically placed call boxes students can use if they feel at risk or spot signs of trouble.

[5]The various security measures in place at academic institutions help decrease risks to the physical well-being of students, faculty, and staff. But the success of any measure depends primarily on the alertness and responsiveness of those it is supposed to protect.

Responding to a Reading

1. What is the thesis of "Toward a Safer Campus"? What is the topic, and what is the assertion?

2. Who do you think the intended audience is, and what is the intended purpose of the essay?

3. What is the primary pattern of development?

4. What are the two secondary patterns?

5. How do the primary and secondary patterns help the writer achieve the intended writing purpose?

6. What approach does the author take to the hook in the introduction? What approach does the author take to the conclusion? Are the hook and the conclusion effective? Explain.

7. **Writing Assignment.** Write a paragraph expressing your reaction to the essay. You might focus on a thought or feeling prompted by something in the essay, or indicate whether you liked or did not like some aspect of it, and why.

WRITING ASSIGNMENTS

For your essay, you have a choice of assignments. The primary pattern of development is indicated, but feel free to include any secondary patterns that help you explain or prove your thesis and achieve your writing purpose.

By now, you have found procedures for planning, writing, and rewriting that work well for you, and you should rely on them as you write this essay. However, if you get stuck along the way, try a different procedure to break the block. In addition, use the Checklist for an Essay on page 170 and the Tips for Composing Your Essay on page 173.

1. **Narration:** Narrate an account of a time you learned something important about yourself, a friend, or a relative.

2. **Description:** Describe a place that causes you to feel a strong emotion.

3. **Illustration:** Illustrate one of these sayings: "Appearances can be deceiving" or "Be careful what you wish for, because you may get it."

4. **Process analysis:** Explain how to do something difficult with ease and grace, such as end a relationship, remain calm during an exam, deal with road rage, or cope with writer's block.

5. **Definition:** Write a definition of *hero,* of *superstar,* or of *inner strength*.

6. **Comparison and contrast:** Compare and contrast or just contrast the way men and women are portrayed in two different television programs.

7. **Cause-and-effect analysis:** Write a cause-and-effect analysis of one fact of college life, such as exams, required courses, roommates, grades, athletics, or dating.

8. **Classification:** Classify ways to meet people or ways to deal with difficult people.

9. **Argument:** Argue for or against requiring public school students to wear uniforms. Alternatively, argue for or against requiring a foreign language for college graduation.

10. **Combine Patterns:** Using cause-and-effect analysis and process analysis (and other patterns, if you like), explain why and how students cheat.

11. **Respond to an Image:** Sports are important in American life. Explain the role of some aspects of sports in American life and assess whether that role is positive or negative. The image on page 192 may give you ideas.

SUCCEEDING IN COLLEGE

Meet New People and Seek New Experiences

It's human nature to gravitate toward people similar to yourself, because these are the people you are most comfortable around. It is also natural to engage in activities you already know you like and are good at. However, college is a time to stretch and grow, so make an effort to interact with people different from you and to try new activities. You will learn much about yourself and others. Here are some tips to get you started.

- **Talk to international students.** Most likely, some students in your classes are from countries you know little about. Make a lunch date with one or more of these students. Learn about their countries and customs. Become aware of their perspectives and share yours in return. The experience will broaden you and add a valuable dimension to your education.

- **Talk to your instructors.** Each term, pick an instructor you think you can learn more from and set up an appointment to chat in his or her office. Discuss the course, your goals, and your interests. In no way should you make a pest of yourself, but one or two talks each term will teach you much.

- **Use your electives to take something new.** If you never had an anthropology course, but anthropology has intrigued you, now is the time to try it out in an introductory course. If you are afraid of the grade you might earn, look into a pass/fail option.

- **Try a new sport or a new exercise or a new activity.** Your student center and recreation center offer many activities to try, from rock climbing to theater trips.

Write about It

Write about ways you can try new activities and meet new people to enrich your college education. Or if you have already done so, write about your experience.

For more practice with essays, go to www.mywritinglab.com.

CHAPTER 15
Identifying Subjects and Verbs

Much of your success learning and applying grammar rules will depend upon your ability to identify subjects and verbs. If you have trouble identifying subjects and verbs, this chapter will help you. If you already identify subjects and verbs successfully, this chapter will reinforce your understanding and perhaps teach you a few new points. First, take the following pretest to assess your current level of understanding.

Pretest

Underline each subject once and each verb twice. If you are unsure, do not guess; just move on. Check your answers in Appendix II.

1. Before work, Jeffrey's mother packed his school lunch.

2. Tuition at this school is the second lowest in the state.

3. Marcos has eaten peanut butter sandwiches for lunch every day this week.

4. Mother returned to school and studied business administration.

5. Many people in this city do not know about the proposed industrial park.

6. Joan and her brothers bought their parents a DVD player for their anniversary.

7. The carton of Grandmother's clothes is in the attic.

8. Jacques has been studying for his law school entrance examination.

9. Are the keys still in the car?

(continued on next page)

10. There will be no excuse for tardiness.

11. Please answer me.

12. At last the holidays are over, and all of us can relax and recover.

13. The students in the reference room of the library are making too much noise.

14. There can be no accidents this time.

15. At the end of the summer, my parents and I will move to Texas and buy a small horse ranch.

SUBJECTS AND VERBS

A sentence has both a subject and a verb. A **subject** is one or more words telling who or what the sentence is about. A **verb** is one or more words telling what the subject does or how the subject exists.

s	v
<u>Babies</u>	<u>cry</u>

Babies: tells who the sentence is about, so this word is the subject

cry: tells what the subject does, so this word is the verb

IDENTIFYING VERBS

You may find the subject and verb of a sentence more easily if you first find the verb and then go on to find the subject. The verb is the word or words that change form to show present, past, and future times (known as **tenses**).

> I walk five miles every day.

In this sentence, the verb is *walk*. We know this because *walk* is the word that changes form to show present, past, and future time.

present tense:	Today I *walk*.
past tense:	Yesterday I *walked*.
future tense:	Tomorrow I *will walk*.

Because verbs indicate time, you can locate them with a simple test. Speak the words *today I, yesterday I,* and *tomorrow I* before a word or word group. If the result is sensible and if that word or word group changes form, it is a verb. Try the test with this sentence:

> The wide receiver fumbled the football.

Can we say, "Today I *the*"? "Yesterday I *the*"? "Tomorrow I *the*"? No, we cannot, so *the* is not a verb. Can we say, "Today I *wide*"? Can we say, "Today I *receiver*"? "Today I *football*"? No, of course not, so *wide, receiver,* and *football* are not verbs. Notice, however, what happens if we apply the test to *fumbled*:

> Today I *fumble.*
> Yesterday I *fumbled.*
> Tomorrow I *will fumble.*

Fumble changes form to indicate different tenses (times), so it is a verb.

NOTE: A few verbs (like *cost*) do not change form to show time.

Action Verbs

The most common kind of verb is the **action verb,** which shows activity, thought, or process. Here are some examples:

Action verbs showing activity: hit, yell, dance, kick, walk, run, eat, play (The trees *sway* in the breeze.)

Action verbs showing thought: think, consider, wonder, remember, want, ponder (Pat *judges* people harshly.)

Action verbs showing process: learn, try, read, enjoy (I can *explain* her anger.)

Linking Verbs

Another kind of verb is the **linking verb,** which joins (links) the subject to something that renames or describes that subject. Here are two examples:

Roberto *is* the best skier in the group. [The verb *is* does not show action. Instead it links the subject *Roberto* with words that describe the subject—"the best skier in the group."]

Roberto	is	the best skier in the group.
↓	↓	↓
subject	linking verb	describes Roberto

Yolanda *was* my best friend. [The verb *was* does not show action. Instead it links the subject *Yolanda* with words that rename the subject—"my best friend."]

Yolanda	was	my best friend.
↓	↓	↓
subject	linking verb	renames Yolanda

Review the following chart of linking verbs so you will recognize them in your own sentences. Notice that linking verbs are most often forms of the verb *to be* (such as *am, is, are, was, were*) or verbs that relate to the senses (such as *taste, smell, sound, touch*).

LINKING VERBS

am	was	appear	taste
be	were	feel	smell
is	been	seem	look
are	being	sound	become

Helping Verbs

An action verb or linking verb can appear with another verb, called a **helping verb.** Here are some examples:

> Grandma Ramirez *can speak* three languages. [The action verb is *speak*; the helping verb is *can*.]
> The train *will be* late. [The linking verb is *be*; the helping verb is *will*.]

Review the following chart of helping verbs so you will recognize them in your own sentences.

HELPING VERBS

am	been	could	have
be	being	will	has
is	may	should	had
are	must	do	shall
was	might	did	
were	can	does	

Notice that some verbs are on both the linking and helping verb lists (*am, is, are, was, were,* for example). When these verbs appear alone, they are linking verbs. When they appear with other verbs, they are helping verbs.

linking verb: The food *is* too spicy.

helping verb: The tree *is* dropping its leaves.

Be aware that a sentence can have more than one helping verb.

two helping verbs: The plane *has been* delayed.

three helping verbs: I *will have been* gone by then.

Finally, know that *have, has, had* are usually helping verbs, but the following examples show two times when they are action verbs:

> A cat *has* kittens. (*Has* means "gives birth to.")
> We *have* lunch at noon. (*Have* means "eat.")

KINDS OF VERBS

Kind	Function	Examples
action verbs	show activity, movement, thought, or process	The bride and groom *dance* beautifully.
		Everybody *hopes* for the best.
		I *try* hard every day.
linking verbs	join the subject to something that renames or describes the subject	Our teacher *is* also a captain in the National Guard.
		The piano *sounds* out of tune.
helping verbs	appear with an action or linking verb	The play *will* not begin on time.

Practice 15.1

Identify each underlined verb as an action verb (av), helping verb (hv), or linking verb (lv). The first two are done as examples.

[1]More than 260,000 people <u>are buried</u> at Arlington National Cemetery, which <u>conducts</u> approximately 5,400 burials each year. [2]The average number of funerals held there <u>is</u> twenty a day. [3]Of all the national cemeteries in the United States, Arlington <u>has</u> the second-largest number of people buried there. [4]Calverton National Cemetery on Long Island <u>holds</u> the distinction of being the largest. [5]At the cemetery, there <u>can be</u> as many as 7,000 burials a year.

[6]The first graves in Arlington National Cemetery <u>were dug</u> by James Parks. [7]Parks <u>was</u> a former Arlington Estate slave. [8]He <u>was born</u> on the property and <u>can claim</u> to be the only person buried in the cemetery who <u>came</u> into this world on the property. [9]He <u>is interred</u> in Section 15.

Practice 15.2

Underline every verb in the following paragraph.

[1]Almost everyone can recognize the opening of Ludwig van Beethoven's *Fifth Symphony*. [2]The composer may have expected its popularity. [3]However, he would have been surprised about one particular use of his composition. [4]During World War II, the first four notes became a rallying cry for the Allies. [5]The first three short notes and the one longer note sounded like the Morse code for the letter *V*—three dots and a dash. [6]The Allies had adopted the *V* as the symbol for victory. [7]Beethoven's first four

notes from the *Fifth Symphony* were played every night between programs of the British Broadcasting Corporation and extensively in the United States as well. [8]Clearly, the music had a stirring effect.

◼

Sentences with More Than One Verb

In a sentence, the action verb or the linking verb is called the **main verb.** If the main verb (the action or linking verb) appears with a helping verb, the verbs together are called the **complete verb.**

sentence:	The candidates will debate the issues next Tuesday.
main verb (an action verb):	debate
helping verb:	will
complete verb:	will debate
sentence:	The children do seem cranky.
main verb (a linking verb):	seem
helping verb:	do
complete verb:	do seem

A single sentence can have more than one complete verb. In the following examples, each complete verb is italicized, each main verb is underlined, and each verb is labeled as an action verb (av), linking verb (lv), or helping verb (hv).

> av av
> Paul *sat* at the window and *waited* for Maria.
> hv av lv
> My sister *had arrived* by noon, but I *was* too sick to see her.
> av av
> As the storm *pounded* the coastal town, volunteers *evacuated* residents
> hv av hv av
> who *had ignored* earlier warnings that winds *could damage* property and life.

NOTE: Be careful of descriptive words such as *not, just, never, only, already,* and *always.* These words are not verbs, although they often appear with verbs.

Earl will not agree to such a scheme. (The verb is *will agree.*)

NOTE: A verb that follows *to* is known as an **infinitive.** The infinitive form will never be part of the complete verb functioning with the subject.

I hesitated to answer the question. (The complete verb is *hesitated,* not *answer,* which follows *to.*)

Practice 15.3

Underline each complete verb. Remember, a verb that follows *to* is not part of the complete verb, and descriptive words are not part of the verb.

Example

Frederick Douglass <u>was born</u> in 1818, <u>lived</u> as a slave, <u>lived</u> free, and <u>died</u> in 1895.

1. Because he was a slave, Douglass was sent to live several places, and he had little contact with his family as a result.

2. The wife of one of his owners taught Douglass how to read and how to write.

3. Douglass would have remained a slave, but after several attempts to escape, he finally succeeded in 1838.

4. He made it to New York, married a free African American woman, and settled in New Bedford, Massachusetts.

5. Douglass became active in the abolitionist movement, traveled widely, and was highly acclaimed for his powerful speeches about the need to end slavery.

Practice 15.4

Underline each complete verb. Remember, a verb that follows *to* is not part of the complete verb, and descriptive words are not part of the verb.

Example

Frederick Douglass <u>wrote</u> about his life as a slave when he <u>penned</u> his autobiography, *Narrative of the Life of Frederick Douglass, an American Slave*.

1. Because he had not been born a free man, when Frederick Douglass wrote his autobiography he put his life in danger.

2. If he had been caught, Douglass would have immediately been returned to slavery.

3. To avoid capture, Douglass left the United States and traveled abroad, where he gave lectures and where friends finally bought his freedom so he was able to return to the United States.

4. Back in the United States, Douglass started a publication in which he argued for the end of slavery.

5. He also recruited African Americans to fight in the Union army, and he later advised President Lincoln about how he should free the slaves.

Review Practice 15.5

Underline each complete verb.

[1]Unlike hurricanes and winter storms, thunderstorms affect relatively small areas. [2]The typical thunderstorm spans fifteen miles in diameter and lasts an average of thirty minutes. [3]Nearly 1,800 thunderstorms are occurring at any moment around the world—that is, 16 million a year. [4]Despite their small size, all thunderstorms are dangerous. [5]They can produce lightning, which kills more people each year than tornadoes. [6]Heavy rain from thunderstorms can lead to flash flooding. [7]Furthermore, strong winds, hail, and tornadoes are also associated with some thunderstorms.

IDENTIFYING SUBJECTS

FAQ

Q: Why should I know how to identify subjects and verbs?

A: You must be able to identify subjects and verbs in order to write effective sentences and avoid errors with pronouns, verb forms, fragments, run-ons, and comma splices.

The **subject** of a sentence is who or what the sentence is about. You can locate the subject by asking "who or what?" before the verb. The answer will be the subject of the sentence. Consider this sentence:

> Ivan earned the highest grade on the history midterm.

The verb in this sentence is *earned*. To find the subject, ask, "who or what earned?" The answer is "*Ivan* earned." Therefore, *Ivan* is the subject. Now look at this sentence.

> Before Easter my cat was ill.

The verb is *was*. Ask "who or what was?" and the answer is *cat*. *Cat,* then, is the subject of the sentence.

CAUTION: Some words can be subjects in some sentences and verbs in others. *Run* is such a word.

run as verb:	I *run* five miles before breakfast every day.
run as subject:	My morning *run* was refreshing.

Practice 15.6

Underline the subject once and the complete verb twice. To find the verb, locate the word or words that change form to show time; to find the subject, ask "who or what?" before the verb.

Example

> Every <u>child</u> <u><u>is</u></u> familiar with Cracker Jack.

1. The snack was created by F. W. Rueckheim at the Chicago World's Fair in 1893.

2. The popular snack got its name from a popular expression of the day.

3. People used to say "crackerjack" to mean "great."

4. The toy prize was added to Cracker Jack boxes in 1912.

5. Cracker Jack's popularity has not declined over the years.

Practice 15.7

Underline the subject once and the complete verb twice. To find the verb, locate the word or words that change form to show time; to find the subject, ask "who or what?" before the verb.

Example

> <u>Champagne</u> <u><u>is</u></u> often <u><u>drunk</u></u> at celebrations.

1. Surprisingly, this alcoholic beverage was invented by Dom Perignon, a Benedictine monk.

2. The cleric was put in charge of the vineyards at his monastery in 1668.

3. During his tenure there, Perignon developed sparkling wines.

4. These wines were named for the Champagne section of France.

5. Also, Dom Perignon has come to be the name of a very prestigious and expensive bottle of wine.

Sentences with Prepositional Phrases

A **preposition** shows how two things relate to each other in time or space.

> The wallet was *behind* the couch. [*Behind* is a preposition; it shows how the wallet and couch are positioned in space: One is behind the other.]
> We had dinner *before* the concert. [*Before* is a preposition; it shows how dinner and the concert are positioned in time: One was before the other.]

You can identify many (but not all) prepositions if you think of a box and a baseball. Any word that can describe the relationship of the baseball to the box is a preposition. The baseball can be *in* the box, *on* the box, *near* the box, and *under* the box; so *in, on, near,* and *under* are prepositions. Following is a chart of some common prepositions.

FAQ
Q: English is my second language, and I'm having trouble with prepositions. What can I do?

A: As you read your assignments and the newspaper, and as you listen to classmates and television, notice prepositions and how they are used. Eventually, you will get a feel for them.

COMMON PREPOSITIONS			
about	before	inside	through
above	behind	into	to
across	between	like	toward
after	by	of	under
along	during	off	up
among	for	on	with
around	from	out	within
at	in	over	without

A **prepositional phrase** is a preposition and the words that work with it. Here are examples of prepositional phrases. The prepositions are underlined as a study aid.

<u>about</u> this time	<u>among</u> my best friends	<u>at</u> noon
<u>by</u> tomorrow	<u>into</u> the lake	<u>to</u> me
<u>in</u> the back	<u>over</u> the rainbow	<u>on</u> the dog

The subject of a sentence will *never* be part of a prepositional phrase. Therefore, to find the subject of a sentence, you can cross out all prepositional phrases first. The subject will be among the remaining words.

> The leader ~~of the scouts~~ is a wilderness expert. (The subject is <u>leader</u>.)
>
> A box ~~of old clothes~~ is ~~on the kitchen table~~. (The subject is <u>box</u>.)

If you do not eliminate prepositional phrases in the preceding sentences, you might be fooled into thinking the subject of the first sentence is *scouts* and that the subject of the second sentence is *clothes*.

Practice 15.8

Cross out the prepositional phrases and underline the subject.

Example

> The <u>rise</u> ~~of popular media~~ has affected the political process.

1. From television to the Internet, the dissemination of political information is vast and fast.

2. Candidates in both major political parties now raise money on the Internet.

3. Most politicians at every level of government maintain websites to communicate with their constituencies.

4. The popularity of YouTube adds a new dimension to campaigning.

5. A critical element in politics, the mass media keep candidates under the microscope.

Practice 15.9

Cross out the prepositional phrases and underline the subject.

Example

> The <u>power</u> ~~of the media~~ in politics cannot be overstated.

1. Political life in the media age can be daunting.

2. Any misstep by a politician instantly appears on YouTube, cable news programs, and websites in a never-ending loop.

3. Of all Ronald Reagan's talents, one of the most important was his ability to use media effectively.

4. The correlation between the media and political events is interesting to examine.

5. For example, media images of the Vietnam War helped fuel the antiwar sentiment.

Sentences with Inverted Order

The subject usually comes before the verb, as in this example:

>   *S*   *V*
>
> The children romped with the playful dog.

Sometimes the subject comes *after* the verb. Then the sentence has **inverted order.** A sentence that asks a question has inverted order.

> V   S
> Is the soup hot enough?

In this sentence, the verb *is* comes first. When we ask "who or what is?" we get the answer *soup,* so *soup* is the subject. In this case, the subject comes after the verb.

A sentence that begins with *there is, there are, there was, there were, here is, here are, here was, here were* will also have inverted order.

> V   S
> There were twenty people on a waiting list for that apartment.

The verb is *were,* and the subject is *people.* (*Were* is the verb because it changes form to indicate different tenses, and *people* is the subject because it answers the question "who or what were?")

Practice 15.10

For each sentence, underline the subject once and the verb twice. Remember, find the verb first and then find the subject by asking "who or what?" before the verb.

Example

> Here are the folders.

1. Is the storm over yet?

2. There are twelve people in this elevator.

3. Was your week in Ft. Lauderdale relaxing?

4. In the kitchen drawer were three dirty knives.

5. Here are the missing files.

Practice 15.11

For each sentence, underline the subject once and the verb twice. Remember, find the verb and then find the subject by asking "who or what?" before the verb.

Example

> There are only three people here.

1. Is the exam next Tuesday or next Wednesday?

2. On the windowsill sat the fat calico cat.

3. There is some confusion about the new graduation requirements.

4. Are you free for dinner Thursday night?

5. Beside the peaceful brook sat Rusty and his dog.

Sentences with More Than One Subject

A sentence can have more than one subject:

The *money* and the *credit cards* were stolen from my wallet.

The verb in this sentence is *were stolen*. When we ask "who or what were stolen?" we get the answer *money* and *credit cards*. Thus, *money* and *credit cards* are both subjects. Now study this sentence:

Greg slid into home plate as the shortstop made a play at second base.

This sentence has two verbs: *slid* and *made*. When we ask "who or what slid?" we get *Greg* for an answer; when we ask "who or what made?" we get *shortstop* for an answer. Therefore, this sentence has two subjects: *Greg* and *shortstop*.

Practice 15.12

Each sentence has more than one subject. Underline each of these subjects. Begin by finding the verb or verbs and then ask "who or what?"

Example

Both <u>Senator Polanski</u> and <u>Governor Perry</u> favor the proposed jobs bill.

1. The school board and the leaders of the teachers' union met behind closed doors for most of the afternoon.

2. Police work is rewarding, but police officers do not make much money.

3. Too many accidents have occurred at the junction of Routes 11 and 45, so a traffic light will be installed.

4. The singer and her accompanist performed an encore in response to the standing ovation.

5. The rain fell for hours, and soon the small streams began to flood low-lying areas.

Practice 15.13

Each sentence has more than one subject. Underline each of these subjects.

Example

Your <u>time</u> and your <u>energy</u> are needed on this project.

1. The rabbit and her young fled in panic when the lawn mower ran over their burrow.

2. Both the manager and the assistant manager apologized for the poor service.

3. The fire alarm sounded, so the students filed out of the room in an orderly fashion.

4. I planted a garden in my backyard, but the rabbits ate most of my crops.

5. Two robins and three sparrows fed contentedly at the bird feeder outside the kitchen window

Sentences That Are Commands or Requests

A sentence can issue a command or make a request.

command: Have the leaves raked by dinner time.

request: Close the door for me, please.

In sentences that are commands or requests, the subject often goes unstated. Instead, the subject is understood to be *you*.

command: You have the leaves raked by dinner time.

request: You close the door for me, please.

Practice 15.14

On a separate sheet, write four sentences with unstated subjects that are understood to be *you*. Two sentences should issue a command and two should make a request.

Example

Park your car on the left side of the driveway, so I have room to pull out.

Review Practice 15.15

Underline the subjects in the sentences in the following paragraph.

[1]There are more than two billion quarts of ice cream eaten in the United States each year. [2]With that figure, you would think ice cream originated in the United States, but the treat was first created in the Orient. [3]Marco Polo encountered it there and brought the idea back to Italy. [4]From Italy, recipes for the confection were carried to France. [5]In France, ice cream became very popular with the nobility. [6]An effort was made to keep the recipes for ice cream a secret from the common people. [7]The first factory for the manufacture of ice cream was started in Baltimore in 1851, but the real development of ice cream did not occur until after 1900, with the advent of refrigeration. [8]There is sugar in ice cream, but the treat is still a fairly nutritious food. [9]One-third pint of vanilla ice cream has as much calcium as one-half cup of milk. [10]Protein and vitamin B are also plentiful in vanilla ice cream.

Tips

IDENTIFYING SUBJECTS AND VERBS

- It is usually easier to find the verb first.
- Remember that linking verbs do not show action; they are forms of *to be* (*am, is, are*) or sensory verbs (*taste, smell, sound*).
- In commands or requests, the subject *you* may be implied (understood but unstated).
- **If English is not your first language,** remember that helping verbs come *before* action verbs, and that a word can come between the helping verb and action verb.

>   hv   av
> My roommate *will study* with us tonight.
>
>   hv   av
> My roommate *will* not *study* with us tonight.

Post Test

In both A and B, underline the subjects once and the complete verbs twice. You will have to draw on everything you have learned so far about subjects and verbs. If the subject is understood, write it in.

A.

1. Six of us had decided to travel to Bowling Green for the big game.

2. For the past year, Juan, Lisa, and Maria have volunteered to work in the children's hospital for three hours every week.

3. The first American to orbit the earth was John Glenn.

4. Luis will never agree to your plan, but you may convince Margo.

5. As the price of cigarettes rises, more people will quit smoking.

6. The trees in Vermont have already changed color.

7. The quarterback faked a pass and then ran up the middle for a five-yard gain.

8. Why are you going alone on your vacation?

9. Behind the old barn there is a beautiful patch of clover in bloom.

10. Take this book and return it to the library.

11. Here is the report, but I must have it back in a week.

12. On the top shelf of my closet are the clothes for the rummage sale.

13. More people must be told about organ donation programs, for such programs save lives.

14. Since Mario quit smoking, he has become irritable and generally unpleasant.

15. As more people become comfortable with computers, information will be processed faster than ever.

16. To me, swearing is offensive.

17. The pile of dirty clothes in the closet is beginning to smell.

18. You must add the eggs before you add the flour and salt.

19. Peter, Helen, and David decided that they would never campaign for Jeffrey in the student council election.

20. The issue of fair play must be considered in this case.

B.

¹People have dreams every night. ²The early dreams usually last only a few minutes, but the dream just before morning can be as long as an hour. ³This is the dream we are most likely to remember. ⁴There are conflicting explanations for dreams. ⁵Freud thought that dreams hide worrisome ideas. ⁶He said that troublesome thoughts would wake us if they were not disguised as something else. ⁷However, many scientists and dream researchers disagree. ⁸They have said that dreams are caused by the jumble of electrical impulses in the brain at night. ⁹Dreams occur when the brain tries to make sense of these confusing impulses. ¹⁰For example, if you dream that you cannot move, your brain may be trying to explain the paralysis of deep sleep.

LEARNING FROM TEXTBOOKS

The textbooks you read in college are essential to your success. In this feature, you will be asked to connect what you have learned in this book to the kind of reading you do as a student and the kind of writing you see in your textbooks. The following excerpt was taken from a college political science textbook. Read it and answer the questions that follow.

What Is Federalism?

[1]**Federalism** is a way of organizing a nation so that two or more levels of government have formal authority over the same area and people. [2]It is a system of shared power between units of government. [3]For example, the state of California has formal authority over its inhabitants, but the national government can also pass laws and establish policies that affect Californians. [4]We are subject to the formal authority of both the state and the national governments.

1. For what audience and purpose is the paragraph intended?

   _____

   _____

2. The title is in the form of a question. What is the subject and what is the verb? How does the title help the textbook authors achieve their purpose?

   _____

   _____

   _____

3. One of the subjects of sentence 1 is in boldface. How does the boldface type help the authors achieve their purpose? What is the other subject of the sentence?

   _____

   _____

   _____

4. In sentence 3, the opening phrase indicates that an example follows. How does that example help the authors achieve their purpose?

   _____

   _____

   _____

5. How many prepositional phrases appear in sentence 1? In sentence 2?

   _____

6. In sentence 5, underline the subject once and the complete verb twice.

Write about It

Our Constitution established a system of federalism in which each state maintains much authority over its citizens, although the centralized national government has some authority in certain matters. In a paragraph, contrast the advantages or disadvantages of this system of shared authority with a system that gives all the authority to the national government.

SUCCEEDING IN COLLEGE

Learn Strategies for Reading and Studying Textbooks

When you read your textbooks, pay attention to the verbs, because they can affect meaning significantly. Consider, for example how meaning is different in these sentences:

- Researchers *believe* that birth trauma can cause attention deficit disorder.

- Researchers *suspect* that birth trauma can cause attention deficit disorder.

- Researchers *doubt* that birth trauma can cause attention deficit disorder.

Reading and studying textbook material requires special strategies. Some of the following may work for you. If you need additional help, visit your campus reading lab or study skills center.

- Preview the material to get a sense of what is in store. Read chapter introductions, headings, captions, and charts. If the chapter closes with a summary, read that summary.

- Read long or difficult material in stages. Try three to five pages in the morning, another three to five in the afternoon, and so on.

- Look up words you do not understand.

- Read the material more than once. The first time, concentrate on what you do understand and do not worry about material you do not understand. In subsequent readings, work to understand more. If there is still material that you do not understand, ask questions in class or during your instructor's office hours.

- At the end of every section, look away from the book and review in your mind what you have read.

- Take notes on or highlight important points.

- Write to "set" the material. Summarize what you have read, outline the material, write and answer study questions, or list main points and important supporting details.

Write about It

Study five pages from a textbook from another class, using two or more of the procedures above—preferably ones that you have not tried before. Then, in a paragraph, evaluate the success of the strategies you tried. Be sure to explain why you think the strategies did or did not work for you.

For more practice with identifying subjects and verbs, go to www.mywritinglab.com.

CHAPTER 16

Using Coordination and Subordination

can't stand alone

I f you can use coordination and subordination effectively, you can express yourself with precision and in a pleasing style. This chapter will help you learn what you need to know, but first take the following pretest to assess your current level of understanding.

Pretest

An **independent clause** has a subject and a verb and can be a sentence; a **dependent clause** has a subject and a verb but cannot be a sentence. **Coordination** joins two independent clauses in a sentence. **Subordination** joins an independent clause and a dependent clause in a sentence. Write a *C* if the sentence has coordination; write an *S* if it has subordination. If you are unsure, do not write anything. Check your answers in Appendix II.

1. _____ William decided to become a vegetarian, even though he loved beef.

2. _____ None of the new fall television series has become a runaway hit, but I do not know why.

3. _____ After she took a nap, Louise felt ready to begin studying.

4. _____ I am moving out of the residence hall, and I am renting a house with friends.

5. _____ Before the last note sounded, the audience jumped up and applauded.

6. _____ The committee deliberated for more than an hour before it reached a decision about the new bylaws.

7. _____ Timothy sprained his ankle, but he refuses to use crutches.

8. _____ The plumber did not have the right tools on the truck to fix the problem with the pipes, so he went back to his shop.

9. _____   Marta decided that she would rather be happy than right, so she apologized to Curt.

10. _____   Surprisingly, the mayor decided not to run for reelection; she may consider a senate bid next year.

IDENTIFYING CLAUSES

A **clause** is a group of words with both a subject and a verb (see Chapter 15 on how to identify subjects and verbs). The following word groups are clauses (the subjects are underlined once, and the verbs are underlined twice).

> the <u>snow</u> <u>fell</u> softly
> after the <u>marathon runner</u> <u>crossed</u> the finish line
> <u>Helen</u> <u>was</u> not <u>invited</u> to the reception
> before the <u>storm warnings</u> <u>were issued</u>

The following word groups are *not* clauses because they do not have both a subject *and* a verb. (Word groups that do not have both a subject *and* a verb are **phrases.**)

> seeing the log in his path
> in the pantry
> behind the sofa in the den
> frightened by the snarling dog

NOTE: Look again at the lists of clauses and phrases and notice that length has nothing to do with whether a word group is a clause or a phrase.

Practice 16.1

Place an *X* next to each clause. Remember, a clause has both a subject and a verb.

1. __N__   before Lorenzo could finish his sentence

2. __N__   around the corner from my house

3. __N__   against the wishes of her parents and friends

4. __Y__   she means well

5. __N__   wishing I could help you more

6. __Y__   the lead singer was the best performer in the show

7. __Y__   federal funds were requested to repair the dam

8. __N__   not wanting to intrude on Martha's privacy

9. __y__ the construction foreman took full responsibility for the damages

10. __y__ a hawk soared in the distance

Two Kinds of Clauses

A clause that can be a sentence is an **independent clause;** a clause that cannot be a sentence is a **dependent clause.** The following clauses are independent clauses because they can be sentences. In fact, if you add capital letters and periods, you *do* have sentences.

independent clause:	the movie ended very late
sentence:	The movie ended very late.
independent clause:	freedom of speech is our most valuable liberty
sentence:	Freedom of speech is our most valuable liberty.
independent clause:	her advice was not very helpful
sentence:	Her advice was not very helpful.

The following are dependent clauses. They have subjects and verbs (all clauses do), but they cannot stand alone as sentences.

dependent clause:	because the union went on strike
dependent clause:	after the doctor examined the patient's throat
dependent clause:	when the pitcher threw his best curveball

Practice 16.2

Write *DC* next to each dependent clause and *IC* next to each independent clause.

1. __DC__ after Tony checked the locks on the doors

2. __DC__ when he tried desperately not to show fear

3. __IC__ we asked the committee to reconsider its report

4. __IC__ the board of trustees raised tuition

5. __DC__ when the last vote was counted

6. __DC__ because the summer drought created a food shortage

7. __IC__ I left for the appointment ten minutes late

8. __DC__ before the movers lifted the chest of drawers in the attic

9. __IC__ the consumer price index points to a recession

10. __DC__ since Jan was awarded two scholarships

COORDINATION

Coordination is the proper joining of two independent clauses in one sentence. (Remember, independent clauses can stand as sentences.)

Joining Independent Clauses with Coordinating Conjunctions

You can join independent clauses in one sentence with a comma and one of the following **coordinating conjunctions**:

FAQ

Q: Is there an easy way to remember the coordinating conjunctions?

A: Think of "fanboys." Each letter stands for one of the coordinating conjunctions: *for, and, nor, but, or, yet, so.*

COORDINATING CONJUNCTIONS

and	or	so
but	for	yet
		nor

Here are two independent clauses:

> The traffic light at Fifth and Elm is not working.
> No major accidents have been reported.

Here are the independent clauses properly joined in one sentence with a comma and the coordinating conjunction *but:*

independent clause
↓
The traffic light at Fifth and Elm is not working, but no major

independent clause
↓
accidents have been reported.

Here are two other independent clauses:

> Jake's frustration was building quickly.
> He decided to get away for the weekend and relax.

These independent clauses can be properly joined with a comma and coordinating conjunction *so:*

independent clause
↓
Jake's frustration was building quickly, so he decided to

independent clause
↓
get away for the weekend and relax.

With a comma and coordinating conjunction, you can do more than join independent clauses. As the following chart explains and illustrates, you can show the relationship between the clauses.

Relationships Shown with Coordinating Conjunctions

1. and (shows addition)

   Three of us wanted to visit the museum, and two of us wanted to see a play.

2. but (shows contrast)
   yet (shows contrast)

   Your plan is a good one, but we do not have the money to implement it.
   Your plan is a good one, yet we do not have the money to implement it.

3. or (shows an alternative or choice)

   Professor Jennings explained that we could write a ten-page research paper, or we could take a final examination.

4. for (means "because")

   The linoleum floor in the basement was buckling, for water had seeped in during the spring rains.

5. so (means "as a result")

   The new model cars are in the showrooms, so now is the time to get a good deal on last year's models.

6. nor (means "not either one")

   My keys are not on the table, nor are they in my coat.

NOTE: When independent clauses are joined by *nor,* the verb comes before the subject in the second clause.

With a clear understanding of the relationships coordinating conjunctions show, you can join independent clauses according to the following chart.

Coordination: Joining Independent Clauses with a Comma and a Coordinating Conjunction

Two independent clauses can be joined as a single sentence with a comma and a coordinating conjunction.

independent clause + comma and coordinating conjunction + independent clause

, and
, but
, or
, for
, so
, yet
, nor

Practice 16.3

To join the independent clauses properly in a sentence, place a comma and write an appropriate coordinating conjunction on the blank.

Example

People often think of the stock market as one entity ,but [yet] a number of different stock markets exist.

1. The stock and bond markets offer opportunities to businesses *and* they offer opportunities to investors.

2. Issuing stocks helps companies , *for* it allows them to raise money.

3. Investors can benefit , *for* they share in the success of a company.

4. Stocks give investors partial ownership in a company _____ bonds are a form of debt financing.

5. A stock exchange can be a physical facility _____ it can be a computer network.

6. Individuals can buy stock through an organized stock exchange _____ they can purchase stock over-the-counter through a dealer exchange.

7. Industry self-regulation should govern the stock market _____ state and federal laws must ensure honesty in the industry.

8. The Truth in Securities Act of 1933 requires full disclosure of financial information _____ the general public gets accurate information about stocks and bonds.

9. The 1988 Insider Trading and Securities Fraud Act facilitates investor lawsuits _____ the 1995 Private Securities Litigation Act encourages penalties against frivolous investor lawsuits.

10. Many other laws protect investors _____ securities fraud still occurs _____ investors must be cautious.

Practice 16.4

Join the independent clauses into one sentence, using a comma and coordinating conjunction.

Example

To earn tuition money, Josef dropped out of school for a semester.
He took a job as a nurse's aid.

To earn tuition money, Josef dropped out of school for a semester, and he took a job as a nurse's aid.

1. Maria and John are poor choices to head the committee.
They are disorganized and unreliable.

_____

_____

2. The plot of the movie was boring and predictable. , but
   The actors were fresh and engaging.

   _____

   _____

3. You can borrow my laptop to type your term paper. , or
   You can pay someone to do it for you.

   _____

   _____

4. The National Weather Service issued a thunderstorm warning.
   The umpire postponed the Little League championship game.

   _____

   _____

5. Michael passed the ball to Jeff. , and
   Jeff kicked it into the net to score the winning goal.

   _____

   _____

6. Many people thought videocassette recorders would seriously hurt the movie industry.
   The opposite proved to be true.

   _____

   _____

7. Currently, no cure exists for myasthenia gravis.
   Researchers are working hard to help those afflicted with this neurological disorder.

   _____

   _____

8. Those in need of extra help can visit the Tutoring Center.
   They can go to the Student Services Office.

   _____

   _____

9. Self-hypnosis can help people suffering from stress.
It is an effective relaxation technique.

_____

_____

10. Lorenzo began a rigorous exercise program.
He had to lose ten pounds before winter practice drills began.

_____

_____

11. With the new state funds, the school board hired three teachers.
They decided to remodel the high school library.

_____

_____

12. Thirty students were accepted into the medical program., *but*
Only two-thirds of them will eventually graduate.

_____

_____

13. Not everyone enjoyed the theater department's production.
Those who did raved about it.

_____

_____

14. Be sure to determine what you need before buying a computer., *or/for*
You could end up with a system that does not fill your needs.

_____

_____

15. Fifty percent of the student body was absent with the flu., *but*
The principal still did not cancel classes.

_____

_____

Practice 16.5

Create more coordination in the paragraph by combining sentences 2 and 3, sentences 4 and 5, sentences 6 and 7, sentences 8 and 9, sentences 10 and 11, and sentences 12 and 13. To combine each pair of sentences, add a comma and an appropriate coordinating conjunction. Cross out periods and capital letters as necessary.

Example

Adolescence is a difficult time, so teenagers ~~. Teenagers~~ need their friends.

[1]When people become teenagers, they begin to need intimacy in their friendships. [2]Adolescents are eager to share their hopes and fears. [3]They enjoy trading secrets with others they trust. [4]Furthermore, teens have a stronger need for close friends than younger people. [5]They spend more time away from their parents. [6]Some parents fear the influence friends exert on their teenagers. [7]Contrary to popular belief, peer pressure is not necessarily stronger than family ties. [8]Still, friends are very important to teens. [9]They help them make key decisions about college and careers. [10]Also, friends help them sort out right decisions from wrong ones. [11]Friends provide "reality checks" for adolescents. [12]Some teen friendships are short-lived. [13]Others last long into the teenagers' adulthood.

Practice 16.6

On a separate sheet, write eight sentences. Each sentence should have two independent clauses joined with a comma and a coordinating conjunction. Use each coordinating conjunction at least once.

Joining Independent Clauses with Conjunctive Adverbs

You can join independent clauses in one sentence with a semicolon, one of the following **conjunctive adverbs,** and a comma.

CONJUNCTIVE ADVERBS

but	and	so
; however,	; furthermore,	; thus,
; nevertheless,	; moreover,	; consequently,
; nonetheless,	; therefore,	

Here are two independent clauses (word groups that can be sentences):

The editorial in Sunday's paper made a good point.
It will not change many people's minds.

Here are the independent clauses properly joined in one sentence with a semicolon, the word *however,* and a comma:

independent clause ↓ … independent clause ↓

The editorial in Sunday's paper made a good point; however, it will not change many people's minds.

Here are two other independent clauses:

> Next fall, tuition will increase by 10 percent.
> The cost of living in a dorm will rise by 5 percent.

These independent clauses can be properly joined with a semicolon, the word *furthermore,* and a comma:

independent clause   independent clause

Next fall, tuition will increase by 10 percent; furthermore, the cost of living in a dorm will rise by 5 percent.

With a semicolon, conjunctive adverb, and comma, you can do more than join independent clauses. As the following chart explains and illustrates, you can show the relationship between the clauses.

Relationships Shown with Conjunctive Adverbs

1. however (means "but")
   nevertheless (means "but")
   nonetheless (means "but")

   > The snow plows worked through the night to clear the roads; however, many streets were still impassable.
   > The snow plows worked through the night to clear the roads; nevertheless, many streets were still impassable.
   > The snow plows worked through the night to clear the roads; nonetheless, many streets were still impassable.

2. furthermore (means "in addition")
   moreover (means "in addition")

   > To save money, the transit authority must raise fares; furthermore, it plans to reduce the number of buses in operation.
   > To save money, the transit authority must raise fares; moreover, it plans to reduce the number of buses in operation.

3. therefore (means "as a result")
   thus (means "as a result")
   consequently (means "as a result")

   > I am hoping to earn a scholarship my sophomore year; therefore, I must maintain a B average.
   > I am hoping to earn a scholarship my sophomore year; thus, I must maintain a B average.
   > I am hoping to earn a scholarship my sophomore year; consequently, I must maintain a B average.

FAQ

Q: The words in the conjunctive adverb list are also mentioned as transitions on pages 56–57. Why?

A: Conjunctive adverb is the words' part of speech. *Transition* is the words' function. Thus, these words are conjunctive adverbs that can function as transitions.

With a clear understanding of the relationship conjunctive adverbs show, you can join independent clauses according to the following chart.

Coordination: Joining Independent Clauses with a Semicolon, Conjunctive Adverb, and Comma

Two independent clauses can be joined in a single sentence with a semicolon, a conjunctive adverb, and a comma.

independent clause	+	semicolon and conjunctive adverb and comma	+	independent clause

; however,

; nevertheless,

; nonetheless,

; furthermore,

; moreover,

; therefore,

; thus,

; consequently,

Practice 16.7

Join the independent clauses with a semicolon, an appropriate conjunctive adverb, and a comma.

Example

In the nineteenth century, the invention of a safe elevator made the skyscraper

possible _; furthermore,_ the Chicago fire of 1871 contributed to the development of tall buildings.

1. In the mid-nineteenth century, steam-operated elevators were used in warehouses
   to move goods and materials _, however,_ they were not considered safe for people.

2. In 1853, Elisha Otis invented a safety feature to keep elevators from falling should
   a cable break _Therefore_ people were no longer afraid to ride elevators.

3. The elevator became safer _, thus_ it became more practical for tall
   buildings with the later invention of an electric motor-driven elevator.

4. In 1871, the Great Fire burned much of Chicago _____ there was a
   need for rebuilding on a huge scale.

5. The fire created a need for building _, In addition,_ Chicago was experiencing a population boom.

6. The amount of land available could not meet demand _____ the only
   solution was to build up.

7. To build up high enough to meet demand, new building techniques were devised
   _____ the skyscraper was born.

8. The method for building skyscrapers, devised by George Fuller, involved creating steel cages and concrete columns to support the weight of the building

_____ the cages and columns had to support the contents and people in the building.

9. The first skyscraper, completed in 1885, was Chicago's Home Insurance Building

, However it was demolished in 1931.

10. At ten stories and 238 feet, the Home Insurance Building was small by today's standards _____ it caused quite a sensation in its day.

Practice 16.8

Join the independent clauses in one sentence with a semicolon, an appropriate conjunctive adverb, and a comma.

Example

Emilio is a charming child.
He is a loyal, caring friend.

Emilio is a charming child; furthermore, he is a loyal, caring friend.

_____

1. For years there were more teachers than teaching jobs. however,
   Now this trend is beginning to reverse itself.

_____

_____

2. To locate the escaped convict, the police set up roadblocks. Also, In addition, Thus
   They conducted a house-to-house search.

_____

_____

3. New signs have been put up on campus. Therefore,
   Finding most of the buildings is easier.

_____

_____

4. Good writing skills are important for success in college.
   They are just as important on the job.

_____

_____

5. The school tax levy was defeated by voters.
   No new school texts can be purchased this year.

   _____

   _____

6. The new automobile assembly plant will be open by November.
   The unemployment rate in this area should drop.

   _____

   _____

7. Carlo was accepted into graduate school to study chemistry.
   He was awarded a scholarship for academic excellence.

   _____

   _____

8. Louise has been a hospital volunteer for three years. *However*
   Now she has decided to apply for a paid position.

   _____

   _____

9. Writers who wait for inspiration may never get much done.
   Writers who freewrite for ideas will make more progress.

   _____

   _____

10. Gary was in top condition for the marathon.
    He still did not expect to place in the top ten.

   _____

   _____

11. Susan pretended she was not bothered by losing her job.
    Those close to her knew she was depressed.

   _____

   _____

12. The assembly-line workers ended their two-week strike.
    The plant would be back in operation by mid-afternoon.

   _____

   _____

13. Ivana earned a scholarship for her high math grades.
    She won a scholarship to play on the women's basketball team.

    _____

    _____

14. Some students become overly nervous when they take exams. *Therefore,*
    They are too tense to perform well.

    _____

    _____

15. The firefighters were granted a **5** percent pay raise. *However,*
    They still make less than they deserve.

    _____

    _____

    ■

Joining Independent Clauses with a Semicolon

When the relationship between the two independent clauses is so clear that you do not need to show their relationship with a conjunction, you can join the clauses with a semicolon.

    independent clause + semicolon + independent clause

Here are two independent clauses (word groups that can be sentences):

> Many breeds of dogs are good with children.
> Other breeds should not be around them.

Here are the two independent clauses properly joined in one sentence with a semicolon:

            independent clause   *independent clause*
                   ↓   ↓
Many breeds of dogs are good with children; other breeds should not be around them.

If you use a semicolon to join clauses, double-check to be sure you have independent clauses on *both* sides of the semicolon.

	dep clause	*indep clause*
no:	When I stopped eating sugar;	I felt better in a week.

	dep clause	*indep clause*
yes:	When I stopped eating sugar,	I felt better in a week.

	indep clause	*indep clause*
yes:	I stopped eating sugar;	I felt better in a week.

Practice 16.9

Follow each independent clause with a semicolon and another independent clause. Be sure your independent clause is very closely related to the one already given.

Example

The rain will continue for another four days ; most secondary roads will be flooded.

1. Economic issues concern most voters ; Furthermore, military _____

_____

2. An increasing number of people get their news from Internet sites ; Therefore, the newspaper do not make more money _____

3. In an economic downturn, many people go back to school _____

_____

4. Frank noticed a hole in the sleeve of his shirt ; Therefore, he bought a new one

5. Computers have changed the way we shop ; Thus, they not shopping outside any more.

6. By the end of next week, the factory will close _____

_____

7. In order to cut down on litter, the city has instituted a $500 fine for improper disposal of trash _____

_____

8. Sometimes, I prefer to stay in on Saturday night ; however, on Sunday I can go out

9. The police chief promised to reduce crime in the downtown business district ; Therefore, they still arrest those gang members

10. The theater troupe is starting a summer camp for young people _____

_____

Review Practice 16.10

On a separate sheet, rewrite the following paragraph by joining some sentences with coordination. Then read your revised version out loud to notice how much more smoothly it reads than the original. (More than one satisfactory revision is possible.)

[1]In 1920, Josephine Dickinson was newly married. [2]She was a willing cook. [3]She was somewhat clumsy and kept injuring herself in the kitchen. [4]Her husband, Earl, a cotton buyer for the local Johnson and Johnson plant, found himself constantly tending to Josephine's little cuts and burns. [5]One night, Earl tried to design a bandage that would stay in place. [6]He unrolled a length of sterile gauze along the middle of the tape. [7]Then he wrapped the whole assembly in crinoline. [8]As needed, Josephine could cut an appropriate length from the roll. [9]She could peel off the crinoline and apply the bandage. [10]Earl told a company manager about his invention, which soon emerged as Johnson and Johnson's Band-Aid. [11]At first, sales were slow. [12]They soon gained momentum, thanks to a campaign giving Band-Aids to the Boy Scouts and butchers.

SUBORDINATION

An **independent clause** has a subject and a verb and can be a sentence. A **dependent clause** has a subject and a verb but cannot be a sentence.

independent clause: the doctor explained the symptoms

dependent clause: when the doctor explained the symptoms

A dependent clause is introduced by one of the **subordinating conjunctions,** words like those listed in the following chart.

Subordinating Conjunctions		
after	before	until
although	even though	when
as	if	whenever
as if	in order to	where
as long as	once	whereas
as soon as	since	wherever
as though	so that	whether
because	unless	while

Joining an Independent Clause with a Dependent Clause

A dependent clause and an independent clause can be joined in the same sentence. This joining is called **subordination.**

dependent clause: since the polls do not close for another hour

independent clause: we do not know the election results

Now here are the dependent clause and independent clause in one sentence:

Since the polls do not close for another hour, we do not know the election results.

In the preceding example, the dependent clause comes before the independent clause. You can also place the independent clause first:

We do not know the election results since the polls do not close for another hour.

Here are another dependent clause and independent clause:

dependent clause: when I graduated from high school
independent clause: I expected to join the army.

Now here are the dependent clause and independent clause in one sentence:

When I graduated from high school, I expected to join the army.

or

I expected to join the army when I graduated from high school.

PUNCTUATION NOTE: When the dependent clause comes before the independent clause, place a comma after the dependent clause. This rule is illustrated in the previous example sentences.

Practice 16.11

Each sentence has an independent clause and a dependent clause. Underline the dependent clause once and the independent clause twice. Draw a circle around the subordinating conjunction that introduces the dependent clause. (Notice the commas after the dependent clauses at the beginning of sentences.)

Example

The economy of the United States changed (when) the cotton gin was invented.

1. When the eighteenth century began, cotton was not a cash crop for American planters.

2. Because the seeds were sticky, they could not be easily separated by hand.

3. The problem of quickly separating the seeds from the cotton lint was not solved until Eli Whitney invented the cotton gin.

4. After the cotton gin was invented, demand for cotton increased on the world market.

5. With the cotton gin, a laborer could clean fifty pounds of cotton a day, whereas the same laborer could clean only one pound by hand.

6. Southern cotton planters made a great deal of money (except during the panic of 1837) since production increased and prices were high.

7. Although the southern planter made money from cotton, the northern factory owner also benefited.

8. The southern planter made money from growing cotton while the northern factory owner made money from turning it into cloth.

9. The cotton trade was a major force in the United States economy until the Civil War broke out and even beyond that.

19 century

10. The Confederacy was able to obtain loans from abroad as long as foreign powers accepted cotton as security for the loans.

Practice 16.12

Join the independent clause and dependent clause into a single sentence. Place the dependent clause first or last according to the directions given. (Place a comma after a dependent clause that comes before the independent clause.)

Example

(Place the dependent clause first.)

while the teacher explained cell division

the class took notes furiously

While the teacher explained cell division, the class took notes furiously.

1. (Place the dependent clause last.)

because she had a frightening dream

the child woke up crying

2. (Place the dependent clause first.)

until you exercise regularly and quit smoking

you will be short of breath

3. (Place the dependent clause last.)

since she was not sure what she wanted to do after high school

Tasha decided to enlist in the navy

4. (Place the dependent clause first.)
   although I loved the book
   I hated the movie version of *Hitchhiker's Guide to the Galaxy*

   Although I love the book, I hate _____

5. (Place the dependent clause last.)
   before he auditioned for a role in *Rent*
   Juan took six weeks of voice lessons *before the.*

Practice 16.13

Change one of the independent clauses to a dependent clause by placing an appropriate subordinating conjunction in front of it. Then join the new dependent clause and the remaining independent clause into a single sentence. Place some of the dependent clauses first and some of them last. Also, place a comma after a dependent clause that comes first.

Example

Diane and Mohammed moved to Virginia.
Seth and Janet were afraid they would not see them again.

Because Diane and Mohammed moved to Virginia, Seth and Janet were afraid they would not see them again.

1. Cass was unsure of what courses she should take next semester.
   She made an appointment with her academic advisor.

2. Kevin apologized for being inconsiderate.
   Miguel still could not forgive him.

3. The senator has no money to finance a reelection campaign.
   He decided not to seek a second term in office.

4. The employer improved working conditions.
   The union has vowed to remain on strike.

   _____

   _____

5. Many people believe anger is a destructive emotion.
   I find it to be a healthy, adaptive one.

   _____

   _____

Practice 16.14

On a separate sheet, rewrite the following paragraph by joining some sentences with appropriate subordinating conjunctions to create subordination. Then read your revised version to notice how much more smoothly it reads than the original. (More than one revision is possible.)

[1]A talent scout met Margaret Mitchell, the author of *Gone with the Wind*. [2]He was in Atlanta to find new writers. [3]He had been told that Mitchell was writing a very important book. [4]However, Mitchell wrote for her own satisfaction. [5]She would not show the talent scout her book. [6]He was about to leave the city. [7]Mitchell changed her mind and called him from the lobby of his hotel. [8]He arrived downstairs to find the 4 feet 11 inch Mitchell sitting on a sofa dwarfed by two piles of manuscript stacked to her shoulders. [9]The manuscript was very large. [10]He had to buy an extra suitcase to lug it back to New York. [11]His publishing company, Macmillan, snapped up the novel. [12]*Gone with the Wind* sold 50,000 copies in one day and won the Pulitzer Prize. [13]Macmillan's decision proved to be a wise one.

Practice 16.15

On a separate sheet, write five sentences that join one independent clause and one dependent clause.

Joining an Independent Clause with a Relative Clause

One kind of dependent clause begins with one of these words:

who, whose (to refer to people)

which (to refer to things and animals)

that (to refer to people or things)

These words are called **relative pronouns,** and the dependent clauses they introduce are called **relative clauses.**

The second method of subordination involves joining an independent clause and a relative clause, like this:

sentence:	The boy who won the award is my son.
independent clause:	the boy is my son
relative clause:	who won the award

Here are other examples:

sentence:	The class that I am taking is time-consuming.
independent clause:	the class is time-consuming
relative clause:	that I am taking

sentence:	Jocelyn, whose art is displayed in the student gallery, will paint your portrait.
independent clause:	Jocelyn will paint your portrait
relative clause:	whose art is displayed in the student gallery

sentence:	You may use my car, which needs gas.
independent clause:	you may use my car
relative clause:	which needs gas

If a relative clause is needed to identify who or what is referred to, it is **restrictive.** If the relative clause is not needed to identify who or what is referred to, it is **nonrestrictive.**

restrictive:	The police officer *who saved the child from drowning* is my neighbor.

"Who saved the child from drowning" is needed for identifying the police officer. Without the clause, we cannot tell which police officer is referred to.

nonrestrictive:	Officer Manuel, *who saved the child from drowning,* is my neighbor.

"Who saved the child from drowning" is not needed for identifying the police officer because the person's name is given.

PUNCTUATION NOTE: Set off nonrestrictive (not needed for identification) relative clauses with commas:

Bridgett, *who scored fifteen points,* was the most valuable player.
That man on the bench, *whose name I forget,* is suspicious looking.
That movie, *which appeals to me,* is playing at the Strand.

Do not set off restrictive clauses:

Any employee *who works for me* must have good computer skills.
The watch *that I found* looks valuable.
The child *whose balloon broke* began to cry.

Practice 16.16

Combine the sentences by turning the second sentence into a relative clause that begins with *who, whose, which,* or *that.* Place the relative clause after the subject of the first sentence. Be prepared to explain your use of commas.

Examples

The mayor does not plan to run for reelection.

The mayor does not get along with the city council.

The mayor, who does not get along with the city council, does not plan to run for reelection.

The kitten is now a member of my family.

I found the kitten last week.

The kitten that I found last week is now a member of my family.

1. The large oak tree must be cut down.
The tree was struck by lightning.

The large oak tree which was truck by lightning

2. The book of Longfellow's poems is very old and valuable.
I found the book in Grandfather's attic.

The book of Longfellow's poems which I found in G . . . . is very old and valuable

3. Frank Mussillo has decided to retire at the end of the summer.
Frank Mussillo has been fire chief of our town for thirty years.

4. The Theatre Guild's production of *Porgy and Bess* has been held over for another week.
The production is playing to packed houses every night.

5. The house needed more repairs than they realized.
Pilar and David bought the house. which needed more repairs
that

6. The woman offered to give me directions.
   The woman noticed my confusion.

   The woman who noticed my ... offered to give me directions.

7. Marty finally sold a short story to a literary magazine.
   Marty has been writing in his spare time for ten years.

   Marty, who has been ... , finally sold a

8. Aunt Maria's arrival was a pleasant surprise to all of us.
   The arrival was unexpected.

9. The police officer questioned the witnesses.
   The police officer was off duty.

   The police officer who was off ... , questioned

10. The man offered to draw us a map.
    The man noticed we were lost.

Practice 16.17

On a separate sheet, write ten sentences of your own with relative clauses. Remember to use commas with clauses that are not needed for identification.

Review Practice 16.18

The following paragraph can be improved with coordination and subordination. On a separate sheet, rewrite the paragraph according to the directions given at the end.

¹A Florida hotel called Jules' Undersea Lodge is located under the ocean. ²The hotel is the size of a small house. ³The hotel *which* can accommodate six people. ⁴*After* You are ready to depart for the hotel. ⁵A guide puts your belongings in a

waterproof suitcase and secures it with screws to keep out water. ⁶Then the guide takes you by boat to a platform from which you dive into the water. ⁷Breathing fresh air pumped through a hose held in your mouth, you swim underwater to the lodge. ⁸A guide carries your suitcase. ⁹The guide swims with you. ¹⁰The hotel itself has two bedrooms, a kitchen, and a living room. ¹¹The kitchen has a microwave and a fully stocked refrigerator. ¹²The living room has a DVD player and television. ¹³You can relax in the lodge. ¹⁴You can go diving outside. ¹⁵You are ready to leave. ¹⁶A guide swims with you back to the platform.

a. Join sentences 2 and 3 by making sentence 2 a relative clause.

b. Join sentences 4 and 5 by adding a subordinating conjunction to sentence 4 and making it a dependent clause.

c. Join sentences 8 and 9 by making sentence 9 a relative clause.

d. Join sentences 11 and 12 by adding a comma and coordinating conjunction.

e. Join sentences 13 and 14 by adding a comma and coordinating conjunction.

f. Join sentences 15 and 16 by adding a subordinating conjunction to sentence 15 and making it a dependent clause.

Tips

USING COORDINATION AND SUBORDINATION

- Read your draft aloud. If it sounds choppy or sing-song, try including more coordination and subordination.
- If you use a semicolon to join clauses, double-check to be sure you have independent clauses on *both* sides of the semicolon.
- If you are unsure whether a clause is independent or dependent, speak it aloud. If it sounds as if something is missing, the clause is likely dependent.
- If you are unsure whether a relative clause is restrictive or nonrestrictive, try omitting it. If the person or item referred to is still clearly identified, the clause is probably nonrestrictive.
- **If English is not your first language,** be careful not to use a pronoun in a relative clause that repeats the subject of the independent clause.

  no: My garden, which *it* is full of weeds, needs attention.

  yes: My garden, which is full of weeds, needs attention.

- **If English is not your first language,** remember that when you use *nor* for coordination, word order changes, and all or part of the verb comes before the subject.

  Kwame cannot eat wheat, nor can he eat peanuts.

On a separate sheet, rewrite the next passage to include coordination and subordination. Then read both the original and revision aloud to notice how much better the coordination and subordination make the revision sound. (Many revisions are possible.)

[1]Meredith West and Andrew King studied cowbirds for many years. [2]West and King are scientists in North Carolina. [3]A male cowbird sings. [4]The female cowbird lets him know what songs she likes without making a sound. [5]She likes a song. She lifts her wing.

[6]Cowbirds in different parts of the country sing different tunes. [7]West and King put male cowbirds from North Carolina with female cowbirds from Texas. [8]The males learned to sing Texas cowbird songs. [9]The scientists were puzzled. [10]The males learned these songs. [11]The females did not make a peep. [12]They videotaped the birds. [13]They saw that the females would flash a wing when they liked a song. [14]The males would repeat the song. [15]The females liked it. [16]Now, if the birds could just learn some Jonas Brothers tunes.

LEARNING FROM TEXTBOOKS

The following excerpt, which comes from a college sociology textbook, defines *symbol*. Read the paragraphs and answer the questions that follow.

[1]As humans wrestle with the meanings of their material environment, we attempt to represent our ideas to others. [2]We translate what we see and think into symbols. [3]A **symbol** is anything—an idea, a marking, a thing—that carries additional meanings beyond itself to others who share in the culture. [4]Symbols come to mean what they do only in a culture; they would have no meaning to someone outside. [5]Take, for example, one of the most familiar symbols of all, the cross. [6]If one is Christian, the cross carries with it certain meanings. [7]But to someone else, it might be simply a decoration or a reference to the means of execution in the Roman era. [8]And to some who have seen crosses burning on their lawns, they may be a symbol of terror. [9]That's what we mean when we say that symbols take on their meaning only inside culture.

[10]Symbols are representations of ideas or feelings. [11]In a single image, a symbol suggests and stands in for something more complex and involved. [12]A heart stands for love; a red ribbon signifies AIDS awareness and solidarity; the bald eagle represents the American national character.

[13]Symbols can be created at any time. [14]Witness the recent and now widely known red AIDS ribbon or the pink ribbon for breast cancer awareness. [15]But many symbols developed over centuries and in relative isolation from one another. [16]In the case of older symbols, the same ones may mean completely different things in different cultures. [17]For example, the color red means passion, aggression, or danger in the United States while it signifies purity in India and is a symbol of celebration and luck in China. [18]White symbolizes purity in the West, but in Eastern cultures is the color of mourning and death.

1. Which sentences include coordination? What method of coordination do each of these sentences use (a coordinating conjunction, a conjunctive adverb, or a semicolon)?

_____

_____

_____

_____

2. Which sentences include subordination? What method of subordination do each of these sentences use (joining an independent and dependent clause or joining an independent clause with a relative clause)?

_____

_____

_____

_____

3. Why do the textbook authors use a semicolon for coordination (instead of a coordinating conjunction) in sentences 4 and 12?

_____

_____

4. Why are the relative clauses in sentences 3 and 8 *not* set off with commas?

_____

_____

5. What subordinating conjunctions introduce dependent clauses in the passage?

_____

_____

6. How do the coordination and subordination help students understand and learn the textbook content?

_____

_____

_____

Write about It

Countries can have powerful symbols that mean different things to different people. For example, in the United States, the Vietnam War Memorial likely means one thing to a veteran of the Vietnam War, another thing to a family who lost a loved one in the war, and something else to a teenager who has little firsthand knowledge of the war. Select one symbol important to citizens of the United States, such as the American flag or the Statue of Liberty, and write a definition that explains what it means to you. Are others likely to share that meaning?

SUCCEEDING IN COLLEGE

Know How to Talk to Instructors about Your Grades

From time to time, you will want to talk to your instructor about your grade. You may be seeking clarification so you better understand why you earned a particular grade, or you may be seeking a grade adjustment. Most instructors are receptive to conversations about your grade. However, you should follow the appropriate etiquette for such discussions.

First, grade discussions are confidential, so meet in your instructor's office, either during office hours or at a scheduled appointment. Remember that instructors are human and unlikely to respond well to anger, accusations, or rudeness, so be respectful. If you are seeking clarification about a grade, open with something like this: "Thank you for seeing me. I want to discuss my last test because I am hoping you can help me understand why I did not get a higher grade." If you are seeking a grade adjustment, you can say something like this: "I've studied my exam and your responses, and I believe my grade should be a bit higher. Would you be willing to discuss that with me?"

If you are seeking a grade adjustment, be prepared to state your case. Explain politely why you believe you deserve a higher grade. Then listen—really listen—to your instructor's response. Your instructor could have an excellent justification for the grade that never occurred to you. However, if you are not satisfied with your instructor's response, learn your school's procedure for resolving grade disputes and follow it exactly.

Write about It

Find out your school's procedure for resolving disputes between students and faculty. Do you think the procedure is a good one? Why or why not?

For more practice with coordination and subordination, go to www.mywritinglab.com.

CHAPTER 17
Avoiding Sentence Fragments

Sentence fragments look like sentences because they have periods and capital letters; however, they are really not sentences, so you should avoid them. If you currently know little about avoiding fragments, this chapter will help you. If you already do a good job of avoiding fragments, this chapter will reinforce your understanding and perhaps teach you a few new points. Before getting under way, take the following pretest to determine your current level of understanding.

FAQ
Q: Other writers often use fragments. Why can't I?

A: Fragments often appear in certain kinds of writing, particularly advertising. However, they are rarely acceptable in college papers. Professional writers may use fragments to achieve a special effect. If you want to use a fragment for a particular effect, consult with your instructor first.

Pretest

Write *S* on the blank if the pair of word groups includes only sentences, and write *F* if the pair includes a sentence fragment. Do not guess. If you are unsure, do not write anything. Check your answers in Appendix II.

1. __F__ I enjoy one activity more than any other. Eating Mexican food.

2. __F__ Rico's dog likes playing hide-and-seek. And playing with balls too.

3. __F__ Although many people do not appreciate Sondra's sense of humor. I think she is very funny.

4. __S__ After I took a study skills course, I learned to take better notes. Now my grades are improving steadily.

5. __F__ One thing will convince Marion to study. The threat of flunking out of school.

6. __F__ Pilar having spoken too soon. Regretted her action.

7. __F__ Apologizing for the misunderstanding. Jeffrey asked for another chance.

8. __S__ Before you go on a job interview, you should learn something about the company offering the job. This information will enable you to ask intelligent questions.

(continued on next page)

9. _F_ Bitten by the acting bug. My sister went to New York to try for a career on the stage.

10. _F_ Some people refuse to believe the earth's resources are dwindling. Even though the evidence is all around them.

IDENTIFYING SENTENCE FRAGMENTS

To be a **sentence,** a word group must have a subject, a verb, and a sense of completeness. If any one of these elements is missing, the word group cannot be a sentence. A **sentence fragment** is a word group being passed off as a sentence because it has a capital letter and a period. However, a fragment cannot really stand as a sentence because it lacks one of the essential elements: a subject, a complete verb, or a sense of completeness.

The italicized words in the following examples are fragments.

fragment (subject missing):	The gale force wind toppled power lines. *And interrupted radio communications.*
fragment (complete verb missing):	*The mother wondering what the children could be up to.* She quietly peeked into the bedroom.
fragment (lacks sense of completeness):	*When the band played its last song.* The audience cheered wildly.

Missing Subject Fragments

To be a sentence, a word group must have its own subject. Without a subject, a word group is a fragment.

> The sales clerk told us she would be with us in a minute. *But spent ten minutes with another customer.*

The italicized words are a fragment because they contain no subject for the verb *spent.* The subject in the preceding sentence *(sales clerk)* cannot operate outside its own sentence. (If you need help finding subjects and verbs, study Chapter 15.)

Here is another example:

> Dr. Barolsky passed out the exam papers. *Then announced we would have one hour to complete the questions.*

The italicized words are a fragment because they contain no subject for the verb *announced.* The subject in the preceding sentence (*Dr. Barolsky*) cannot operate outside its own sentence.

To correct fragments that result from missing subjects, you have two options:

(*option 1*) Join the fragment to the sentence before it.

fragment:	The sales clerk told us she would be with us in a minute. *But spent ten minutes with another customer.*
sentence:	The sales clerk told us she would be with us in a minute but spent ten minutes with another customer.

Now the verb *spent* has a subject: *sales clerk*.

(*option 2*) Add a subject so the fragment becomes a sentence.

fragment: Dr. Barolsky passed out the exam papers. *Then announced we would have one hour to complete the questions.*

sentence: Dr. Barolsky passed out the exam papers. Then he announced we would have one hour to complete the questions.

Now the verb *announced* has a subject: *he*.

Practice 17.1

Each pair of word groups has one sentence and one fragment. Underline the fragment. Then rewrite to eliminate the fragment, using the option given in parentheses.

Example

(option 1) In 2007, the world's population was over 6.6 billion people. And had grown by 2 billion people in the previous twenty-five years.

In 2007, the world's population was over 6.6 billion people and had grown by 2 billion people in the previous twenty-five years.

1. (option 1) Population growth is slowing. But is continuing to grow nonetheless.

    ~~It's~~ Population growth is slowing, but it is continuing to grow nonetheless.

2. (option 2) The world population is increasing by 76 million persons per year. By 2050, could reach 9.1 billion.

    ~~It could~~ The world population is increasing by 76 million people per year. By 2050, it will reach by 9.1

3. (option 2) About 2.5 billion people will be added to the population by 2050. Furthermore, will be added in developing nations.

    It About 2.5 billion people will be added to the population by 2050. Furthermore, it will ...

4. (option 1) Billions of people in these developing countries already live in poverty. And lack the sufficient resources to meet their basic needs for food, clothing, and shelter.

    _____

    _____

5. (option 2) Unable to meet their basic needs, over 20,000 people already die each day in these developing countries. Moreover, will become more desperate with a population increase.

_____

_____

6. (option 1) The twin problems of population growth and poverty must be addressed. And must be addressed soon.

_____

_____

Practice 17.2

On a separate sheet of paper, rewrite to eliminate the four fragments created by missing subjects. If you have trouble finding the fragments, try reading the paragraph slowly, from last sentence to first sentence.

[1]One modern convenience we tend to take for granted is the shopping cart. [2]This device was invented by Sylvan Goldman, who lived in Oklahoma City. [3]And ran a grocery store there. [4]Goldman felt sorry for customers. [5]He watched them struggling as they shopped and tried to hold onto their purchases. [6]He hit upon an idea to help them. [7]And built the first crude shopping cart. [8]First, he fastened two folding chairs together. [9]Then put wheels on the legs and baskets on the seats. [10]The contraption looked weird. [11]But worked. [12]From that point on, shopping became easier. [13]The next time you push a shopping cart, think of Sylvan Goldman.

Incomplete Verb Fragments

A fragment will result if you do not include a necessary helping verb. (See page 196 on helping verbs.)

fragment:	Jane going to the store.
sentence:	Jane is (or was) going to the store. [The helping verb *is* (or *was*) is added.]

In general, *-ing* verb forms and past participle verb forms, which often end in *-ed,* (see pages 300–301 for an explanation of past participles) must appear with a helping verb, or the result will be a fragment.

-ing fragment:	The baby sleeping soundly in the crib.
sentence:	The baby is (or was) sleeping soundly in the crib.
past participle fragment:	The police officer angered by the driver's attitude.
sentence:	The police officer was (or is) angered by the driver's attitude.

To correct fragments that result from incomplete verbs, you have two options.

(*option 1*) Add the missing helping verb. Choose from *is, are, was, were, have, has,* or *had*—whichever is appropriate.

fragment:	The sun setting in the west.
sentence formed by adding helping verb:	The sun is setting in the west.

(*option 2*) Change the *-ing* or past participle form to the simple present or past tense, whichever is appropriate.

fragment:	The baby sleeping soundly in the crib.
sentence with simple present tense verb:	The baby sleeps soundly in the crib.
fragment:	The police officer angered by the driver's attitude.
sentence with simple past tense verb:	The driver's attitude angered the police officer.

Practice 17.3

Change each fragment to a sentence using the method of correction given in parentheses.

Examples

(option 1) The university's faculty promotions committee considering the promotion requests of fifty instructors.

The university's faculty promotions committee is considering the promotion requests of fifty instructors.

(option 2) The adolescent boys devouring everything in the refrigerator.

The adolescent boys devoured everything in the refrigerator.

1. (option 2) Before the second half began, the coach reminding the front line to avoid offsides penalties.

   Before ———————, the coach reminded

2. (option 2) The president's speech was enthusiastically received. Both Democrats and Republicans vowing to help pass the legislation requested.

   were vowing   vowed

3. (option 1) The union leaders want to call attention to their political agenda. Therefore, they taken a hard-line stand during the negotiations.

_____

_____

4. (option 1) Many people believe that we are not the only life forms in the universe. They noting frequent UFO sightings and other unexplained events as proof.

Many people _____ , They notice frequent

_____

5. (option 2) A female named Hatshepsut being an ancient Egyptian pharoah.

_____

_____

6. (option 1) The hawk riding the air currents and soaring majestically.

is

_____

_____

Practice 17.4

Revise to eliminate the four fragments that result from incomplete verbs. If you have trouble finding the fragments, try reading the paragraph slowly from last sentence to first.

[1]When Allesandra makes up her mind, it is permanent. [2]Nothing proves that point more than the following story about her broken engagement. [3]Allesandra broken off her engagement with Roberto. [4]Roberto hoping to win her back, so he sent her 1,480 roses. [5]This amounted to one rose for each day of the more than four years they were engaged. [6]One day after the arrival of the roses, Allesandra dining in a restaurant with her family. [7]Roberto arrived on horseback to deliver the last rose in person. [8]He made an impassioned plea to the woman to resume the engagement. [9]Allesandra, however, not interested. [10]She said, "no thanks," and continued eating her meal.

Missing Subject and Verb Fragments

Some fragments lack both a subject and a complete verb. In the examples that follow, the fragments are italicized.

Gloomy weather always depresses me. *Also snowy weather.*
All the Smiths are very considerate. *Particularly in times of trouble.*
Unable to assemble Leo's bike. Dad was frustrated.
I walked across campus. *Reading my biology notes.*

To correct fragments that result from missing subjects and verbs, you have two options.

(*option 1*) Some fragments can be corrected by joining them to sentences before or after them.

fragment:	*Unable to assemble Leo's bike.* Dad was frustrated.
sentence:	Unable to assemble Leo's bike, Dad was frustrated.
fragment:	I walked across campus. *Reading my biology notes.*
sentence:	I walked across campus reading my biology notes.

(*option 2*) Some fragments can be corrected by adding the missing subject and verb.

fragment:	Gloomy weather always depresses me. *Also snowy weather.*
sentence:	Gloomy weather always depresses me. I am also depressed by snowy weather.
fragment:	All the Smiths are very considerate. *Particularly in times of trouble.*
sentence:	All the Smiths are very considerate. They are particularly considerate in times of trouble.

Practice 17.5

Each pair of word groups contains one fragment and one sentence. First, underline the fragment. Then rewrite to eliminate the fragment, using either option 1 or option 2.

Example

<u>In Colorado.</u> President Woodrow Wilson suffered a stroke.

In Colorado, President Woodrow Wilson suffered a stroke.

1. President Woodrow Wilson suffered a serious stroke. During a speaking tour of Colorado in 1919.

_____

_____

2. From the time of his stroke until the end of his term seventeen months later. First Lady Edith Wilson controlled all access to the president.

_____

_____

3. Edith Wilson was very knowledgeable about foreign policy. Also domestic policy.

_____

_____

4. President Wilson considered his wife a trusted advisor. Even before his stroke.

_____

_____

5. Except for the President's wife and personal physician. No one really knew how bad Wilson's condition was for quite some time.

_____

_____

6. The First Lady guarded President Wilson's door, admitting no one. Not even cabinet members or trusted advisors.

_____

_____

Practice 17.6

On a separate sheet of paper, revise to eliminate the five fragments that result from missing subjects and verbs. If you have trouble finding the fragments, read the paragraph slowly from last sentence to first.

¹There are fundamental differences between the alligator and the crocodile. ²The head of the alligator is shaped like a spade. ³The crocodile has a pointy nose. ⁴With protruding teeth. ⁵Living in swampy areas of the southeastern United States. ⁶The alligator is particularly numerous in Louisiana and parts of Florida. ⁷The crocodile, however, likes salt water, and in the United States is found only in south Florida. ⁸The alligator is dark brown. ⁹Also yellow markings. ¹⁰The crocodile is olive green and black. ¹¹While there are differences, both animals benefit the environment. ¹²Offering refuge to many species during floods. ¹³Their nests are important. ¹⁴Also, their droppings add vital nutrients to the water. ¹⁵Thus, these animals, which offer little threat to humans, should be protected. ¹⁶To preserve the balance of nature.

Dependent Clause Fragments

In Chapter 16, you learned that a **dependent clause** has a subject and a verb, but it cannot be a sentence because it is incomplete.

dependent clause fragment:	*s v* When Jorge was a child.
sentence:	When Jorge was a child, he had several health problems.

The following are dependent clause fragments. Read each one aloud to hear that it cannot stand as a sentence because it is incomplete.

After the meeting was over.

Before we can leave on our vacation.

Although Jessie admitted he made a mistake.

Since I have begun taking college courses.

Dependent clauses begin with **subordinating conjunctions,** one of the words or short phrases in the list that follows. When you check your work for fragments, pay special attention to word groups that begin with one of these words or short phrases. Be sure the necessary completeness is there.

SUBORDINATING CONJUNCTIONS

after	before	until
although	even though	when
as	if	whenever
as if	in order to	where
as long as	once	whereas
as soon as	since	wherever
as though	so that	whether
because	unless	while

Some dependent clause fragments begin with the relative pronouns *who, whose, which,* or *that,* so watch for word groups that begin with one of these words. (For more on this subject, see pages 229–230.)

fragment:	Who lives next door to my parents.
fragment:	Which is in North Carolina.
fragment:	That I told you about.

To correct dependent clause fragments, you can often join the fragment to a sentence that appears before or after it.

fragment:	*After the meeting was over.* We all went out for coffee.
sentence:	After the meeting was over, we all went out for coffee.
fragment:	My self-esteem has improved. *Since I have begun taking college courses.*
sentence:	My self-esteem has improved since I have begun taking college courses.
fragment:	This is the Italian restaurant. *That I told you about.*
sentence:	This is the Italian restaurant that I told you about.

Practice 17.7

Each pair of word groups includes one dependent clause fragment and one sentence. Underline the fragment and correct it by joining it to the sentence.

Example

Because 800 to 1100 tornadoes occur in the United States each year. Everyone should learn about tornado safety.

Because 800 to 1100 tornadoes occur in the United States each year, everyone should learn about tornado safety.

1. Although tornadoes have occurred in every state, Texas, Oklahoma, and Kansas are usually hardest hit.

_____

_____

2. These states are the hardest hit. Because humid winds come from the Gulf of Mexico.

These _____ because humid _____

_____

3. The Gulf winds mix with dry winds. Which do not come from the Gulf of Mexico.

The _____ which do not _____

_____

4. Since the majority of tornadoes come and go quickly. They cause little harm.

Since _____, they cause little _____

_____

5. The strongest tornado measures an F5. Which means the storm has winds over 360 miles an hour.

_____

_____

6. Even if it is just an F0 or an F1 storm. Any tornado has the potential to cause harm.

_____

_____

Subject, verb, dependent clause

Practice 17.8

On a separate sheet of paper, revise to eliminate the six dependent clause fragments. If you have trouble finding the fragments, try reading the paragraph slowly from last sentence to first.

[1]Motown, the most successful black-owned American record company, was founded in 1960 in Detroit by Berry Gordy Jr. [2]Who began as a song-writer in the mid-1950s. [3]Led by the writing talents of Smokey Robinson, who also sang with the Miracles. [4]Motown artists were an important presence on the record charts in the 1960s and 1970s. [5]A reference to "Motor Town" (Detroit), Motown came to signify a particular performance style. [6]A Motown song often featured elaborate structures, heavy rhythms, and background orchestras. [7]Because the company kept a tight rein on the image of its performers. [8]It often prescribed their manners and style of grooming. [9]Live performances required carefully controlled choreography and elaborate costumes. [10]Which added up to the Motown-style package. [11]Clearly, the formula was a success. [12]Because it made stars of many performers, including Diana Ross and the Supremes, Stevie Wonder, Marvin Gaye, the Jackson Five, and Lionel Richie. [13]At its best, Motown represented the best of mass-produced, black-derived pop music. [14]Although its later productions were more obviously the products of a musical assembly line. [15]Motown was largely responsible for introducing the sounds of contemporary black music to a white audience.

Review Practice 17.9

On a separate sheet, rewrite to eliminate the sentence fragments.

[1]All families should plan and practice how to escape from their homes in the event of a fire. [2]Especially at night. [3]Because every minute spent in a burning house means extra danger. [4]Escape routes should be planned and practiced periodically. [5]Family members should practice crawling through the house in the event rooms are filled with smoke. [6]Also learning how to move through the house in darkness. [7]In addition, family members should plan where to meet outdoors. [8]And what to do when they get there. [9]If families plan and practice their escape, a house fire does not have to mean complete tragedy. [10]To learn more about fire safety in the event of a house fire. [11]Contact your local fire department.

FAQ

Q: When two correction options are possible, how do I know which to use?

A: Use the method that works better with your other sentences, perhaps because it improves your sentence variety. If both methods work equally well, it does not matter which you use.

Tips

AVOIDING SENTENCE FRAGMENTS

- Read backwards from your last sentence to your first. You will be less likely to overlook fragments by mentally connecting them to other sentences.
- Notice word groups with *-ing* and *-ed* verb forms. Be sure each verb is complete.
- Check every "sentence" beginning with a subordinating conjunction or a relative pronoun (*who, whose, which, that*) to be sure it really is a sentence.

(continued on next page)

- If you compose at the computer, reformat your paper into a list of sentences. Is each one complete? Of course, reformat your paper after checking.
- **If English is not your first language,** remember that although a sentence does not have to have a subject in some languages, in English a sentence must have both a subject and a verb.

Post Test

On a separate sheet, rewrite the paragraphs to eliminate the fragments.

A. [1]The California condor looks very strange. [2]When perched in a tree. [3]It has a bald head and a wrinkled neck. [4]And a large black, feathered body. [5]Near the ground, the bird is hilariously awkward. [6]It lumbers on takeoffs, and it crashes on landings. [7]In the air, however, the bird is a breathtaking sight. [8]Its wings spreading out nine feet. [9]It can soar at an amazing 80 miles an hour. [10]At one time, one wild condor was left in California. [11]Scientists managed to capture it when it swooped down to feed on a dead goat. [12]The scientists took it to the San Diego Zoo. [13]Where it lived with thirteen other condors. [14]These condors, along with fourteen in the Los Angeles Zoo, the only remaining California condors in the world. [15]Scientists captured these birds. [16]To protect them from being shot or poisoned.

B. [1]Learning how some familiar foods got their names can be interesting. [2]Graham crackers, for example. [3]Were named after Reverend Sylvester Graham. [4]Graham encouraged people to eat special diets. [5]In the nineteenth century. [6]Sometimes, foods are named after the people who invented them. [7]Eggs Benedict being one example. [8]The popular breakfast food was named after a New York businessman, Sam Benedict, who came up with the concoction one night at the famous Waldorf-Astoria hotel. [9]The name Sanka is derived from the French phrase *sans caffeine*. [10]Which means "without caffeine." [11]Although foods are often associated with people. [12]They are also associated with cities. [13]Lima beans, for example, named after Lima, Peru, and brussels sprouts named for Brussels, Belgium. [14]Mayonnaise got its name from Mahon, the Mediterranean city. [15]Where it was first made.

LEARNING FROM TEXTBOOKS

The following material from a college criminal justice textbook appears as a marginal note like the FAQs in this book. Read the excerpt and answer the questions.

police subculture

A particular set of values, beliefs, and acceptable forms of behavior characteristic of American police with which the police profession strives to imbue new recruits. Socialization into the police subculture commences with recruit training and continues thereafter.

1. What is the purpose of this material?

   _____

   _____

2. Why does the author place this material in the margin of the textbook? How does that placement help the author achieve his purpose?

   _____

   _____

3. The text below the heading "police subculture," includes one fragment and one sentence. Underline the sentence once and the fragment twice.

4. As the marginal note on page 237 explains, writers sometimes use fragments intentionally. Why do you think the textbook author used a fragment?

   _____

   _____

Write about It

Define some subculture, such as that of college athletes or military personnel. Describe one or more "values, beliefs, and acceptable forms of behavior," such as the way college athletes behave when losing or the way military personnel act toward superior officers.

SUCCEEDING IN COLLEGE

Use Fragments and Other Short Forms in Note-taking

Avoid sentence fragments in your formal college writing. However, when you take lecture notes, speed is important, so writing fragments can be useful. For example, assume your business instructor says, "The service industry is becoming increasingly computerized and interactive." You can write this fragment in your notes:

Service industry becoming more computerized and interactive.

In the interest of speed, you can shorten further with abbreviations by writing just the first or the first two or three syllables of words, like this:

Serv. indus. becoming more comp. &interact.

Sometimes, the easiest way to abbreviate is with symbols rather than shortened words. For example, assume your business instructor says, "A databank is an electronic storage file." You can write a note with a symbol, like this:

Databank = electron. storage file.

Following is a chart of some common abbreviations and symbols you can use.

abbreviation or symbol	meaning
e.g.	for example
vs	versus
w/	with

(continued on next page)

SUCCEEDING IN COLLEGE (continued)

abbreviation or symbol	meaning
w/o	without
#	number
&	and
%	percentage
>	greater than
<	less than
=	is/equals
≠	is not/does not equal

Write about It

Select a page from one of your textbooks and take notes on it by using fragments and other shortened forms. Then close your book and rewrite your notes in complete sentences.

For more practice with avoiding sentence fragments, go to www.mywritinglab.com.

CHAPTER 18

Avoiding Run-On Sentences and Comma Splices

Run-on sentences and comma splices are a problem because they can confuse readers by blurring sentence boundaries. You may currently know very little about how to avoid sentences that are run together without punctuation (run-ons) or with just a comma (comma splices), and that is not a problem because this chapter will help you learn what you need to know. On the other hand, you may already know more than you realize, in which case this chapter will reinforce your understanding and perhaps teach you a few new points. The following pretest will help you assess your current level of understanding.

Pretest

If the word group is a run-on because sentences are run together without punctuation, write *RO* on the blank; if it is a comma splice because sentences are improperly linked by a comma, write *CS* on the blank; if it is correct, write *C* on the blank. Do not guess. If you are unsure, do not write anything. Check your answers in Appendix II.

1. **CS** I heard a siren, I pulled my car to the edge of the road.
2. **RO** The sudden spring rains caused flash flooding the townspeople moved to higher ground. *— Independent clause.*
3. **RO** Roberto's singing career is going very well he has signed a contract with an important talent agent.
4. **C** If I had the opportunity, I would travel to Europe.
5. **RO** The last day of the month is the best time to buy a car at that time dealers are anxious to reduce their inventory.
6. **CS** People are changing their eating habits, more of us are restricting fat and cholesterol.
7. **RO** Because I spilled bleach on it, the shirt is ruined.

C

(continued on next page)

8. __C__ I do all my grocery shopping on Sunday to avoid the crowds.

9. __Cs__ Martha subscribes to ten magazines she doesn't know where to put them all.

10. __C__ To be sure that your car runs well, change the oil regularly.

IDENTIFYING RUN-ON SENTENCES AND COMMA SPLICES

If two independent clauses (word groups with subjects and verbs that can be sentences) are run together without any punctuation, the error is called a **run-on sentence.** If the independent clauses are joined by just a comma, the error is called a **comma splice.** (You can review independent clauses on page 212)

Here are two independent clauses (word groups that can be sentences):

> Randy could not wait to tell everyone his good news.
> He got the job he wanted so badly.

If you run the independent clauses together, the result is a **run-on sentence:**

run-on: Randy could not wait to tell everyone the good news he got the job he wanted so badly.

If you join these independent clauses with just a comma, the result is a **comma splice:**

comma splice: Randy could not wait to tell everyone the good news, he got the job he wanted so badly.

Correcting Run-ons and Comma Splices with a Period and Capital Letter

One way to eliminate a run-on sentence or comma splice is to use a period and capital letter to make each independent clause a separate sentence.

run-on: I left the party at 11:00 then I went to a movie.

correction: I left the party at 11:00. Then I went to a movie.

comma splice: Darla is the perfect person for the job, she is reliable, intelligent, and efficient.

correction: Darla is the perfect person for the job. She is reliable, intelligent, and efficient.

Practice 18.1

Eliminate each run-on or comma splice by adding a period and capital letter. Two sentences are correct.

Example

"pan out." It

You have probably heard the expression ~~"pan out," it~~ is used when things work out satisfactorily.

1. When a plan goes well, you can say that "everything panned out."   *Correct.*

2. When a plan does not go well, you can say the opposite. You can say that "things did not pan out."

3. "Pan out" is a gold-mining term. One method of finding gold is to take a handful of sand and place it in a little pan.

4. By sloshing the water back and forth in the pan, miners cause the lighter sand, dirt, and pebbles to slide over the edge.   *Correct.*

5. The heavier gold stays in the pan. Thus it "pans out."

6. We do not often pause to think about common expressions. Their origins can be very interesting, however.

Practice 18.2

Eliminate the three run-on sentences and comma splices by using periods and capital letters.

[1]Bill Haley was the first real rock-and-roll star. His recording of "Crazy Man Crazy" was the first rock-and-roll record to make *Billboard's* pop music charts. [2]Although he started out as a country singer, Haley decided to make a bid for teen appeal in the mid-1950s. [3]When his "Rock Around the Clock" became the theme song for the movie *The Blackboard Jungle* in 1955, Haley scored big with teen audiences. He was at this point a genuine rock-and-roll star. [4]For the next two years he had a dozen top-40 hits, these included "See You Later Alligator" and "Burn That Candle." [5]When Haley died in 1981, he was 55, and he had sold 60 million records.

FAQ

Q: Why do run-ons and comma splices matter?

A: When readers cannot easily tell where your sentences begin and end, they can become confused about where ideas start and stop.

Correcting Run-ons and Comma Splices with a Comma and Coordinating Conjunction

You can eliminate a run-on sentence or comma splice by joining the independent clauses with a comma and one of the following coordinating conjunctions.

COORDINATING CONJUNCTIONS		
and	or	so
but	for	yet
	nor	

run-on:	The hamburger was not completely cooked I asked the waiter to take it back to the kitchen.
correction:	The hamburger was not completely cooked, so I asked the waiter to take it back to the kitchen.
comma splice:	This compact disc player costs more than that one, it is worth the extra expense.
correction:	This compact disc player costs more than that one, but it is worth the extra expense.

Practice 18.3

Eliminate the run-ons and comma splices by adding commas and coordinating conjunctions. One sentence is correct. In some cases, more than one coordinating conjunction can be selected.

Example

One name above all is associated with the dictionary, ∧*and* that name is "Webster."

1. Many dictionaries bear the name "Webster," Noah Webster does not have anything to do with these books.

2. Webster published the first major dictionary in the United States in the early 1800s, his name is practically synonymous with "dictionary."

3. His rights to dictionaries ran out many years ago, the word "Webster's" entered the public domain.

4. Anyone can now use Webster's name in connection with a dictionary, regardless of the author or publisher.

5. Any company can call its dictionary "Webster's," many companies do.

6. We will most likely think of Noah Webster whenever we check a word in a dictionary, he is the one whose name means "dictionary."

Practice 18.4

Use commas and coordinating conjunctions to eliminate the four run-ons and comma splices.

[1]Exercise does not have to be unpleasant. [2]If you follow some simple guidelines, you can enjoy the road to fitness. [3]First pick a form of exercise you like, walking, swimming, running, bicycling, or whatever. [4]You should set goals for yourself, you should make those goals a little harder as you move along. [5]You should swim a bit farther, you should run a little longer each day. [6]It is important to go slowly at first, you might sustain an injury. [7]To avoid injuries, you should also do warm-up and cool-down stretching exercises. [8]Finally, exercise with a friend, you can encourage each other and enjoy the companionship.

Correcting Run-Ons and Comma Splices with a Semicolon

A second way to eliminate a run-on or comma splice is to use a semicolon to join the independent clauses. Use this correction method when the relationship between the independent clauses is so clear that it does not need to be shown. (See also page 223.)

run-on:	None of us wanted to go out we were all too tired.
correction:	None of us wanted to go out⍽;⍽we were all too tired.
comma splice:	Jim and Clarice bought a house that is a hundred years old, they will have to work hard to fix it up.
correction:	Jim and Clarice bought a house that is a hundred years old⍽;⍽they will have to work hard to fix it up.

A run-on or comma splice can also be corrected with one of the following **conjunctive adverbs** used with a semicolon and a comma.

CONJUNCTIVE ADVERBS

; however,	; furthermore,	; thus,
; nevertheless,	; moreover,	; consequently,
; nonetheless,	; therefore,	

---

run-on:	The examination was harder than I expected I believe I passed it.
correction:	The examination was harder than I expected⍽; however,⍽I believe I passed it.
comma splice:	On April Fools' Day my son put a rubber snake in my bed, he poured salt in my coffee.
correction:	On April Fools' Day my son put a rubber snake in my bed⍽; furthermore,⍽he poured salt in my coffee.

CAUTION: When you use a semicolon to avoid a run-on sentence or comma splice, be sure you have an independent clause on *both sides* of the semicolon.

incorrect:	Carol decorated the Christmas tree; before Philippe got home from work. (An independent clause does not appear after the semicolon.)
correct:	Carol decorated the Christmas tree before Philippe got home from work.

Practice 18.5

Eliminate the run-ons and comma splices by adding semicolons. Three sentences are correct.

Example

Some laws currently on the books are wacky; it is hard to understand why.

1. For example, stores in Providence, Rhode Island, are not allowed to sell tooth-brushes on Sunday; however, they can still sell toothpaste.

2. In Paraguay, dueling is illegal if both parties are blood donors.

3. In Atwoodville, Connecticut, people cannot play Scrabble while waiting for a politician to speak, now that is an odd ordinance.

4. According to the Recruitment Code of the U.S. Navy, anyone "bearing an obscene and indecent" tattoo will be rejected.

5. The U.S. patent laws prohibit granting patents on useless inventions, That law is not always enforced.

6. Items in the catalogs mailed to me prove that many useless items are patented.

Practice 18.6

Add semicolons to eliminate the three run-on sentences and comma splices.

[1]An increasing number of employers are providing day-care centers at their places of business they have learned that employees are more productive when they do not have to worry about baby-sitting arrangements for their children. [2]In addition, when child-care is on company premises, employees do not have to call off work when the babysitter fails to show up. [3]Many companies are learning that on-site day-care is a valuable fringe benefit. [4]Employees are less likely to change their places of employment when day-care is available this means companies do not have to worry about rapid employee turnover. [5]Undoubtedly, more and more companies will be providing day-care facilities, they are a benefit to both employer and employee.

Warning Words and Phrases

Pay special attention to the following words and phrases. When you edit and come across one of these words or phrases, check to see if it is joining independent clauses. If it is, use a semicolon before the warning word or phrase.

as a result	furthermore	moreover	similarly
consequently	hence	nevertheless	then
finally	however	next	therefore
for example	in addition	on the contrary	thus

Practice 18.7

If the word group is a run-on, write *RO* on the blank; if it is a comma splice, write *CS;* if it is a correct sentence, write *C*. Circle the warning word or phrase.

Example

   RO   We do not often pay attention to movie sound effects (however,) they are an important aspect of many films

1. _____ Henri completed the committee report for his fraternity, then he took it to the chapter president.

2. _____ Carla's cavity was so deep she had to have two shots of novocaine consequently she could not feel the right side of her face for three hours.

3. _____ We waited most of the morning for Joan to arrive; finally, we just left without her.

4. _____ Not everyone understands Dad's sarcastic sense of humor; as a result, some people feel insulted when he teases them.

5. _____ In addition to losing my keys last week, I misplaced my good leather gloves.

6. _____ First you should choose an advisor in your major field of study, next you should select an advisor in your minor field of study.

7. _____ Dr. Schultz is sick with the flu therefore our midterm has been postponed until next week.

8. _____ The football team lost three games in a row as a result of errors by the defensive squad.

Review Practice 18.8

Edit to eliminate the run-on sentences and comma splices, using any of the correction methods explained in this chapter.

[1]Margaret Chase Smith was the first woman elected to both the United States House of Representatives and the United States Senate. [2]Her husband, a Republican congressman from Maine, died in 1940, Mrs. Smith replaced him in the House of Representatives. [3]She served in the House for eight years. [4]She was elected to the Senate in 1948 she was reelected in 1954 and 1960. [5]In 1950 she was one of the first senators to oppose Senator Joseph McCarthy. [6]In 1965 she campaigned for the Republican presidential nomination, she was the first woman to do so. [7]Smith was an influential legislator during her years in Congress, moreover, she was not put off by the fact that at the time, politics was largely the domain of males. [8]In fact, Smith helped pave the way for other women to enter the political arena at the national level.

FAQ

Q: Can I find run-ons and comma splices by looking for long sentences?

A: No, run-ons and comma splices can be very short. For example, this short word group is a comma splice: Joan left, Henri did not. Also, long sentences are not necessarily run-ons or comma splices. For example, this long sentence is correct: When the tornado struck the Midwestern town, the early warning system functioned so well that all residents were able to take cover, and no loss of life was reported.

Tips

AVOIDING RUN-ON SENTENCES AND COMMA SPLICES

■ Count the number of independent clauses in every word group you are calling a sentence. If you have two or more, be sure they are correctly joined.

■ Remember, a comma by itself cannot join independent clauses; it must appear with a coordinating conjunction.

■ If you compose at the computer, use the search or find function to locate the warning words and phrases. Then determine whether each one you find is joining independent clauses. If it is, use a semicolon.

■ **If English is not your first language,** remember that although commas can legitimately join independent clauses in several other languages, in English they cannot.

Post Test

Edit to eliminate the run-on sentences and comma splices. You may use any or all of the correction methods explained in this chapter.

A. [1]Many schools have alcohol-awareness programs to steer children away from drinking, however, parents need to be involved as well. [2]Parents can do a number of things, for example, they can discuss drinking scenes in programs and movies they watch with their children. [3]Parents should ask questions such as "Why do you think grown-ups drink?" and "Can grown-ups have fun without drinking?" [4]Because children may become confused seeing adults drink when they have been told to say no, parents should explain the health risks associated with alcohol and the fact that the legal drinking age is 21. [5]It is also a good idea to emphasize positive reasons for saying no: Children need to keep their heads clear for school, they also need to keep their bodies healthy for athletics. [6]Parents can also role-play with their children. [7]Give them a glass of water and have them practice saying "No thanks." [8]Parents must be actively involved, they cannot leave the full responsibility to the schools.

B. [1]The children's song "Pop Goes the Weasel" does not mean what many people think it does. [2]In England in the seventeenth and eighteenth century, a weasel was a tool used by hat makers, they used it to apply the fabric to the outside of a hat. [3]"Pop" was a slang term it meant "to pawn something." [4]When the hatter in the song runs out of money, he pawns his hatter's tool. [5]In other words, "That's the way the money goes pop goes the weasel." [6]As you can now see, the song has nothing to do with a furry animal, nor does it relate to an animal bursting.

LEARNING FROM TEXTBOOKS

The following is an excerpt from a college nutrition textbook. Read it and answer the questions that follow.

[1]Hunger exists in every nation of the world; however, the causes vary. [2]In wealthy nations, it is usually caused by unequal distribution of abundant food to people who are poor. [3]In developing nations, unequal distribution can be a factor, but the most common

causes are natural disasters, war, overpopulation, poor farming practices, lack of infrastructure, and disease.

Natural Disasters

[4]In the summer of 2004, a drought in western Africa brought life-threatening undernutrition to about 20% of the population of Niger and Mali. [5]Such natural disasters often result in widespread hunger because they destroy substantial amounts of local crops in a short time. [6]Drought and other natural disasters, including floods, tsunamis, high winds, hurricanes, frosts, and infestations by insects, worms, or microbes can even result in **famine,** a severe food shortage affecting a large percentage of the population in a limited geographic area at a particular time.

1. Is sentence 5 a run-on sentence? Why or why not?

   _____

   _____

2. Is the semicolon in sentence 1 used correctly? Explain why or why not.

   _____

   _____

3. Rewrite sentence 3 so that a conjunctive adverb correctly joins the independent clauses. Be sure to punctuate correctly.

   _____

   _____

4. Combine sentences 4 and 5 into one sentence, without creating a comma splice or run-on sentence.

   _____

   _____

5. Textbook authors often present overviews of contents so you will know in advance which topics will be covered and in what order. Find the overview in this excerpt and then predict what topic will be addressed next, after natural disasters.

   _____

Write about It

Undernutrition in poor countries claims the lives of 98 of every 1000 children. Do you think that we in the United States have a responsibility to do something about this high death rate? Write an argument that states and defends your assertion.

Make Inferences When You Read

When writers join independent clauses by a semicolon alone, you must determine on your own how the ideas in the clauses relate to each other. You may need to reflect for a moment or even read between the lines. When you assess stated ideas to draw conclusions about what is not stated but merely suggested, you are making an **inference.**

For example, read the following sentence, and reflect for a moment to make an inference about the relationship between the ideas in the independent clauses:

> Americans are weary of the preferential treatment given to special interest groups contributing large amounts of money to political campaigns; Congress will have to consider additional campaign finance reform soon.

Did you infer that the relationship between the ideas in the clauses is one of cause and effect, that the idea in the second independent clause is a result of the idea in the first independent clause?

When you read your textbooks and other college materials, you will often need to make inferences, and not just when semicolons separate independent clauses. When you make these inferences, make reasonable ones supported by the clues in the text. Consider this passage, for example:

> Americans are becoming increasingly frustrated by the amount of violent crime in this country and the apparent failure of the judicial and penal systems to stem the violence. Seeking a quick fix, we are demanding harsher penalties, even to the extent of trying youthful offenders as adults. Despite the fact that studies confirm the utter futility of locking away our youngest criminals, we demand harsher sentences, even life imprisonment for young teens convicted of murder.

You can reasonably infer from the material that the writer believes that trying juveniles as adults is a bad idea, but you cannot infer that the writer believes we want vengeance against youthful offenders, because no evidence in the text supports that inference.

Write about It

Photocopy an article from a magazine or newspaper. Note one inference you can make from the article and explain why you can reasonably make that inference.

For more practice with avoiding run-on sentences and comma splices, go to www.mywritinglab.com.

CHAPTER 19

Writing Sentences with Variety and Parallelism

Sentence variety and parallel structure are important to good sentence style, and this chapter will teach you what you need to know. If you already are competent in these areas, this chapter will reinforce your understanding and perhaps teach you a few new points. Before beginning, take the following pretest to assess your current level of understanding.

Pretest

1. If the group of sentences has sentence variety (that is, has varied sentence openers), write *yes* on the blank. If it does not have sentence variety, write *no*. If you are unsure, do not guess; leave the space blank. Check your answers in Appendix II.

   a. ___No___ If we educate people about the importance of recycling, more people will recycle. When we increase the amount of recycling, we can live on the land more gently. Because we must take care with our resources, we must try to live more gently on the land.

   b. ___yes___ More people will recycle if we educate them about the importance of recycling. Of course, if we increase the amount of recycling, we can live on the land more gently. Then, we will take better care of our resources.

   c. ___no___ Children today are at risk from inadequate health care. Unfortunately, the government is not taking the risk seriously enough, so clearly we need to lobby our legislators on the matter.

   d. ___yes___ Sadly, children today are at risk from inadequate health care. Unfortunately, the government is not taking the risk seriously enough. Clearly, we need to lobby our legislators on the matter.

2. Place a check mark next to the better sentence in each pair. If you are unsure, do not guess; leave both spaces blank. Check your answers in Appendix II.

   a. ___✓___ The twins are energetic, talented, and personable.

   _____ The twins are energetic, talented, and they are personable.

   (continued on next page)

261

b. _____ Cal's blood test showed that he had high cholesterol and a triglyceride level that was too high.

_____✓_____ Cal's blood test showed that both his cholesterol and triglyceride levels were high.

c. _____ The new house is not only beautiful but it is energy efficient.

_____✓_____ The new house is not only beautiful but energy efficient.

d. _____✓_____ Either Hank will spend his savings on a trip to Europe, or he will use the money to buy a car.

_____ Hank will either spend his savings on a trip to Europe, or he will use the money to buy a car.

SENTENCE VARIETY

To improve the flow of your writing and have a mature style, use a variety of sentence structures. This mix of sentence structures is known as **sentence variety.** You have already learned about subordination and coordination. When you use these, you are contributing to sentence variety. In addition, you can achieve sentence variety by using the sentence structures described on the following pages.

Begin with One or Two -*ly* Words

Words that end in -*ly* are **adverbs.** Adverbs describe verbs.

adv

Mother <u>carefully</u> eased the heavy cake pans out of the oven.

Carefully describes how Mother eased the pans out of the oven. An -*ly* word can be an excellent way to open a sentence:

Carefully, Mother eased the heavy cake pans out of the oven.
Hoarsely, the cheerleaders shouted for a touchdown.
Patiently, Dr. Vardova explained differential equations.

PUNCTUATION NOTE: When you begin a sentence with an -*ly* word (adverb), place a comma after the word. This rule is illustrated in the previous sentences.

You can also begin a sentence with two -*ly* words:

Slowly and steadily, the workers slid the refrigerator into the narrow space next to the stove.
Quickly yet cautiously, Frank crossed the narrow bridge.
Loudly but politely, she explained her complaint to the manager.
Softly, sweetly, the nurse sang a lullaby to the infant.

As you can tell from the preceding examples, two -*ly* words can be separated with *and, but, yet,* or a comma.

PUNCTUATION NOTE: Two *-ly* words (adverbs) are separated with a comma when no word is between them. Also, when a pair of *-ly* words begins a sentence, place a comma after the second *-ly* word. This rule is illustrated in the previous example sentences.

Practice 19.1

Begin the following sentences with *-ly* words (adverbs) of your choice. At least two sentences should begin with a pair of *-ly* words.

Example

The frustrated sales clerk explained for the third time why she could not give the customer a refund.

Loudly, the frustrated sales clerk explained for the third time why she could not

give the customer a refund.

1. Valerie arranged the roses and mums in the antique vase.

Carefully, Valerie arranged the roses and mums in the antique vase.

2. Ted maneuvered the car around the fallen rocks.

Carefully, Ted maneuvered the car around the fallen rock.

3. Dominic cradled his newborn daughter in his arms.

Caughtly gently,

4. Jeffrey ran around the bases after hitting his third home run of the season.

Quickly,
Suddently,

5. The first-grade teacher showed the class how to write cursive letters.

Luckily,
Kindly,

6. Dr. Chun performed his duties as head of the art institute.

Proudly, Dr. Chun performed his duties as head as of the art institute.

7. Jan entered the classroom ten minutes after the lecture had begun.

Slowly, Nervously, Jan entered the classroom...

8. I shouted at the truck driver who changed lanes and cut me off.

Angrily, I shouted at the truck...

Practice 19.2

On a separate sheet, write two sentences of your own that begin with an *-ly* word (adverb) and two sentences that begin with a pair of *-ly* words. Remember to use commas correctly.

Begin with an *-ing* Verb or Phrase

The *-ing* form of a verb is the **present participle.** The present participle can be used as a descriptive word and can be an effective sentence opening.

Whistling, John walked past the cemetery.

Whistling is the *-ing* form of the verb *whistle*. In the preceding sentence, it describes John. Opening some of your sentences with present participles contributes to sentence variety. Here are more examples:

Crying, the child said that he fell off his bicycle.
Coughing, Maria left the classroom to get a drink of water.
Limping, I crossed the street.

You can also begin a sentence with an *-ing* verb phrase (**present participle phrase**). An *-ing* verb phrase is the present participle (*-ing* verb form) and one or more words that work with it. Here is a sentence that opens with a present participle phrase:

Whistling softly, John walked past the cemetery.

The present participle phrase is *whistling softly,* which describes John.

By opening some of your sentences with present participle phrases, you can achieve sentence variety. Here are more examples:

Crying pitifully, the child said that he fell off his bicycle.
Coughing into her handkerchief, Maria left the classroom to get a drink of water.
Limping more than usual, I crossed the street.

CAUTION: The *-ing* word or phrase should appear immediately before the word or phrase it describes, or the result will be rather silly, like this:

Dancing in the moonlight, the band played a romantic song.

Dancing in the moonlight is a present participle phrase that is not followed by a word it can logically describe. As a result, the sentence says that the band was dancing in the moonlight. (For more on this point, see **dangling modifiers** on pages 360–361.)

PUNCTUATION NOTE: When you begin a sentence with a present participle or a present participle phrase, follow the participle or phrase with a comma. The previous example sentences illustrate this rule.

Practice 19.3

Begin the following sentences with the *-ing* words (present participles) of your choice. At least two sentences should begin with *-ing* verb phrases. Remember to place commas correctly.

Example

Mother prepared Thanksgiving dinner for fourteen people.

Working feverishly, Mother prepared Thanksgiving dinner for fourteen people.

1. Donna explained why tax reform would hurt the middle class.

    understanding   the situation

2. Juanita accepted her award for scholastic achievement in mathematics.

    Crying and shaking, Juanita accepted

3. Pete and Lorenzo tried to tell us what was so funny.

    Laughing,
    Smiling,

4. Jalil bench-pressed 250 pounds.

    overwhelming, jalil bench-pressed

5. Diana planted tulip and daffodil bulbs in her spring garden.

Properly, _____

_____

6. The collie ran across the yard.

Barking, The collie ran across the yard.

_____

7. Dr. Dominic announced that everyone passed the exam.

excitingly, _____

_____

FAQ

Q: How can I tell if my writing needs sentence variety?

A: Read your writing out loud, or have someone else read it to you. If it sounds choppy or sing-songy, it needs sentence variety.

8. The ten-year-old was bored by the pastor's sermon.

_____

_____

Practice 19.4

On a separate sheet, write two sentences of your own that begin with an *-ing* verb (present participle) and two sentences that begin with an *-ing* verb phrase (present participle phrase). Be sure to follow the *-ing* verb or verb phrase with a word the participle can describe. Also, remember to use commas correctly.

Begin with an *-ed* Verb or Phrase

The *-ed* form of a verb is the **past participle.** The past participle can be used as a descriptive word and as an effective sentence opening.

> Frightened, the child crawled in bed with his parents.

Frightened is the *-ed* form of the verb *frighten*. In the preceding sentence, it describes the child. By opening some of your sentences with past participles, you can contribute to sentence variety in your writing. Here are more examples:

> Tired, Dad fell asleep while watching the Raiders game.
> Irritated, Mandy threw her books on the floor.
> Excited, Leonid told his friends about his good fortune.

You can also begin a sentence with an *-ed* verb phrase (**past participle phrase**). An *-ed* verb phrase is the past participle (*-ed* verb form) and one or more words that work with it.

> Frightened by the dark, the child crawled in bed with his parents.

In this case, the past participle phrase is *frightened by the dark,* which describes the child.

Opening some of your sentences with past participle phrases will help you achieve sentence variety. Here are more examples:

> Tired after raking the leaves, Dad fell asleep watching the Raiders game.
> Irritated by her low exam grade, Mandy threw her books on the floor.
> Excited about being promoted to manager, Leonid told his friends about his good fortune.

CAUTION: The *-ed* verb or phrase should appear immediately before the verb or phrase it describes, or the result will be a silly sentence, like this:

> Delighted by the victory, a celebration was in order.

Delighted by the victory is a past participle phrase that is not followed by a word it can logically describe. As a result, the sentence says that a celebration was delighted by the victory. (For more on this point, see **dangling modifiers** on pages 360–361)

PUNCTUATION NOTE: When you begin a sentence with an *-ed* verb (past participle) or an *-ed* verb phrase (past participle phrase), follow the *-ed* verb or verb phrase with a comma. The previous example sentences illustrate this rule.

Practice 19.5

Open the sentences with *-ed* verbs (past participles) of your choice. Begin at least two sentences with *-ed* verb phrases. Remember to place commas correctly.

Example

The referee threw the coach out of the game.

Angered, the referee threw the coach out of the game.

1. The kitten curled into a furry ball and fell asleep.

   Tired, the kitten curled into a furvoy ball
   exshauted, the kitten . . .

2. Three-year-old Bobby ran crying to his nursery school teacher.

   cried, the three year-old bobby ran to his. . .
   melted, the three . . .

3. Maria sprinted frantically after the man who stole her purse.

Scared,

Angered,

4. The tenants voiced their complaints to the apartment manager.

angered, the tentants voiced their...

reported, the voiced tentant...

5. Lorenzo reached over and turned off the blaring alarm.

scarred, Lorenze...

scared frightened...

6. The steak was worth the twenty dollars I paid for it.

enjoyed,...

Pleased...

7. The police officer told Alicia she was lucky to get off with just a warning.

her calmed...

relieved...

8. The cookies were too burned to sell at the charity bazaar.

Practice 19.6

On a separate sheet, write two sentences of your own that begin with *-ed* verbs (past participles) and two sentences that begin with *-ed* verb phrases (past participle phrases). Be sure to follow the *-ed* verb or verb phrase with a word the participle can describe. Also, remember to use commas correctly.

Begin with a Prepositional Phrase

A **preposition** shows how two things relate to each other in time or space. (See page 201 for a more detailed explanation of prepositions.) Following is a chart of common prepositions.

COMMON PREPOSITIONS

about	before	inside	through
above	behind	into	to
across	between	like	toward
after	by	of	under
along	during	off	up
among	for	on	with
around	from	out	within
at	in	over	without

A **prepositional phrase** is a preposition and the words that work with it. Here are examples of prepositional phrases. The prepositions are underlined as a study aid.

<u>in</u> May	<u>across</u> the street	<u>toward</u> the end <u>of</u> the book
<u>behind</u> me	<u>during</u> the concert	<u>inside</u> the oven
<u>on</u> top	<u>out of</u> bounds	<u>without</u> a doubt

Beginning some of your sentences with prepositional phrases will help you achieve sentence variety. Here are examples of sentences that begin with prepositional phrases:

> Under the kitchen table, Rags sat contentedly chewing on his bone.
> In the spring, the senior class will travel to Washington.
> From now on, everyone in this state must wear a seat belt.

PUNCTUATION NOTE: A prepositional phrase that begins a sentence is usually followed by a comma.

> Between the oak trees, two squirrels were chasing each other.
> By noon, all the sale items were sold.

Practice 19.7

Underline the prepositional phrases in the following sentences. (Several of the sentences contain more than one prepositional phrase.)

Example

The infant began crying <u>in the middle</u> <u>of the night</u>.

1. At ten o'clock, the church bells chimed in unison.

2. Charlie announced that there was a thief among us.

3. The truth of the matter is that no one cares.

4. With the help of everyone, the fund-raiser can be a huge success.

5. By daybreak, a foot of snow had fallen in our city.

Practice 19.8

Combine the two sentences into one sentence that begins with one or more prepositional phrases in the second sentence. Remember to use commas correctly.

Example

"Colonel" Harlan Sanders held odd jobs.
He held odd jobs for twenty-five years with only a sixth-grade education.

For twenty-five years with only a sixth-grade education, "Colonel" Harlan

Sanders held odd jobs.

1. Harlan Sanders opened a small gas station and restaurant.
He opened it in Corbin, Kentucky, in 1929.

In 1929, Harlan

2. His cooking grew so popular that he opened Sanders Café.
He opened the café after a short time.

After a short time,

3. Both the war and a new interstate led to a decline in customers.
The decline in customers came during World War II.

During World War II,

4. Mounting debts required Sanders to sell the restaurant, but he franchised his cooking method and secret seasoning.
He sold the restaurant in 1956.

In 1956,

5. He had sold more than 600 franchises, and he sold his company but remained its spokesperson.
He sold them about four years later.

four years later,

Practice 19.9

On a separate sheet, write four sentences that begin with prepositional phrases. Remember to place a comma after each phrase.

Review Practice 19.10

On a separate sheet, rewrite the paragraphs to add more sentence variety. Use a combination of the techniques you have learned: *-ly* openers, *-ing* verb openers, *-ed* verb openers, and prepositional phrase openers. You may change word order, and you may also begin some sentences with the subject.

A.   Amelia Earhart and her navigator tried to fly around the world during the summer of 1937. They were supposed to stop at Howland Island to refuel, but they never arrived. The pilot radioed compass readings hoping to be guided in. These, sadly, were the last words heard from Earhart. The plane was declared lost at sea after a long naval search. A number of theories have been advanced to explain Earhart's disappearance. Some say Earhart was spying for the United States. They say she was shot down over the Marshall Islands, which were held by Japan. Others say a navigational error caused Earhart to miss Howland Island and crash at sea. Still others say the plane ran out of gas and crashlanded. The real cause of Earhart's disappearance will probably never be learned, although people will always admire the courage of the first woman to fly across the ocean.

B.   Walter Gregg and his family should have taken a drive on the afternoon of March 11, 1958. They hung out at home instead. They were around to see their house demolished by an atomic bomb as a result. The bombing occurred when the bomb bay doors of a U.S. Air Force jet accidentally opened, and an atomic warhead fell out. The bomb crashed through the roof of the Greggs' house outside Florence, South Carolina. It obliterated the residence and gouged out a thirty-five-foot crater in the backyard. The explosion, luckily, was nonnuclear. What detonated was the TNT in the bomb's trigger device. The Greggs were slightly injured by flying debris. They accepted a $54,000 settlement from the government.

PARALLELISM: WORDS IN SERIES AND PAIRS

Parallelism refers to balance. For your sentences to have the necessary parallelism or balance, words that form pairs or series should all have the same form. Here is an example:

Ian enjoys skating and reading.

Two words form a pair: *skating* and *reading*. Since both words have the same form (*-ing* verb forms), the sentence has the necessary parallelism or balance.

Here is another example of a sentence with parallelism. This time, there is balance among words that form a series:

Janet and Rico found the movie fresh, funny, and surprising.

Three words form a series: *fresh, funny,* and *surprising*. Since each of these words has the same form (each is an adjective that describes *movie*), the sentence has the necessary parallelism.

Now here is a sentence that lacks parallelism:

The doctor told the patient to avoid salt and that he should get more exercise.

Two elements form a pair: *to avoid salt* and *that he should get more* exercise. The first element is a verb phrase; the second is a clause. Because the elements in the pair are different forms, the sentence lacks parallelism. To achieve the necessary balance, the sentence needs two verb phrases or two clauses:

> The doctor told the patient to avoid salt and to get more exercise. (two verb phrases)

> or

> The doctor told the patient that he should avoid salt and that he should get more exercise. (two clauses)

Here is another sentence that lacks parallelism:

> This course demands patience, dedication, and a student must know how to research.

Three elements form a series: *patience, dedication,* and *a student must know how to research.* The first two elements are nouns, but the third element is a clause. Because all the elements in the series do not have the same form, the sentence lacks parallelism. Here is the sentence revised to achieve parallelism:

> This course demands patience, dedication, and research ability. (three nouns)

Practice 19.11

The underlined element in the pair or series is not parallel. Rewrite the sentence to achieve parallelism.

Example

Joan's aptitude test revealed ability in math and <u>she was good at learning foreign languages</u>.

Joan's aptitude test revealed ability in math and foreign languages.

1. The citizens' committee criticized the mayor's proposal because of its complexity and <u>it was expensive</u>.

   the citizens' committee critized the mayors proposal because of it's complexity & its price.

2. To save money on his living expenses, Gustav got a roommate, <u>ate out less</u> often, ~~he fired his~~ cleaning person, and he clipped coupons to use at the grocery store.

   And gustav got a roomate, ate out less often

3. Before agreeing to the surgery, Delores decided she would get a second opinion and <u>to see if she feels better in two weeks</u>.

Delores decided she wants the second opinion to see if she feels better in two weeks.

4. The proposal for renovating the downtown business district suggests eliminating one-way streets, instituting on-street parking, and <u>we should reface some of the other buildings</u>.

_____

_____

5. My family prefers a week at the ocean in a condominium to <u>spending a week in the mountains in a cabin</u>.

spend a week in the mountain cabin.

_____

6. By three months, most infants will recognize their mother's voice, hold their heads up unassisted, and <u>three-month-old infants will grasp at objects placed within their reach</u>.

and will grasp at objects placed within their reach.

7. My piano teacher gave me a choice between playing one difficult piece or <u>I could play two less difficult ones</u>.

playing one difficult piece or play less two difficult ones.

8. Geography 102 was canceled because the enrollment was low and <u>because of the illness of the instructor</u>.

_____

_____

Practice 19.12

Complete each sentence with a parallel element.

Example

Tony swaggered in, tipped his hat, and *smiled at everyone in the room.*

1. Most people expect Gregory to win the race for Student Government president because of his intelligence, integrity, and _____

_____

2. I like spending a quiet Saturday evening alone better than _____

_____

3. Marta approached the stage with her heart pounding, her palms sweating, and

_____

_____

4. To pass the course, Professor Lloyd explained that we would have to write a research paper, that we would have to pass a midterm examination, and that

_____

_____

5. Several committee members wanted to raise money with a rummage sale, but most wanted _____

_____

6. Chez enjoyed the novel, but I found it predictable, sluggish, and _____

_____

7. Lee has always liked small, informal weddings better than _____

_____

8. If you are not sure what courses to take next semester, you can consult the college catalog or _____

_____

Practice 19.13

Find and correct the faulty parallelism in the following paragraph.

[1]Leonardo da Vinci, who lived from 1452 to 1519, was one of the world's great geniuses. [2]No one before him or who has lived after has achieved so much in so

many fields. [3]He was an outstanding painter, sculptor, and he was also an architect. [4]He designed bridges, highways, weapons, costumes, and he invented scientific instruments. [5]He also invented the diving bell and tank, and he designed flying machines, although they could not be built with the materials of the time. [6]Da Vinci approached science and art in the same methodical manner: He made sketches to help him solve problems. [7]He saw no difference between planning a machine and how he would plan a painting. [8]Probably the most famous painting in the world, the *Mona Lisa,* was painted by Leonardo da Vinci in Florence.

PARALLELISM: PAIRS OF CONJUNCTIONS

Some conjunctions work in pairs.

CONJUNCTIONS THAT WORK IN PAIRS

either . . . or	not only . . . but [also]
neither . . . nor	whether . . . or
both . . . and	if . . . then

For parallelism, put the words that follow the second conjunction in the same form as the words that follow the first conjunction.

> Either I will earn enough money to pay my tuition, or I will ask my parents for a loan.

The words that follow *either* have the same form as the words that follow *or* (both word groups are clauses). Thus, parallelism is achieved.

Here is another example:

> Working full-time while going to school full-time is both tiring and foolish.

The word that follows *both* has the same form as the word that follows *and* (both words are modifiers). As a result, parallelism is achieved.

Now here is an example of a sentence that lacks parallelism:

> This stretch of beach is not only beautiful, but it is private as well.

In this example, *not only* is followed by *beautiful* (a descriptive word), and *but* is followed by *it is private as well* (a clause). Because the conjunctions are not followed by words in the same form, the sentence lacks parallelism. To achieve parallelism, follow each conjunction with words in the same form:

> This stretch of beach is not only beautiful but private.

Practice 19.14

Complete each of the following sentences with a parallel element.

Example

To pass Calculus II either I must get a tutor, or

I must go to the math lab.

1. Luis will either trade his car in for a new model or _____

_____

2. Either I will move to the city or _____

_____

3. Professor Amin decided both to postpone the examination for a week and

_____

_____

4. Kwesi hopes not only to graduate a semester early but _____

_____

5. The principal can neither enforce the dress code to the board of education's satis-

faction nor _____

_____

6. To improve economic conditions, the governor must not only attract new industry

to our state but also _____

_____

7. Jonathan is either helping those less fortunate than he or _____

_____

8. Juanita is not only a good listener but _____

_____

Review Practice 19.15

On a separate sheet, rewrite the following paragraph to eliminate problems with parallelism.

[1]Friendships at work have their own set of guidelines. [2]You should understand the difference between work friends and friends who are personal. [3]Conversations with work friends focus mostly on office personalities, politics, and they center on work-related problems. [4]You should neither confide personal information nor problems to work friends. [5]To avoid complications, try to socialize mostly with coworkers who are at your level in the hierarchy. [6]Unequal status can lead to envy, suspicion, or sometimes cause favoritism. [7]Proceed carefully with office friendships with members of the opposite sex. [8]Avoid any hint of romance, either during work hours or there should be no hint after work hours. [9]If you follow these guidelines, you can enjoy friendships at work without unpleasant complications.

Tips

WRITING SENTENCES WITH VARIETY AND PARALLELISM

- Read your draft aloud or listen as someone reads it *to* you. If you hear something that sounds clumsy or "off," see if you need to add sentence variety or correct a parallelism problem.
- Remember that adding coordination and subordination, which you learned about in Chapter 16, can help you achieve sentence variety.
- If you compose at the computer, use your search function to locate the conjunctions that work in pairs. Then you can check that you have the same structures after both the first and second conjunction.
- **If English is not your first language,** use the prepositions *in, on,* and *at* correctly to show time and place.

  a. Use *in* for seasons, months, and years without a specific date.

  > *In* 1999, Stavros will graduate with two degrees.
  > I usually take my vacation *in* the winter.

  b. Use *on* for a specific day or date.

  > *On* the first of March, Joseph begins his new job.
  > This office will close *on* Friday.

  c. Use *in* for a period of the day.

  > My exercise class meets *in* the early evening.

  d. Use *at* for a specific location and *in* for a location surrounded by something else.

  > The dentist you should see is located *at* 3150 Fifth Avenue.
  > Gregory lived *in* Salzburg for a semester.

Post Test

On a separate sheet, revise the paragraph to improve parallelism and sentence variety.

[1]Checkers is at least 5,000 years old. [2]It was played in early Egypt, in ancient Greece, and it was played in early Rome. [3]The earliest form of the game on

(continued on next page)

record was played with twelve pieces on each side. [4]The first known book about checkers was published in 1547 in Spain. [5]The game was likely brought to Spain by the Moors. [6]The Moors probably got the game in Arabia. [7]Checkers is called "draughts" in England. [8]Checkers is both fun and it is easy to play. [9]It is popular all over the world. [10]Many educators believe the game helps people develop foresight, think critically, and that it improves concentration.

LEARNING FROM TEXTBOOKS

The following is an excerpt from a college business textbook chapter about business ethics and corporate social reponsibility. Read the excerpt and answer the questions that follow.

[1]In nearly every company, the manner in which employees and executives handle information is one key to avoiding harm to others. [2]Because these people often have access to information that outsiders don't have, they have a responsibility not to take advantage of the situation. [3]Specifically, buying or selling a company's stock based on information that outside investors lack is known as **insider trading,** which is not only unethical but also illegal. [4]Insider trading is a good example of the ethical trouble that businesspeople can get into when they face a **conflict of interest,** a situation in which a choice that promises personal gain compromises a more fundamental responsibility. [5]If you're in charge of buying a new computer system for your company and you select the vendor who gave you Super Bowl tickets instead of the vendor who offered a better deal for your company, you would be guilty of a conflict of interest.

1. To analyze the variety of sentence openers, answer the following:

   a. Which sentence begins with the subject? _____

   b. Which sentence begins with a prepositional phrase? _____

   c. Which sentences begin with a dependent clause? _____

   d. Which sentence begins with an adverb? _____

2. How does the sentence variety help you learn the material?

   _____

   _____

3. How is parallelism achieved in sentence 3?

   _____

   _____

4. How does parallelism help you learn the material?

_____

_____

Write about It

Conflicts of interest can occur in settings other than business. Mention a conflict of interest a person can experience in the classroom or with friends. Use process analysis to explain how the conflict should be resolved and why it should be resolved that way. Alternatively, classify different kinds or levels of conflicts of interest.

SUCCEEDING IN COLLEGE

Keep a Learning Log

In Chapter 1, you learned about keeping a journal. Journaling in a learning log can also help you remember important content in your courses. A learning log is *not* the notebook where you record your class notes. It is a separate notebook in which you record your *reactions* to course content, class lectures, discussions, and reading. In a learning log, you relate course content in one class to course content in another class, to your own experience, and to your own thinking. For example, if you read something by Benjamin Franklin in your American literature class, you may be reminded about something you learned about him in a history class, and you can write that down in your learning log. Or if you learn about attention deficit disorder in your education class and you know someone with this disorder, you can compare your observations of that person with what you learned in class. If you disagree with something said in class, you can also write about that disagreement.

Keeping a learning log can "set" your learning so you better remember course content. It can also help you become a better learner by helping you discover which learning strategies work best for you. Keep track in your log of how you study and compare test results to your study strategy to determine if you should make changes. For example, note in your log that you studied for your psychology test in a study group. If you did not do well on the test, you may not want to use a study group to prepare for the next test. If you are having trouble taking notes in physics class, write about the problem, perhaps noting that the instructor speaks too softly or too fast. Then you can devise a solution: sitting in front of the class and using a tape recorder, for example.

Write about It

Keep a learning log for three days. Then write about whether or not the log helps you learn content or become more informed about your study strategies. Be specific about why you find the log helpful or why you do not.

For more practice with writing sentences with variety and parallelism, go to www. mywritinglab.com.

CHAPTER 20

Choosing Words Carefully

I f you have problems with word choice, this chapter will help you learn what you need to know to express yourself more effectively. If you do not have problems with word choice, this chapter will reinforce what you already know and perhaps teach you a few new points. The following pretest will help you assess how much you currently know about choosing words carefully.

Pretest

Place a check mark next to the better sentence. Do not guess. If you are unsure, do not write anything. Check your answers in Appendix II.

1. a. _____ The movie was interesting and absorbing.

   b. _____ The movie was absorbing.

2. a. _____ After final exams are over, I am going to chill out for a week.

   b. _____ After final exams are over, I am going to relax for a week.

3. a. _____ After a massage, Jan no longer felt stiff.

   b. _____ After a massage, Jan no longer felt stiff as a board.

4. a. _____ Turn left at the house that is beige in color and travel two blocks north to find the house where my sister lives alone by herself.

   b. _____ Turn left at the beige house and travel two blocks north to find the house where my sister lives by herself.

5. a. _____ Because of the fog, I can't see anything more than five feet in front of me.

   b. _____ Because of the fog, I can't see nothing more than five feet in front of me.

WORDINESS

Unnecessary words—**wordiness**—weaken your style. When you revise, eliminate wordiness by pruning away words that add no meaning and words that are repetitious.

Words that add no meaning are **deadwood,** and you should revise to eliminate deadwood.

Sentences with Deadwood	**Revisions**
Two different kinds of cake were offered.	Two different cakes were offered. (*Kinds of* adds no meaning.)
	or
	Two kinds of cake were offered.
Diane's new Corvette is red in color.	Diane's new Corvette is red. (Can *red* be anything but a color?)
We rushed quickly to see what was wrong.	We rushed to see what was wrong. (*Rushing* has to be done quickly.)

Another form of wordiness is purposeless **repetition.** Consider this sentence:

> To relax before my exam, I watched and viewed a movie.

Viewed repeats the idea included in *watched,* so *viewed* is purposeless repetition. Here is the sentence revised to eliminate the repetition:

> To relax before my exam, I watched a movie.

Here are more examples to study:

Sentences with Repetition	**Revisions**
Carol finally realized and understood that she had to help herself.	Carol finally realized that she had to help herself.
	or
	Carol finally understood that she had to help herself. (*Realized* and *understood* mean the same.)
Some people think and believe that drug abuse is our nation's most serious problem.	Some people think that drug abuse is our nation's most serious problem.
	or
	Some people believe that drug abuse is our nation's most serious problem. (*Think* and *believe* mean the same.)

Practice 20.1

Revise the following sentences to eliminate wordiness.

Example

In the year of 1912, Theodore Roosevelt was campaigning in the city of Milwaukee.

In 1912, Theodore Roosevelt was campaigning in Milwaukee.

1. A would-be assassin who wanted to kill Roosevelt shot him on the right side part of his chest.

2. Much of the force of the bullet was absorbed by the President's eyeglass case and by the fifty-page speech he was carrying double-folded in two in his breast pocket.

3. The end result was that the bullet lodged just short of his lung, and, driping blood, the President pulled and tugged himself up to the podium.

4. In our modern world today, Secret Service agents would have whisked and rushed the President away, but Roosevelt was the type of person who carried on no matter what.

5. He announced and said he planned to deliver the speech as long as he still had life in his body.

6. He spoke for ninety minutes of time, but was unable to refer to or check his text.

7. There was a gaping, wide hole in the pages where the bullet had torn through them.

_____

_____

8. Roosevelt was luckily fortunate that he did not succumb to his wound.

_____

_____

Practice 20.2

Cross out deadwood and unnecessary repetition to eliminate wordiness.

¹The first metal coins were minted in about approximately 800 B.C. ²Before that time in history, all trade had been done by barter. ³For example, a toolmaker craftsman might barter and trade tools in exchange for meat or clothing to wear. ⁴As civilization developed, trade became more intricately complex, and barter became too clumsily awkward. ⁵A trader needed easily carried tokens that were small in size, but the tokens had to be valuable. ⁶So the first coins were made of metal, in particular gold and silver metal. ⁷This simple invention of money made trade much simpler.

DOUBLE NEGATIVES

These words are negatives because they communicate the idea of *no*:

Negatives

no	none	hardly
not	nowhere	scarcely
no one	nobody	
never	nothing	

any contraction form with *not* (*can't, don't, won't,* etc.)

In English, only one negative is used to express a single negative idea.

incorrect (two negatives):	I *can't* see *no* reason to go.
correct (one negative):	I can see *no* reason to go.
correct (one negative):	I *can't* see any reason to go.
incorrect (two negatives):	Dee would *never* tell *no* one.
correct (one negative):	Dee would *never* tell anyone.
correct (one negative):	Dee would tell *no one*.
incorrect (two negatives):	The boys could *not hardly* eat.
correct (one negative):	The boys could *hardly* eat.
correct (one negative):	The boys could *not* eat.

The preceding examples show that eliminating one negative may mean changing *no one* to *anyone*, *nowhere* to *anywhere*, *never* to *ever*, and *no* or *none* to *any*.

The following sentences contain double negatives. First underline each negative. Then revise each sentence by eliminating one negative.

Example

The board member came under attack because he is <u>not never</u> at the meetings.

The board member came under attack because he is never at the meetings.

1. Paul didn't do nothing to start the fight.

_____

_____

2. I gave the cashier $20.00, but I didn't get no change.

_____

_____

3. Mom couldn't find nowhere to hide the Christmas presents.

_____

_____

4. Some people won't ask nobody for nothing.

_____

_____

5. The street department hardly never swept the streets this fall.

_____

_____

SLANG

Slang expressions are very informal usages unsuitable for most formal writing. Slang can originate with one group of people, say musicians or artists, and spread to the larger population. Slang often originates with young people and makes for colorful, vital speech. However, until a slang expression works its way into the language of the general population (if it ever does), avoid it in your college writing, unless you need it to create a special effect.

Here are examples of slang expressions. Because slang changes quickly, many of them may no longer be current by the time you read them.

dooced (getting fired for something written in a weblog)	loose rap (lies told to impress member of the opposite sex)
drop the needle (play a vinyl record)	party foul (something unacceptable done at a social gathering)
the 411 (the information)	trick out (modify a car with parts and features after it is purchased)
pass the bone (share knowledge)	
Steez (style)	Hulk out (to become angry or violent)

Practice 20.4

List as many slang expressions as you can think of. Next, pick two of the slang expressions and use each of them in a separate sentence. Then rewrite the sentences, eliminating the slang and substituting language more appropriate to formal writing.

CLICHÉS

Clichés are overused expressions. At one time they were fresh and interesting, but years of overuse have made them tired and dull. Here is a partial list of clichés. Studying it will help you become sensitive to the kinds of expressions to avoid.

over the hill	sadder but wiser	crack of dawn
free as a bird	last but not least	busy as a beaver
cold as ice	fresh as a daisy	light as a feather
hour of need	shadow of a doubt	slowly but surely
white as snow	call it quits	down in the dumps

Practice 20.5

Write three clichés not on the list.

1. _____

2. _____

3. _____

Practice 20.6

Rewrite the sentences, substituting fresh phrasings for the underlined clichés.

Example

I dread going shopping with Dotty because she is <u>like a bull in a china shop.</u>

I dread going shopping with Dotty because she is so clumsy that she is always

bumping into displays and breaking things.

1. If I were you, I would not <u>bet the rent</u> that Julian will keep his promise.

   _____

   _____

2. <u>In a nutshell,</u> the comedian is not very funny because his jokes are <u>as old as the hills.</u>

   _____

   _____

3. Trying to find my contact lens in the dark was like <u>looking for a needle in a haystack.</u>

   _____

   _____

4. It is a <u>crying shame</u> that more is not being done to help the homeless.

   _____

   _____

5. Nina and Jacob <u>worked their fingers to the bone</u> completing their wedding plans.

   _____

   _____

   ■

VOCABULARY BUILDING

The more words you know, the more precisely and effectively you can express yourself. Vocabulary lists for study are available in any vocabulary-building book in your campus bookstore or library. You can also develop and learn your own list with these procedures.

1. Using a notebook, index cards, or computer file, write down unfamiliar words you encounter in your textbooks and lectures. Also write down new words you discover in your reading of magazines and newspapers and that you hear on television or the radio. Write, too, the sentence you read or heard each word in.

2. In a paper or online dictionary, check the pronunciation of the word if you are uncertain of it and the meaning of the word. Copy these down. If there is more than one

meaning, copy the one that fits the use of the word in the sentence you read or heard.

3. Study your notebook, cards, or computer file each day. Learn the new words and review the old ones.

4. When possible, learn meanings through association. For example, to learn that *ostracize* means "to banish or expel," you may associate it with an ostrich, which banishes itself by poking its head in the sand. Also, learn clusters of words. For example, once you have learned what *luminous* means, learn *luminance, illuminate, luminary,* and *luminosity.* To discover word clusters, look for related words around each word you check in the dictionary.

5. Use the words you learn as you speak, write, and think, so they become a natural part of your vocabulary.

6. Many words share common **prefixes** (beginnings) and **suffixes** (endings). Study the meanings of prefixes and suffixes as an aid to learning meanings. To do this, consult a vocabulary book in the library or study skills center.

Practice 20.7

1. For a day, record in a small notebook, on index cards, or in a computer file any words you see or hear that you do not know, following the directions given in the previous discussion.

2. Buy a copy of *Time* or *Newsweek* and read three articles, or read the articles online. List every word that is not familiar to you. Add some of these words to your notebook, index cards, or computer file. Read at least one article in the magazine each day and add unfamiliar words to your notebook, cards, or file.

Review Practice 20.8

On a separate sheet, revise the paragraph to improve word choice by eliminating problems with wordiness, double negatives, slang, and clichés.

[1]A man who was a chocolate maker and who went by the name of Clarence Crane tried to make a mint that would boost and increase his candy sales in summer when heat would melt his chocolate. [2]To make a long story short, Crane was in a drugstore to get a bottle of flavoring. [3]He didn't know nothing about how pills were made at the time. [4]However, he noticed the druggist using a pill-making machine. [5]It was manually operated by hand and made pills that were flat and round in shape. [6]A lightbulb went off in Crane's head. [7]He got an idea that became the bomb when he decided to use the pill-making machine to punch out the middle of his mints. [8]And that is how the lifesaver candy was created.

FAQ

Q: Are there any other ways I can increase my vocabulary?

A: Read something you enjoy, such as magazines, detective fiction, or online newspapers, for at least fifteen minutes every day, and your vocabulary will improve over time.

Tips

CHOOSING WORDS CAREFULLY
- Focus on word choice during revising rather than during drafting.
- Pare down phrases to words. For example, "for this reason" can become "because" and "at this time" can become "now."

(continued on next page)

Tips for Choosing Words Carefully (continued)

- To increase your vocabulary, work crossword puzzles.
- If you use a computer, visit http://www.dictionary.com to have a different word and definition e-mailed to you each day. Or you might enjoy learning new words with the visual dictionary at http://visual.merriam-webster.com, where you can get pictures of words.
- **If English is not your first language,** do not hesitate to ask native speakers of English to define any words they use that you are not sure of.
- **If English is not your first language,** this site can help with vocabulary, slang, and clichés: http://www.manythings.org/.

Post Test

Underline problems with wordiness, double negatives, slang, and clichés in the following passage. Then rewrite on a separate page to eliminate the problems.

[1]In a class, I learned about the history of writing. [2]Nobody scarcely knows when writing originally began, although we do have a sense of how it developed. [3]Humans began making pictures to record hunting, wars, and tribal life. [4]Pictures and images were also used for messages. [5]A picture of the sun meant a day; two marks next to the picture meant two days. [6]Such signs are called *pictographs*. [7]Eventually pictographs were simplified. [8]For example, Egyptians used a wavy line to mean "a body of water," and the Chinese used an ear between two doors to mean "listen." [9]These markings are called *ideographs*.

[10]Eventually, the Egyptians, who were smart as a whip, developed a system of signs, called *hieroglyphics,* that included a phonetic system that was big-time cool. [11]With this writing, signs represented sounds rather than objects or ideas. [12]As civilization advanced and progressed, humans needed more signs, so they came up with the bright idea of a system of spelling words according to sound. [13]For example, the English word "belief" would be spelled with a picture of a bee and a leaf. [14]These signs are called *phonograms*.

[15]The next stage in the development of writing was the invention of the alphabet. [16]Both the Egyptians and the Babylonians eventually used alphabets of single letters. [17]From their writing came the Greek and Latin alphabets, which are used by most modern people of today who hang their hats outside Asia.

LEARNING FROM TEXTBOOKS

The following excerpt was taken from a college biology textbook, from a chapter titled "Conservation Biology." Read the paragraph and answer the questions that follow.

[1]Several researchers estimate that at the current rate of destruction, over half of all currently living plant and animal species will be gone by the end of this century.

²Why should we care about the loss of biodiversity? ³Perhaps the purest reason is what Harvard biologist E. O. Wilson calls *biophilia,* our sense of connection to nature and other forms of life. ⁴Many people also share a moral belief that other species have an inherent right to life. ⁵But in addition to ethical and aesthetic reasons for preserving biodiversity, there are practical ones as well. ⁶We depend on other species for food, clothing, shelter, oxygen, soil fertility—the list goes on and on. ⁷In the United States, 25% of all prescriptions dispensed from pharmacies contain substances derived from plants. ⁸For instance, drugs called vincristine and vinblastine, which come from the rosy periwinkle, are effective against Hodgkin's disease and certain other forms of cancer. ⁹Rosy periwinkle is a flowering plant native to Madagascar, of an island in the Indian Ocean east of Africa. ¹⁰Separated from the mainland for more than 150 million years, Madagascar is home to some 8,000 species of flowering plants, 80% of which occur nowhere else in the world. ¹¹With an estimated 200,000 species of plants and animals, Madagascar is among the top five most biologically diverse countries in the world. ¹²Unfortunately, most of Madagascar's species are in serious trouble. ¹³In the 2,000 years that humans have lived on the island, Madagascar has lost 80% of its forests and about 50% of its native species.

1. The passage does not include a definition of *biodiversity,* used in sentence 2. However, you can probably figure out the meaning from clues in the passage and in the word itself. What do you think *biodiversity* means? Now check a dictionary to see how close you came.

_____

_____

2. What words appear in the passage that you currently cannot define? Look up the meaning of those words. Which ones do you think you can incorporate into your vocabulary on a regular basis?

_____

_____

3. Try to come up with an association to help you remember one of the words from your answer to number 2 and briefly explain your association.

_____

_____

4. As a student reading a biology textbook, explain how you would react if sentence 7 were written this way: In our country, the United States of America, 25%—a full quarter—of all prescription medications dispensed and filled from pharmacies have in them some form of substance that is extracted from the biological entities of plants.

_____

_____

Write about It

Using cause-and-effect analysis, explain why "in the 2,000 years that humans have lived on the island, Madagascar has lost 80% of its forests and about 50% of its native species."

SUCCEEDING IN COLLEGE

Learn Specialized Vocabulary

Each subject you take will have its own specialized vocabulary, which you must learn, use, and spell correctly. In particular, you will notice that the introductory courses required of first- and second-year students include a great deal of terminology that will be new to you. As you encounter this vocabulary in your classes, make a point of mastering it.

- Listen for your instructor to shift tone of voice, slow down, or repeat a term to emphasize important vocabulary.

- Write down the terms your instructor mentions or writes on the board, along with the meanings of those terms. Be sure to get the spelling right.

- If your instructor does not define a term or if you have questions about the vocabulary, ask for help in class.

- Learn the words in your textbooks that are italicized, boldfaced, or printed in a second color.

- If your textbook has a glossary in the back, use it as a source of definitions.

- Learn specialized vocabulary with the procedures for vocabulary building explained on pages 286–287.

Write about It

Read the first chapter of one of your textbooks and write out the answers to these questions:

1. How many new, specialized vocabulary terms are there?

2. Are these terms italicized, boldfaced, or written in a different color?

3. Does the book have a glossary?

Write the definitions of the new, specialized vocabulary terms, and learn their meanings, spellings, and pronunciations.

For more practice with choosing words, go to www.mywritinglab.com.

COMPREHENSIVE POST TEST

■ Identifying Subjects and Verbs

1. Underline the subject once and the verb twice for each sentence.
   a. The pile of dirty clothes in the laundry room is beginning to smell.
   b. All of Mohammed's conversations focus on his interest in classical music.
   c. By Friday, our American history class will have studied all the major battles of the Civil War.
   d. Can you help me with dinner?
   e. The mayor and her advisors plan to implement a new procedure for hiring city employees.

■ Using Coordination and Subordination

2. Write a *C* if the sentence has coordination; write an *S* if it has subordination; write an *N* if it has neither coordination nor subordination.
   a. __S__ Because heavy thunderstorms kept many people away from the polls, voter turnout was very light on election day.
   b. __C__ Heavy thunderstorms kept many people away from the polls, so voter turnout was very light on election day.
   c. __S__ Because of heavy thunderstorms, voter turnout was light on election day.
   d. __C__ The eyes of a woodcock are on the top of its head; therefore, it can see backward and upward.
   e. __S__ Since the eyes of the woodcock are on the top of its head, it can see backward and upward.
   f. __N__ With eyes on the top of its head, the woodcock can see backward and upward.
   g. __C__ Jeff Bezos originally wanted to name his Web venture "Cadabra," but he decided on Amazon.com instead.
   h. __S__ Although he originally wanted to name his Web venture "Cadabra," Jeff Bezos decided on Amazon.com instead.
   i. __C__ Jeff Bezos originally wanted to name his Web venture "Cadabra," but decided on Amazon.com instead.

■ Avoiding Sentence Fragments

3. If all the word groups are sentences, write *yes* on the blank. If some are fragments, write the number of fragments on the blank.
   a. __Y__ The P.T.A. was founded in the United States in 1897. Originally called the National Congress of Mothers, It was expanded to include fathers, teachers, and other citizens. Today the P.T.A. being an important support group for public schools.
   b. __N__ The huddle formation used by football teams originated at Gallaudet University. Which is a liberal arts college for deaf people in Washington, D.C. The huddle was used to prevent other schools from reading players' sign language.

c. ___✓___ Another interesting fact is that Alexander Graham Bell was originally an instructor for deaf children. <u>Because he wanted to help his deaf wife</u> and mother to hear. He invented the telephone. You may also be surprised to learn that in the United States, deaf people have safer driving records than hearing people.

d. ___✓___ The first McDonald's opened in Des Plaines, Illinois, in 1955. This prototype restaurant offering hamburgers for 19 cents, fries, soft drinks, and coffee for a dime, and shakes for 20 cents. The Big Mac didn't arrive until 1968, and it cost 49 cents. The quarter-pounder arriving on the scene in 1971. It cost 53 cents.

■ Avoiding Run-On Sentences and Comma Splices

4. If all the sentences are correct, write *yes* on the blank. If they include run-ons or comma splices, write the number of mistakes on the blank.

a. ___RO___ Guion S. Bluford, Jr., was the first African American to fly in space during the Space Shuttle Challenger mission STS-8 of August 30–September 5, 1983. Bluford, who holds a Ph.D. in aerospace engineering, flew a second time aboard the shuttle from October 30 to November 6. The first black man to fly in space was Cuban cosmonaut Arnaldo Tamayo-Mendez, he flew aboard Soyuz 38 and spent eight days on the Soviet space station.

b. ___✓___ People get goose bumps when they are cold for a reason. These bumps are the result of the contraction of muscle fibers in the skin; the muscular activity produces more heat, which raises the body temperature. Thus, goose bumps are nature's way of helping us warm up.

■ Writing Sentences with Variety and Parallelism

5. Cross out and add words so the passage has sentence variety.
   Diamonds were considered lucky charms at one time. People wore diamonds for good fortune, thinking diamonds protected them from harm. We do not have this superstition today, but diamonds remain popular.

6. Place a check next to the sentences that are correct because they have parallel structure.

a. _____ The agenda for the meeting includes discussion on membership, a vote on the budget, and the nominating committee will present the new slate of officers.

b. ___✓___ The agenda for the meeting includes discussion on membership, a vote on the budget, and the nominating committee's presentation of the new slate of officers.

c. _____ The loan officer wants not only to see a copy of my last pay stub, but he wants to see records of my credit card bills.

d. ___✓___ The loan officer wants to see not only a copy of my last pay stub, but also records of my credit card bills.

e. ___✓___ On Fridays, the special is either poached salmon or fried halibut.

f. _____ On Fridays, the special either is poached salmon or fried halibut.

■ Choosing Words Carefully

7. Fill in the blank with the correct word or phrase from the pair given in parentheses.
   a. (hardly/not hardly) After running her first race, Mia could
      _____ wait to run another one.
   b. (anybody/nobody) I won't bring _anybody_ with me to the concert.

8. Place a check mark next to the better sentence: a or b; c or d; e or f.
   a. _____ After studying with the techniques she learned at the study skills center, Carlotta was chilling before her final exams.
   b. _✓_ After studying with the techniques she learned at the study skills center, Carlotta felt confident before her final exams.
   c. _✓_ On the first day of summer vacation, schoolchildren feel joyously liberated.
   d. _____ On the first day of summer vacation, school children feel free as little birds.
   e. _____ In my opinion, it seems to me that the housing market has cooled because interest rates have climbed.
   f. _✓_ In my opinion, the housing market has cooled because interest rates have climbed.

CHAPTER 21
Using Verbs Correctly

Verbs convey a great deal of meaning, and they can add considerable energy to writing. At the same time, verbs can be tricky because to use them correctly, you need to understand several grammar points, which this chapter will help you learn. If you currently know a great deal about using verbs, this chapter will reinforce your understanding and perhaps teach you a few new points. To assess your current level of understanding, take the following pretest.

Pretest

A. If the underlined verb is correct, write *C* on the blank. If it is incorrect, write *I* on the blank. If you are unsure, do not guess; leave the space blank. Check your answers in Appendix II.

1. _shine_ The sun <u>shone</u> so brightly I couldn't see to drive.

2. _is_ Maria <u>be</u> the one to ask about that.

3. _C_ We <u>had driven</u> two hundred miles when the fuel pump broke.

4. _does_ Larry explained, "A person <u>do</u> what he has to do."

5. _hope_ I <u>hopes</u> I can get a part-time job this summer.

6. _done_ We <u>have did</u> everything you asked.

7. _began_ The teachers <u>began</u> their strike the day after Christmas. _C_

8. _have_ They <u>has told</u> me they do not plan to go with us.

9. _C_ My sister Hannah <u>decided</u> to join the navy.

10. _brough_ Olga <u>brang</u> her botany notes for me to copy.

B. Fill in the blank with the correct present tense form in parentheses.

1. (means/mean) My collection of shells from Ocean City _means_
   a great deal to me.

(continued on next page)

2. (visits/visit) Either Mother or Aunt Harriet ___visits___ Uncle Ned on his birthday.

3. (plans/plan) Both Hans and his best friend ___plan___ to attend Ohio State University.

4. (likes/like) Everyone ___likes___ a good mystery.

5. (practices/practice) The football team ___practices___ twice a day.

6. (decides/decide) The personnel committee ___decides___ whom to hire for the teaching positions.

7. (is/are) Here ___are___ the papers you lost.

8. (wants/want) Each of the children ___want___ to take karate lessons.

9. (works/work) Stavros is one of those people who ___work___ harder than necessary.

10. (sleeps/sleep) The cat, along with her kittens, ___sleep___ in the garage.

C. If the verb tenses change, write *TS* (for tense shift) on the blank. If the tenses are consistent, write *C* on the blank.

1. __C__ The doctor explained that the child's tonsils were infected and had to be removed when the infection was gone.

2. __C__ All of us are prepared for an emergency. We have first-aid kits, flashlights, waterproof clothing, and extra food.

3. __TS__ When the nature guide turned over the leaf, the scouts see the monarch butterfly egg.

4. __TS__ The killer whale feeds on seals, fish, and other whales. It did not attack human beings.

5. __C__ The blue whale can grow to be 100 feet long, although it eats only microscopic animals.

VERB FORMS

As explained in Chapter 15, verbs often change their form to show different times, also called **tenses.** The next sections will tell you more about those verb forms and how to use them.

Regular Verbs

Most English verbs are **regular,** which means they form the past tense by adding *-d* or *-ed*. Here are examples of regular verbs:

Present Tense	Past Tense
love	love<u>d</u>
save	save<u>d</u>
walk	walk<u>ed</u>
yell	yell<u>ed</u>

Regular verbs ending in *y* often change the *y* to *i* before adding *-ed,* like this:

Present Tense	**Past Tense**
study	stud<u>ied</u>
hurry	hurr<u>ied</u>
worry	worr<u>ied</u>

Present Tense Forms for Regular Verbs   When you write or speak of events that occur now, in the present time, you use the **present tense.** In the present tense, your regular verbs should have the forms shown in the following chart. Notice that whether the regular verb adds an *-s* or *-es* depends on the subject of the sentence.

REGULAR VERB FORMS: PRESENT TENSE

Singular		**Plural**
I play.		We play.
You play.		You play.
He plays.		They play.
She plays.	Notice the *-s* or *-es* ending here.	The children play.
It plays.		
The child plays.		

CAUTION: A common error is forgetting the *-s* or *-es* ending for a regular, present tense verb used with *he, she, it,* or any singular noun subject.

no:	Mary *like* chocolate pudding.
yes:	Mary *likes* chocolate pudding.

Practice 21.1

On a separate sheet of paper, rewrite the paragraph, changing the past tense verbs to present tense forms. Be careful to use the *s* or *es* ending when needed. The first sentence is done as an example.

[1]African grasslands <s>supported</s> *support* large numbers of insect-eating and seed-eating birds. [2]The ostrich, one of these birds, survived on fruit, seeds, and small animals. [3]The Kori, the world's heaviest bird, also lived on the grasslands. [4]This bird weighed 110 pounds. [5]Oxpeckers, another grassland bird, perched on the backs of grazing animals and chewed ticks and other parasites they discovered there. [6]Still other grassland birds included bulbuls, shrikes, storks, cranes, and ground hornbills. [7]One of the most interesting birds, the weaverbird, designed elaborate

hanging nests in trees. [8]Unfortunately, large flocks of these birds caused exten-sive damage to African trees. [9]Birds of prey on the grasslands included the vul-ture and the lanner falcon. [10]Indeed, birdwatchers often traveled to this part of the world to observe the rare and wonderful birds.

Practice 21.2

Complete each of the sentences by using a present tense form of a regular verb from the list and any other words you want. Do not use the same verb twice, and be sure to use *-s* or *-es* endings where needed.

play	laugh	organize
smile	move	follow
study	practice	learn
worry	joke	collect

Example

The excited children *play happily in the school yard during recess.*

_____

1. My best friend _____

_____

2. Professor Bauer _____

_____

3. We _____

_____

4. The planning committee _____

_____

5. You _____

_____

6. I _____

_____

7. He _____

_____

8. My younger sister _____

_____

Practice 21.3

Fill in the blanks with the correct present tense form of the verb in parentheses. The first blank is filled in as an example.

Because of my cold, my nose no longer (to function) <u>1 functions</u> as part of my respiratory system. I (to inhale) <u>2_____</u> deeply, but no air (to penetrate) <u>3_____</u> the blocked passages. I (to race) <u>4_____</u> to the bathroom and (to grab) <u>5_____</u> a tissue before I (to sneeze) <u>6_____</u> myself to the floor. Pulling myself up, I (to head) <u>7_____</u> for the kitchen. My throat (to rust) <u>8_____</u>out, and my mouth (to enter) <u>9_____</u> the drought season. Switching on the light, I (to tug) <u>10_____</u> at the refrigerator door, which (to seem) <u>11_____</u> like wrenching a two-ton vault. Struggling for strength, I (to open) <u>12_____</u> the door, (to grab) <u>13_____</u>the orange juice, and (to pour) <u>14_____</u> the liquid. The juice (to burn) <u>15_____</u> my aching throat. I (to reach) <u>16_____</u> for a cold tablet and (to pop) <u>17_____</u> it in. To clear my nose, I (to reach) <u>18_____</u> for the nasal spray. I (to squirt) <u>19_____</u> twice in each nostril and (to tilt) <u>20_____</u> my head back. I (to walk) <u>21_____</u> back to bed, but I (to toss) <u>22_____</u> and (to turn) <u>23_____</u> for hours until exhausted. I (to drift) <u>24_____</u> off to sleep, hoping not to awaken until the cold (to burn) <u>25_____</u> itself out.

■

Past Tense Forms for Regular Verbs   When you write or speak of events that occurred in the past, you use the **past tense.** In the past tense, your regular verbs should have the forms shown in this chart. Notice that unlike the present tense forms, the past tense forms never change—they always end in *-d* or *-ed,* regardless of the subject.

FAQ
Q: What is the problem with "incorrect" verb forms? I hear people use them all the time.

A: Many varieties of English exist. The "incorrect" forms can be acceptable for use with family and friends. They are inappropriate, however, in most school and work situations.

REGULAR VERB FORMS: PAST TENSE

Singular	**Plural**
I played.	We played.
You played.	You played.
He played.	They played.
She played.	The children played.
It played.	
The child played.	

CAUTION: A common error is forgetting the *-d* or *-ed* ending for a regular, past tense verb.

no: Yesterday I *walk* to work.

yes: Yesterday I *walked* to work.

Practice 21.4

On a separate sheet, write a sentence using the regular verb in parentheses in its past tense form. Circle the past tense ending, and use a different subject for each sentence.

Example

(start) The referee start(ed) the sudden death overtime play.

1. (look)
2. (want)
3. (talk)
4. (expect)
5. (discover)

Practice 21.5

On a separate sheet, rewrite Practice 21.3. This time fill in the blanks with past tense forms of the verbs given.

Past Participle Forms for Regular Verbs   The **past participle** is the verb form that is used with the helping verbs *has, have,* and *had*. As shown in the following chart, the past participle of regular verbs is formed in the same way the past tense of regular verbs is formed: by adding *-d* or *-ed*. Notice, however, that the subject of the sentence determines whether you use *has* or *have*.

REGULAR VERB FORMS: PAST PARTICIPLE

Singular	**Plural**
I have played.	We have played.
I had played.	We had played.
You have played.	You have played.
You had played.	You had played.
He has played.	They have played.
He had played.	They had played.
She has played.	The children have played.
She had played.	The children had played.
It has played.	
It had played.	
The child has played.	
The child had played.	

NOTE: As you can tell from the preceding examples, the past participle form does not change even though the form of the helping verb changes.

CAUTION: A common error is forgetting the *-d* or *-ed* ending for the past participle form of a regular verb.

no: The union *has decide* to accept the wage offer.

yes: The union *has decided* to accept the wage offer.

Practice 21.6

Find and correct the errors with the past participle and accompanying helping verbs. The first one is done as an example.

[1]Donna and Rico have ~~plan~~ ^{planned} their wedding for August 16, but suddenly Rico have decided that he wants to elope. [2]At one time, he had agreed that a big wedding would be desirable, but lately he have wonder if a big, splashy affair is too much trouble and expense. [3]Donna, surprisingly, has agree to think about eloping, even though she have wanted a big wedding all her life. [4]Fortunately, the caterer has agreed to return the couple's deposit if they cancel the reception.

Practice 21.7

On a separate sheet, write a sentence using the helping verb and past participle form of the regular verb in parentheses.

Example

    (has + walk) <u>For the past year, Jill has walked three miles a day.</u>

1. (had + jump)

2. (has + change)

3. (had + open)

4. (has + work)

5. (had + apply)

Irregular Verbs

An **irregular verb** does not add *-d* or *-ed* to form the past and past participle forms. Instead, irregular verbs form the past and past participle in a variety of ways. A list of some irregular verbs with their past and past participle forms follows. Study the list and place a star next to the forms you do not already know. Then learn these forms.

Present	Past	Past Participle
be (am/is/are)	was/were	been
become(s)	became	become
begin(s)	began	begun
bend(s)	bent	bent
bite(s)	bit	bitten
blow(s)	blew	blown
break(s)	broke	broken
bring(s)	brought	brought
buy(s)	bought	bought
catch(es)	caught	caught
choose(s)	chose	chosen
come(s)	came	come
cost(s)	cost	cost
do (does)	did	done
draw(s)	drew	drawn
drink(s)	drank	drunk
drive(s)	drove	driven
eat(s)	ate	eaten
fall(s)	fell	fallen
feed(s)	fed	fed
feel(s)	felt	felt

Present	Past	Past Participle
fight(s)	fought	fought
find(s)	found	found
fly (flies)	flew	flown
forget(s)	forgot	forgotten
forgive(s)	forgave	forgiven
freeze(s)	froze	frozen
get(s)	got	got *or* gotten
give(s)	gave	given
go (goes)	went	gone
grow(s)	grew	grown
hang(s)—a picture	hung	hung
hang(s)—a person	hanged	hanged
has (have)	had	had
hear(s)	heard	heard
hide(s)	hid	hidden
hold(s)	held	held
hurt(s)	hurt	hurt
keep(s)	kept	kept
know(s)	knew	known
lay(s)—to place	laid	laid
lead(s)	led	led
leave(s)	left	left
lend(s)	lent	lent
lie(s)—to rest	lay	lain
light(s)	lit	lit
lose(s)	lost	lost
make(s)	made	made
meet(s)	met	met
pay(s)	paid	paid
read(s)	read	read
ride(s)	rode	ridden
ring(s)	rang	rung
rise(s)	rose	risen
run(s)	ran	run
say(s)	said	said
see(s)	saw	seen
sell(s)	sold	sold
send(s)	sent	sent
set(s)	set	set
shake(s)	shook	shaken

Present	Past	Past Participle
shine(s)—to give light	shone	shone
shine(s)—to polish	shined	shined
shrink(s)	shrank	shrunk
sing(s)	sang	sung
sit(s)	sat	sat
sleep(s)	slept	slept
speak(s)	spoke	spoken
spend(s)	spent	spent
stand(s)	stood	stood
steal(s)	stole	stolen
sting(s)	stung	stung
strike(s)	struck	struck
swim(s)	swam	swum
take(s)	took	taken
teach(es)	taught	taught
tear(s)	tore	torn
tell(s)	told	told
think(s)	thought	thought
throw(s)	threw	thrown
wake(s)	woke *or* waked	woken *or* waked
wear(s)	wore	worn
win(s)	won	won
write(s)	wrote	written

FAQ

Q: Where can I find the forms for all the irregular verbs?

A: You can look up an irregular verb in a dictionary to find its past tense and past participle forms.

Present Tense Forms for Irregular Verbs   When you write or speak of events that occur now, use the **present tense.** In the present tense, irregular verbs should have the form shown in the first column of the chart beginning on page 302. You will add *-s* or *-es* to that form, depending on the sentence subjects, as shown in the chart that follows.

IRREGULAR VERB FORMS: PRESENT TENSE

Singular		**Plural**
I drink.		We drink.
You drink.		You drink.
He drinks.		They drink.
She drinks.	Notice the *-s* or *-es* ending here.	The dogs drink.
It drinks.		
The dog drinks.		

CAUTION: A common error is forgetting the *-s* or *-es* ending for an irregular present tense verb used with *he, she, it,* or any singular noun subject.

no: Helga *sing* beautifully.

yes: Helga *sings* beautifully.

Practice 21.8

Rewrite the sentences, changing the underlined past tense verbs to present tense forms. Be careful to use the *-s* or *-es* ending when needed. If you are unsure of the correct form, check the list beginning on page 302.

Example

The golden sun <u>rose</u> over the Atlantic Ocean.

The golden sun rises over the Atlantic Ocean.

1. Matteo always <u>forgot</u> to meet me at the library after class.

   Matteo always forgets to meet me at the library after class.

2. The thoughtful dinner guest <u>brought</u> the hostess a bottle of wine.

   The thoughtful dinner guest brings the hostess a bottle of wine.

3. For a moment the centerfielder <u>lost</u> the ball in the sun, but he <u>caught</u> it anyway.

   For a moment the centerfielder lost the ball in the sun, but he catches it anyways.

4. I <u>knew</u> the answer.

   I know the answer.

5. Jannine <u>left</u> her car keys in the ignition.

   Jannine leaves her car keys in the ignition.

6. When the church bells <u>rang</u>, the congregation <u>rose</u> and <u>sang</u> a hymn.

<u>When the church bells ring, the congregation</u>
<u>rises and sings a hymn.</u>

Practice 21.9

Complete each sentence with a present tense form of an irregular verb from the list beginning on page 302 and any other words you need. Use *-s* or *-es* endings where needed.

Example

The scouts and their leader *take a group of senior citizens shopping every week.*

1. She   <u>always forgets where she places her keys.</u>

2. During the meeting, Boris and I   <u>sneaked out to eat something</u>

3. Before leaving for work, Luis   <u>makes sure he eats.</u>

4. They   <u>always ask me this question.</u>

5. The customer   <u>was being rude and annoying</u>

Present Tense Forms for *Be, Have,* and *Do*   The present tense forms of the irregular verbs *be, have,* and *do* are tricky. The following charts will help you learn these forms.

PRESENT TENSE FORMS OF *BE*	
Singular	**Plural**
I am.	We are.
You are.	You are.
He is.	They are.
She is.	The toys are.
It is.	
The toy is.	

PRESENT TENSE FORMS OF *HAVE*

Singular

I have.

You have.

He has.

She has.

It has.

The child has.

Plural

We have.

You have.

They have.

The children have.

PRESENT TENSE FORMS OF *DO*

Singular

I do.

You do.

He does.

She does.

It does.

The child does.

Plural

We do.

You do.

They do.

The children do.

CAUTION: Use the contraction forms *don't* and *doesn't* carefully. A common mistake is to use *don't (do not)* when *doesn't (does not)* is needed.

no:	The toy *don't* work anymore.
yes:	The toy *doesn't* work anymore.
no:	He *don't* want to work outside.
yes:	He *doesn't* want to work outside.

Practice 21.10

Fill in the blank with the correct present tense form of the verb in parentheses.

Example

(be) This CD _____is_____ very popular among teenagers.

1. (have) He _____has_____ an impressive stamp collection.

2. (be) New Year's Eve parties _____are_____ always a disappointment to me.

3. (do) Many parents _____do_____ not understand their teenage children.

4. (have) I _____have_____ the information you asked for.

5. (do) Jamal _____ *does* _____ the best he can, but I _____ *do* _____ not always recognize that fact.

6. (be) I _____ *will be* _____ here if you need help, and your parents _____ *will be* _____ too.

Past Tense Forms for Irregular Verbs   When you write or speak of events that occurred in the past, you use the **past tense.** In the past tense, use the irregular verb forms in the second column of the list beginning on page 302. Unlike the present tense forms, the past tense forms never change, as shown in the chart that follows.

IRREGULAR VERB FORMS: PAST TENSE

Singular	**Plural**
I drank.	We drank.
You drank.	You drank.
He drank.	They drank.
She drank.	The dogs drank.
It drank.	
The dog drank.	

CAUTION: A common error is using the past participle form (in the third column of the list beginning on page 302) for the simple past tense. Remember, the past participle appears with a helping verb (see pages 301–302).

no:	Jim *done* the work. (past participle without helping verb)
yes:	Jim *has done* the work. (helping verb with past participle)
yes:	Jim *did* the work. (past tense form)

Practice 21.11

Fill in the blank with the past tense form of the irregular verb in parentheses. If you are unsure of the form, check the chart beginning on page 302.

Example

(hold) As Grandma _____ *held* _____ the quilt I made for her, she smiled gratefully.

1. (forget) Michael was embarrassed because he _____ *forgot* _____ his sister's birthday.
2. (hear) When Eleni _____ *heard* _____ about the earthquake in California, she raced home to call her relatives in San Diego.
3. (lend) José is sorry he _____ *lend* _____ Lenny $50 because Lenny never repaid the loan.
4. (begin) Once everyone was seated, the orchestra _____ *began* _____ the overture.

5. (steal) As Aaron Cohen released the pitch, Brett Butler ___stole___ second base.

6. (wake) The alarm on the clock radio sounded at 6:45, and I ___woke___ with a start.

7. (teach) Yesterday Professor Morales ___taught___ us several techniques for successful revising.

8. (buy) The angora sweater I ___bought___ for Nuha is one size too large.

Practice 21.12

Pick five irregular verbs that you do not already know the parts of (use the chart beginning on page 302). Then, on a separate sheet, use the past tense form of each of these verbs in a sentence.

Past Tense Forms for *Be*   The irregular verb *be* is the only verb whose forms vary in the past tense according to the subject of the sentence. The following chart shows you the forms.

PAST TENSE FORMS OF *BE*

Singular	Plural
I was.	We were.
You were.	You were.
He was.	They were.
She was.	The toys were.
It was.	
The toy was.	

Practice 21.13

Fill in the blank with *was* or *were*.

Example

The test results ___were___ surprising.

1. The doctor ___was___ certain that rest and a better diet ___was___ all you needed.

2. I ___was___ eager to join you, but my roommates ___were___ not available to go.

3. They ___were___ certain they passed the quiz, but you ___were___ skeptical.

4. The children ___were___ excited when they found a puppy on the porch.

5. She _____was_____ the first person in her family to go to college, so her parents
_____were_____ very proud of her.

6. We _____were_____ eager to help you stop smoking.

Past Participle Forms for Irregular Verbs   The **past participle** is the verb form used with the helping verbs *has, have,* and *had*. The past participle of irregular verbs is the form in the third column of the list beginning on page 302. As the following chart shows, the subject of the sentence determines whether you use *has* or *have*.

IRREGULAR VERB FORMS: PAST PARTICIPLE

Singular	**Plural**
I have drunk.	We have drunk.
I had drunk.	We had drunk.
You have drunk.	You have drunk.
You had drunk.	You had drunk.
He has drunk.	They have drunk.
He had drunk.	They had drunk.
She has drunk.	The dogs have drunk.
She had drunk.	The dogs had drunk.
It has drunk.	
It had drunk.	
The dog has drunk.	
The dog had drunk.	

NOTE: As you can tell from the preceding examples, the past participle form does not change even though the form of the helping verb changes.

CAUTION: The past participle from must be used with a helping verb; it is not used alone.

no:	I *seen* Nancy. (past participle without helping verb)
yes:	I *have seen* Nancy. (past participle and helping verb)
yes:	I *had seen* Nancy. (past participle and helping verb)
no:	I *seen* her yesterday. (past participle without helping verb)
yes:	I *saw* her yesterday. (past tense form)

Practice 21.14

Fill in the blank with the past participle form of the irregular verb in parentheses.

Example

(bring) Fortunately, Gina has _____brought_____ a first-aid kit.

1. (blow) The strong winds have _____blown_____ since early this morning.
2. (choose) Lars has _____chose_____ to attend St. Bonaventure.
3. (go) The stray dogs had _____gone_____ by the time the dog warden arrived.
4. (lie) Doreen has _____lied_____ down for a while to try to get rid of her headache.
5. (ride) After Peter and Sondra had _____rode_____ the merry-go-round for the fifth time, they wanted some cotton candy.
6. (write) Thousands of angry consumers have _____write_____ the Better Business Bureau to complain about the faulty appliance.

Practice 21.15

On a separate sheet, write a sentence using the helping verb and past participle form of the irregular verb in parentheses. If you are unsure, check the list beginning on page 302.

Example

(has + teach) Dr. Yurak has taught both English and history for twenty years.

1. (had + wake) Waken
2. (has + do) done
3. (had + see) Seen
4. (has + sting) stung
5. (had + stand) Stood
6. (has + be) been
7. (had + meet) met

Review Practice 21.16

Rewrite each sentence twice, first using the past tense form of the underlined irregular verb, then using a past participle form.

Example

The family <u>eats</u> a vegetarian supper of corn chowder and wheat rolls.

a. The family ate a vegetarian supper of corn chowder and wheat rolls.

b. The family has eaten a vegetarian supper of corn chowder and wheat rolls.

1. Mom and Dad <u>hide</u> the eggs for the annual Easter egg hunt.

   a. _____

   _____

   b. _____

   _____

2. Few people <u>understand</u> the significance of the governor's decision.

   a. _____

   _____

   b. _____

   _____

3. The honor guard <u>stands</u> at attention for an hour.

   a. _____

   _____

   b. _____

   _____

4. Jan <u>swims</u> five miles before breakfast.

   a. _____

   _____

   b. _____

   _____

5. The bypass <u>runs</u> all the way to Route 40.

   a. _____

   _____

   b. _____

   _____

SUBJECT-VERB AGREEMENT

A word that refers to one person or item is **singular**; a word that refers to more than one person or item is **plural.**

Singular (refers to one person or item)		Plural (refers to more than one person or item)	
dog	month	dogs	months
desk	I	desks	we
box	he	boxes	they
cup	she	cups	
	it		

To achieve **subject-verb agreement,** use a singular verb with a singular subject and a plural verb with a plural subject. Subject-verb agreement is an issue only with present tense verb forms and the past tense forms of *be—was* (singular) and *were* (plural).

Present tense verb forms add *-s* or *-es* when used with *he, she, it,* or a singular noun. *Was* is used with singular nouns and *I, he, she,* and *it.* The following charts summarize this subject-verb agreement rule.

PRESENT TENSE: MOST VERBS

Singular Subject/Singular Verb	**Plural Subject/Plural Verb**
I move slowly.	We move slowly.
You move slowly.	You move slowly.
He moves slowly.	They move slowly.
She moves slowly.	The dogs move slowly.
It moves slowly.	
The dog moves slowly.	

NOTE: Add *-s* or *-es* to the verb only when the subject is *he, she, it,* or a singular noun.

PAST TENSE: *WAS/WERE*

Singular Subject/Singular Verb	**Plural Subject/Plural Verb**
I was here.	We were here.
You were here.	You were here.
He was here.	They were here.
She was here.	The dogs were here.
It was here.	
The dog was here.	

FAQ
Q: Can I tell whether to use a singular or plural verb by how the sentence sounds?

A: How a sentence sounds is not a reliable guide for choosing a verb form. Instead, identify the subject and then decide on the appropriate singular or plural form.

> **NOTE:**   Use *was* only when the subject is *I, he, she, it,* or a singular noun.

Practice 21.17

1. Fill in each blank with the correct present tense form of the verb in parentheses.

From time to time, you probably (wake up) ᵃ˙_____ with dark circles under your eyes. These circles (indicate) ᵇ˙_____ that you (need) ᶜ˙_____ more sleep. Blood vessels under the eyes (drain) ᵈ˙_____ blood from your head. However, blood circulation (slow) ᵉ˙_____ when you are tired. This slow-down (cause) ᶠ˙_____ the blood vessels to swell. Under the eyes, the skin (thin) ᵍ˙_____ . When blood vessels (swell) ʰ˙_____, you (see) ⁱ˙_____ right through the skin. The darkness you (notice) ʲ˙_____ is actually blood.

2. Fill in the blanks with either *was* (singular) or *were* (plural).

   a. We _____ certain that Jamal _____ not here yet.

   b. You _____ the best person for the job because Joyce _____ not available.

   c. This class _____ difficult, but they _____ able to handle it.

   d. Jane _____ new in town, but she _____ making friends easily.

   e. It _____ too early to leave, but we _____ too tired to stay.

   f. The spring rains _____ over, but the summer heat _____ not here yet.

Practice 21.18

Eliminate the faulty subject-verb agreement in the following paragraph.

¹Lighthouses guide sailors to safe anchorages. ²They also warns them of danger. ³The most famous ancient lighthouse was the Pharos of Alexandria, built in Egypt about 300 B.C. ⁴Early lighthouses was just wooden towers with metal baskets of burning wood or coal hung from poles on the top. ⁵Today, the most powerful light shine from the Créac'h d'Ouessant lighthouse. ⁶It warn of treacherous rocks of northwest France. ⁷Most lighthouses have sirens that blare out coded fog warnings. ⁸However, some lighthouses emits radio signals to guide ships with radio direction finders. ⁹Without lighthouses, the sea would be even more treacherous than it already is.

Compound Subjects

A **compound subject** is a two-part subject with the parts connected by *and, or, either . . . or, neither . . . nor,* or *not only . . . but [also].*

1. If the subjects are joined by *and,* the verb will usually be plural.

   <u>My best friend and I</u> <u>spend</u> spring break in Florida.

2. When the subjects are considered one unit, like *ham and eggs* and *rock and roll,* use a singular verb:

   <u>Rock and roll</u> <u>is</u> here to stay.

3. If the subjects are joined by *or, either . . . or, neither . . . nor,* or *not only . . . but [also],* the verb agrees with the closer subject.

   <u>Either my brothers or my sister</u> <u>is</u> going. (singular verb to agree with the singular *sister*)
   <u>Neither my hat nor my gloves</u> <u>are</u> where I left them. (plural verb to agree with the plural *gloves*)

NOTE: If you do not like the sound of "Either my brothers or my sister is going," reverse the order to place the plural subject second, so you can use a plural verb:

   <u>Either my sister or my brothers</u> <u>are</u> going.

Practice 21.19

Follow each compound subject with the correct present tense form of the verb in parentheses. Then finish the sentence with any other words you care to add.

Example

(taste) The meat and the potatoes *taste overcooked and bland.* _____

1. (know) Neither the club president nor the treasurer _____

   _____

2. (grow) Cotton and tobacco _____

   _____

3. (sing) The choir or the choirmaster _____

   _____

4. (visit) The children and their teacher _____

   _____

5. (have) Neither the encyclopedia nor the dictionaries _____

_____

6. (plan) Not only Sue but also Helen _____

_____

7. (volunteer) Either Mr. Chen or his wife _____

_____

8. (hope) The teacher and her principal _____

_____

Collective Noun Subjects

Collective nouns refer to groups. They are words like these:

congregation	committee	band	faculty
group	team	jury	flock
herd	audience	family	class

1. If the collective noun is considered one group acting as a whole, a singular verb is used.

> At noon, the <u>band</u> <u>boards</u> the bus for the trip to the Rose Parade. (The singular verb is used because band is acting as a whole.)

2. If the members of the group are acting individually, the collective noun takes a plural verb.

> The <u>faculty have</u> debated that issue for years. (The plural verb is used because the individual members of the faculty are acting individually.)

Practice 21.20

On a separate sheet, write sentences using the given collective nouns as subjects and the correct present tense forms of the verbs in parentheses. Be prepared to explain why you used the verb form that you did.

Example

flock (migrate) *The flock migrates to a warmer climate for the winter.*

1. army (attack)
2. family (eat) The family eat together
3. jury (argue) Jury argues the case
4. committee (decide)
5. team (practice)

Indefinite Pronoun Subjects

An **indefinite pronoun** refers to a group without specifying the particular members.

1. These indefinite pronouns always take a singular verb:

anyone	anybody	anything	each
everyone	everybody	everything	one
no one	nobody	nothing	none
someone	somebody	something	

> Anyone <u>is</u> welcome to attend the open house.
> Everything <u>works</u> out eventually.
> Each student <u>writes</u> a term paper during the senior year.
> Somebody <u>helps</u> Grandma clean her house every week.

2. These indefinite pronouns always take a plural verb:

both	many	few	several

> Many <u>believe</u> that Congress will defeat the budget proposal.

3. These indefinite pronouns take either a singular or plural verb, depending on whether the sense of the subject is singular or plural:

all	more	some
any	most	

> Some of my homework <u>is</u> missing. (The verb is singular because the sense of the subject is that one unit is missing.)

> Some of the puzzle pieces <u>are</u> missing. (The verb is plural because the sense is that more than one unit is missing.)

Practice 21.21

Circle the indefinite pronoun subjects and fill in the blanks with the correct present tense form of the verb in parentheses.

Example

(be) (All) of the lost money _____is_____ in the back of the drawer.

1. (believe) Each of us __believes__ the tax increase will improve the economy.

2. (find) Many of the band members __find__ the new director enthusiastic and creative.

3. (be) Everyone ____is____ invited to the tailgate party before the homecoming game.

4. (be) All of the hem ____are____ torn from the skirt.

5. (seem) None of the proposals __seems__ adequate to solve the problem.

6. (be) Some of the desserts _are_ low in fat and sugar.

7. (go) Everything _goes_ wrong when I am in a hurry.

8. (taste) All of the vegetables _taste_ underseasoned to me.

9. (expect) Nobody _expects_ you to be perfect.

10. (feel) All of the clothes _feel_ soft.

Phrases between the Subject and Verb

Phrases, particularly prepositional phrases (see pages 201–202), often come between the subject and verb. Do not be fooled by these phrases, for they do not affect subject-verb agreement.

The <u>theme</u> of the stories <u>is</u> middle-class greed. (A singular verb is used to agree with the singular subject *theme*. The phrase *of the stories* does not affect agreement.)

Practice 21.22

After each subject and phrase, write a present tense verb and any other words you want to add. (Use forms of the verb *to be* no more than twice.) Underline the subject once and the verb twice; draw a line through the phrase between the subject and verb.

Example

The <u>carton</u> <s>of records</s> <u>is blocking</u> the entrance to the room. _____

_____

1. The people on the bus _____

_____

2. Many paintings by that artist _____

_____

3. The students from Sri Lanka _____

_____

4. The scouts, along with their scoutmaster, _____

_____

5. The group of children _____

_____

6. The mistakes on the last page of the essay _____

_____

7. The seats in the tenth row _____

_____

8. The ragweed in the fields _____

_____

9. One of the kittens _____

_____

10. The container of sewing materials _____

_____

◼

Inverted Order

When a sentence has **inverted order,** the subject comes *after* the verb. (See pages 202–203 for more on inverted order.) Inverted order often occurs when a sentence begins with *here* or *there*. The following sentences have inverted order. The subjects are underlined once, and the verbs are underlined twice.

> Here <u>are</u> the <u>items</u> for the charity garage sale.
> There <u>is</u> only <u>one movie</u> suitable for children.

Even if a sentence has inverted order, the subject and verb must agree.

Practice 21.23

Complete the following sentences, being sure your subjects and verbs agree.

Example
   Here is *an unusual painting.* _____

1. Here are _____

_____

2. There is _____

_____

3. There are _____

_____

4. There were _____

_____

5. There was _____

_____

■

Who, Which, That

Who, which, and *that* are **relative pronouns** that refer to nouns. (See pages 229–230)
Use a singular verb when *who, which,* or *that* refers to a singular noun. Use a plural verb
when *who, which,* or *that* refers to a plural noun. Study these two examples:

Peter is one of those students *who study* constantly. (The plural verb is used
because *who* refers to the plural noun *students*.)

This is the book *that has* the surprise ending. (The singular verb is used
because *that* refers to the singular noun *book*.)

Practice 21.24

Draw an arrow from *who, which,* or *that* to the noun it refers to. Then fill in the
blank with the correct present tense form of the verb in parentheses.

Example
(follow) Vashti is a person who _____*follows*_____ every rule to the letter.

1. (do) A person who _____ not understand trigonometry will have trouble
   with physics.

2. (support) The beams that _____ this section of roof are beginning to rot.

3. (believe) Dr. Perni is one of those instructors who _____ her students can
   succeed.

4. (divide) This is the lake that _____ the property in half.

5. (scare) This is the kind of movie that always _____ me.

Review Practice 21.25

Find and eliminate the subject-verb agreement problems in the following passage,
drawing on everything you have learned and crossing out and rewriting as necessary.

[1]Beluga whales live in groups called pods, which are social units that may con-
sists of two to twenty-five whales. [2]Both males and females makes up a pod,

although mothers with calves often form separate pods during calving season. ³A pod of belugas hunt and migrate together as one group.

⁴The behavior of belugas are interesting to observe. ⁵One of their most common behaviors are vocalizing. ⁶Also, during calving season, adult belugas at sea have been observed carrying objects such as planks, nets, and even caribou skeletons on their heads and backs. ⁷Females in zoological habitats have also been seen carrying floats or buoys on their backs after losing a newborn. ⁸Experts thus theorize that this carrying is surrogate behavior. ⁹Belugas, which exhibits a great deal of curiosity toward humans, often swim up to boats. ¹⁰They seem as interested in us as we are in them.

■

TENSE SHIFTS

As you have learned, verb tenses express different times. If you move from one verb tense to another without a good reason to indicate a different time, you create a problem called **tense shift.**

tense shift:	When I *left* the house this morning, I ~~go~~ *went* to school.
explanation:	The first verb *(left)* is in the past tense to show that an event occurred before the present. However, the second verb *(go)* shifts to the present tense for no reason.
correction:	When I *left* the house this morning, I *went* to school.
explanation:	Both verbs are now in the past tense, so the tense shift is eliminated.

Some tense shifts are not a problem because a change of time is called for. Consider the following example:

appropriate tense shift:	"Frankfurters" *are* named for the city where they *were* first made: Frankfurt, Germany.
explanation:	The present tense *are* is used because frankfurters are named *in the present*. The past tense *were* is used because frankfurters were first made *in the past*.

Practice 21.26

Underline the verbs and then eliminate each inappropriate tense shift by crossing out the problem verb and writing the correct form above it.

Example

In the mid-nineteenth century, doctors <u>operated</u> with their bare hands in their street

clothes, and instruments ~~are~~ *were* not sterilized.

1. In the 1860s, the British surgeon Sir Joseph Lister pioneered sanitary operating room procedures. At the time, the post-operative mortality rate in many hospitals is over 90 percent.

2. For surgical dressing, doctors use sawdust, and instruments were not sterilized; they were just washed with soap and water.

3. When Lister gave a speech in Philadelphia in 1876, he expresses his views on germs; however, no one seems interested, except a Missouri physician named Joseph Lawrence.

4. Lawrence went back to his lab and develops an antibacterial liquid, which was manufactured locally.

5. To honor Lister, the man who pioneers sterile conditions, the liquid was named Listerine.

Practice 21.27

Eliminate inappropriate tense shifts by changing verb tenses where necessary. Remember not all tense changes are a problem. Eliminate only the inappropriate shifts.

[1]A ground ball that takes a bad hop is a baseball infielder's nightmare. [2]For example, in a 1960 World Series game, a New York Yankees player, Tony Kubek, was hit in the throat by a bad-hop grounder; an important run scored, and Kubek has to leave the game.

[4]Sometimes, bad-hop grounders are less serious. [5]In a 1948 Boston Red Sox–Philadelphia Athletics game, the Sox are at bat against the Athletics. [6]The Red Sox had Ted Williams on third base and Billy Goodman at bat. [7]Goodman hits a twisting grounder toward Athletics shortstop Eddie Joost, who got in front of the ball, but he couldn't handle it. [8]It hits his glove, runs up his arm, and disappears into the sleeve of his shirt. [9]Joost dropped his glove and began to search all over for the ball, but it is under his shirt. [10]He pulled his shirttail out of his pants, and the ball drops and rolls away. [11]Goodman reaches first as a result. [12]Williams, who could have scored easily, was still standing on third base, laughing too hard to run.

Review Practice 21.28

Edit to eliminate the problems with verbs in the following paragraph. You will need to draw on everything you learned in this chapter.

[1]A team of scientists raise fleas in laboratories to learn more about how these pests caused disease in humans and to learn about effective ways to control the insects. [2]The fleas be kept in special jars that contain sieves. [3]These fleas lay eggs in the jars, and the eggs drops through the sieves. [4]The scientists collects the eggs so they can raise more fleas from them. [5]Each of the jars also have tubes that carries warm water to heat blood that is contained underneath a skin-like sheath. [6]The fleas

bite through this sheath to drink the blood, which is served as their food.

[7]Interestingly, these laboratory breeding grounds for fleas are called *fake pups*.

Tips

USING VERBS CORRECTLY

- When a phrase comes between the subject and verb, you may find it easier to choose the verb form if you substitute a pronoun, like this:

  The box under the clothes *is/are* mine.
  It *is* mine.

- To determine the correct verb when a sentence has inverted order, rewrite the sentence so it is in normal order.

  "Here (*is* or *are*) the car keys" becomes "The car keys *are* here."
  "Where (*was/were*) you going?" becomes "You *were* going where?"

- **If English is not your first language,** be aware that some plural nouns may be singular in function, and therefore take a singular verb. Here are some examples:

mathematics	news	politics
measles	physics	scissors

  The news from Wall Street *worries* me.
  Mathematics *is* my favorite subject.

- **If English is not your first language,** be aware that when the complete verb is made up of two words, you do not add *-s* or *-es* to the second verb:

  no: My mother <u>can *helps*</u> me with my tuition bill.
  yes: My mother <u>can *help*</u> me with my tuition bill.

Post Test

A. Find and correct the verb errors in the following paragraph.

[1]Before Barry Bonds, Henry Louis Aaron, known as "Hank," be ~~was~~ American baseball's all-time champion home run hitter. [2]He enters ~~ed~~ the record books on April 8, 1974, when he breaked ~~broke~~ Babe Ruth's record of 714 home runs. [3]Aaron then went on to hit a total of 755 homers before he complete his twenty-three-year major-league career. [4]Aaron begin playing professionally for all-black teams in Mobile and Indianapolis, but he sign ~~ed~~ with the National League's Milwaukee

(continued on next page)

Braves when he be [was] 18. [5]He had reach [reached] the major leagues when he were [was] only 20 and quickly become [became] one of the game's finest players. [6]He play [played] for the Braves almost exclusively, first in Milwaukee and then in Atlanta. [7]Along with a lifetime batting average of 305, Aaron had 2,297 runs batted in. [8]He was the National League's most valuable player in 1957 and lead [led] the league in home runs and runs batted in. [9]A favorite with fans, Aaron done [did] much to generate enthusiasm for the game he loved to play.

B. Change the underlined past tense verbs to present tense verbs.

[1]After the noon rush hour, Leo's Pizzeria <u>was</u> [is] a mess. [2]The once clean stainless-steel table where pizzas <u>were</u> [is] made <u>was</u> [is] splattered with sauce and flooded with oil. [3]On the table, crusty dough and hardening strands of moz-zarella <u>contributed</u> [contribute] to the mess, which included crumbled plastic dough bags dripping with oil. [4]A mountain of dirty dishes <u>sat</u> [sit] in wait, threatening to topple if someone <u>did</u> [does] not come soon to wash them. [5]A collection of torn pizza boxes, strewn across the counter, <u>hid</u> [hide] spatulas, used and abandoned. [6]Blackened pizzas, burned and forgotten during the rush, <u>filled</u> [fill] the air with the scent of charcoal. [7]Added to this smell <u>were</u> [are] the watering onions near the ovens. [8]The flour used to make the crusts <u>covered</u> [cover] everything in the room with a fine dust. [9]Anyone who <u>entered</u> [enters] the kitchen would surely think twice before eating at Leo's.

LEARNING FROM TEXTBOOKS

The following excerpt was taken from a college environmental science textbook. Read the paragraphs and answer the questions that follow.

[1]From the dawn of human history until the beginning of the 1800s, population increased slowly and variably, with periodic setbacks. [2]It was roughly 1830 before world population reached the 1 billion mark. [3]By 1930, however, just 100 years later, the population had dou-bled to 2 billion. [4]Barely 30 years later, in 1960, it reached 3 billion, and in only 15 more years, by 1975, it had climbed to 4 billion. [5]Thus, the population doubled in just 45 years, from 1930 to 1975. [6]Then, 12 years later, in 1987, it crossed the 5 billion mark! [7]In 1999, world population passed 6 billion, and it is currently growing at the rate 76 million people per year. [8]This rate is equivalent to adding to the world every year the combined popula-tions of California, Texas, and New York.

[9]On the basis of current trends (which assume a continued decline in fertility rates), the U.N. Population Division (UNPD) medium projection predicts that world population will pass the 7 billion mark in 2012, the 8 billion mark in 2024, and the 9 billion mark in 2047

and will reach 9.1 billion in 2050. [10]At that point, world population will still be increasing by 34 million per year. [11]After that, it is all guesswork.

1. Why does the textbook author state the population for so many different years, rather than just note what it was in 1830 and what it is likely to be in 2050?

   _____

   _____

2. In what tenses are each of the following sentences written?

   a. sentences 1 and 2 _____

   b. sentence 8 _____

   c. sentence 10 _____

3. There are a number of tense shifts in the paragraphs. Are any of these tense shifts inappropriate? Explain.

   _____

   _____

4. In sentence 2, why is *was* used rather than *were*?

   _____

5. In the following sentences which words are the past participle forms?

   a. sentence 3 _____

   b. sentence 4 _____

Write about It

Population growth on the scale explained in the textbook excerpt will certainly have an impact. Using cause-and-effect analysis, discuss one effect of the increased number of people on the planet. You might consider the effect on resources, public policy, housing, food, or climate change, for example.

SUCCEEDING IN COLLEGE

Ask Questions and Engage in Class Discussions

When you ask questions in class, you clear up problems for yourself and for others. You can make sure you understand important material, and you may even raise a point that otherwise might not be mentioned. When you engage in class discussions, you become part of a community of learners and an active participant in academic dialogue. You make a contribution to your

(continued on next page)

class, sharpen your critical thinking skills, and set your learning. And in very large classes, you help your instructor remember you.

Despite the importance of asking questions and engaging in class discussions, some students are reluctant to speak in class because they are shy or fearful. If you hesitate to speak in class, you should work to overcome your reluctance because there is much to gain from class participation. The following tips can help.

- Sit in the front of the room. Asking questions from the front of the room is easier because you can make eye contact with your instructor. You won't see students sitting behind you, so you will be less likely to feel intimidated.

- Listen thoughtfully. Pay attention to the questions and comments already made, so you do not duplicate them. If you do need to ask a question asked previously, acknowledge that you heard the answer but need more explanation.

- Think first. Form your question or comment, reflect on it a moment, and then raise your hand. If it helps, write down your question or comment.

- If questions or comments occur to you while you are doing your homework, write them down to ask in class.

- Do not hesitate. If you wait to ask a question or make a comment, thinking that someone else will do it, the class may end and you may miss your opportunity.

Write about It

Explain how you feel about asking questions and speaking in class. If you like, you can consider the following questions: Do you speak often? Are you comfortable or uncomfortable? Are you more comfortable in some classes than others? Why do you feel the way you do? What kinds of classes make it easy or hard for you to speak up?

For more practice with using verbs, go to www.mywritinglab.com.

CHAPTER 22
Using Pronouns Correctly

To use pronouns correctly, you need to understand several grammar points. If you do not know all of them, do not be concerned, because this chapter will help you. On the other hand, you may currently know a great deal about using pronouns correctly, in which case this chapter will reinforce your understanding and perhaps teach you a few new points. To assess your current level of understanding, take the following pretest.

Pretest

Fill in the blanks with the correct pronoun form in parentheses, and then check your answers in Appendix II. Do not guess; if you are unsure, do not put anything in the blank.

1. (I, me) My sister and _____ are attending the same college.

2. (they, them) Each morning I walk farther than _____.

3. (I, me) Because there was a fly in the soup, the manager gave my date and _____ a free dinner.

4. (her, their) Each of the mothers complained that _____ children watched too much television.

5. (his or her, their) All of the students were instructed to bring _____ books and notes to the examination.

6. (its, their) The book of old photographs fell off _____ shelf.

7. (its, their) The committee felt _____ authority should be extended to making and enforcing rules.

8. (who, whom) That is the person _____ I told you about.

9. (I, me) The police officer told the other driver and _____ that she could not determine who caused the accident.

10. (its, their) One of the dresses has lost _____ shape.

PRONOUN-ANTECEDENT AGREEMENT

A **pronoun** takes the place of a noun or refers to a noun (a **noun** names a person, place, idea, emotion, or item).

The noun the pronoun stands for or refers to is the **antecedent.** In the following examples, an arrow is drawn from the pronoun to the noun antecedent:

Some <u>consumers</u> do not understand <u>their</u> legal rights.

<u>Michelle</u> understood that if <u>she</u> did not find a suitable babysitter, <u>she</u>

would not be able to return to college.

The oak <u>tree</u> must be diseased, for <u>it</u> is dropping <u>its</u> leaves.

A pronoun must be singular if the word it refers to (the antecedent) is singular. The pronoun must be plural if the antecedent is plural. Matching singular pronouns with singular antecedents and plural pronouns with plural antecedents creates **pronoun-antecedent agreement.**

singular pronoun/singular antecedent: The <u>child</u> cried because

<u>she</u> broke <u>her</u> favorite toy.

plural pronoun/plural antecedent: The basketball <u>players</u>

cheered when <u>they</u> won the game in double overtime.

Here is a chart of singular and plural pronouns.

PRONOUNS

Singular	**Plural**
I, me, my, mine	we, us, our, ours
he, she, it, him, her	they, them, their, theirs
his, hers, its	

Pronouns That Are Both Singular and Plural

you, your, yours

Practice 22.1

Fill in each blank with a pronoun from the "Pronouns" chart. Then draw an arrow from the pronoun to its antecedent. The first one is done as an example.

At 4:00 A.M., Gregory was awakened by the blare of [1] _____*his*_____ smoke

detector. [2] _____ was dazed at first, but quickly [3] _____ realized that the house was on fire. Gregory's room mates downstairs had also been awakened, and 4_____ were shouting to Greg to get out of the house. However, Greg realized that Mike and his sister Darla were still asleep in the attic, so 5_____ ran upstairs to get 6_____. Greg pounded on 7_____ door to wake 8_____ up. Then, the three of them began descending the stairs to the front door. Before they reached 9_____, Darla was overcome by smoke and Mike had to carry 10_____ part of the way. The three of them escaped just in time, for as they exited there was an explosion upstairs and fire shot through the windows. Firefighters blame the fire on a space heater. 11_____ was placed too close to some rags and ignited 12_____. 13_____ said the boys are fortunate that 14_____ detector was working. Everyone is safe, but Darla suffered from smoke inhalation, so 15_____ had to be hospitalized.

Compound Subject Antecedents

A **compound subject** is a two-part subject with the parts connected by *and, or, either . . . or,* or *neither . . . nor, not only . . . but [also].* Follow these rules when a pronoun refers to all or part of a compound subject.

1. When the noun antecedents are joined by *and,* the pronoun will usually be plural.

    My *father and mother* sold <u>their</u> house and moved into an apartment. (*Their* is plural because it refers to two people, *father and mother.*)

2. If the noun antecedents are joined by *or, either . . . or,* or *neither . . . nor,* the pronoun agrees with the closer antecedent.

    Ivan or *Ralph* will lend me <u>his</u> car to use while mine is in the shop. (The singular *his* is used to agree with *Ralph,* the closer antecedent.)

    Neither the president nor his *advisors* believe <u>they</u> can get the disarmament bill through Congress. (The plural *they* is used to agree with *advisors,* the closer antecedent.)

    Either Jeff or his *brothers* will bring <u>their</u> extension ladder over so I can clean the gutters around the house. (The plural *their* is used to agree with *brothers,* the closer antecedent.)

NOTE: To avoid an awkward-sounding (but grammatically correct) sentence, place the plural part of a compound subject last.

awkward: Either the scouts or the scout leader will bring *his* leaf identification manual.

natural sounding: Either the scout leader or the scouts will bring *their* leaf identification manual.

Practice 22.2

Fill in the blank with the correct pronoun.

Example

Neither the mayor nor city council members are spending ___*their*___ own money for reelection campaigns.

1. The students and their teacher decorated _____ classroom for the Martin Luther King, Jr., memorial celebration.

2. Joyce and Burt handed in _____ research papers early.

3. Either my mother or my grandmother will make _____ chocolate chip cookie recipe for the family reunion.

4. Neither the teachers nor the school board members changed _____ positions after hours of negotiating.

5. I thought Rico or Elliot would offer to bring _____ Coleman stove on the camping trip.

6. The Hummel figurine and the Royal Copenhagen plate were carefully removed from _____ gift box.

Collective Noun Antecedents

A **collective noun** refers to a group. These words are collective nouns:

audience	faculty	herd
band	family	jury
committee	group	team

1. If the sense of the collective noun is that the group is acting as one unit, the pronoun that refers to the collective noun should be singular.

   The <u>committee</u> was unsure of <u>its</u> assignment.

> **NOTE:** If you find it awkward to use the singular *its,* add "members of" before the collective noun and use a plural verb and pronoun:
>
> The members of the committee were unsure of their assignment.

2. If the members of the group are acting individually, the pronoun that refers to the collective noun should be plural:

   The <u>committee</u> argued about <u>their</u> differing opinions.

Practice 22.3

Circle the collective noun antecedent. Then fill in the blank with the singular *its* or the plural *their*.

Example

The women's softball (team) scored _____its_____ third upset of the season against the top-ranked team in the league.

1. The jury debated all night in order to resolve _____ different views of the evidence.

2. The audience shouted _____ approval by calling for an encore.

3. After the curtain fell on the third act, the cast came out and took _____ bow.

4. The coach reminded the team to bring _____ playbooks to every practice.

5. The orchestra lifted _____ instruments, signaling that the concert was about to begin.

6. At the general membership meeting, the committee reported _____ findings.

■

Indefinite Pronoun Antecedents

An **indefinite pronoun** refers to a group without specifying the particular members. An indefinite pronoun can be an antecedent for another pronoun.

1. These indefinite pronouns are always singular, so pronouns that refer to them should also be singular:

anyone	everybody	nothing
everyone	nobody	something
no one	somebody	each
someone	anything	one
anybody	everything	none

Everyone should bring <u>his or her</u> notebook to the lecture.

Each of the priests is volunteering <u>his</u> time to help at the battered persons' shelter.

None of the mothers brought <u>her</u> children to the meeting.

NOTE: As the last two examples illustrate, a prepositional phrase that comes after the indefinite pronoun does not affect pronoun-antecedent agreement. (See also "Phrases after the Antecedent" on page 334.)

2. These indefinite pronouns are always plural, so pronouns that refer to them should also be plural:

both   ·   many   few   several

Few understand all <u>their</u> rights under the law.

Many believe <u>their</u> educational backgrounds are not adequate.

3. These indefinite pronouns are either singular or plural. Pronouns that refer to one of them should be singular if the meaning of the indefinite pronoun is singular, and plural if the meaning of the indefinite pronoun is plural.

all   more   some
any   most

All of the class finished <u>their</u> research papers. (The plural pronoun is used because the antecedent *all* has a plural sense.)

All of the report fell out of <u>its</u> folder. (The singular pronoun is used because the antecedent *all* has a singular sense.)

Practice 22.4

Fill in the blanks with the correct pronoun: *his, her, its, they,* or *their.*

Example

All of the contestants hoped ___*their*___ entries would be judged the best of the show.

1. Most of the curtain has slipped off ___it's___ rod.
2. Many of the protesters shouted that ___their___ civil rights had been violated.
3. To pass inspection, you must be sure that everything is in ___it's___ place.
4. Each of the boys on the varsity basketball team is expected to keep ___~~their~~ his___ grades up to a B average.
5. The salesclerk was alarmed because one of the expensive designer dresses was missing from ___it's___ hanger.
6. Very few of the contestants believed ___they___ had much of a chance to win.

Nonsexist Usage

In the past, writers would use the masculine forms *he, his, him,* and *himself* to refer to nouns and indefinite pronouns that included both males and females. Thus, sentences like the following were frequently written and spoken:

Each student is expected to bring <u>his</u> book to class.

Every person has <u>his</u> own opinion.

Everybody described <u>his</u> career goals.

Although this use of the masculine pronoun is grammatically correct, it excludes women. To avoid using a masculine pronoun to refer to groups that include both men and women, you have three options.

1. Use *he or she, him or her, his or hers, himself or herself*.

   Everybody described <u>his or her</u> career goals.

   Using pairs of pronouns works in many situations. However, if this solution becomes cumbersome, use one of the two solutions that follows.

2. Use plural forms.

   All the students described their career goals.

3. Reshape the sentence to avoid the pronoun.

   Every person described a career goal.

FAQ

Q: Can I use *he, him,* and *his* with singular antecedents that include females?

A: Using masculine pronouns to refer to singular antecedents that include females is grammatically correct, but many readers will consider this usage sexist.

Practice 22.5

Rewrite each sentence to eliminate sexist pronoun usage. Refer to the three preceding suggestions for how to do this, and try to use each suggestion twice.

Example

None of the people who entered the writing contest had his manuscript returned.

The people who entered the writing contest did not have their manuscripts returned.

1. Anyone who cannot reach his goal is sure to feel frustrated. *his/her.*

   Anyone who cannot reach their goal is sure to feel frustrated.

2. Every~~one~~ *People* who entered the poetry contest ~~is~~ *are* convinced that hi~~s~~ *their* poem will win the $500 prize.

   Everyone who entered the poetry contest is convinced they'll win a $500 prize.

3. Anyone who puts his money in a savings account now will earn very little interest.

[handwritten: their]

Anyone who puts his/her money in a savings account ...

4. No one in the audience felt the play was worth the price he paid.

[handwritten: they]

Audience members felt the play was not worth the price they paid.

5. Each of the investment brokers advised his clients to avoid the risks of penny stocks.

[handwritten: their]

The investment brokers advised his/her clients to avoid the risks of penny stocks

6. Someone has left his chemistry book and notes on the desk.

[handwritten: their]

Someone has left his/her chemistry book and notes on the desk.

Phrases after the Antecedent

A prepositional phrase can come after the antecedent (see pages 201–202 on prepositional phrases). The phrase will not affect pronoun-antecedent agreement.

The can of sardines sits on <u>its</u> side in the cupboard. (The prepositional phrase *of sardines* does not affect agreement. The singular *its* is used to agree with the singular *can*.)

Each of the windows had slipped off <u>its</u> track. (The prepositional phrase *of the windows* does not affect agreement. The singular *its* is used to agree with the singular *each*.)

The students in the class asked if <u>their</u> test would be given on Wednesday. (The prepositional phrase *in the class* does not affect agreement. The plural *their* is used to agree with the plural *students*.)

Practice 22.6

Draw a line through each prepositional phrase after the antecedent. Then fill in the blanks with the correct pronoun. You will choose between *its* or *their*.

Example

The canopy ~~of tropical rain forests~~ provides ___*its*___ birds with food.

A host gets

1. A host of birds gets _____*it's*_____ nourishment from the nectar, fruit, and seeds that the canopy provides.

2. The brightly colored birds in the Amazon get _____*it's*_____ *their* supply of fruit from plentiful trees.

3. One of the strangest birds of the Amazon is the hoatzin; _____*their*_____ *it's* claws are on _____*its*_____ wings.

4. One of the birds making _____*their*_____ *it's* home in the Amazon rain forest is the harpy eagle.

5. Many birds with an unusual characteristic of some kind make _____*its*_____ *their* home in the African rain forests.

6. A particular type of bird called the African hornbill makes _____*their*_____ home in Africa but not in South America.

it's

Review Practice 22.7

Circle the letter of the correct sentence.

1. a. Because hypertension (high blood pressure) is the cause of 1.5 million heart attacks a year, everyone should learn if <u>he or she has</u> it.

   b. Because hypertension (high blood pressure) is the cause of 1.5 million heart attacks a year, everyone should learn if <u>they have</u> it.

2. a. Most people with hypertension have no symptoms, so <u>they do</u> not know they are afflicted.

   b. Most people with hypertension have no symptoms, so <u>he or she does</u> not know they are afflicted.

3. a. For example, neither my uncle nor my father discovered <u>their</u> high blood pressure until it was almost too late—after having a major heart attack.

   b. For example, neither my uncle nor my father discovered <u>his</u> high blood pressure until it was almost too late—after having a major heart attack.

4. a. As a result, our family has <u>their</u> blood pressure checked regularly.

   b. As a result, our family has <u>its</u> blood pressure checked regularly.

5. a. One of my family members discovered <u>her</u> hypertension after experiencing vision changes.

   b. One of my family members discovered <u>their</u> hypertension after experiencing vision changes.

6. a. Other people discover <u>their</u> high blood pressure when they investigate chest pains, shortness of breath, or swollen ankles.

   b. Other people discover <u>his or her</u> high blood pressure when they investigate chest pains, shortness of breath, or swollen ankles.

PRONOUN REFERENCE

When a pronoun does not refer clearly to its antecedent, confusion can occur. The next sections help you avoid such confusion.

Unclear Reference

When the reader cannot tell which antecedent a pronoun refers to, the problem is **unclear reference.** Here is a sentence that has unclear reference because the pronoun could refer to two nouns:

> Kathy was having lunch with Sasha when she heard the news.

Because the pronoun reference is unclear, the reader cannot tell whether Kathy or Sasha heard the news. Here is another example:

> After I put the cereal and orange juice on the table, my dog jumped up and spilled it.

What was spilled, the cereal or the orange juice? Because the pronoun reference is unclear, the reader cannot tell for sure.

To solve a problem with unclear reference, you may have to use a noun instead of a pronoun:

> Kathy was having lunch with Sasha when Sasha heard the news.
>
> After I put the cereal and orange juice on the table, my dog jumped up and spilled the juice.

Practice 22.8

Rewrite the following sentences to solve problems with unclear pronoun reference.

Example

Lenny told Jake that he would have to return the book by Friday.

Lenny told Jake to return the book by Friday.

1. I put the chicken in the oven and the broccoli in the microwave. An hour later it burned.

   I put the chicken in the oven and the broccoli in the microwave. An hour later the chicken

2. Tatiana carefully removed the vase from the coffee table before dusting it.

   the vase

3. My mother explained to my sister that she had to leave for school in an hour.

_____ *that my sister had to leave* _____

_____ *My mother told my sister that she had to leave for* _____

school in an hour.

4. Before Jack could give Marvin his class notes, he fell asleep.

_____ *Marvin* _____

_____

5. As I was placing the ceramic bowl on the glass table, it broke.

_____ *ceramic broke* _____

_____

Unstated Reference

Unstated reference occurs when a pronoun refers to an unwritten or unspoken antecedent. To solve the problem, state the unstated form.

unstated reference:	Joel is known as a patient tutor. It is a trait the other tutors admire. (*It* is meant to refer to *patience*, but that word does not appear—*patient* does.)
correction:	Joel is known as a patient tutor. <u>His patience</u> is a trait the other tutors admire.
unstated reference:	Because Anika is so insecure, she has very few friends. It causes her to seek constant approval. (*It* is meant to refer to *insecurity*, but that word does not appear—*insecure* does.)
correction:	Because Anika is so insecure, she has very few friends. <u>Her insecurity</u> causes her to seek constant approval.

Unstated reference also occurs when *this, that, which, it,* or *they* has no specified antecedent. To solve the problem, add the missing word or words.

unstated reference:	During my last physical examination, the doctor urged me to lower my salt intake. This means my food tastes bland. (*This* has no stated antecedent.)
correction:	During my last physical examination, the doctor urged me to lower my salt intake. <u>This change</u> means my food tastes bland.
unstated reference:	The auto workers and GM negotiated all night, but it failed to produce a contract. (*It* has no stated antecedent.)
correction:	The auto workers and GM negotiated all night, but <u>the session</u> failed to produce a contract.

Unstated reference will occur when *they* or *you* has no stated antecedent. To solve the problem, add the missing word or words.

unstated reference:	I called the billing office to complain about my bill, but they said it was correct. (*They* has no stated antecedent.)
correction:	I called the billing office to complain about my bill, but <u>the clerk</u> said it was correct.
unstated reference:	Worker dissatisfaction occurs when you do not let employees participate in decision making. (*You* has no stated antecedent.)
correction:	Worker dissatisfaction occurs when <u>employers</u> do not let employees participate in decision making.

NOTE: *You* and *your* address the reader directly. Use these pronouns only when you mean to address the reader; do not use them for general statements that apply to more people than the reader.

no:	At election time, <u>you</u> always see politicians promising things they can't deliver.
yes:	At election time, voters always see politicians promising things they can't deliver.
yes:	At election time, politicians are always promising things they can't deliver.

Practice 22.9

Revise the sentences to eliminate the unstated reference problems.

Example

Because he had a tension headache, Nick was irritable. It made him very difficult to be around.

Because he had a tension headache, Nick was irritable. His irritability made him very difficult to be around.

1. The comedian told several ethnic jokes. It annoyed most of the audience.

   The comedian told several ethnic jokes, the joke the annoyed most of the audience.

2. The movie was excessively violent and too long. This caused most of the critics to review <u>it</u> badly.

   the movie   the length and violence

3. The paint had a few blisters in it near the ceiling, but for the most part, they did an excellent job.

the painters

_____

_____

4. I went to see my advisor, but they said that he was sick.

the receptionist .

_____

_____

5. Ivan felt nervous about the upcoming examination. It made sleep difficult for him.

his nervousness

_____

_____

6. During finals week, you always know that students are working hard.

everyone

_____

_____

7. The police officer explained to the suspects that they had a right to an attorney, which is guaranteed by law.

_____

_____

8. Corrine is a very talented artist. It helped her earn a scholarship to the state art institute.

Her talent helped her earn

_____

_____

<hr>

Review Practice 22.10

Eliminate the problems with pronoun reference in the following paragraph. The first one is done as an example.

Its density

[1]Saturn, the second largest planet in the solar system, is the least dense [2]It is the reason Saturn would float in an ocean, if there were one big enough. [3]They say that the planet's mass is 95 times the mass of the Earth. [4]Saturn radiates about 80 percent more energy than it receives from the sun. [5]However, you cannot attribute the excess energy to a particular cause just yet. [6]Saturn's diameter is almost 75,000 miles, but the planet is 10 percent narrower at its poles. [7]It is a consequence of its

rapid rotation. [8]Saturn and Jupiter are similar in atmospheric appearance, but it has dark and light cloud markings and swirls and curling ribbons. [9]A thick haze mutes these markings. [10]Helium and hydrogen compose most of the atmosphere, with about 80 percent made up of it. [11]The most remarkable feature of Saturn, however, is its rings, made up of billions of water-ice particles orbiting around the planet. [12]With winds measured at 1,100 miles per hour near its equator and temperatures ranging between 176 degrees and −203 degrees, the planet is far from hospitable.

SUBJECT, OBJECT, AND POSSESSIVE PRONOUNS

Pronouns can be used as subjects, as objects, or as possessive forms.

SUBJECT, OBJECT, AND POSSESSIVE PRONOUNS		
Subject	**Object**	**Possessive**
I	me	my/mine
we	us	our/ours
you	you	your/yours
he	him	his
she	her	her/hers
it	it	its
they	them	their/theirs

Subject Pronouns

A pronoun is the **subject** of a sentence or clause when it tells who or what the sentence or clause is about (see page 200 for more on identifying subjects). When a pronoun functions as the subject, you must use one of the subject pronouns in the previous chart.

> *He* slammed the car door on John's finger.
> Because *I* am ill, *they* must go alone.
> During summer school, *she* took a word-processing course.
> *They* ate quickly and left.
> In the spring and summer, *I* walk five miles a day.

Object Pronouns

A pronoun can be the **object of a verb.** The object of a verb is the word that receives the action the verb expresses.

> Daniela carried *it* upstairs.

The verb is *carried. It* receives the action of the verb *carried,* and is therefore the object of that verb.

To find the object of a verb, ask "whom or what?" *after* the verb. Here are some examples:

> Pat ate *it.* (Ask "ate whom or what?" and the answer is *it,* so *it* is the object of the verb.)
> Ida always understands *him.* (Ask "understands whom or what?" and the answer is *him,* so *him* is the object of the verb.)
> The ending of the book surprised *me.* (Ask "surprised whom or what?" and the answer is *me,* so *me* is the object of the verb.)

A pronoun can also be the **object of a preposition.** The object of a preposition follows a preposition. A preposition is a word like *to, in, at, near,* or *around.* (See pages 201–202 on prepositions.) In the sentences that follow, the italicized pronouns function as objects of prepositions:

> Janine put the chair next to *us.* (The preposition is *to.*)
> The annoyed pitcher threw the ball at *me.* (The preposition is *at.*)
> Raul always wants to be near *her.* (The preposition is *near.*)

Sometimes the preposition is not stated; instead, it is understood to be *to* or *for.* This often happens after the verbs *give, tell, buy, bring,* and *send.*

FAQ
Q: What is an indirect object?

> The instructor gave *him* the answer. (The instructor gave the answer to *him.*)
> Mother sent *me* a rose for my birthday. (Mother sent a rose *to me* for my birthday.)
> I bought *him* the book. (I bought the book *for him.*)

A: An indirect object is the object of the preposition *to* or *for.* These prepositions may be unstated, as in "I gave *him* a cookie."

When a pronoun functions as an object, use one of the object pronouns in the chart on page 340.

Possessive Pronouns

A pronoun can also be **possessive;** that is, it can show ownership, as in these sentences:

> Diane lets *her* cat sleep in bed with *his* cat toys.
> Wise investors never put all of *their* money in one stock.

NOTE: Notice that *its* is the possessive pronoun, not *it's. It's* is a contraction form that means "it is" or "it has."

possessive:	The dog buried *its* bone.
contraction:	I believe *it's* too late to call Vincenzo.

Who and Whom

Who is a subject pronoun and *whom* is an object pronoun. Thus, use *who* for a subject of a sentence or clause and *whom* for the object of a verb or preposition.

subject of sentence:	*Who* wants to eat dinner now?
subject of clause:	Josef is the one *who* can help you.
object of verb:	The person *whom* you need works in this office.
object of preposition:	To *whom* should I mail the form?

Practice 22.11

Above each underlined pronoun, write *S* if it is a subject pronoun, *O* if it is an object pronoun, or *P* if it is a possessive pronoun.

¹Danny is someone <u>whom</u> I could never trust. ²<u>I</u> lent <u>him</u> my car because <u>his</u> was in the shop, but little did <u>I</u> know that <u>I</u> would never see <u>it</u> again. ³Danny drove <u>my</u> car to the gas station, but when <u>he</u> went inside to pay, <u>he</u> foolishly left the keys in the ignition and the door unlocked. ⁴While he was inside, a thief jumped in and drove off. ⁵Unfortunately, the guy was more than a car thief, for he used my car in an armed robbery an hour later. ⁶The police caught up with <u>him</u>, but a high-speed chase ensued, followed by a crash. ⁷<u>My</u> car ended up down a ravine. ⁸It has been two years since the incident, and the car still has not been returned to <u>me</u>. ⁹My father and I have tried to get it back, but the police told <u>us</u> that <u>they</u> need <u>it</u> for the upcoming trial. ¹⁰<u>We</u> can try again when the trial is over. ¹¹The wheels of justice may turn slowly, but the wheels of my car are not turning at all.

Practice 22.12

Fill in the blanks with a correct subject, object, or possessive pronoun. Write *S* if you have used a subject pronoun, *O* if you have used an object pronoun, or *P* if you have used a possessive pronoun. In the first and last sentences, choose *who* or *whom*.

Roy was a high school quarterback for ¹_____ the future looked bright. As a sophomore, ²_____ broke the school passing records, and as a junior ³_____ led ⁴_____ team to a conference championship. Many college scouts were watching ⁵_____, and ⁶_____ were ready to offer ⁷_____ rather impressive scholarships. Unfortunately, an incident occurred in Roy's senior year. Two hefty players on an opposing team sacked Roy at the line of scrimmage. ⁸_____ tackled ⁹_____ so hard that ¹⁰_____ was knocked unconscious and rushed to the hospital. He had a concussion, but ¹¹_____ came out of it just fine. However, when I went to see Roy in the hospital, he told ¹²_____ that he had no desire to play football again. When Roy got out of the hospital, ¹³_____ friends and coaches tried to change his mind, but ¹⁴_____ were unable to persuade ¹⁵_____ to go back to the game. Roy was just too afraid of getting hurt again. Roy went to college, but ¹⁶_____ had to give up his athletic schol-arship. He does not seem to have any regrets, though. In fact, when I last spoke to ¹⁷_____ he told ¹⁸_____ he was sure he had done the right thing.

¹⁹_____ would have thought Roy could be happy without football?

Subject and Object Pronouns in Compounds

And or *or* can link a pronoun to a noun to form a **compound.**

Bob and *me*	the children and *us*	the children or *I*
the boy and *I*	Gloria and *he*	Conchetta or *them*

If the pronoun is part of a compound that acts as a subject, use a subject pronoun. If the pronoun is part of a compound that acts as the object of a verb or the object of a preposition, use an object pronoun.

> *Bob and I* bought season tickets to the Steelers' games. (The italicized compound is the subject of the sentence, so the subject pronoun is used.)
> The car almost hit *Bob and me*. (The italicized compound is the object of the verb, so the object pronoun is used.)
> The coach was angry with *Bob and me*. (The italicized compound is the object of the preposition *with,* so the object pronoun is used.)

To decide if a subject or object pronoun is needed in a compound, mentally cross out everything in the compound except the pronoun. Then decide if the remaining pronoun is a subject or an object.

> ~~The children and~~ I went to the movie.
> ~~The children and~~ me went to the movie.

When everything but the pronoun is crossed out in each compound, you can tell that the pronoun is part of the subject. Thus, the subject form *I* is needed:

> The children and I went to the movies.

Here is another example:

> Professor Hernandez explained to ~~Colleen, Louise, and~~ I that our project was well researched and informative.
> Professor Hernandez explained to ~~Colleen, Louise and~~ me that our project was well researched and informative.

With everything in the compound except the pronoun crossed out, you can see that the pronoun is part of the object of the preposition *to*. Therefore, an object pronoun is needed:

> Professor Hernandez explained to Colleen, Louise, and me that our project was well researched and informative.

FAQ
Q: Can I tell which pronoun to use according to how the sentence sounds?

A: Sound is an unreliable way to choose a pronoun.

NOTE: When a noun and pronoun form a compound, place the pronoun at the end of the compound.

no:	I and the teacher disagreed about the correct answer.
yes:	The teacher and I disagreed about the correct answer.
no:	The boat belongs to me and Joyce.
yes:	The boat belongs to Joyce and me.

> ### Practice 22.13

Fill in each blank with the correct subject or object pronoun in parentheses.

Example

(she, her) Kurt and_____*she*_____ ran a mile in the snow.

1. (I, me) The salesclerk gave Jim and _____ the wrong packages.

2. (we, us) The band was too loud for Dikla and _____, so we left.

3. (I, me) Sora and _____ searched the piles of sweaters for my size.

4. (we, us) The movers or _____ will pack the dishes in the kitchen.

5. (they, them) I gave you and _____ the directions to the farm that sells fresh produce.

6. (he, him) Dr. Amin wants Julia and _____ as lab assistants.

7. (she, her) To make money for college, Wanda and _____ worked all summer as table servers.

8. (I, me) Give the library books to Hans or _____ to return for you.

Subject and Object Pronouns Paired with Nouns

When a pronoun is paired with its noun antecedent, you can decide whether a subject or object pronoun is needed by mentally crossing out the noun and deciding whether the remaining pronoun is a subject or object. For example, crossing out the nouns in the following sentences will help you choose the correct pronoun:

> We ~~nonsmokers~~ favor banning smoking in public places.
> Us ~~nonsmokers~~ favor banning smoking in public places.

With the nouns crossed out, you can see that the pronoun acts as a subject, so the subject pronoun *we* is needed. This makes the first example the correct sentence. Now look at these sentences:

> Smokers are sometimes inconsiderate of we ~~nonsmokers~~.
> Smokers are sometimes inconsiderate of us ~~nonsmokers~~.

With the nouns crossed out, you can see that the pronoun is the object of the preposition *of*, so the second sentence is correct because it uses the object pronoun *us*.

> ### Practice 22.14

For each pair of sentences, cross out the paired noun and decide if a subject or object pronoun is needed. Then place a check next to the correct sentence.

Examples

___✓___ We ~~students~~ believed that the tuition hike was unfortunate but necessary in light of increasing costs.

_____ Us ~~students~~ believed that the tuition hike was unfortunate but necessary in light of increasing costs.

1. _____ Some of we golfers were unhappy with the condition of the course.

   _____ Some of us golfers were unhappy with the condition of the course.

2. _____ None of the legislators considered the impact of the tax increase on we, the middle-class property owners.

   _____ None of the legislators considered the impact of the tax increase on us, the middle-class property owners.

3. _____ Dr. Wren asked I, the only one who did not understand the problem, to put my answer on the board.

   _____ Dr. Wren asked me, the only one who did not understand the problem, to put my answer on the board.

4. _____ We new pledges must stick together if we are going to make it through the fraternity initiation.

   _____ Us new pledges must stick together if we are going to make it through the fraternity initiation.

5. _____ The club charter prevents we new members from holding office for a year.

   _____ The club charter prevents us new members from holding office for a year.

Subject and Object Pronouns in Comparisons

The words *than* and *as* can be used to show comparisons.

> Marta is friendlier *than* Lorraine. (Marta's friendliness is compared to Lorraine's friendliness.)
> Larry is not as good at math *as* John. (Larry's math ability is compared to John's math ability.)

Notice that when *than* or *as* is used to show comparison, words that could finish the comparison go unstated.

> Marta is friendlier than Lorraine.

> > could be

> Marta is friendlier than Lorraine *is*.

> Larry is not as good at math as John.

> > could be

> Larry is not as good at math as John *is*.

When a pronoun follows *than* or *as* in a comparison, decide whether to use a subject or object pronoun by mentally adding the unstated words. Which sentence uses the correct pronoun?

> Marcus is a better basketball player than *I*.
> Marcus is a better basketball player than *me*.

To decide which pronoun is correct, mentally add the unstated word or words:

> Marcus is a better basketball player than I am.
> Marcus is a better basketball player than me am.

With the unstated *am* added, you can see that the pronoun functions as the subject of the verb *am*. Since *I* is a subject pronoun, the first example is correct. Here is another example:

> The news report disturbed Harriet as much as *I.*
> The news report disturbed Harriet as much as *me.*

To decide on the correct pronoun, add the unstated words:

> The news report disturbed Harriet as much as it disturbed I.
> The news report disturbed Harriet as much as it disturbed me.

With the unstated words *it disturbed* added, you can see that the pronoun functions as the object of the verb *disturbed*. Since *me* is an object pronoun, the second example is correct.

Correct pronoun choice in comparisons is important because the pronoun can affect meaning. Here is an example:

> Carol always liked Julio more than I.
> Carol always liked Julio more than me.

FAQ

Q: I always hear sentences like "Larry is not as good at math as me." Why is that wrong?

A: In informal speech and writing, "Larry is not as good at math as me" is common. For formal writing and speech, use "Larry is not as good at math as I."

The first sentence means that Carol liked Julio more than I liked Julio. The second sentence means that Carol liked Julio more than she liked me.

Practice 22.15

Fill in the blank with the correct pronoun in parentheses. If you are unsure, mentally rewrite each sentence, supplying the unstated words.

Example

(they, them) Juanita and I do not enjoy NASCAR racing as much as __*they*__ .

1. (we, us) Carol and I were annoyed to discover that Ted and Janet had better seats for the concert than __we did__ .
2. (I, me) Making friends has always been easier for Eleni than __it has been for me__
3. (he, him) Studying together helps you as much as __him__ .
4. (she, her) I believe in the power of positive thinking more than __she does__ .
5. (we, us) On opening night, Francis was less nervous than __we were__ .
6. (I, me) Since you do not care for classical music as much as __I do__ , you should meet me after the concert for dinner.

PERSON SHIFT

When you write or speak about yourself, you use these pronouns: *I, we, me, us, my, mine, our,* and *ours.* They are called **first-person pronouns.**

> *I* hated to leave, but *I* had to get *my* car home by 10:00.

When you write or speak directly to a person, you use these pronouns: *you, your,* and *yours.* They allow you to address directly the person you are writing or speaking to. These pronouns are **second-person pronouns.**

> *You* should bring *your* first draft to class on Thursday.

To write about people or things that do not include yourself or a person you are addressing, you use *he, she, it, they, him, her, them, his, hers, its, their,* and *theirs.* These are **third-person pronouns.**

> *She* told *him* to pick *her* up at 7:00.

Following is a chart of first, second, and third person pronouns.

FIRST-, SECOND-, AND THIRD-PERSON PRONOUNS

First-Person	Second-Person	Third-Person
I	you	he
we		she
me	your, yours	it
us		they
my, mine		him
our, ours		her
		them
		his
		her, hers
		its
		their, theirs

If you move inappropriately from one person to another person within a sentence or longer passage, you create a problem called **person shift**:

> *I* attend aerobics classes three times a week. The exercise helps *you* relax.
> (The shift is from the first person *I* to the second person *you*.)

Here is the example rewritten to eliminate the person shift:

> *I* attend aerobics classes three times a week. The exercise helps *me* relax.
> (Both *I* and *me* are first person pronouns.)

To avoid person shifts, remember that nouns are always third person, so pronouns that refer to nouns should also be third person.

person shift:	*Salesclerks* have a difficult job. *You* are on *your* feet all day dealing with the public. (The shift is from the third-person *salesclerks* to the second-person *you* and *your*.)
shift eliminated:	*Salesclerks* have a difficult job. *They* are on *their* feet all day dealing with the public. (The third-person pronouns *they* and *their* refer to the third person *salesclerks*.)

> **NOTE:**   The most frequent problems with person shift occur when writers shift from the first person or third person to the second person *you* as illustrated in the previous example. When using *you,* be sure that you are really addressing the reader and not shifting from a first- or third-person form.

Practice 22.16

Rewrite the sentences to eliminate troublesome person shifts.

Example

Chemistry was not as hard as I thought it would be. You just had to keep up with the reading and ask questions when you did not understand.

Chemistry was not as hard as I thought it would be. I just had to keep up with the

reading and ask questions when I did not understand.

1. It was a mistake for me to try to teach my son to drive because you lose patience quickly when working with your own children.

   _____ my _____

   _____ I _____

2. Learning to use a computer was time-consuming for me. You had to study the user's manual and practice often.

   _____

   _____

3. I realize too much sun is not good for your *my* skin, but every summer I neglect to use sunscreen.

   _____

   _____

4. Before high school seniors select a college, you *they* should visit several campuses and speak to the admissions counselors.

   _____

   _____

5. Many doctors believe women should take calcium supplements. Doing so can help you guard against osteoporosis.

   them _____

   _____

Practice 22.17

Cross out pronouns that create troublesome person shifts and write the correction above the line.

[1]Some people are saying that men are less willing to mentor women in the workplace because of charges of sexual harassment. [2]However, male employees can still coach and support women to help them advance their careers. [3]First, companies should have formal mentor programs. [4]You should assign experienced employees to show newer employees the ropes. [5]That way, no one will suspect that the mentoring is anything other than a professional work arrangement. [6]Second, employers should draw up rules for people in the mentoring program. [7]Then, you do not have to wonder if your behavior will be seen as inappropriate. [8]You just follow the rules for mentoring and you will know that your behavior is acceptable. [9]Finally, new employees should have more than one mentor when possible to avoid the suspicion that people are pairing up. [10]If these guidelines were introduced into the workplace, both employees and employers would be comfortable with mentoring. [11]You would not have to worry that charges of sexual harassment would be leveled.

Review Practice 22.18

Cross out the incorrect pronouns and write the correction above the line.

[1]The first tombstones were used by Bushmen whom believed that every dead body had evil spirits living in them. [2]A tribe would place a heavy stone on a grave because they believed it would prevent the spirit from rising. [3]Also, a tribe member would place the stone to mark the spot so you could avoid it.

[4]The ancient Greeks used gravestones, and they were usually heavily ornamented. [5]The early Hebrews marked its graves with stone pillars. [6]The Greeks and them were among the earliest users of gravestones. [7]The Egyptians took even greater measures than them. [8]They marked burial spots with tombs and pyramids. [9]Over the years, different people have used different things to mark its graves. [10]There are those who erect tall pillars of ornamental stone and those for whom a grave is marked with simple slabs of wood or stone.

[11]As Christianity spread, the marking of graves with crosses became common. [12]Decorating graves with flowers and wreaths is also common among Christians, but it goes back to the ancient Greeks, who used wreaths made of gold. [13]During

the early days of Christianity, they made wreaths of ribbon and paper and gave them to the church as a memento of the person whom died.

Tips

USING PRONOUNS CORRECTLY
- When editing, check every pronoun to be sure each has a clear antecedent.
- Memorize which indefinite pronouns are singular, which are plural, and which can be either singular or plural. Then you can more easily use pronouns to refer to these words.
- Remember that *I* and *we* refer to the writer, and *you* refers to the reader.
- If you compose at the computer, use your search function to locate *it* and *they*. Then you can check to be sure each of these words has a stated antecedent.
- **If English is not your first language,** remember that the indefinite pronouns *some* and *any* are used in a generic sense.

    Do you have *any* paper? (No specific paper is requested.)
    Do you have *my* paper? (Specific paper is requested.)
    I would enjoy *some* cake. (Any cake will do.)
    I would enjoy *your* cake. (A specific kind of cake would be enjoyed.)

It's okay

Post Test

A. Cross out each incorrect pronoun and write in the correction.

¹Most volunteer youth coaches find it a rewarding experience because ~~you~~ *They* can make an important contribution to the lives of young people. ²To make coaching a positive experience, coaches must remember several points. ³First, successful coaches' priorities should be having fun and learning; they should not emphasize winning above all. ⁴~~You~~ *They* should remember that the players are kids first and athletes second. ⁵Coaches should know the players and respect their limits. ⁶For example, ten-year-olds should not be asked to lift weights. ⁷This could harm young bodies. ⁸They say that successful coaches allow for a wide range of abilities and resist the temptation to field only the best players. ⁹Most important of all, however, is making sure that the kids feel they are a valued part of a team.

B. Cross out each incorrect pronoun and write the correct one above it.

¹A person who lives in constant fear of becoming a victim of crime can solve ~~their~~ *his/her* problem easily—by turning off ~~their~~ *his/her* television. ²Several years ago, a set of

studies was done. ³They showed that when people watch a great deal of television, they suffer an exaggerated sense of fear. ⁴Apparently, all the murder and mayhem on the small screen make frequent TV viewers feel at risk. ⁵Thus, someone who spends most of their time in front of the set will worry far more about being victimized by crime than someone who watches little or no television. ⁶Women and children may find his or her fears even greater. ⁷It is because women on television are most often shown as the victims of violent crime, and young children do not recognize the unrealistic nature of much programming. ⁸Thus, you feel more threatened than other viewers. ⁹Obviously, the studies show that parents of a young child should limit his or her child's viewing time.

LEARNING FROM TEXTBOOKS

The following excerpt comes from a college history textbook chapter on the Great Depression. Read the paragraph and answer the questions that follow.

¹In human terms, the Depression dealt a devastating blow to large numbers of Americans: crushing poverty, hunger, humiliation, and loss of dignity and self-worth. ²Many felt a profound shame that they could no longer earn a living and support their families. ³The few jobs available often went to the young, strong, well fed, and well groomed. ⁴In 1934, an Oklahoma woman poured out her heart in a letter to President Roosevelt: "The unemployed have been so long without food-clothes-shoes-medical care-dental care etc— we look pretty bad—so when we ask for a job we dont' get it. ⁵And we look and feel a little worse each day—when we ask for food they call us bums—it isent our fault . . . no we are not bums." ⁶Yet the shabby appearance of the jobless helped neither their self-respect nor their work prospects. ⁷In another letter to the president, an unemployed worker from Oregon explained the difficult choices: "We do not dare to use even a little soap when it will pay for an extra egg (or) a few more carrots for our children." ⁸These letters were among thousands of requests for help sent to FDR.

1. Direct quotations appear in sentences 4, 5, and 7. How do these sentences help the textbook authors achieve their writing purpose?

   _____

   _____

2. Name the indefinite pronoun antecedent in sentence 2. What pronouns refer to that antecedent? Are those pronouns singular or plural? Why?

   _____

   _____

(continued on next page)

LEARNING FROM TEXTBOOKS (continued)

3. Underline the pronouns in sentence 4 and label each one *S* if it is a subject pronoun, *O* if it is an object pronoun, and *P* if it is a possessive pronoun.

4. Underline the pronouns in sentence 5 and label each one *S* if it is a subject pronoun, *O* if it is an object pronoun, and *P* if it is a possessive pronoun.

5. Throughout the paragraph, the pronouns shift between first and third person. Are these shifts a problem? Explain.

_____

_____

Write about It

One of the facts the paragraph highlights is that how people look when they apply for jobs is important. Discuss another situation in which people are judged by their appearance and argue whether or not judging people by their appearance is fair in this situation.

SUCCEEDING IN COLLEGE

Know How to Write on a Deadline

In college and on the job, you will often need to produce a satisfactory piece of writing in a limited amount of time. When faced with a deadline, you may feel stress, and that stress can make it even harder for you to write well. The trick to meeting a deadline is to get organized and use the time you do have to best advantage.

Above all, do not panic and do not delay. Get going immediately by making a schedule. Work backwards from your deadline date. For example, if your deadline date is next Friday, schedule editing and proofreading on Thursday, revising on Wednesday, and so on. The closer your deadline is, the tighter your schedule will be and the more you will do in a single day.

Under the pressure of a deadline, you may be tempted to skip steps in the writing process, but that is a mistake. You will not be able to spend as much time generating ideas, drafting, rewriting, and editing, but you should work through each of these steps to whatever extent time allows. Furthermore, you should not abandon resources that have helped you in the past. If reliable readers help you evaluate your draft, use them in deadline situations—just give them less to do and less time to do it in.

Write about It

Discuss the role deadlines play in your life. You may consider the following questions if you like, or any others you think lend insight into how deadlines affect you:

• In general, are deadlines (not just for writing projects) present in your life very often?

• Are the deadlines for important projects?

• How do deadlines make you feel?

• How well do you perform when faced with a deadline?

For more practice with using pronouns, go to www.mywritinglab.com.

CHAPTER 23
Using Modifiers Correctly

adj ̆ adv
group of words

Modifiers are descriptive words that help you express yourself in a precise and interesting way. If you do not currently use modifiers well, this chapter will explain what you need to know. If you already use modifiers correctly, this chapter will reinforce your understanding and perhaps teach you some new points. Before getting under way, you should assess your current level of understanding by taking the following pretest.

Pretest

If the underlined modifier is used correctly, write *yes* on the blank. If the underlined modifier is not used correctly, write *no* on the blank. Do not guess; if you are unsure, do not write anything. You can check your answers in Appendix II.

1. _softly_ Whistling <u>soft</u>, Chuyen worked in the kitchen.

2. _C_ Professor Smith <u>quickly</u> explained the directions before he passed out the exam questions.

3. _badly_ The splinter in Fluffy's paw caused her to limp <u>bad</u>.

4. _C_ The <u>frustrated</u> toddler pounded her fists against the floor and screamed in rage.

5. _____ Les is <u>more happier</u> now that he has changed his major to physical therapy.

6. _____ Diana plays the cello <u>good</u>. *well*

7. _C_ Ivan felt his history midterm was the <u>easiest</u> test he had taken this semester.

8. _____ <u>Whistling as he walked down the street</u>, Tom's mood could not have been better.

(continued on next page)

9. _C_ <u>Wondering which route to take</u>, Katrina pulled to the side of the road and studied the map.

10. _____ The second day I had the flu, I felt <u>worser</u> *worse* than I did the day before.

ADJECTIVES AND ADVERBS

A word or word group that describes another word or word group is a **modifier.** In the following sentences, the modifiers are italicized. An arrow points to the word the modifier describes.

The *cloudy* sky threatened rain.

The pitcher threw a *sinker* ball.

The *marathon* runner was breathing *heavily*.

Modifiers that describe nouns and pronouns are **adjectives.** In the following sentences, the adjectives are italicized and an arrow is drawn from the adjective to the word it describes:

Janet spilled *hot* coffee.   (*Hot* describes the noun *coffee.*)

Michael is *shy.*   (*Shy* describes the noun *Michael.*)

She seems *angry.*   (*Angry* describes the pronoun *she.*)

Adverbs are modifiers that describe verbs, adjectives, or other adverbs. Adverbs often tell *how, when,* or *where.*

The lecturer spoke *briefly.* (*Briefly* describes the verb spoke; it tells *how* the lecturer spoke.)

The lecturer spoke *very* briefly. (*Very* describes the adverb *briefly* it tells *how* briefly.)

I just finished an *extremely* difficult job. (*Extremely* describes the adjective *difficult*; it tells *how* difficult.)

I just finished an extremely difficult job *yesterday.* (*Yesterday* describes the verb *finished*; it tells *when* the job was finished.)

The car stalled *there.* (*There* describes the verb *stalled*; it tells *where* the car stalled.)

Practice 23.1

Draw an arrow from each bracketed modifier to the word described. Above each bracketed modifier, write *adj* if the modifier is an adjective or *adv* if the modifier is an adverb.

Example

     adj   adj   adv

[Detroit native] Berry Gordy founded the [famous] Motown Records [in the 1960s].

1. [Initially], Gordy signed talent from the [African American] population of Detroit.

2. Gordy had an [infallible] instinct for making [black] music [widely] popular among both black and white listeners.

3. He exerted [firm] control over [all] recordings and produced a [stylistic] consistency that came to be known as Motown sound.

4. With its [increasing] popularity, Motown music [quickly] became [less] popular among black listeners, and Motown artists began to perform for [largely] [white] audiences.

5. African American audiences saw Motown music as a [heavily] diluted [pop] sound, and the black audience that [first] gave Motown music its recognition began to lose interest.

-ly Adverbs

Many adjectives can be made into adverbs by adding an *-ly* ending.

Adjective	Adverb
glad	gladly
painful	painfully
quick	quickly
loud	loudly

      The *painful* tooth kept me awake all night. (*Painful* is an adjective describing the noun *tooth*.)
      The dog limped *painfully* into the garage. (*Painfully* is an adverb describing the verb *limped*.)

NOTE: Be careful to use the adverb form when the modifier describes a verb, adjective, or adverb.

no: Marvin ran quick into the house.

yes: Marvin ran *quickly* into the house. (Use the adverb form because the modifier is describing a verb.)

Practice 23.2

Circle the correct form in each set of parentheses. Then draw an arrow to the word described.

Example

Archaeologists study the pyramids (frequent/**frequently**).

Egyptian tombs were not always as grand as the pyramids. The first Egyptians were buried (shallow/**shallowly**) under a pile of rocks in desert pits. The bodies were wrapped (tight/**tightly**) in goatskin or reed mats, and the desert's hot sand preserved them rather (adequate/**adequately**). Personal goods were placed (close/**closely**) around the body. Then around 3000 B.C., kings and officials began to build large, flat-topped tombs made of sunbaked mud and bricks, which provided protection against the (**harmful**/harmfully) effects of nature. Each of these tombs had a (**vast**/vastly) burial chamber and (**large**/largely) rooms filled with goods. Around 2700 B.C. came the invention of stone architecture and the first pyramid, called the Step Pyramid. The tomb of King Djoser lies buried under the structure. Like later pyramids, it had two purposes. It was both a royal tomb and a temple for worshipping the dead king. The pyramids of Egypt are a (**massive**/massively) reminder of the pharaohs' power and a creative ancient civilization.

before Christ

A.D.
vast = very large

Practice 23.3

On a separate sheet, use each adjective and adverb in its own sentence. Draw an arrow from the adjective or adverb to the word it describes.

1. easy
2. easily
3. comfortable
4. comfortably
5. fearful
6. fearfully

Good/Well

Good is an adjective, so it describes nouns and pronouns. *Well*—except when it means "healthy"—is an adverb, so it describes verbs, adjectives, and other adverbs.

It saddens me that Felipe is moving because he is a *good* friend. (*Good* is an adjective describing the noun *friend*.)

Two weeks after my surgery, I felt *well* again. (Here, *well* means "healthy" and is
   an adjective describing the pronoun *I*.)

For a beginner, you skate very *well*. (*Well* is an adverb describing the verb *skate*.)

FAQ
Q: What's the difference between "I feel well" and "I feel good"?

A: "I feel good" means "I am in a good mood." "I feel well" means "I feel healthy." Remember that *well* rhymes with the first syllable of *healthy*.

NOTE: Be careful not to use *good* as an adverb.

no: Maria did good on her test.

yes: Maria did well on her test. (*Well* is an adverb describing the
                        verb *did*.)

Good is also used as an adjective after verbs like *seem, feel, look,* and *taste* (verbs
related to the senses):

I feel good today. (Here, *good* suggests "in good spirits" and describes the
   pronoun *I*.)
The food tastes good. (*Good* describes the noun *food*; no action is being
   described.)
The cool breeze feels good. (Again, no action is described; *good* describes
   breeze.)

Practice 23.4

Fill in each blank with *good* or *well*, whichever is correct.

1. The children's production of *Hansel and Gretel* was _____ well _____ staged, and
   the sets were particularly _____ good _____.

2. The horse I bet on ran _____ well _____ until the home stretch, and then she did not
   do very _____ well _____.

3. Although I have been taking my allergy medicine, I still do not feel _____ well _____

4. Nao plays the clarinet _____ well _____ enough to have his first recital, even though
   he has had only a dozen lessons.

5. With her red hair, Marsha looks _____ good _____ in green.

Comparative and Superlative Forms

Adjectives and adverbs can be used to show how two or more things compare to
each other.

Katherine is *thinner* than Mario. (The adjective *thinner* compares how thin
   Katherine and Mario are.)

The audience is cheering *more loudly* now. (The adverb *more loudly* compares how loudly the audience is cheering now with how loudly it cheered at some point in the past.)

Lee is the *tallest* member of the basketball team. (The adjective *tallest* compares Lee's height with the height of the other team members.)

The **comparative** form of an adjective or adverb compares two things. The **superlative** form compares more than two things. The comparative form of adjectives and adverbs is usually made by adding *-er* or using the word *more* before the modifier. The superlative form is usually made by adding *-est* or using the word *most* before the modifier.

COMPARATIVE AND SUPERLATIVE FORMS

Modifier	Comparative	Superlative
loud	louder	loudest
heavy	heavier	heaviest
young	younger	youngest
annoyed	more annoyed	most annoyed
beautiful	more beautiful	most beautiful
intelligent	more intelligent	most intelligent

modifier:	Joy and Ned bought a *large* house. (no comparison here)
comparative:	Joy and Ned bought a *larger* house than Kay and Tom. (two houses are compared)
superlative:	Joy and Ned bought the *largest* of the three houses they looked at. (more than two houses are compared)
modifier:	Etty spoke *persuasively*. (no comparison here)
comparative:	Etty spoke *more persuasively* than Carl did. (two people are compared)
superlative:	Etty spoke the *most persuasively* of all the candidates. (more than two candidates are compared)

Keep the following guidelines in mind when you form the comparative and superlative forms of modifiers:

1. With one-syllable modifiers, use *-er* and *-est*.

sad	sadder	saddest
loud	louder	loudest
near	nearer	nearest

2. With three-syllable words, use *more* and *most*.

usual	more usual	most usual
rapidly	more rapidly	most rapidly
important	more important	most important

3. With adverbs of two or more syllables, use *more* and *most*.

quickly	more quickly	most quickly
clearly	more clearly	most clearly
freely	more freely	most freely

4. With two-syllable adjectives ending in *-y,* change the *y* to *i* and add *-er* and *-est*.

happy	happier	happiest
angry	angrier	angriest
easy	easier	easiest

5. With some two-syllable adjectives that do not end in *-y,* use *-er* and *-est,* and with some, use *more* and *most*.

foolish	more foolish	most foolish
careful	more careful	most careful
quiet	quieter	quietest

6. Never use an *-er* form with *more* or an *-est* form with *most*.

no: Maria is *more happier* now that she quit her job.

yes: Maria is *happier* now that she quit her job.

no: Lionel is the *most foolhardiest* child I know.

yes: Lionel is the *most foolhardy* child I know.

The following comparative and superlative forms are irregular. Memorize them or check this chart each time you use them.

IRREGULAR COMPARATIVE AND SUPERLATIVE FORMS

Modifier	Comparative	Superlative
good	better	best
well	better	best
bad	worse	worst
badly	worse	worst
many	more	most
much	more	most
some	more	most
little	less	least

The base form of a modifier appears in parentheses. Fill in the blank with the correct comparative or superlative form (whichever is called for).

Example

(expensive) The Toyota is ___more expensive___ than the comparably equipped Jetta.

1. (young) My sister is two years ___younger___ than I.
2. (loud) When I banged on the wall to request quiet, the person in the next apartment turned the radio up ___louder___.
3. (quickly) Of all the runners in the race, Dana is expected to run the ___quickliest___.
4. (talented) Of the two actors auditioning for the role, Stavros is the ___most talentest___.
5. (easy) John drew Henry a map showing an ___easier___ way to get to the lake than taking Route 11.
6. (bad) Christmas is the ___worst___ holiday for those who have no friends or family.

Practice 23.6

The base form of a modifier appears in parentheses. Fill in the blank with the correct comparative or superlative form.

Example

(good) I like studying in the library ___better___ than studying in my room.

1. (bad) Of all the movies playing in town this week, you selected the ___worst___ one to see.
2. (well) Since I began to exercise regularly, I feel ___better___ than I ever did before.
3. (some) ___More___ of us are going to our twenty-year reunion than went to the ten-year reunion.
4. (good) The score Jamie got on his third algebra quiz was the ___best___ one he has earned this term.
5. (bad) Lying to a friend is bad; refusing to admit the lie is ___worse___.
6. (good) John believes that the movie version of *The Da Vinci Code* is ___better___ than the book.

DANGLING MODIFIERS

A modifier without a logical sentence subject to describe is a **dangling modifier.** Dangling modifiers are a problem because they create silly or confusing sentences like this:

> *Standing at the street corner,* a car splashed mud all over my new coat.
> (*Standing at the street corner* has no logical sentence subject to describe. Therefore, it seems that the *car* was standing at the street corner.)

Because *standing at the street corner* has no sensible subject to describe, it is a dangling modifier. Here is another example:

> *Tired after a hard day of classes,* sleep was needed. (*Tired after a hard day* has no logical subject to describe, so it seems that *sleep* was tired.)

Dangling modifiers can be eliminated two ways. First, you can supply a logical sentence subject for the modifier to describe just after the modifier.

dangling modifier:	Feeling depressed, an evening with friends was needed. (Was the evening depressed?)
correction:	Feeling depressed, Colleen needed an evening with friends. (Now *feeling depressed* has a logical subject to describe—Colleen.)
dangling modifier:	Unsure of which choice to make, an academic advisor was needed. (Was the advisor unsure of which choice to make?)
correction:	Unsure of which choice to make, I needed an academic advisor. (Now *unsure of which choice to make* has a logical subject to describe—*I*.)

A second way to eliminate a dangling modifier is to change the modifier to a dependent clause. (Dependent clauses are discussed on page 212.)

dangling modifier:	Walking across the street, a truck turned the corner and narrowly missed me. (Was the truck walking across the street?)
correction:	While I was walking across the street, a truck turned the corner and narrowly missed me. (The opening modifier is rewritten as a dependent clause.)
dangling modifier:	When entering the bar, an ID must be shown. (Does the ID enter the bar?)
correction:	When a person enters the bar, an ID must be shown. (The opening modifier is rewritten as a dependent clause.)

Practice 23.7

On a separate sheet, rewrite each sentence to eliminate the dangling modifier.

Example

Wondering what to do, an idea struck me.

Wondering what to do, I was struck by an idea.

1. Exhilarated by the sunny day, a walk in the park sounded like a good idea.

2. Feeling the chill in the air, a roaring fire in the fireplace sounded perfect.

3. Before beginning to make the Mississippi mud cake, all the ingredients were assembled on the kitchen counter.

4. Frightened by the menacing dog, my knees began to shake.

5. Unsure of the best course of action, the decision was difficult.

6. Making no errors in the field and batting the best they have all season, the game was easily won by the Meadville Tigers.

MISPLACED MODIFIERS

A modifier placed too far away from the word it describes is a **misplaced modifier.** Misplaced modifiers are a problem because they create confusing or silly sentences. (As you will see in the first example below, prepositional phrases can be modifiers.)

misplaced modifier:	Andrea bought a silk dress at a thrift shop with a broken zipper. (Did the thrift shop have a broken zipper? It seems so because *with a broken zipper* is too far from *dress,* the word the modifier is meant to describe.)
misplaced modifier:	The litterbug threw a plastic wrapper out of the car window driving down Route 81. (Was the car window driving down Route 81? It seems so because *driving down Route 81* is too far from *litterbug,* the word the modifier is meant to describe.)

To eliminate a misplaced modifier, move the modifier as close as possible to the word it describes:

Andrea bought a silk dress with a broken zipper at a thrift shop. (*With a broken zipper* is now next to *dress,* the word the modifier describes.)

Driving down Route 81, the litterbug threw a plastic wrapper out of the car window. (*Driving down Route 81* is now next to *litterbug,* the word the modifier describes.)

Practice 23.8

Rewrite the sentences to eliminate the misplaced modifiers.

Example

Lydia said she wanted a hamburger on the phone.

On the phone, Lydia said she wanted a hamburger.

1. The children stuck in the hospital for Halloween got candy from the visiting clown that was chocolate.

   candiest

   Stuck in the hospital, the children got chocolate from the visiting clown.

2. Carlo asked Henry to help him fix his flat tire in the restaurant.

   At the restaurant, Carlo asked Henry to fix his flat tire.

3. At a garage sale, I bought a lovely end table for my apartment with drawers.

   At a garage sale, I bought a lovely end table with drawers for my apartment.

4. Gregory gave an electronic keyboard to his brother with a memory and playback functions.

> Gregory gave an electronic keyboard ~~to t~~ with a memory and playback function to his brother.

5. For the New Year's Eve celebration, Jorge borrowed noise makers from his roommate with colored streamers.

> For the New Year's eve celebration, Jorge borrowed noise makers with colored streamers from his roommate.

Review Practice 23.9

Eliminate the errors with modifiers by crossing out and writing above the line. You will have to draw on everything you learned in this chapter. The first one is done as an example.

[1]Sybil Bauer (1903–1927), one of the ~~most~~ best backstroke swimmers, won the Olympic gold medal and eleven national championships. [2]She probably would have won more championships if there had been more events when she was swimming competitive. [3]Going into the 1924 Olympics, world records for every backstroke distance were held by Bauer. [4]In fact, in an informal meet in 1922, she swam four seconds more fast than the men's record. [5]Unfortunately, that time was not recognized because the meet was not sanctioned. [6]In the 1924 Olympics, Bauer won the only backstroke event, the 100-meter, easy. [7]Her time was more than four seconds more fast than the silver medalist's. [8]Sadly, Bauer was stricken with cancer and died premature at twenty-four. [9]In six years of competitive swimming, she set twenty-four records. [10]Imagine what she could have accomplished had she lived even longer.

Tips

USING MODIFIERS CORRECTLY

■ Check your adjectives. If any of them describe an action (a verb) or a modifier (an adjective or adverb), make them into adverbs, often by adding -*ly*.
■ Check each time you use *more* or *most,* to be sure the word does not appear with a modifier ending in -*er* or -*est*.
■ Look hard at sentence openings. If they are modifiers, be sure they do not dangle.

(continued on next page)

Tips for Using Modifiers Correctly (continued)

■ If you are unsure of the correct comparative or superlative form, look up the base form in the dictionary. If something other than *-er* or *-est* is used, those forms will be given.

■ To be sure you have used *good* or *well* correctly, mentally draw an arrow from the word to what it describes.

■ **If English is not your first language,** remember to place adverbs in the following order:

1. adverbs of direction and place
2. adverbs of manner or means
3. adverbs of frequency
4. time expressions

> *place · means · frequency · time*
> The play will be performed <u>downtown by the local theater nightly for one weekend</u>.

■ Place adjectives in the following order:

1. adjectives of number
2. adjectives of judgment
3. adjectives of size or shape
4. adjectives of color

> *number judgment size color*
> <u>Two beautiful large brown</u> terriers are asleep on the lawn.

Post Test

Eliminate the errors with modifiers by crossing out and writing above the line.

[1]Johnny Heisman, for whom the Heisman Trophy is named, was one of football's inventivest coaches. [2]One of his most odd inventions was the hidden-ball trick. [3]Once a player asked him if it was illegal to hide a ball during a play in 1895. [4]Heisman knew it was not against the rules, and he wondered how it could be done. [5]Thinking the ball could be hidden under a running back's jersey, a play was devised by Heisman and two of his players. [6]As the ball was snapped to "Tick" Tichenor, the rest of the team would drop back and form a circle around him. [7]Then Tichenor would drop to one knee and slip the ball quick under his jersey. [8]The team would run to the right, and the defenders would follow them. [9]Then Tichenor would get up quick and run the other way. [10]Trying the trick against Vanderbilt, a touchdown was scored. [11]More tighter uniforms and more faster play have made the hidden-ball trick more hard to perform. [12]The bizarre play is rarely used today.

LEARNING FROM TEXTBOOKS

The following excerpt comes from a college business textbook. Read the paragraphs and answer the questions that follow.

Learning from Business Blunders

Oops: [1]On the surface, it looked like Hallmark Cards did everything you're supposed to do. [2]Its researchers, monitoring the demographic bulge of the baby boom generation, created the Time of Your Life product line to appeal specifically to people reaching the 50-year milestone in life. [3]Their careful customer research showed that while boomers might be aging, they don't want to think of themselves as old. [4]In response, the product line featured youthful, healthy images of people in the prime of life. [5]The products were displayed in a special Time of Your Life section in Hallmark stores. [6]Hallmark had succeeded with other product lines aimed at specific groups of customers, such as Mahogany (African-American themes) and Tree of Life (Jewish themes). [7]Time of Your Life sounded like another winner, but the product line was a flop.

What You Can Learn: [8]While the products themselves may have been right on the mark in terms of customer wants and needs, the final piece of the puzzle—the retail presentation—put people off. [9]Boomers who didn't want to think of themselves as old weren't about to shop in the "old people's" section of the card store. [10]Marketers need to consider the entire consumer experience; a mistake at any stage can doom the entire effort.

1. Identify each of the following as adjectives or adverbs in the passage and indicate the words they describe:

   a. sentence 2—demographic _____

   b. sentence 2—specifically _____

   c. sentence 3—careful _____

   d. sentence 4—youthful _____

   e. sentence 4—healthy _____

2. Prepositional phrases can be used as adjectives and adverbs. Identify each of the following as adjectives or adverbs in the passage and indicate the words they describe:

   a. sentence 1—On the surface _____

   b. sentence 2—in life _____

   c. sentence 6—with other product lines _____

   d. sentence 10—at any stage _____

3. Rewrite sentence 2, placing "monitoring the demographic bulge of the baby boom generation" first. Be careful to avoid writing a dangling modifier.

   _____

   _____

(continued on next page)

LEARNING FROM TEXTBOOKS (continued)

4. What adjectives and adverbs should Hallmark use to make people feel good about themselves at age 50?

_____

_____

Write about It

The textbook authors say that "a mistake at any stage can doom the entire effort." Narrate a time outside of the context of business when this point was true for you or someone else.

SUCCEEDING IN COLLEGE

Study Visual Aids

You may be tempted to skip over visual aids such as photographs, charts, graphs, and tables in your textbooks, but don't. By offering a visual depiction of important points, photographs, charts, graphs, and tables can help you understand and remember important information.

The following strategies can help you make the most of visual aids in your textbooks:

- Identify the main point the visual aid is making. Is a chart showing that more women than men have undiagnosed heart disease? Is a table of data showing you which states spend the most money on education? Is a photograph showing you the conditions in a nineteenth-century New York tenement apartment?

- Read the caption of the visual aid for the main point or explanatory information.

- Study the details by identifying the people, scenes, and moods in photographs; the headings on columns in charts and tables; and the labels for horizontal and vertical axes of graphs.

- Connect the information in the visual aid to the chapter. Does the visual aid illustrate a point made in the text, or does it introduce a new point?

Write about It

Find one photograph and one other visual aid in one or two of your textbooks. Using the above strategies, explain what can be learned from each of these visual aids.

For more practice with using modifiers, go to www.mywritinglab.com.

CHAPTER 24
Using Capital Letters and Punctuation Correctly

When used correctly, capital letters and punctuation marks help writers convey meaning. Therefore, the more you know about how to capitalize and punctuate, the better able you are to use these tools to help express your ideas. This chapter will help you learn what you need to know to capitalize and punctuate to the best advantage. First, to assess your current level of understanding, take the following pretest.

Pretest

A. If all the necessary capital letters appear, write *yes* on the blank; if one or more capitals are missing, write *no*. Do not guess; if you are unsure, do not write anything. Check your answers in Appendix II.

1. _N_ My dog, Laddie, ran away last week, but he was seen near lake jewel.

2. _N_ My favorite holiday is memorial day because it signals the start of summer.

3. _N_ This semester my favorite class is psychology, although I am also enjoying Western Civilization 303.

4. _Y_ Ever since I was a child, I have eaten Kellogg's Rice Krispies for breakfast along with Minute Maid orange juice.

5. _N_ Last summer, I was sure the Cleveland indians would be in the pennant race.

B. Add a period, question mark, or exclamation point, whichever is most appropriate. Check your answers in Appendix II.

6. My advisor asked me when I planned to graduate ?

7. The hysterical child screamed, "My dog has been hit by a car." (Put the punctuation inside the quotation mark.)

8. I wondered why Janie never introduced me to her family.

9. How many eggs do you add to the cake batter ?

10. Joey was voted the most valuable player in the game.

(continued on next page)

367

C. If the sentence is punctuated correctly with commas, write *yes* in the blank; if not, write *no*. Do not guess; if you are unsure, do not write anything. Check your answers in Appendix II.

11. _N_ After storming onto the floor and arguing with the referee Coach Bennett received a technical foul.

12. _N_ The withered, ivy plant could not be saved, so I tossed it in the trash.

13. _N_ I left for Nashville, Tennessee, on August 22, 1983.

14. _Y_ Uncertain yet eager, Josh began his first day as a camp counselor.

15. _N_ When we have children of our own we come to understand how our own parents worried, sacrificed, and planned to ensure our own futures.

16. _N_ Without telling the children where they were going, we picked them up at school, put them in the car, and headed for Virginia Beach Virginia.

17. _Y_ Rosa was well prepared for the test and feeling confident, so she was sure she did well.

18. _N_ Suddenly, and unexpectedly, the string snapped, and the kite drifted off.

19. _N_ George, in my opinion is trustworthy, and he is certainly a hard worker.

20. _N_ Because the spring was unusually dry the crop yield was low, and produce prices rose.

D. If the semicolon is used correctly, write *yes* in the blank; if it is not used correctly, write *no*. Do not guess; if you are unsure, do not write anything. Check your answers in Appendix II.

21. _Y_ I told you not to go; it's too bad you didn't listen to me.

22. _N_ People who do not vote; do not understand how a democracy functions.

23. _Y_ My mother was born in Alexandria, Virginia; my father was born in Denver, Colorado; my sister was born in Tucson, Arizona; and I was born in Detroit, Michigan.

24. _Y_ The wedding was a disaster; by the end of the evening, the bride and groom were not speaking to each other.

25. _N_ When the lifeguard put up the gale warning flags; everyone left the beach.

E. If the sentence is punctuated correctly with a colon, parentheses, or dash, write *yes* in the blank. If not, write *no*. If you are unsure, do not write anything. Check your answers in Appendix II.

26. _N_ We went to the restaurant at eight o'clock, but it was closed. (I'm not really sure why.) *take out dấu ngoặc*

27. _N_ The topic of my research paper is: why eating disorders are more common among females than males.

28. _Y_ Franklin Roosevelt said this: "The only thing we have to fear is fear itself."

29. _Y_ My earliest memory of my father—and it is indeed a pleasant one—is of him putting me on his shoulders and parading around the house.

30. __Y__ Drexel (what an unusual name) has a sister named Drexine (good grief!).

F. If the sentence is punctuated correctly with apostrophes, write *yes* in the blank; if not, write *no*. If you are unsure, do not write anything. Check your answers in Appendix II.

31. __No__ The hat I found belongs to one of the boy's.

32. __Y__ I can't understand why Carmen is so angry at Ralph.

33. __No__ Its' been quite some time since I've had a vacation.

34. __N__ In the '50s life was simpler.

35. __Y__ Both senators' bills died in committee.

36. __Y__ Someone's car is double-parked and sure to be ticketed.

37. __Y__ My boss's top priority right now is increasing efficiency in all departments.

38. __Y__ All of her *e*'s look like *i*'s to me.

CAPITAL LETTERS

Most often, capital letters are used to identify something specific. The capital letters in *Fifth Avenue* signal that Fifth Avenue is a *specific* street: the capital letters in *General Motors* signal that General Motors is a *specific* car manufacturer.

1. Capitalize the names of people and animals.

Lucy	Fido	Madonna
Douglas	Rover	George Bush

but

Do not capitalize words such as *man, boy, girl, woman, cat, rock star, collie,* and *child*.

> Mohan bought a sheepdog he named Hairy.

2. Capitalize the first word of a sentence.

> The door slammed shut on Henry's finger.

3. Capitalize the first word of a direct quotation.

> Doreen explained, "You must get an advisor's signature before you can register for this course."

but

> "You must get an advisor's signature," Doreen explained, "before you can register for this course." (Do not capitalize *before* because it does not begin a sentence that is a direct quotation.)

4. Always capitalize *I*.

> Curt and I felt I had a good chance of winning the competition.

5. Capitalize titles before people's names.

Mayor Morales	Judge Fulks	Senator Glenn
Reverend Jones	Rabbi Mendel	Captain McKenna
Professor O'Brien	Uncle Raymond	President Lincoln

but

Do not capitalize titles used without the names.

a mayor	the judge	a senator
a reverend	a rabbi	the captain
a professor	my uncle	a president

> The instructor, Professor Chang, introduced the guest lecturer, Councilman Luntz, who used to be a senator.

6. Capitalize months, days of the week, and holidays.

January	Tuesday	Easter

> The first Monday in September is Labor Day.

7. Capitalize specific geographic locations, including specific cities, states, countries, bodies of water, roads, and mountains.

Georgia	Columbus, Ohio	Lake Erie
Route 86	Stark County	Atlantic Ocean
Mt. Rushmore	Grand Canyon	France
Colorado River	Northwest Territory	Pike's Peak

but

Do not capitalize general geographic locations.

state	city	the country
a lake	the mountain	north of town
the ocean	a river	my county

> We left the city at ten and headed west. By late afternoon, we had arrived in St. Louis to see the Mississippi River.

8. Capitalize the names of nationalities, religions, languages, and the adjective forms of these words.

English	Judaism	Spanish
Catholic	Thai food	Chinese
African dance	French restaurant	Latin American music

> This town has excellent Japanese restaurants and art galleries with extensive European collections.

9. Capitalize names of organizations, companies, colleges, and buildings.

Fraternal Order of Police	General Foods
Democratic Party	Yale University
Empire State Building	American Cancer Society

but

organization	university
political party	building

> When I was in New York for the Modern Language Association conference, I stayed near the Empire State Building.

10. Capitalize historic events and documents.

Gettysburg Address	the Roaring Twenties
the Reformation	Battle of the Bulge
the Declaration of Independence	the Korean War
World War I	the Constitution

> The television show M*A*S*H was set during the Korean War, but it was first shown during the Vietnam War.

FAQ

Q: Can I omit capital letters in e-mail?

A: Informal e-mail between friends and family is often written without capital letters. However, follow the capitalization rules in more formal e-mail, such as that written for school or work.

11. Capitalize the names of sacred books and words referring to God. Also capitalize pronouns that refer to God.

the Lord	the Talmud	the Scriptures
the Trinity	the Koran	Jehovah
the Old Testament	the Torah	the Bible

> The man prayed to the Almighty for His help.

12. Capitalize the names of specific course titles, but not the general names of courses unless they are languages.

History 101	French	Survey of English Literature
Chemistry 709	Italian	Business Management

but

sociology	accounting	mathematics

> My geography course was not as difficult as I expected it to be, but Child Psychology 210 and German were very hard.

13. Capitalize the brand names of products but not the general names of product types.

Aim toothpaste	Jell-O	Tretorn sneakers
Marlboro	Toyota	London Fog raincoat

but

toothpaste	gelatin	tennis shoes
cigarettes	car	raincoat

At the grocery store, I remembered to get the Roman Meal bread, but I forgot the ice cream and Hershey's syrup.

14. Always capitalize the first and last word of a title. In between, capitalize everything except articles (*a, an,* and *the*), conjunctions (words like *and, but, or, for, so, if, as*), and prepositions (words like *of, at, in, near, by*). If the title has a colon, capitalize the first word after the colon.

Gone with the Wind	*Star Trek II: The Wrath of Khan*
"A Modest Proposal"	*Around the World in Eighty Days*
A Farewell to Arms	"Politics and the English Language"

In English class we read *Tender Is the Night*.

15. Capitalize words that show family relationships if names can be substituted for these words.

Ask Mother what she wants for her birthday. (We can say, *Ask Lucille what she wants for her birthday*.)

During World War II, Grandpa was a medic. (We can say, *During World War II, Charles was a medic*.)

but

Ask my mother what she wants for her birthday. (We do not say *Ask my Lucille what she wants for her birthday*.)

During World War II, my grandpa was a medic. (We do not say *During World War II, my Charles was a medic*.)

Practice 24.1

a. Fill in the blanks according to the directions given in parentheses.

Example

(Use a street.) For most of my life, I lived on <u>Elm Avenue.</u>

1. (Use the title of a movie; underline the title to indicate italics.) If you are interested in good entertainment, be sure to see <u>*Transformers*</u>

2. (Use the title of a book; underline the title.) In literature class, I read <u>*The boy named "It".*</u>

3. (Use the specific title of a course.) Besides composition, this term I am taking <u>*algebra*</u>

4. (Use the general name of a course other than a language.) So far in college, my
   favorite course has been _____ *Stitistics* _____

5. (Use a holiday.) The holiday that I enjoy the least is _____ *Christmas* _____

6. (Use a date.) My birthday is _____ *April 3rd,* _____

7. (Use the brand names of three specific products and use the general name
   of one other product.) At the grocery store, I spent $30.00 on
   _____ *Suave shampoo.* _____

8. (Use a specific geographic location.) This summer, I would very much like to see
   _____ *the Statue of Liberty.* _____

9. (Use a specific historic period or event.) In history, I enjoyed studying about
   _____ *The great depression.* _____

10. (Use a congressperson's title and last name.) When I learned that the legisla-
    ture was considering raising the speed limit, I wrote a letter of protest to
    _____ *Jan Schakowsky.* _____

11. (Use *mother* or *father* as a substitute for a name.) As I was growing up,
    _____ *my mother* _____ taught me to take responsibility for my actions.

12. (Use *mother* or *father*.) As I was growing up, my _____ *father* _____
    taught me to take responsibility for my actions.

b. Add necessary capital letters, and omit unnecessary ones.

1. Roberto Walker Clemente (1934–1972) was one of Major League Baseball's
   greatest players. In fact, he was the first latin American player to be admitted
   into the national baseball hall of fame. L

2. Born in Carolina, Puerto Rico, on august 18, 1934, Clemente was the youngest
   child of Melchor and Luis Clemente. Clemente's Father was a foreman for the
   local Sugar Company, while his Mother worked at the plantation house.

3. Clemente played baseball during High School, but he also pursued track and
   javelin. He was considered a potential olympic competitor in track and field.
   Local businessman Roberto Marin recruited Clemente to play for the brooklyn
   dodgers. Over the course of his career, Clemente accumulated 3,000 hits. His
   3,000th hit came on september 30, 1972.

4. About his career, Clemente said, "i am convinced that god wanted me to be a baseball player." In addition to his induction into the national baseball hall of fame,
   Clemente was inducted into the black athletes hall of fame, and he was pictured
   on a u.s. postage stamp. He was even asked to run for the Mayor of San Juan.

5. Clemente was also known for his acts of charity and for mentoring young
   hispanic ballplayers. In 1972, he decided to visit Managua, Nicaragua, to help

earthquake victims. Moments after his plane took off, it crashed and sank into the atlantic ocean, killing everyone on board. Thousands of memorial gifts were sent, generating enough money to build Ciudad Deportiva, where Puerto Rican boys could cultivate their athletic ability under the guidance of professional athletes.

END PUNCTUATION

The **period** (.), **question mark**(?), and **exclamation point**(!) signal the end of sentences.

The Period

Use a period (.) to end a sentence that makes a statement, makes a request, or issues an order.

a statement:	Because of the heavy rains, the lowlands are flooded.
a request:	Bring me the evening paper, please.
an order:	Leave me alone so I can study.

The Question Mark

Use a question mark (?) to end a sentence that asks a direct question.

Will you lend me your history notes?
Is this seat taken?
How can I help you if you refuse my advice?

However, use a period—not a question mark—to end a sentence with an indirect question. An **indirect question** is a statement, even though it notes that someone asked a question.

indirect question:	I wonder where I will be in ten years.
direct question:	Where will I be in ten years?
indirect question:	The waiter asked whether we wanted dessert.
direct question:	The waiter asked, "Do you want dessert?"
indirect question:	Kevin wanted to know whether he could go.
direct question:	May I go?

The Exclamation Point

Use an exclamation point (!) after a statement or command that shows strong feeling or surprise.

a command with strong feeling:	Get out of the car before the engine catches on fire!
a statement with strong feeling:	I will get even with you if it is the last thing I do!
a statement with surprise:	I couldn't believe I earned the highest grade ever scored on the exam!

NOTES: 1. Do not overuse exclamation points. If you must use them often, your words are not conveying the message.

2. Do not use an exclamation point with a period or question mark.

no:	Are you sure you want to go?!
yes:	Are you sure you want to go?
no:	I am amazed at her nerve.!
yes:	I am amazed at her nerve.
yes:	I am amazed at her nerve!

FAQ
Q: Can I use more than one exclamation point at the end of a sentence if I want to show very strong emotion?

A: Use only one exclamation point at the end of a sentence.

Practice 24.2

On a separate sheet, write sentences according to the directions given, ending each sentence with a period, question mark, or exclamation point as appropriate.

1. Write a sentence you might hear spoken on campus; be sure the sentence makes a statement.

2. Write a direct question you might ask a waiter in a restaurant.

3. Write a sentence that asks an indirect question. Begin the sentence with "Shelly asked whether."

4. Write a sentence that expresses great anger or fear.

5. Write a sentence that expresses a request a parent might make of a child.

6. Write a sentence that expresses a command a fire chief might give to firefighters; the command should express strong emotion.

COMMAS

Commas (,) are important because they separate sentence elements to make the reader's job easier.

Commas with Dates

With dates, use a comma to separate the day and the year.

I expect to graduate June 14, 2012.
On June 14, 2012, I will graduate.

NOTE: One form of writing dates does not use commas. Do not use commas if the day precedes the month and year.

I expect to graduate 14 June 2012.

If no day is given, there is no comma between the month and the year.

Julia began working for the United Parcel Service in January 2000.

Do not use a comma between the month and the day.

no: My birthday is May, 4, 1969.

yes: My birthday is May 4, 1969.

Commas with Places and Addresses

Use commas to separate the names of cities and states.

When they retired, my parents moved to Naples, Florida.

or

My parents moved to Naples, Florida, when they retired.

Place a comma between the street address and the city. There is no comma before the zip code.

Garth's Flower Shop is located at 311 West Palm Lane, Warren, Ohio 44484.

Practice 24.3

On a separate sheet, write sentences as directed.

1. Write a sentence that begins with "I live at." Include your complete street address, city, state, and zip code.

2. Write a sentence that gives the city and state of a place you want to visit. Begin the sentence with "I would like to visit."

3. Write a sentence that gives the month and year you began college. Begin the sentence with "I began college."

4. Write a sentence that gives your complete date of birth. Begin the sentence with "I was born."

Commas with Words, Phrases, and Clauses in a Series

A **series** is three or more words, phrases, or clauses. All but the last item in a series should be followed by a comma.

words in a series:	I realized I had forgotten my *shampoo, brush, and pajamas.*
phrases in series:	I have *lost weight, toned my muscles, and increased my flexibility.*
clauses in a series:	*You can take these books back to the library, you can pick up my dry cleaning, and you can wash the car.*

FAQ

Q: Can I place a comma wherever I pause or draw a breath in speech?

A: This method is an unreliable way to use commas. The only reliable method is to learn the rules.

> **NOTE:** When all the items in a series are separated by *and* or *or,* do not use commas.
>
> The dessert cart held fancy *pies and cakes and tortes.*
> Place the plant *in the kitchen window or on the television or coffee table.*

Practice 24.4

Use each series or pair in a sentence, being careful to use commas correctly.

Example

the spaghetti the veal and the broiled chicken

The waiter explained that the specials of the day were the spaghetti, the veal, and the

broiled chicken.

1. the hardback or the paperback

_____

_____

2. the noise the pollution and the crowds

_____

_____

3. a fever a sore throat a stuffy nose and body aches

_____

_____

4. the food was overpriced the service was slow and the seating was uncomfortable

_____

_____

5. a relaxing bath or an invigorating shower

_____

_____

6. swept the downstairs and washed the clothes and cleaned the garage

_____

_____

Commas with Coordination

Coordination means that two word groups that can stand alone as sentences (**independent clauses**) are joined by *and, but, or, for, so, nor,* or *yet* (**coordinating conjunctions**). Coordination is explained more fully on pages 213-214.

Place a comma before a coordinating conjunction that joins two independent clauses.

> Jillian gently picked up the baby chick, and she stroked it lovingly.
> I would ask you to join me, but you are busy.
> Our current basketball coach will probably be fired, for he has won only a fourth
>   of his games the past two years.
> The corporate offices of Raphael Industries will move to our town, so we can
>   expect a decrease in our unemployment rate.

> **NOTE:** Do not place a comma every time you use a coordinating conjunction. Many times these conjunctions do not connect independent clauses. When they do not, no comma is used.
>
> > The Corvette raced down the street and sped around the corner.
> > (No comma is used because *and* does not join two independent clauses, only two verb phrases.)

> **NOTE:** Remember that independent clauses cannot be joined by a comma alone—the comma must be used with the coordinating conjunction, or you will have a comma splice. (See page 252.)

Practice 24.5

Circle every coordinating conjunction. When the conjunction joins independent clauses, add a comma before it. The first one is done as an example.

¹You will never find the pot of gold at the end of the rainbow, (for) rainbows do not end. ²They are actually circles and the arc of color you see is just a small part of the rainbow. ³In order for a rainbow to form, sunshine and air loaded with water are needed. ⁴The sunlight looks white but white light really is made up of all colors. ⁵The water in the air bends the light and separates it into the colors so you see a rainbow. ⁶How much of the rainbow you see depends on where the sun is in the

sky. [7]When the sun is high, most of the rainbow is below the horizon yet when the sun is lower, more of the rainbow is visible. [8]When the sun is near the horizon, an observer on a high mountain or in an airplane may be lucky enough to see the whole rainbow circle. [9]Occasionally, the light of the moon forms a rainbow. [10]However, the moon's light is faint so the lunar rainbow's colors are faint and difficult to see.

Commas with Introductory Elements

An **introductory element** is a word, phrase, or clause that comes before the sentence subject. Follow an introductory element with a comma. In the following examples, the subjects are underlined as a study aid.

comma after introductory word:	Carefully, <u>the child</u> placed the precious china doll on the shelf.
	Whistling, <u>Kobina</u> sanded the cupboard doors.
comma after introductory phrase:	Playing both offense and defense, <u>Mario</u> was the most valuable member of the football team.
	In the middle of the night, <u>the smoke alarm</u> went off and roused all of us from our beds.
comma after introductory dependent clause:	When the steel mills closed, <u>over a thousand people</u> were out of work.
	If the union does not get a pay raise, <u>its members</u> will take a strike vote.

Practice 24.6

Add commas after introductory elements in the following paragraph and cross out any incorrect commas.

[1]In Babylon some 4,000 years ago the first paved roads appeared. [2]As people, began living in town and trading with their neighbors they needed better means of transport. [3]A cart could not cross wild country because it could break an axle or sink into mud or sand. [4]Thus paved roads were developed in response to a need. [5]Undoubtedly, the greatest road-builders were the ancient Romans. [6]Built by army engineers Roman roads were made of stones and gravel and ran straight from town to town. [7]The roads were sloped so that rain would drain away to the sides. [8]A marvel of engineering these roads were used by Roman armies to march across the empire and keep the peace.

Commas with Interrupters

An **interrupter** is a word or phrase that interrupts the flow of a sentence. Interrupters are not necessary for understanding the main idea. Some common interrupters are

I believe	by all means	to tell the truth
incidentally	by the way	I am sure
in fact	it seems to me	if you ask me
believe it or not	as a matter of fact	without a doubt

Interrupters are set off from the rest of the sentence with commas.

> The physical education requirement, *if you ask me,* should be abolished. (The interrupter comes in the middle of the sentence, so there is a comma before and after it.)
> *By the way,* Kwame has decided to run for a seat on the student council. (The interrupter comes at the beginning of the sentence, so a comma is placed *after* it.)
> Mayor Juarez has no choice but to lay off some city workers, *it seems to me.* (The interrupter comes at the end of the sentence, so a comma is placed *before* it.)

Transitions are often considered interrupters and are set off from the rest of the sentence with commas. (Transitions are explained on pages 56–57.)

> *As a result,* Donofrio won the election by a 50 percent margin. (The transtion comes at the beginning of the sentence, so a comma is placed *after* it.)
> Dr. Wright, *however,* disagrees with my view. (The transition comes in the middle of the sentence, so a comma is placed *before and after* it.)

Nonessential elements are also interrupters and set off from the rest of the sentence with commas. A **nonessential element** is a word, phrase, or clause that is not necessary for identifying the person, item, or place referred to. Here are examples of sentences with nonessential elements:

> Asa, *my oldest brother,* joined the Air Force. (*My oldest brother* is nonessential because it is not needed to identify who joined the Air Force; *Asa* does that.)
> The woman next door, *determined to strike out on her own,* quit her job and moved to Tennessee. (*Determined to strike out on her own* is nonessential because it is not needed to identify who quit her job and moved to Tennessee; *the woman next door* does that.)
> Xenia, Ohio, *which was once devastated by a tornado,* is now thriving. (*Which was once devastated by a tornado* is nonessential because it is not needed to identify what is now thriving; *Xenia, Ohio,* does that.)

The same word group can be nonessential in one sentence and essential in another. Here is an example:

> Alexis Ellington, *who won three major poetry contests,* will read some of her poems on campus this Friday night. (*Who won three major poetry contests* is nonessential for identifying who will read her poems, so commas are used.)
> A woman *who won three major poetry contests* will read some of her poems on campus this Friday night. (*Who won three major poetry contests* is now essential for identifying who will read her poems; therefore, no commas are used.)

Practice 24.7

Insert commas where they are needed to set off interrupters.

[1]According to psychologists drive reduction theory is a powerful motivational concept. [2]Clark Hull and Donald Hebb who formulated the theory state that certain drives motivate us to act. [3]We try for example to avoid or eliminate hunger, thirst, and sexual frustration. [4]In other words avoiding these unpleasant states compels us to behave in certain ways. [5]Obviously some drives are more powerful than others. [6]Thirst for instance is more powerful than hunger—and for a good reason. [7]Human beings can survive just a few days without water but over a month without food. [8]Thus natural selection the fundamental biological imperative ensured that our drive to quench thirst was more powerful than our drive to satisfy hunger. [9]For the most part drive reduction theory states that humans are motivated to maintain homeostasis which is equilibrium. [10]To maintain homeostasis, we eat when hungry, drink when thirsty, and try to avoid sexual frustration. [11]How motivated we are to act depends on the strength of our drives obviously.

Commas with Coordinate Modifiers

Use a comma to separate coordinate modifiers not already separated by *and*. **Coordinate modifiers** describe the same word equally.

> Be careful on the *wet, slippery* floor. (*Wet* and *slippery* are coordinate modifiers because they both describe *floor,* so a comma is placed between them.)

> Modifiers are coordinate if you can place *and* between them.

> Davey could not part with his *old, faded* shorts because he wore them in the state basketball championships. (You can say *old and faded shorts,* so the modifiers are coordinate, and a comma is used.)

> I asked the waiter for *fresh apple* pie for dessert. (You would not say *fresh and apple pie,* so the modifiers are not coordinate, and no comma is used.)

Another way to test if modifiers are coordinate is to reverse their order. If you can reverse their order, the modifiers are coordinate. In the preceding examples, *old, faded shorts* can be changed to *faded, old shorts,* so the modifiers are coordinate. However, *fresh apple pie* cannot be changed to *apple fresh pie,* so the modifiers are not coordinate.

NOTE:	Do not use a comma between coordinate modifiers separated by *and.*
no:	The speaker was given a warm, and enthusiastic welcome.
yes:	The speaker was given a warm and enthusiastic welcome.

Practice 24.8

On a separate sheet, use each pair of modifiers and the noun in a sentence of your own. If the modifiers are coordinate and *not* already separated by *and,* place a comma between them.

1. hot blinding sun

2. cut bleeding knee

3. elegant silk scarf

4. steaming chicken soup

5. sensitive and caring nurse

6. warm gentle breeze

Commas with Direct Address

In **direct address,** you use the name of the person or animal you are speaking to. Names used in direct address are set off with commas.

> *Marvin,* I need to borrow your class notes.
> If you ask me, *Harriet,* we should leave now.
> Stop rolling in the clean laundry, *you silly cat.*

Do not set off the name of a person or animal spoken *about;* set off only the names of persons or animals spoken *to.*

direct address:	Carla, let me use your car for an hour. (Carla is spoken *to.*)
no direct address:	Carla will let me use her car for an hour. (Carla is spoken *about.*)

Practice 24.9

On a separate sheet, write six sentences of your own. Two sentences should have direct address at the beginning, two should have direct address in the middle, and two should have direct address at the end.

Review Practice 24.10

Place commas where they are needed in the following paragraphs.

A.   [1]Language which is a set of symbols and sounds by which we communicate and think helps us form our identities. [2]In the thirteenth century Frederick II who was the Emperor of the Holy Roman Empire performed an experiment. [3]He wanted to discover the "natural language of man" so he took some newborn babies and did not allow anyone to speak to them. [4]The babies were well cared for in every other way. [5]The babies perhaps not surprisingly died. [6]Humans need to interact with others to survive and language helps accomplish the interaction. [7]Interestingly language is not solely a human trait. [8]Other animals use sounds gestures facial expressions and touch to communicate with each other. [9]Non-human language relates immediate important events in the present—nearby food sources or the presence of danger for example. [10]Human language on the other hand can be used to transmit culture.

B.   [1]Paul Revere was born on January 1 1735 in Boston Massachusetts. [2]He was the third child of a silversmith Apollos De Revoire. Apollos a French Huguenot had come to Boston as a boy. [3]When he was older he changed his name to the simpler Revere. [4]Young Paul became an excellent craftsman in fine metals. [5]In 1757 he married Sarah Orne. [6]When she died in 1773 Revere married Rachel Walker. [7]He had eight children by each wife but five of them died in infancy. [8]Revere was an early member of the Sons of Liberty and he was one of the leaders of the Boston Tea Party in 1773. [9]On the night of April 18–19 1775 Paul Revere rode to warn American patriots northwest of Boston that the British intended to raid Lexington and Concord. [10]As a result of Revere's warnings the Lexington Minutemen were ready for the British and for the important historic battle that launched the American Revolution. [11]During the war Revere engraved the printing plates for the first currency for Massachusetts set up a powder mill and served in the local militia. [12]In 1792 he opened a foundry to cast cannons and bells. [13]At sixty-five he learned how to roll sheet copper and became the first man in the United States to do this. [14]His copper sheets in fact were used on the famous ship *Old Ironsides*. [15]Revere died in Boston on May 10 1818.

SEMICOLONS

The **semicolon** (;) joins grammatically equal sentence elements. It most often joins independent clauses, but it can also be used to avoid confusion in certain series.

Semicolons to Join Independent Clauses

Semicolons can join **independent clauses** (word groups that can stand alone as sentences). For a discussion of independent clauses, see page 212.

> The table has been in my family for four generations; it was given to me by my mother.

The fund-raising drive was a success; we collected enough pledges to keep the soup kitchen open another year.

When you use a semicolon, be sure you have independent clauses on *both* sides. A semicolon cannot separate an independent clause from a word group that is not an independent clause.

no: Because Hank was having trouble with math; he decided to hire a tutor. (The word group before the semicolon is not an independent that can stand alone as a sentence.)

Semicolons can also be used with conjunctive adverbs to join independent clauses, as shown in the following chart. This rule is discussed in detail on pages 218–220.

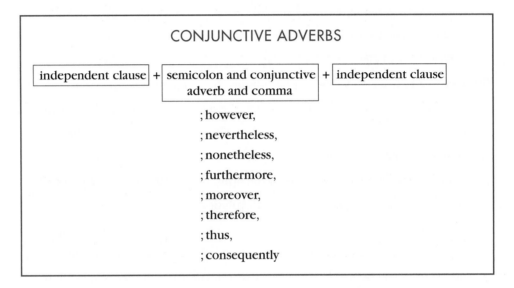

CONJUNCTIVE ADVERBS

independent clause + semicolon and conjunctive adverb and comma + independent clause

; however,
; nevertheless,
; nonetheless,
; furthermore,
; moreover,
; therefore,
; thus,
; consequently

Some people agreed with the speaker's remarks; however, most seemed to disagree.

State aid to public schools has been cut drastically; therefore, it will be necessary to pass a school levy.

Practice 24.11

Place semicolons where they are needed in the following sentences.

Example

The December snowfall set a record; however, it was never necessary to close the schools.

1. A person who runs for public office must endure considerable scrutiny every facet of a politician's life is subject to examination.

2. Louisa was finally realizing her dream she was about to open her own toy and hobby shop.

3. I took my complaint to three company officials nonetheless, no one was sure how to help me.

4. The driver failed to see the stop sign partially hidden by the bushes as a result, he narrowly missed hitting an oncoming van.

5. My son studied ecology in his fourth-grade science class he then convinced me to recycle aluminum and paper.

Semicolons with Items in a Series

A semicolon can join items in a series when the series already has commas in it.

> The menu featured omelets, pancakes, and sausage for breakfast; hero sandwiches, soup, and burgers for lunch; and pasta, steak, and fish for dinner.

Practice 24.12

Place semicolons where they are needed in the following sentences. In some cases, you will replace commas with semicolons.

Example

> The City Council voted to create tax incentives, which will attract new businesses; to build a new high school, which will alleviate crowding; and to increase pay for safety forces, which will attract more police officers.

1. The team's infield is strong: Jakes, a senior, plays first base Juarez, a sophomore, plays second base Wallace, a junior, plays third base and Sniderman, a freshman, plays shortstop.

2. Tony looked for his Christmas presents in the linen closet, where they were hidden last year, in the attic, where years of castoffs were stored and in the garage, where Dad has his workroom.

3. At the flea market, I bought an old chair, which should fit in my living room a weathered porch swing, which I plan to refinish and a broken record player, which I have no use for at all.

4. On the cruise, my parents met a couple from Juneau, Alaska, a woman from Nashville, Tennessee, and a family from Great Neck, New York.

5. The model home has a gourmet kitchen, which includes stainless steel appliances, an open floor plan, which was designed by a famous architect, and a large lot, which sits on a cul-de-sac.

Review Practice 24.13

In the following paragraph, add semicolons where they are needed and strike out semicolons that are incorrectly used.

¹Every summer I go to the beach, and usually there is some mishap. ²I have cut myself on shells, which is always a danger because I walk barefoot, received a severe sunburn, which made me very sick, and gotten sand in my eye, which caused a nasty abrasion on my cornea. ³Last summer for the first time, I was stung by a jellyfish. ⁴I was standing in shallow water; when I felt the painful sting. ⁵Fortunately, I had just read an article about how to deal with jellyfish stings; so I knew just what to do. ⁶Quickly, I scooped up some sand, then rubbed it on the sting under water. ⁷This helped wash away any remaining jellyfish nettles. ⁸Next, I went to my room and applied alcohol this neutralized the majority of the toxins. ⁹(I could have also used vinegar or meat tenderizer.) ¹⁰Finally, I washed the area with soap and fresh water. ¹¹In the case of a severe jellyfish sting, especially if there are allergic reactions, I would have consulted a physician or gone to an emergency ward; additional help may have been necessary. ¹²For the next twenty-four hours, I felt a bit nauseated, somewhat headachy, and a little feverish however, after that, I was fine.

COLONS, PARENTHESES, AND DASHES

The **colon** (:) introduces a long list, a quotation, or an explanation. **Parentheses** [( )] enclose material that is downplayed. The **dash** (—) signals a long pause for emphasis or dramatic effect.

The Colon

1. Use a colon to introduce a list.

   The doctor told me to avoid the following: salt, chocolate, caffeine, and artificial preservatives.
   I got a job for these reasons: bills, bills, and more bills.

2. Use a colon to introduce material that explains something in the main clause.

   The evening ended on a bad note: A prankster pulled the fire alarm, and the building had to be evacuated.

3. Use a colon to introduce an example of something in the independent clause.

   Jake has become a compulsive buyer: Just yesterday he spent a hundred dollars on a silk shirt and fifty dollars on a leather belt.

4. Use a colon to introduce a quotation.

   Herman Melville wrote one of the most famous opening sentences in literature: "Call me Ishmael."

NOTE: Do not use a colon after a linking verb (see pages 195–196), after a preposition (see pages 201–202), or between a verb and its object (see pages 340–341).

no:	Michael is: bright, motivated, and talented. (The colon appears after a linking verb.)
yes:	Michael is bright, motivated, and talented.
no:	I looked for my lost wallet in: the house, the car, and the office. (The colon appears after a preposition.)
yes:	I looked for my lost wallet in the house, the car, and the office.
no:	At the outlet mall, Karen bought: pottery, baskets, and shoes. (The colon comes between the verb and its object.)
yes:	At the outlet mall, Karen bought pottery, baskets, and shoes.

NOTE: As the previous examples show, if the colon is followed by an independent clause, capitalize the first word of the clause; otherwise, use lowercase.

Parentheses

Use parentheses [( )] to enclose material that you want to downplay or deemphasize. Often material in parentheses is a side comment.

> My physics teacher (Dr. Garner) has agreed to give me extra help before the final exam.
> Translators (the unsung heroes of the literary world) must preserve the meaning and intent of the original work.
> Before beginning assembly, check to be sure you have all the parts (twelve in all).

The Dash

Use a dash (—) to signal a long pause for emphasis or dramatic effect.

> My flight was canceled because of bad weather—what an annoyance that proved to be.
> Eight of us—all wearing heavy winter coats—squeezed into the car. Carla—an extremely talented violinist—is the youngest member of the symphony orchestra.

NOTE: If you want to downplay material, parentheses can sometimes be used in place of a colon. If you want to emphasize the material, dashes can sometimes be used.

colon:	Harvey cares about just one person: himself.
parentheses to downplay:	Harvey cares about just one person (himself).
dash to emphasize:	Harvey cares about just one person—himself.

Practice 24.14

Add colons, parentheses, and dashes to the following passage, and be prepared to explain your reason for each addition. (The passage can be punctuated correctly in several different ways.)

¹The elevator is the product of centuries of development, beginning with the ancient Greeks. ²The Greeks knew how to lift objects using pulleys grooved wheels that ropes can slide over and winches machines that have broad drums with ropes fastened to them. ³Turning the drum with a crank winds the rope up on the drum or lets it out; running the rope over a pulley allows a load to be raised or lowered.

⁴In the seventeenth century came the "flying chair," which was designed to carry people to the top floors of a building by means of a system of weights and pulleys. ⁵Because it operated outside the building, the flying chair never became popular a fact that does not surprise most people.

⁶During the last half of the nineteenth century, elevators were in existence, but they were mostly used for freight. ⁷Steam power was used to turn the hoisting drums of these elevators. ⁸People did not use these elevators much for one reason they were afraid the rope holding the elevator might snap, and the elevator would go crashing down. ⁹Then Elisha Otis invented a safety device that prevented this accident from happening, and elevators became popular. ¹⁰Also, at this time, hydraulic power fluid under pressure began to be used to raise and lower elevators. ¹¹Finally, the electric elevator, which is what is used today, was developed by the German engineer, Werner von Siemens.

APOSTROPHES

Apostrophes (') serve two main purposes: They signal ownership, and they signal that letters or numbers have been omitted in contractions and other forms.

Apostrophes for Possession

Possession means ownership. One way to show possession is with a phrase beginning with *of,* and the other way is with an apostrophe.

> The brightness *of the sun* makes it difficult to drive. (The brightness belongs to the sun.)
> The *sun's* brightness makes it difficult to drive. (The brightness belongs to the sun.)
> The office *of the vice president* is on the second floor. (The office belongs to the vice president.)

The *vice president's* office is on the second floor. (The office belongs to the vice president.)

The paw *of the dog* is badly cut. (The paw belongs to the dog.)

The *dog's* paw is badly cut. (The paw belongs to the dog.)

A number of rules govern how to use the apostrophe to show possession.

1. Add an apostrophe and an *s* to all singular nouns and to plural nouns that *do not* end in *s*.

Singular Noun or Plural Noun that Does Not End in *s*	Add '*s*	Possessive Form
Bill	Bill's	Bill's coat
car	car's	car's driveshaft
children	children's	children's toys
teacher	teacher's	teacher's desk
men	men's	men's clothing
Doris	Doris's	Doris's job

2. Add an apostrophe to plural nouns ending in *s*.

Plural Noun Ending in *s*	Add an Apostrophe	Possessive Form
brothers	brothers'	brothers' room
shoes	shoes'	shoes' laces
babies	babies'	babies' diapers

3. When a word is hyphenated, add the apostrophe after the last part of the word.

This is my mother-in-law's car.

All of my editor-in-chief's decisions were carefully made.

4. With two or more nouns, use the apostrophe after the last noun to show joint possession. Use the apostrophe after each noun to show individual possession.

Carol and Dan's son will go to Italy this summer as part of the Children's International Summer Village program. (The son belongs to both Carol and Dan; this is joint ownership.)

Carol's and Dan's businesses are enjoying excellent growth. (Carol and Dan each have a business; this is individual ownership.)

5. Use an apostrophe and *s* to make indefinite pronouns possessive. An **indefinite pronoun** refers to a group without specifying the particular members. (See pages 331–332.)

Someone's car is parked so near to mine that I cannot get in on the driver's side.

Everyone's responsibility is to help the poor.

6. Do not use apostrophes with possessive pronouns. These words already show ownership, so no apostrophe is needed.

POSSESSIVE PRONOUNS

Singular	**Plural**
my, mine	our, ours
your, yours	your, yours
his	their, theirs
her, hers	
its	

yes: The winning number is his.

no: The winning number is his'.

NOTE: *Its* is a possessive pronoun, so no apostrophe is needed to show ownership. *It's* is a contraction form of "it is" or "it has." There is no form *its'*.

possessive: The dog keeps licking *its* paw as if something is wrong.

contraction: *It's* difficult to give up sugar.

Practice 24.15

Fill in the blank with the correct possessive form; use the information in parentheses as a guide.

Example

(The dog belongs to Mona.) _____Mona's_____ dog will weigh over a hundred pounds when it is grown.

1. (The questions belong to the students.) The instructor was careful to answer all the

   _____ questions.

2. (The mattress belongs to the bed.) I have trouble sleeping in the dorm because my

   _____ mattress is too soft.

3. (The blades belong to the knives.) All of the steak _____ blades are too dull to cut easily.

4. (The paycheck belongs to Phyllis.) A mistake was made in _____ paycheck, and she was shorted $20.00.

5. (The laces belong to the shoes.) Both of the _____ laces broke when I tried to tie them.

6. (The ring belongs to my sister-in-law.) My _____ square-cut emerald ring is a family heirloom worth a great deal of money.

7. (The help belongs to everyone.) _____ help is needed if the fund-raiser is to be a success.

8. (Rhonda and Helen made different mistakes.) _____ and _____ mistakes are easy to correct.

9. (Rhonda and Helen have the same expectations.) _____ and _____ expectations are too high.

10. (The van belongs to Morris.) _____ van has 100,000 miles on it, but he has no plans to trade it in.

11. (The fillings belong to the teeth.) Most of my _____ fillings are loose.

12. (The natural resources belong to the country.) The _____ natural resources must be protected.

13. (The leg belongs to the table.) The _____ leg is marred because the cat uses it as a scratching post.

14. (The gloves belong to several boys.) The _____ gloves were left in a pile to dry by the radiator.

15. (The book belongs to the teacher) The _____ book was left on the desk.

Apostrophes for Contractions

A **contraction** is formed when two words are joined to make one. When the words are joined, at least one letter is omitted. An apostrophe stands for the missing letter or letters.

FAQ
Q: Some teachers don't like students to use contractions. Why?

A: Contractions are not suitable for formal academic writing. However, many teachers will allow them in writing that is not formal. Ask your teacher whether you can use them, if you are unsure.

COMMON CONTRACTIONS

Two Words	Contraction	Missing Letter(s)
are not	aren't	o
is not	isn't	o
does not	doesn't	o
have not	haven't	o
can not	can't	no
could not	couldn't	o
they will	they'll	wi
she will	she'll	wi
he will	he'll	wi
who is	who's	i
who has	who's	ha
will not	won't	irregular: ill/o
would not	wouldn't	o

(continued on next page)

we are	we're	a
they are	they're	a
she had	she'd	ha
he would	he'd	woul

Practice 24.16

Fill in the blank with the contraction form of the words in parentheses.

Example

(I am) _____I'm_____ changing my major to computer technology because the job opportunities are excellent in that field.

1. (we are) Although Higgins is a longshot candidate, _____ still planning to campaign for him.

2. (do not; you are) _____ look now, but the person _____ talking about just walked in the room.

3. (do not; I am) If I _____ get at least a *C* in my circuits class, _____ going to change my major to computer science.

4. (would not) Juanita turned down the job offer because she knew she _____ like the hours.

5. (he has; does not) Now that _____ had a year of physical therapy, Lee

   _____ have trouble with his back.

6. (It is) _____ possible to be happy living anywhere as long as you have good friends.

7. (she will) Pilar called to say _____ be an hour late.

8. (I will) _____ help you in any way I can as long as you cooperate with me.

9. (who is) Jamison is the attorney _____ likely to be appointed a municipal judge.

10. (Who has) _____ been borrowing my CDs without my permission?

Other Uses for the Apostrophe

1. The apostrophe can stand for missing numbers.

   I graduated with the class of '91. (The apostrophe stands for the missing *19.*)

2. The apostrophe can stand for missing letters in informal speech or dialect.

   Grandpa always said, "Feelin' sorry fer yerself is a waste of time."
   "Bring 'em wit' ya," Mike shouted.

3. The apostrophe is used with an *s* to form the plural of letters. No apostrophe is used to form the plural of numbers, words used as terms, symbols, and abbreviations.

Plural of letters:	How many *s*'s are in *embarrass*?
Plural of numbers:	Be more careful about how you make your *4s*.
Plural of words used as terms:	All your *theres* are used incorrectly.
Plural of symbols:	Write out the word *percent* instead of using *%s*.
Plural of abbreviations:	There are three M.D.*s* here tonight.

Practice 24.17

Place apostrophes where needed. Some sentences are correct.

1. In the 90s, a computer revolution occurred.

2. The second grader was having trouble learning how to make *rs*.

3. Gary announced, "The best things in life are eatin, sleepin, and partyin."

4. The English department hired three new Ph.D's to teach full time.

5. Marta was having trouble with her *thens* and *thans*.

Review Practice 24.18

Place apostrophes where they are needed in the following sentences. One sentence requires an apostrophe and an *s*.

1. The quarterbacks spectacular pass sparked the offenses scoring drive.

2. Once youve owned a car with a CD player, youll never buy a car without one again.

3. Chris short story was accepted for publication by one of this countrys leading magazines.

4. The Cs that Dana earned kept her off of the deans list.

5. Johns and Marthas problems arent going to be solved overnight; it will take years of counseling before theyre able to understand and alter their behavior.

6. Three companies employees were honored with Chamber of Commerce awards of excellence.

7. My sister-in-laws business, which she started in the late 70s, is now grossing over two hundred thousand dollars a year.

8. Angelo snapped, "Were comin; dont be so impatient."

9. The teams locker room was jammed with reporters, following the upset victory over the Division I champs.

10. The cab drivers strike is a problem for those visiting the city.

QUOTATION MARKS

Quotation marks (" ") most frequently signal that someone's spoken or written words are being reproduced. They also indicate titles of short published writings.

Quotation Marks with Exact Spoken or Written Words

When you reproduce the exact words someone spoke or wrote, enclose the words in quotation marks. A sentence with someone's exact words usually has two parts: a statement of who spoke or wrote the words and the words themselves. The sentence is punctuated according to where in the sentence the exact words appear, as the following examples show.

1. Exact words after the statement of who spoke or wrote the words:

   > Judy warned me, "Be sure to study hard for the chemistry exam because it's a real killer."
   > *A Tale of Two Cities* begins, "It was the best of times."
   > I asked Mario, "Will you join me for lunch tomorrow?"

   a. A comma separates the statement of who spoke from the exact words.

   b. The first word of the exact words is capitalized.

   c. The period or question mark appears inside the final quotation marks.

2. Exact words before the statement of who spoke or wrote the words:

   > "There is a reason for everything," Eleni always said.
   > "Take me to your leader," the alien ordered.
   > "Will I ever be promoted?" the weary office worker wondered.

   a. If the exact words do not ask a question, a comma appears before the final quotation marks.

   b. If the exact words ask a question, a question mark appears before the final quotation marks.

   c. The first word after the exact words is not capitalized unless it is a person's name.

3. Exact words before and after the statement of who spoke or wrote the words:

   > "Before we begin today's lecture," said Dr. Sanchez, "let's review yesterday's material."
   > "I think we can go now," I said. "The rain has stopped."
   > "Are you sure," I asked, "that we can come along?"

   a. A comma appears after the first group of exact words, inside the quotation marks.

   b. If the first group of exact words does not form a sentence, a comma appears after the statement of who spoke or wrote the words. The second group of exact words does not begin with a capital letter.

   c. If the first group of exact words forms a sentence, a period appears after the statement of who spoke or wrote the words. The second group of exact words begins with a capital letter.

   d. A period or question mark appears inside the final quotation marks.

4. A person's thoughts are punctuated like exact words:

> I asked myself, "How did I get into this mess?"
> "I know I can do it," I thought.

5. Before using quotation marks, be sure you really have someone's exact words.

use quotation marks:	Jane said, "I hate snow."
do not use quotation marks:	Jane said that she hates snow. (No one's exact words are repeated here.)
use quotation marks:	The lawyer said, "I will settle the case."
do not use quotation marks:	The lawyer said that he would settle the case. (No one's exact words are repeated here.)

Practice 24.19

On a separate sheet, write sentences according to the directions given.

1. Write a sentence that you recently heard spoken on campus. Place the exact words after the statement of who spoke.

2. Write a sentence you recently spoke to a friend. Place the exact words after the statement of who spoke.

3. Write a sentence that includes a question a teacher has asked you. Place the exact words before the statement of who spoke.

4. Write a sentence that includes words a waiter might say. Place the exact words before the statement of who spoke.

5. Write two sentences that you might speak to a classmate before an exam. Place the exact words before and after the statement of who spoke.

6. Write a sentence a grandparent might speak. Use the words "When I was young" to begin the exact words. Place the exact words before and after the statement of who spoke.

7. Write a sentence that includes a question you might ask your doctor. Place the exact words after the statement of who spoke.

8. Write a sentence that includes words you would think to yourself after waiting for fifteen minutes in a traffic jam.

Quotation Marks with Titles of Short Published Works

Quotation marks enclose the titles of short published works: the titles of magazine and newspaper articles, essays, short stories, short poems, songs, and book chapters.

Titles of longer works, such as books, magazines, newspapers, record albums, television shows, plays, and movies are underlined in handwriting but placed in italics (slanted type) in typed copy.

Use Quotation Marks	Italicize
"Araby" (a short story)	*Gone with the Wind* (a novel/film)
"That Lean and Hungry Look" (an essay)	*Arsenic and Old Lace* (a play)
"Art at Its Best" (newspaper article)	*Wall Street Journal* (a newspaper)
"Ode to the West Wind" (a short poem)	*Twentieth-Century American Poets* (a book)
"Root Beer Rag" (a song)	*Streetlife Serenade* (an album)

Practice 24.20

On a separate sheet, write two sentences. Each one should include the title of a magazine or newspaper article.

Review Practice 24.21

Add the missing punctuation and capitalization in the following paragraph.

[1]In 1791 the bill of rights was added to the u.s. constitution. [2]The bill of rights ensures americans liberties, including freedom of speech freedom of religion and protection against arbitrary searches and seizures of property. [3]Interestingly americans tend to believe in some of their rights more in theory than in practice. [4]For example americans say they believe in freedom of speech but they do not want to let the ku klux klan speak in their neighborhood or allow their public schools teachers to speak on issues such as these atheism homosexuality or abortion. [5]Most civil libertarians opinions are that few rights are absolute we must balance civil liberties and societys other values. [6]Another necessary balance is the balance between national government and state government. [7]The bill of rights which was written to restrict national government conflicted with states rights until the fourteenth amendment was ratified in 1868. [8]That amendment states the following No state shall make or enforce any law which shall abridge the privileges or immunities of citizens of the united states, nor shall any state deprive any person of life liberty or property without due process of law; nor deny to any person within its jurisdiction the equal protection of the laws.

Tips

USING CAPITALS AND PUNCTUATION CORRECTLY

- Use a dictionary to check capitalization and spelling of contractions.
- Identify the sentence subject and then look in front of it. Words before the subject are introductory and are followed by a comma.
- If you are unsure whether an element is an interrupter, read the sentence without it. If the remaining words still form a sentence, and important meaning is not lost, the element is likely an interrupter to be set off with commas.
- If you compose at the computer, use your search function to locate the coordinating conjunctions *and, but, or, nor, for, so, yet.* If there is an independent clause on *both* sides of the conjunction, use a comma before it. You can also search for each semicolon to check for independent clauses on both sides of the punctuation mark.
- **If English is not your first language,** be aware that English capitalization and punctuation are not the same as in many other languages. Ask a writing center tutor to work with you.

Post Test

Drawing on everything you have learned in this chapter, add the missing capitalization and punctuation in the following passage.

[1]Although she died in the early 60s, Marilyn Monroe continues to fascinate the american public. [2]The actress combined glamour with wholesomeness and sex appeal with innocence to create a legend summed up in a single word Marilyn. [3]As Carl Sandburg explained, she wasnt the usual movie idol.

[4]Born as Norma Jeane Mortenson on June 1 1926 in Los Angeles California the actress first called herself Norma Jeane Baker and then Marilyn Monroe. [5]Her film debut was in Scudda-Hoo! in 1948 and her career blossomed with small parts in all about eve in 1950 and the <u>asphalt jungle</u> in the same year. [6]Her gift for comedy became apparent in Gentlemen prefer blondes 1953 and How to Marry a millionaire 1953. [7]Part of her humor lay in the idea that her gorgeous blonde character didnt seem to understand why people thought she was beautiful or funny.

[8]Monroes life was scrutinized by the press her marriages to baseball great Joe DiMaggio and playwright Arthur Miller were widely publicized. [9]She was always troubled by her lack of privacy. [10]To convince the world that she was

more than a blonde bombshell Monroe took acting lessons and starred in complex films like Bus Stop 1956 and The Misfits 1961.

[11]Monroes career was cut short when she died in Los Angeles from an overdose of sleeping pills on August 5 1962. [12]However her sudden death seemed only to enhance the mystique of the actress.

LEARNING FROM TEXTBOOKS

The following excerpt comes from a college government textbook. Read the paragraphs and answer the questions that follow.

[1]When the Social Security program began in the 1930s, 65 was the retirement age. [2]Although this age was apparently chosen arbitrarily, it soon became the mandatory retirement age for many workers. [3]Although many workers might prefer to retire while they are still healthy and active enough to enjoy leisure, not everyone wants or can afford to do so. [4]Social Security is not—and was never meant to be—an adequate income, and not all workers have good pension plans or retirement savings plans.

[5]Although many elderly people wished to work, employers routinely refused to hire people over a certain age. [6]Graduate and professional schools often rejected applicants in their 30s on the grounds that their professions would get fewer years—and thus less return—out of them. [7]This policy had a severe impact on housewives and veterans who wanted to return to school.

[8]As early as 1967, Congress banned some kinds of age discrimination. [9]In 1975, civil rights law denied federal funds to any institution discriminating against people over the age of 40 because of their age. [10]Congress amended the Age Discrimination in Employment Act in 1978 to raise the general compulsory retirement age to 70. [11]Now compulsory retirement has been phased out altogether.

1. Why are commas used in the following sentences?

   a. sentence 1 _____

   b. sentence 4 _____

   c. sentence 8 _____

2. Why is there no comma in sentence 7 to set off the clause that begins with *who*?

   _____

   _____

(continued on next page)

LEARNING FROM TEXTBOOKS (continued)

3. Why are dashes used in sentences 4 and 6? How do those dashes help students understand the content of the passage?

_____

_____

4. In sentences 1 and 6, why are *1930s* and *30s* written, rather than *1930's* and *30's* (with apostrophes)?

_____

_____

5. Explain why the following are capitalized:

a. Social Security (sentence 1) _____

b. Congress (sentence 8) _____

c. Age Discrimination in Employment Act (sentence 10) _____

Write about It

As the textbook excerpt explains, there is currently no mandatory retirement age. Do you think that is a good idea? Or should people be required to retire at a particular age? Argue your assertion.

SUCCEEDING IN COLLEGE

Improve Your Concentration

To study successfully, you must be able to concentrate so you can comprehend material, analyze it, and recall it as necessary. If you need to improve your ability to concentrate, here are some simple steps to take.

- Eliminate distractions. You may think you can study with the television on or with your roommate practicing yoga postures in the same room, but visual and auditory distractions interfere with concentration. Take advantage of quiet hours in your residence hall, find a quiet place on campus to study, or rent a study carrel at the library.

- Respect your concentration span. If your mind regularly begins to wander after a half hour of reading, schedule five minute breaks every thirty minutes. If you get restless after an hour at your desk, take a short walk and come back to your work.

- Respect your personal rhythms. If you are more alert in the morning, study early. If you concentrate better before a meal, study then.

(continued on next page)

SUCCEEDING IN COLLEGE (continued)

- Build your concentration span gradually. Study for thirty minutes before taking a break, and add five minute blocks until you can concentrate for an hour.

- Create variety. Try studying two subjects, each for thirty minutes, rather than one subject for an hour. Do some work that requires writing, and follow it with work that requires reading.

- Take a meditation class. Meditating helps you learn to concentrate. You may find a meditation class on campus or at your local community center.

Write about It

Explain how well you currently concentrate, and describe your distractions. Is your ability to concentrate sufficient for your academic tasks this term? Why or why not? Alternatively, explain a process for improving a student's ability to concentrate on academic tasks.

For more practice with capitalization and punctuation, go to www.mywritinglab.com.

Eliminating Problems with Frequently Confused Words and Spelling

CHAPTER 25

Eliminating Problems with Frequently Confused Words and Spelling

Some English words are so similar that people mistake them for each other. However, these mistakes, along with spelling errors, can distract a reader, so this chapter is designed to help you avoid them. First, to help you assess your current level of understanding, take the following pretest.

Pretest

If the underlined word is correct, write *yes* on the blank; if it is not, write *no*. If you are unsure, leave the space blank. Check your answers in Appendix II.

1. ____N____ I bought <u>an</u> *a* historical novel to read on vacation.

2. ____N____ Emil would <u>of</u> *have* joined us, but he had to work.

3. ____Y____ There were six <u>misspelled</u> words in the paragraph.

4. ____Y____ Jane has lied so often that no one <u>believes</u> her any longer.

5. ____Y____ The <u>effect</u> of the tax increase will not be known right away.

6. ____Y/N____ The factory <u>use</u> to employ twice as many people as it does now.

7. ____Y____ The speeding truck <u>passed</u> me at over 80 miles an hour.

8. ____N____ We are <u>suppose</u> *ed* to have a midterm exam <u>on</u> Friday.

9. ____N____ The <u>less</u> *fewer* problems we have, the happier I am.

10. ____Y____ Of all the items on the menu, Jake can't decide <u>among</u> the salmon, prime rib, and chicken marsala.

FREQUENTLY CONFUSED WORDS

The words given here sometimes present problems for writers.

A/An

1. *A* is used before a consonant sound. (See pages 417–420 on vowels and consonants.)

> *a* tree, *a* friendly face, *a* unicycle (despite the opening vowel, this word begins with a consonant sound)

2. *An* is used before a vowel sound.

> *an* apple, *an* ice cream cone, *an* hour (despite the opening consonant, this word begins with a vowel *sound*)

Practice 25.1

FAQ

Q: Will my computer's grammar or spell checker find errors with frequently confused words?

A: Your spell checker will not distinguish between soundalikes such as *here* and *hear.* Your grammar checker may find some errors with frequently confused words, but you cannot rely on it to find all of them. You must, therefore, learn the frequently confused words.

1. Fill in the blanks with *a* or *an*.

a. _____*A*_____ friendly stranger gave us directions.

b. Ivan gave _____*an*_____ interesting interpretation of the short story.

c. _____ uncle of mine is _____*a*_____ sheriff in _____*a*_____ county west of here.

d. Laughter is _____ universal language.

e. _____ sink full of dirty dishes awaited me when I returned from _____ meeting of the Art Guild.

f. _____ unicorn is _____ mythical beast.

2. On a separate sheet, write two sentences using *a* and two using *an*.

Accept/Except

1. *Accept* means "to receive."

> I *accept* your offer of help with thanks.

2. *Except* means "leaving out" or "excluding."

> All the votes *except* those from Precinct Z have been counted.

TIP
Think of the *ex* in *except* and *excluding.*

Practice 25.2

1. Fill in the blanks with *accept* or *except*.

a. I cannot _____*accept*_____ your explanation.

b. It is not easy to _____ defeat with dignity.

c. Everyone _____*exc*_____ Joanie found the movie dull.

   d. No teacher will _____ a paper as sloppy as this.

   e. _____ for the first number, the concert was very good.

   f. The examination was easy _____ for the last essay question.

2. On a separate sheet, write two sentences using *accept* and two using *except*.

Advice/Advise

1. *Advice* is a noun meaning a suggestion or opinion.

   > In her column, Ann Landers gave *advice*.

2. *Advise* is a verb meaning to give advice.

   > The doctor *advised* Harriet to quit smoking.

TIP
Remember, if you have a vice, you need *advice*.

Practice 25.3

1. Fill in the blanks with *advice* or *advise*.

   a. You should follow my ___advice___ and go back to school.

   b. Why should I ___advise___ you if you won't do as I say?

   c. If you reject my ___advice___ I will offer no more help.

   d. Anton's _____ is always sound because he thinks problems through so carefully.

   e. I cannot _____ you without more information.

   f. No one can _____ you on matters of the heart.

2. On a separate sheet, write two sentences with *advice* and two with *advise*.

Affect/Effect

1. *Affect* is a verb meaning "to influence."

   > The steelworkers' strike has begun to *affect* the local economy.

2. *Effect* is usually a noun meaning "result."

   > The *effects* of the plant layoffs will be serious.

3. *Effect* is sometimes a verb meaning "to bring about."

   > Councilman Page will try to *effect* a change in the city charter.

Practice 25.4

1. Fill in the blanks with *affect* or *effect*.

   a. The _____ of the drought will be felt in the marketplace early this fall.

b. I hope my decision to resign from the committee will not have a negative

_____ on the committee's work.

c. The store owners petitioned the mall management to _____ a change in Christmas shopping hours.

d. What people eat for breakfast can _____ how they perform all morning.

e. An __effect__ of an oil shortage is higher gasoline prices.

f. Childhood traumas _____ us as adults.

2. On a separate sheet, write two sentences using *affect* as a verb, two using *effect* as a noun, and two using *effect* as a verb.

All Ready/Already

1. *All ready* means "all set," or "prepared."

    The crew was *all ready* to set sail.

2. *Already* means "by this time."

    Do not apply for the job because the position has *already* been filled.

TIP

The expressions *all ready* and *all set* both have two words.

Practice 25.5

1. Fill in the blanks with *all ready* or *already*.

    a. The party was _____ over, and the guest of honor had not arrived.

    b. I just cleaned this closet, and _____ it is cluttered.

    c. The water skier waved his hand to the driver to signal he was _____.

    d. Harry and Pilar were _____ to go, but I still had to make a phone call.

    e. _____ Hank is whining, and we just got here.

    f. As soon as Lateefa completes her last economics course, she will be

    _____ to graduate.

2. On a separate sheet, write two sentences using *all ready* and two using *already*.

All Right/Alright

In formal usage, *all right* is considered the acceptable form. Avoid *alright* in college papers.

Among/Between

1. Use *between* for two people or things.

    There are many differences *between* working in a fast-food restaurant and working in a fancy restaurant.

2. Use *among* for more than two people or things.

> The argument *among* the students lasted most of the class period.

Practice 25.6

1. Fill in the blanks with *among* or *between*.

   a. _____ the students in the class, only Mario earned an A on the final exam.

   b. It is difficult for me to choose _____ teaching and research for my career.

   c. The competition _____ the three teams is friendly.

   d. My antique necklace is _____ my most prized possessions.

   e. Ten-year-old Anna could not decide _____ the red bicycle and the green one.

   f. Just _____ you and me, I do not trust Lee.

2. On a separate sheet, write two sentences using *among* and two using *between*.

Been/Being

1. *Been* is the past participle of *be*. It is usually used after *have, has,* or *had*.

   > It has *been* years since I have seen Joel.

2. *Being* is the *-ing* (present participle) form of *be*. It is usually used after *am, is, are, was,* or *were*.

   > Wanda is *being* careless when she leaves her purse there.

NOTE: Do not use *been* without *have, has,* or *had*.

no: I been working hard.

yes: I have been working hard.

Practice 25.7

1. Fill in the blanks with *being* or *been*.

   a. Although I have _____ absent, I studied the assignments.

   b. The child does not understand that she is _____ rude.

   c. The Chens had _____ gone a week before they remembered they forgot to stop their mail.

   d. I am _____ inducted into the honor society tonight.

e. Ned has _____ more than patient.

f. Six families are _____ relocated to make way for the new road.

2. On a separate sheet, write two sentences with *been* and two with *being*.

Beside/Besides

1. *Beside* means "alongside of."

> Park the car *beside* the garage.

2. *Besides* means "in addition to."

> *Besides* being too small, the house was poorly located.

Practice 25.8

1. Fill in the blanks with *beside* or *besides*.

a. _____ the coffee cup was a stale donut.

b. _____ the creek, the collie lay sleeping peacefully.

c. Mother hid the children's Christmas presents in the chest _____ the bed.

d. Few people _____ you and me realize that Randy is insecure.

e. _____ having a headache, I feel sick to my stomach.

f. What is the restaurant's specialty, _____ pasta?

2. On a separate sheet, write two sentences using *beside* and two using *besides*.

Can/Could

1. *Can* is used for the present tense to mean "am/is/are able to."

> If I get an income tax refund, I *can* buy a stereo.

2. *Could* is used for the past tense to mean "was/were able to."

> I thought I *could* finish by noon, but I was wrong.

Practice 25.9

1. Fill in the blanks with *can* or *could*. To determine if you need present or past tense, check the tense of the other verb in the sentence, or look for clues such as *yesterday* or *now*.

a. Before I _____ walk, I was reading.

b. When I was sixteen, I _____ stay up all night and feel great the next

day; now I _____ sleep for eight hours and still be tired.

c. The photographer was certain he _____ restore the old family picture
I found in Grandma's steamer trunk.

d. I _____ never be sure if Sam is telling the truth or lying.

e. Jenny is sure she _____ help us draft a newsletter.

f. Last year I _____ not afford a vacation, but this year I

_____ manage a week at the ocean.

2. On a separate sheet, write two sentences using *can* and two using *could*.

Fewer/Less

1. Use *fewer* for items that can be counted.

The number of students who passed the midterm was *fewer* than usual.

2. Use *less* for something considered as a unit, and for something that cannot be counted.

There is *less* concern for the homeless than there should be.

Practice 25.10

1. Fill in the blanks with *fewer* or *less.*

a. The older I get, the ___*less*___ I worry about minor matters.

b. If you take vitamin C, you may get ___*fewer*___ colds.

c. _____ accidents occurred on Fifth Avenue this year than last year.

d. The movie had _____ violent scenes than I expected.

e. If more people would exercise, there would be _____ depression in
the world.

f. With _____ sex discrimination in the workplace, more women are
executives.

2. On a separate sheet, write two sentences using *fewer* and two using *less.*

Good/Well

1. *Good* is an adjective, so it only describes nouns and pronouns.

Lester is a good drummer. (*Good* describes the noun *drummer.*)

2. *Good* is used as an adjective after sensory verbs such as *seem, feel, look,* and *taste.*

The steaming soup tasted *good.* (*Good* describes the noun *soup.*)

3. *Well* is an adverb, so it describes verbs.

> Bonnie sings *well*. (*Well* describes the verb *sings*.)

4. *Well* also refers to health.

> Tanya does not feel *well* enough to join us.

See also pages 356–357.

Practice 25.11

1. Fill in the blanks with *good* or *well.*

   a. This is a ___good___ time to plant a garden.

   b. I hope I do as ___well___ as you did in the time trials.

   c. I did not do very ___well___ on my chemistry exam because I did not understand covalent bonding ___good___ enough.

   d. The movie was not as _____ as I expected it to be.

   e. Isabella played a _____ tennis match today; I wish I had played as _____.

   f. The _____ behavior of the children earned them a treat.

   g. After eating five cookies, I do not feel _____.

   h. The warm sun feels _____ on my face.

2. On a separate sheet, write two sentences with *good* and two with *well.*

It's/Its

Tip
Do not use *it's* unless you can substitute *it is* or *it has.*

1. *It's* is the contraction form and means "it is" or "it has."

   > *It's* time to head for home.
   > *It's* been a pleasure serving you.

2. *Its* is the possessive form, so it shows ownership.

   > The rubber tree plant is dropping *its* leaves.

Practice 25.12

1. Fill in the blanks with *it's* or *its.*

   a. _____ a sure bet that the store will close if _____ merchandising policies don't improve.

   b. The head librarian announced that the library has increased _____ holdings by 30 percent.

   c. _____ hard to believe, but _____ been three years since we met.

   d. If ___*its*___ work you want, you have come to the right place.

   e. _____ a shame, but Cinema Sixty has changed _____ policy of showing only first-run features.

   f. The company decided to reduce ___*its*___ costs by switching from television to direct-mail advertising.

2. On a separate sheet, write two sentences using *it's* and two using *its*.

                                                                                                                                                   ▬

Of/Have

Do not substitute *of* for *have. Have* is a helping verb (see page 196), and *of* is a preposition (see pages 201–202).

Incorrect	Correct
could of	could have
will of	will have
would of	would have
should of	should have
may of	may have
must of	must have
might of	might have

Passed/Past

1. *Past* refers to a previous time. It can also mean "by."

     It is not possible to change the *past*.

     Past experiences affect us in the present.

     I drove *past* your house yesterday.

2. *Passed* is the past tense of the verb *to pass,* and means "went by" or "handed."

     As Rico *passed* Cathy's desk, he gave her a rose.

     The teacher *passed* the specimen around so all could see it.

TIP
Think of the letters *p* and *t,* as in *past* and *previous time.*

Practice 25.13

1. Fill in the blanks with *past* or *passed.*

   a. When the police officer ___*passed*___ the warehouse, she saw the flames.

   b. The ___*past*___ too often intrudes on the present.

   c. As the marching band ___*passed*___ the reviewing stand, thunderous applause erupted.

d. We should forgive Kurt for his _past_ mistakes.

e. The relay runner ___passed___ the baton to his teammate, who quickly ___passed___ the runner in first place.

f. In times ___past___ it was safe to walk at night.

2. On a separate sheet, write two sentences with *past* and two with *passed*.

Quiet/Quit/Quite

1. *Quiet* means "silence/silent" or "calm."

   Some people can work with a radio on, but I need *quiet*.

2. *Quit* means "stop" or "give up."

   Even if I wanted to *quit* school, my parents would not let me.

3. *Quite* means "very" or "exactly."

   I am *quite* sure no one lives here.

   That is not *quite* the point I am making.

Practice 25.14

1. Fill in the blanks with *quiet, quit,* or *quite*.

   a. If you are ___quite___ certain you can remain ___quiet___ for an hour, I can get my work done.

   b. If you do not ___quit___ smoking soon, you will ___quite___ likely have health problems.

   c. The ___quiet___ in this room is almost eerie.

   d. Martha returned the paint because it was not _____ the color she wanted.

   e. If you are not ___quiet___ certain that you can finish this project, you should probably ___quit___.

   f. Alonzo ___quit___ his fraternity because the parties were too _____.

2. On a separate sheet, write two sentences using *quiet,* two using *quit,* and two using *quite*.

Suppose/Supposed

1. *Suppose* means "assume" or "guess."

   I *suppose* I can be done by six if I hurry.

2. *Supposed* is the past tense form of *suppose*.

   The mayor *supposed* he would win the election by a large margin.

3. *Supposed* means "ought" or "should." In this case, it is preceded by a form of *be* and is always followed by *to*.

   We are *supposed* to clear the cafeteria tables when we are finished eating.

TIP

Always use *supposed* (with the *-ed*) to mean "ought" or "should." *I am suppose to go* is an incorrect form written when the *t* in *to* is allowed to function as the *d* in *supposed*.

Practice 25.15

1. Fill in the blanks with *suppose* or *supposed*.

   a. Franz is _____*supposed*_____ to drive everyone to the party, but where do you _____*suppose*_____ he will get a car?

   b. We all _____*suppose*_____ Matthew would go on to graduate school.   *supposed*

   c. What do you _____*suppose*_____ will happen if the research council does not get   *suppose* the grant it is _____*supposed*_____ to?

   d. Cathy was _____*supposed*_____ to meet me here an hour ago.

   e. Lorenzo is _____*supposed*_____ to bring the chips to the party, but I _____*supposed*_____ he will forget.

   f. Do you _____*suppose*_____ it is possible to finish the cleaning before our guests arrive?

2. On a separate sheet, write two sentences using *suppose* and two using *supposed*.

Then/Than

1. *Then* refers to a certain time.

   I asked Sylvia what she meant; *then* she yelled at me.

2. *Than* is used to compare.

   The chicken is tastier *than* the veal.

TIP

Remember, *then* and *time* have an *e*; *than* and *compare* have an *a*.

Practice 25.16

1. Fill in the blanks with *then* or *than*.

   a. My new apartment is less noisy _____*than*_____ my previous one.

   b. If you arrive _____*then*_____, you will be able to meet my sister.

   c. _____*Then*_____ she said that she would rather arrive late *than* not at all.

    d. You asked for my advice and ___*then*___ refused to take it.

    e. Diana would rather quit school ___*then*___ sell her stamp collection for tuition money.

    f. Getting a campus job is easier ___*then*___ people realize.

2. On a separate sheet, write two sentences using *then* and two using *than*.

There/Their/They're

1. *There* shows direction. It can also come before *are, was, were, is,* or *will be*.

> Put the boxes down over *there*.
>
> *There* are twelve of us helping out at the senior citizens' center.

2. *Their* is a possessive form; it shows ownership.

> The students opened *their* test booklets and began to work.

3. *They're* is the contraction form of *they are*.

> If *they're* leaving now, I should go with them.

Practice 25.17

1. Fill in the blanks with *there, their,* or *they're*.

    a. According to the evening paper ___*there*___ will be a wheat shortage next year.

    b. Henri and Tom said ___*They're*___ not going unless they can bring ___*their*___ video games with them.

    c. If you put the couch over ___*there*___, then ___*there*___ will be enough room for ___*their*___ record collection.

    d. The police officers are concerned because the referendum that would grant ___*their*___ pay raises may not get on the November ballot.

    e. ___*They're*___ asking five hundred dollars for ___*their*___ used piano.

    f. I looked ___*there*___ but I couldn't find ___*their*___ coats.

2. On a separate sheet, write two sentences using *there,* two using *their,* and two using *they're*.

Through/Though/Threw

1. *Through* means "in one side and out the other." It also means "finished."

> It was hard for Grandma to pass the thread *through* the needle.
>
> I will be *through* proofreading my essay in an hour.

2. *Though* means "although"; *as though* means "as if."

> *Though* Alan has never taken lessons, he plays the piano well.
>
> Maria acts *as though* she is mad at the world.

3. *Threw* is the past tense of *throw.*

> The quarterback *threw* an incomplete pass.

Practice 25.18

1. Fill in the blanks with *through, though,* or *threw*.

   a. When she was ___*threw*___ studying, Eleni rested for an hour.

   b. ___*though*___ Hank pretends he does not care, anyone can see ___*through*___ his act.

   c. Cal won a stuffed rabbit when he ___*threw*___ the baseball at the milk bottles on the midway.

   d. ___*though*___ Toni made a basket, the shot did not count because he ___*threw*___ the ball after the buzzer.

   e. Diane strolled ___*through*___ the park as ___*though*___ she did not have any worries.

   f. If we elect Smith, we will have a better chance to work ___*through*___ the police labor dispute.

2. On a separate sheet, write two sentences using *through,* and two using *though,* and two using *threw.*

To/Too/Two

1. *To* means "toward." It can also be part of a verb, as in *to run.*

   > I was going *to* class when I saw Rhonda.
   >
   > I wanted *to* ask you a favor.

2. *Too* means "excessively" or "also."

   > The movie was *too* violent for me.
   >
   > I would like a piece of that cake *too.*

3. *Two* is the number.

   > Only *two* candidates for the school board have experience.

Practice 25.19

1. Fill in the blanks with *to, too,* or *two*.

   a. Before beginning ___*to*___ exercise, stretch for ten minutes.

b. ___*too*___ much smoking and ___*too*___ little exercise make Dan a prime candidate ___*too*___ get a heart attack.

c. The car needed ___*two*___ new tires and a water pump ___*too*___.

d. ___*to*___ tell you the truth, I was not ___*too*___ pleased ___*to*___ be headed ___*to*___ the mall ___*two*___ days before Christmas.

e. The highlight of the trip was going ___*to*___ Disney World for ___*to*___ days.

f. A week is ___*to*___ long for me _____ be gone.

2. On a separate sheet, write two sentences using *to,* two using *too,* and two using *two.*

Use/Used

1. *Use* is a noun that means "purpose." It is also a verb that means "make use of."

> What possible *use* could this have?
>
> How do you *use* this gadget?

2. *Used* is the past tense and past participle form of the verb *to use.* It also means "adjusted" or "accustomed"; in this case, it is followed by *to.*

> The child *used* the towel and threw it on the floor.
>
> I have *used* this product successfully before.
>
> I am not *used* to this kind of treatment.

Practice 25.20

1. Fill in the blanks with *use* or *used.*

a. I am not ___*used*___ to the idea that I am now an adult.

b. I ___*used*___ that shampoo, but I did not like the results.

c. This school does not make sufficient ___*use*___ of computers.

d. A person ___*used*___ to feel safe walking alone at night.

e. We have ___*used*___ that textbook in our English class.

f. I ___*used*___ to wear braces on my teeth.

2. On a separate sheet, write two sentences using *use* and two using *used.*

Where/Were/We're

1. *Where* refers to location.

> Home is *where* a person should feel safe.

2. *Were* is the past tense form of *are*.

> The Raiders *were* ahead until the third quarter.

3. *We're* is the contraction form of *we are*.

> *We're* certain that Mom will do well in school.

Practice 25.21

1. Fill in the blanks with *where, were,* or *we're*.

   a. If you ask me, we do not know ___where___ we are going.

   b. The plans ___were___ changed because ___we're___ uncertain about how long it will take us to drive to Cleveland.

   c. The new federal building will be built ___where___ the old courthouse now stands.

   d. ___we're___ all uncertain about what the future holds and ___where___ we will be this time next year.

   e. Debbie and Lenny ___were___ the best-behaved children at the party.

   f. ___We're___ going, but ___we're___ not happy about it.

2. On a separate sheet, write two sentences using *were,* two using *where,* and two using *we're*.

Will/Would

1. *Will* looks to the future from the present tense.

> Dr. Schwartz believes [present tense] he *will* [at a later date] get his book published.

2. *Would* looks to the future from the past tense.

> Dr. Schwartz believed [past tense] he *would* [at a later date] get his book published.

Practice 25.22

1. Fill in the blanks with *will* or *would*.

   a. Councilwoman Drucker promised that she ___will___ not vote to raise city taxes.

   b. The regional basketball tournament ___will___ be played on our campus this spring.

   c. If you do not stop snapping at people, no one ___will___ want to be around you.

   d. The fans wondered who ___would___ pitch the last inning.

e. The Academic Council plans to announce that graduation requirements _____ change in the near future.

f. The child _____ not leave unless he could take his toy.

2. On a separate sheet, write two sentences using *will* and two using *would*.

Whose/Who's

TIP
Use *who's* only when you can substitute *who is* or *who has*.

1. *Whose* is a pronoun that indicates possession.

> The person *whose* car is double-parked got a ticket.

2. *Who's* is the contraction form of *who is* or *who has*.

> *Who's* on the telephone?
> *Who's* been watching the game?

Practice 25.23

1. Fill in the blanks with *whose* or *who's*.

   a. _____ umbrella was left on the desk?

   b. Dr. Berringer is a teacher _____ lectures are always stimulating.

   c. It is impossible to know _____ been here in the last hour.

   d. They are the couple _____ children broke our window.

   e. _____ the instructor for this course?

   f. I cannot be sure _____ coming to Luis's surprise party.

2. On a separate sheet, write two sentences using *whose* and two using *who's*.

Your/You're

TIP
Use *you're* only when you can substitute *you are*.

1. *Your* is a possessive pronoun and, therefore, shows ownership.

> Remember to bring *your* ticket when you come.

2. *You're* is the contraction form of *you are*.

> *You're* the only person I can trust with this secret.

Practice 25.24

1. Fill in the blanks with *your* or *you're*.

   a. If you really don't want _____ bicycle anymore, Jane will buy it from you.

   b. _____ never really certain what _____ future holds.

   c. _____ best bet is to give Luigi a gift certificate because _____
     never going to find something he doesn't already have.

   d. The key to _____ success will be hard work, not _____
     parents' money.

   e. _____ my best friend, so I know you will help me.

   f. I felt _____ prose was too wordy, so I took the liberty of revising some

     of _____ phrasing.

2. On a separate sheet, write two sentences with *your* and two with *you're*.

                                                     ■

SPELLING

Spelling errors distract readers, so if spelling is a serious problem for you, study the tips and rules that follow.

Spelling Rules

To apply many of the spelling rules, you must know the difference between vowels and consonants.

vowels:	*a, e, i, o, u*
consonants:	*b, c, d, f, g, h, j, k, l, m, n, p, q, r, s, t, v, w, x, z*

Y can be a vowel or a consonant, depending on how it sounds.

y as a vowel:	*funny, shy*
y as a consonant:	*yellow, yes*

Rule 1:

I comes before *e* except after *c*, or when sounding like *a* as in *neighbor* and *weigh*.

The *i* comes before the *e:*

niece, field, grief, believe, friend, relieve, belief

The *e* comes before the *i* because the letters are after *c:*

conceive, ceiling, deceive, receipt, conceit, receive

The *e* comes before the *i* because of the *a* sound:

neighbor, weigh, weight, sleigh

Words with a *shin* sound are spelled *ie* after *c:*

ancient, conscience, efficient, sufficient

Some exceptions to the rule:

either, neither, seize, weird, height, foreign, society

TIP

The following nonsense sentence contains five of the most common exceptions to the ie/ei rule: Either foreigner seized weird leisure.

Rule 2:

Before adding an ending other than *-ing,* change *y* to *i* if there is a consonant before the *y*.

Change *y* to *i* if there is a consonant before the *y:*

study	+	ed	=	studied	plenty	+	ful	=	plentiful
happy	+	ness	=	happiness	cry	+	ed	=	cried
pretty	+	est	=	prettiest	lovely	+	er	=	lovelier

Keep the *y* if there is a vowel before it:

enjoy	+	ment	=	enjoyment	stay	+	ed	=	stayed
play	+	s	=	plays	toy	+	s	=	toys
employ	+	ed	=	employed	destroy	+	er	=	destroyer

Keep the *y* if the ending is *-ing:*

hurry	+	ing	=	hurrying	study	+	ing	=	studying
employ	+	ing	=	employing	cry	+	ing	=	crying
fly	+	ing	=	flying	imply	+	ing	=	implying

Some exceptions to the rule:

day	+	ly	=	daily	lay	+	ed	=	laid
pay	+	ed	=	paid	sly	+	ness	=	slyness
shy	+	ly	=	shyly	gay	+	ly	=	gaily
say	+	ed	=	said					

Rule 3:

When you add an ending to a word that ends with a silent *e*, drop the *e* if the ending begins with a vowel, but keep the *e* if the ending begins with a consonant.

Drop the *e* if the ending begins with a vowel:

hope	+	ing	=	hoping	dine	+	ing	=	dining
pleasure	+	able	=	pleasurable	write	+	er	=	writer
dine	+	er	=	diner	dense	+	ity	=	density
praise	+	ing	=	praising	rhyme	+	ed	=	rhymed

Keep the *e* if the ending begins with a consonant:

hope	+	ful	=	hopeful	complete	+	ly	=	completely
loose	+	ly	=	loosely	state	+	ment	=	statement
hate	+	ful	=	hateful	home	+	less	=	homeless
time	+	less	=	timeless	move	+	ment	=	movement

Some exceptions to the rule:

acknowledge	+	ment	=	acknowledgment
judge	+	ment	=	judgment
mile	+	age	=	mileage

notice	+	able	=	noticeable
argue	+	ment	=	argument
nine	+	th	=	ninth
acre	+	age	=	acreage
awe	+	ful	=	awful
true	+	ly	=	truly
courage	+	ous	=	courageous

Rule 4:

When adding an ending that begins with a vowel to a one-syllable word, double the final consonant if the last three letters of the word are consonant-vowel-consonant (c-v-c).

Double the final consonant if the one-syllable word ends c-v-c:

swim	+	ing	=	swimming	fat	+	est	=	fattest
thin	+	er	=	thinner	skip	+	ing	=	skipping
drop	+	ed	=	dropped	run	+	er	=	runner

Do not double the final consonant if the one-syllable word does not end c-v-c:

eat + ing = eating   burn + er = burner   boil + ed = boiled

Rule 5:

When adding an ending that begins with a vowel to a word of more than one syllable, double the final consonant if the last three letters of the word are consonant-vowel-consonant (c-v-c) *and* if the stress is on the last syllable.

Double the final consonant if the word ends c-v-c and the stress is on the last syllable:

begin	+	er	=	beginner	regret	+	ed	=	regretted
admit	+	ing	=	admitting	prefer	+	ed	=	preferred

Do not double the final consonant if the stress is not on the last syllable:

pardon	+	ed	=	pardoned	ripen	+	ing	=	ripening
labor	+	er	=	laborer					

Do not double the final consonant if the word does not end c-v-c:

evict	+	ing	=	evicting	pretend	+	er	=	pretender
ordain	+	ed	=	ordained					

Do not double the consonant if the stress shifts from the last syllable when the ending is added:

prefer + ence = preference

confer + ence = conference

but

preference (stress shifts from last to first syllable)

conference (stress shifts from last to first syllable)

Rule 6:

Most nouns form the plural by adding *s*. However, if the noun ends in *ch, sh, s, x, z,* or *o*, add *es* to form the plural.

genius + es = geniuses   mix   + es = mixes

potato + es = potatoes   church + es = churches

Some exceptions to the rule:

memos   radios   solos

Rule 7:

When you change the final *y* to *i*, add *es* to form the plural (see Rule 2).

candy + es = candies   party + es = parties   fly + es = flies

but

key   + s = keys   boy + s = boys   toy + s = toys

Practice 25.25

1. To check your understanding of spelling rule 1, fill in the blanks with either *ie* or *ei*. If you are unsure, check a dictionary.

   a. ch _____ _____ f   g. perc _____ _____ ve

   b. br _____ _____ f   h. sh _____ _____ ld

   c. fr _____ _____ ght   i. r _____ _____ gn

   d. ach _____ _____ ve   j. v _____ _____ n

   e. w _____ _____ gh   k. th _____ _____ r

   f. s _____ _____ ge

2. To check your understanding of spelling rules 2–5, add the given endings to the words below. If you are unsure, consult the rule given in parentheses or look up the word in a dictionary.

   a. sorry + er _____ (rule 2)

   b. bat + er _____ (rule 4)

   c. make + s _____ (rule 3)

   d. hammer + ing _____ (rule 5)

   e. hop + ed _____ (rule 4)

f. enjoy + able _____ (rule 2)

g. advertise + ment _____ (rule 3)

h. ask + ing _____ (rule 4)

i. sense + ible _____ (rule 3)

j. slip + ed _____ (rule 4)

k. gossip + ed _____ (rule 5)

l. omit + ing _____ (rule 5)

m. wealthy + er _____ (rule 2)

n. rake + ing _____ (rule 3)

o. ship + ing _____ (rule 4)

p. permit + ed _____ (rule 5)

q. bite + ing _____ (rule 3)

r. marry + ed _____ (rule 2)

s. big + er _____ (rule 4)

t. lazy + ness _____ (rule 2)

3. To check your understanding of rules 6 and 7, write the plural of each noun. If you are unsure, check a dictionary.

a. toy _____

b. brush _____

c. jelly _____

d. mosquito _____

e. television _____

f. veto _____

g. tax _____

h. girl _____

i. enemy _____

j. match _____

Frequently Misspelled Words

The following seventy-five words are often misspelled. Learn to spell every word on the list by making flash cards to study.

1. absence	5. analyze	9. awkward
2. across	6. appreciate	10. beginning
3. actually	7. argument	11. belief
4. a lot	8. athlete	12. business

13. coming	34. intelligence	55. preferred
14. committee	35. knowledge	56. prejudice
15. criticism	36. laboratory	57. privilege
16. definitely	37. leisure	58. pursue
17. dependent	38. length	59. receipt
18. develop	39. library	60. receive
19. discuss	40. marriage	61. religious
20. eighth	41. mathematics	62. rhythm
21. embarrass	42. meant	63. sacrifice
22. especially	43. medicine	64. safety
23. existence	44. necessary	65. scene
24. February	45. neither	66. schedule
25. foreign	46. ninety	67. separate
26. government	47. ninth	68. severely
27. grammar	48. occasionally	69. success
28. guarantee	49. opinion	70. surprise
29. guidance	50. parallel	71. thoroughly
30. height	51. persuade	72. through
31. hoping	52. physical	73. until
32. immediately	53. planned	74. weight
33. independent	54. pleasant	75. written

The Hyphen

Hyphens are most often used to form compound words and to show that a word continues from the end of one line to the beginning of the next. For some word-processing programs, use one horizontal line for the hyphen (–) and two lines for the dash (—).

1. Use a hyphen between words that form a single adjective before a noun.

state-of-the-art stereo   well-known speaker

comparison-contrast essay   run-of-the-mill Sunday

strong-willed child   so-called advice

Do not use a hyphen when the compound comes after the noun:

Fran is a success because she is strong willed.
Fran is a strong-willed woman.

Do not use a hyphen with an *-ly* word:

The slowly moving traffic made me an hour late.

2. Use hyphens between compound numbers from twenty-one through ninety-nine.

thirty-six   seventy-seven   forty-two

3. Use a hyphen between the numerator and denominator in written fractions.

one-fourth   two-thirds

4. Do not use hyphens with most **prefixes** (word beginnings) like *un, inter, mis,* and *dis.*

unnoticed   interrelated   misspell   disengage

5. Use a hyphen after the prefixes *self-, all-, ex-* (meaning *former*), and before the **suffix** (word ending) *-elect.*

self-assured   ex-governor

all-inclusive   mayor-elect

6. Use a hyphen with a prefix before a word that begins with a capital letter.

un-American   pro-Cuban   mid-January

7. Use a hyphen to divide a word at the end of a line, but remember these cautions:

   a. Do not divide one-syllable words.

   b. You should not leave a single letter at the end of the line, so do not divide a word such as *a-void.*

Practice 25.26

Add hyphens where they are needed in the following paragraph.

[1]My mother in law is a first rate artist who will show her paintings at a gallery on the twenty first of the month. [2]Her show will last until mid May. [3]In addition to being a highly acclaimed artist, my mother in law is the ex chair of the United Way campaign in our city and an energetic fund raiser for anti drug campaigns. [4]At sixty seven, she is a remarkable, self possessed, high powered woman whom I admire greatly.

Review Practice 25.27

Eliminate the eleven errors with frequently confused words and spelling in the following paragraph.

[1]Sadly, more and more young children are developing negative body images and starting to diet as a result. [2]However, young children are not suppose to diet. [3]Instead, it's much better if their encouraged to develop healthy attitudes toward food, exercise, and body types. [4]If overwieght children could develop good cating habits and maintain there weight during their formative years, than they will have a good chance of slimming down once they hit the growth spurts of puberty. [5]Its

FAQ

Q: Why do I need to learn how to spell? Can't I just use my computer's spellchecker?

A: Computer spellcheckers have limitations. They do not, for example, distinguish between the frequently confused words and soundalikes, and they include fewer words than most dictionaries. Also, you must know how to spell for those times you are not writing at the computer.

true that the habits children learn at a young age will stay with them long passed childhood and into adulthood. [6]There would be far less eating disorders if children were taught proper nutrition and self acceptance. [7]As a country, were so concerned with being skinny that we teach children—unconsciously or otherwise— to have unrealistic and unhealthy expectations for desireable weight.

Tips

USING FREQUENTLY CONFUSED WORDS AND SPELLING CORRECTLY

- Study your draft word by word, very slowly. Each time you encounter a word that might be misspelled or confused, check it in a dictionary. Never overlook a word even if your suspicion is very slight.
- Keep a list of words you misspell and confuse, and study it daily. You may find it helpful to underline the troublesome parts of words like this.

for<u>eig</u>n

- Learn the correct pronunciation of words. You may misspell *disastrous* if you pronounce it incorrectly as *disasterous.*
- Break words into parts when you spell, like this:

with * hold	class * room	under * standing
under * statement	break * fast	table * cloth
room * mate	shoe * lace	beach * front

- Some words may be easier to handle if you spell them syllable by syllable. For example, *organization* may be easier to spell if you say each syllable as you go: "or ▪ gan ▪ i ▪ za ▪ tion."
- Use memory tricks to help you remember correct spellings and confusing words. For example, *instrument* contains the word *strum,* and you strum a guitar, which is an instrument; *tragedy* contains the word *rage.*
- **If English is not your first language,** the features of your language may make it difficult to learn English spelling. For example, Spanish has no *wh* sound, which could lead you to spell spell *whisper* incorrectly as *wisper.* To compensate, keep a personal spelling list of words you misspell and study it each day. Because soundalikes, such as *too* and *to,* can be difficult to master, reserve a section of your spelling list just for these frequently confused words.

Post Test

Find and correct the twelve errors with frequently confused words and spelling.

[1]The practice of wearing wedding rings goes back to the ancient Egyptians and there habit of sealing a pact with a show of trust. [2]Since a signet ring has

the crest of it's owner, such rings were exchanged as a show of trust. ³If a person excepted the ring, he or she was enterring into a relationship of shared trust. ⁴Eventualy, the practice moved from politics to business. ⁵Now it is a part of marriage ceremonys signifying love and trust among two people.

⁶The practice of using the fourth finger of the left hand as the ring finger dates back to the third century B.C. ⁷At that time, physicains believed that a nerve was suppose to run directly passed this finger and than on to the heart.

LEARNING FROM TEXTBOOKS

The following excerpt comes from a college criminal justice textbook. Read the paragraphs and answer the questions that follow.

¹Recently, a record number of corporations and their executives and former executives have faced high-profile criminal investigations and fraud charges, and both state and federal courts appear determined to impose severe sentences on corporate executives found guilty of white-collar crimes. ²In 2006, for example, in what some called "the biggest business scandal in U.S. history," former Enron executives Kenneth Lay and Jeff Skilling were convicted of conspiracy to commit securities and wire fraud. ³Under Skilling's and Lay's leadership, Enron Corporation rose from relative obscurity to become one of the world's largest corporations. ⁴The Enron scandal, which broke in 2002, reduced the holdings of investment and retirement accounts across the country and around the world, wiping out hundreds of billions of dollars' worth of investor equity and taking a significant toll on the wealth of many Americans.

1. Explain the use of the two hyphens in sentence 1.

   _____

   _____

2. In sentence 1, why is *their* used instead of *there* or *they're*?

   _____

   _____

3. What is the past tense (*-ed*) form of *commit,* which appears in sentence 2? Which rule do you follow to spell this form?

   _____

   _____

(continued on next page)

4. In sentence 2, the word *biggest* appears. Why are there two *g*'s in this word? What rule explains the spelling?

_____

_____

5. Name a word from this paragraph that you can add to your personal spelling list. How can you remember the spelling of this word?

_____

_____

Write about It

In general, do you think corporations in this country victimize consumers or work to benefit them? Use examples to support your assertion.

SUCCEEDING IN COLLEGE

Use Memory Tricks

In this chapter, you learned that memory tricks can help you spell some words and avoid confusing others. You can also use memory tricks to learn content in your other courses. One particularly useful trick is **association** or connecting new material to something you already know. For example, say that for your economics class, you must learn that *laissez-faire* is a form of capitalism whereby people compete with minimal government intervention. You might associate *laissez* with "lazy" and remember that lazy people like to be left alone to loaf, just as government leaves business alone to regulate itself in a *laissez-faire* system.

Another memory trick is to use a **mnemonic device,** which is a saying or name that jogs your memory. Music students often use the mnemonic device, "Every good boy does fine," to remember the lines on a music staff are E, G, B, D, F. Say, for example, you must remember that the structure of a cell nucleus includes the chromatin, nucleolus, and nuclear envelope—CNN, easy to remember if you think of the cable news channel. If you must remember that the parts of a bacteria cell are the flagellum, cytoplasm, capsule, plasma membrane, and ribosome, you might devise a sentence like this, "Funny Cindy captures pink rats."

Write about It

Go to your textbooks and find five sets of facts you need to learn or will need to learn in the future. Then write out five different memory tricks to help you remember those sets of facts.

For more practice with frequently confused words and spelling, go to www. mywritinglab.com.

COMPREHENSIVE POST TEST

■ Using Verbs Correctly

1. If the underlined verb is correct, write *yes* on the blank; if it is incorrect, write *no*.

a. _N_ We <u>been</u> the ones who told Donald that the test was postponed. *were*

b. _N_ The children <u>drunk</u> their milk and then ran outside to play. *drank*

c. _N_ Both of the television documentaries <u>discusses</u> the aftermath of the *discuss* Vietnam War.

d. _N_ Before the sun comes up each morning, everyone in the family <u>exercise's</u> *is* for thirty minutes.

e. _Y_ The box of canned goods <u>are</u> ready to take to the food bank.

f. _Y_ After receiving a standing ovation, the cast of the play <u>was</u> called on stage for another bow.

g. _Y_ Each of the aspiring journalists <u>hopes</u> to get a job on the student newspaper.

h. _N_ *singular* Neither the book nor the movie <u>is</u> suitable for a young audience.

i. _N_ *has* Each of the puppies <u>have</u> black spots on white fur.

j. _____ The a capella choir <u>expects</u> to tour Europe this spring.

k. _N_ After Henri turned in his midterm exam, he <u>checks</u> two answers in his *checked* notes.

l. _N_ The newspaper reporter double-checked his sources and then <u>decides</u> to write the front-page story. *decided.*

■ Using Pronouns Correctly

2. If the underlined pronoun is correct, write *yes* on the bank; if it is incorrect, write *no*.

a. _N_ *he* Katrina and <u>him</u> believe in reincarnation.

b. _Y_ Because Josef trained all summer, he ran the Thanksgiving marathon faster than <u>I</u>.

c. _N_ *it's* None of the radio stations had <u>their</u> license renewed by the Federal Communications Commission.

d. _N_ Because they were talking during the play, someone asked Lee and <u>she</u> to be quiet.

e. _N_ *it's* One of the sweaters slid off <u>their</u> hanger.

f. _Y_ The flock of geese spends several days at the pond behind my house before continuing <u>its</u> southern migration.

g. _Y_ Mario is the artist <u>who</u> painted my portrait.

h. _Y_ Everybody loses <u>his or her</u> way once in a while.

Using Modifiers Correctly

3. If the underlined modifier is correct, write *yes* on the blank; if it is incorrect, write *no*.

   a. __Y__ Doris sneezed so <u>loudly</u> that everyone gasped.

   b. __No__ The ivy needs a trim <u>bad;</u> it is growing across the walkway and up the steps. **badly**

   c. __N__ Now that I have contact lenses, I can see small print <u>more better</u> than I could with glasses.

   d. __N__ __✗__ <u>Understanding the need for review</u>, exercises were an important part of every class.

   e. __N__ I did surprisingly <u>good</u> at the audition, considering I hadn't performed for two years. **well**

   f. __N__ When he was unjustly accused of lying, Jake was the <u>most angry</u> I have ever seen him.

▪ Using Capital Letters and Punctuation Correctly

4. If there are no capitalization errors, write *yes* on the blank. If capitals are missing, or if capitals are used incorrectly, write the number of errors on the blank.

   a. __Y__ At the town meeting, mayor McKelvey spoke about the city's efforts to lure Associated Electronics into the Mahoning Industrial Park. **Y**

   b. _____ The Independence Day celebration at Oak Hill Park is now an annual event. **✗**

   c. _____ If you travel west on Route 46, you will find Mosquito Lake.

   d. __N__ General Motors corporation announced plans to build its new cobalt at its plant in Lordstown, Ohio.

   e. _____ Jon and Kat asked reverend Simon to marry them in Fifth Avenue Baptist Church.

5. If there are no punctuation errors, write *yes* on the blank. If punctuation is missing, or if punctuation is used incorrectly, write the number of errors on the blank.

   a. _____ The congressional candidate spoke in five cities in three days, and made an appearance on two television programs.

   b. _____ Awake, but tired, I managed to pull myself out of bed, stumble down the stairs, and make breakfast.

   c. __Y__ Unaware that the street was being repaved, Tasha turned onto Market Street and found herself in slow moving dense traffic.

   d. _____ Computer grammar checkers, in my opinion, are not very reliable, for they flag errors that do not exist, and fail to flag errors that do exist.

   e. _____ I ordered the chicken marsala, which was tough and bland; my date ordered the prime rib, which was served cold.

   f. __Y__ Many states require schools to administer competency tests to students; some educators object to these high stakes tests.

g. _____ Because of declining revenue, the postal service wants to eliminate Saturday deliveries; this plan worries many people.

h. _____ My favorite search engines are: Alta Vista, Google, and Yahoo.

i. _____ Two issues (gun control and abortion) divide this country more than any others.

j. _____ Two issues—gun control and abortion—divide this country more than any others.

k. __Y__ Marcus's car won't start because it has a dead battery.

l. _____ They're the ones to ask because the ladder you want to borrow is their's.

m. _____ To stimulate holiday sales, the store manager reduced all the toys' prices.

n. _____ The computer technician explained that the repair would be expensive; my machine needed it's motherboard replaced.

o. __Y__ "If we do not increase the sales tax," the mayor explained, "we will have a serious budget deficit in six months."

▨ Eliminating Problems with Frequently Confused Words and Spelling

6. Write the correct word in the blank.

   a. (your/you're) __You're__ the one who has lost __your__ way.

   b. (to/too/two) I would like __to__ go with you, but you already have __too__ many people in the car.

   c. (achieved/acheived) You should be proud of what you have __achieved__ this term.

   d. (mispent/misspent) Because I __misspent__ my savings, I have no money for a vacation.

   e. (happiness/happyness) Money does not buy __happiness__

CHAPTER 26
Writing in Response to College Reading

As a college student, you will read a great deal: textbooks, web pages, novels, essays, supplemental books, and more. In addition, much of your college writing in all your classes will be in response to reading material. This chapter will help you with that reading and writing.

ACTIVE READING

When you read for your own pleasure, it matters only that you have a good time, so you can skip a passage, read with the television on, and ignore words you don't understand. However, when you read your textbooks and other college materials, more is expected of you: You must read attentively for full comprehension. Such attentive reading is **active reading.** Active reading helps you understand the material and form judgments about it by answering the questions in the following box.

Questions an Active Reader Asks

1. What is the author's thesis (central point)?

2. What main ideas support the thesis?

3. Is the support for the thesis adequate and convincing?

4. Is the author expressing facts, opinions, or both?

5. What is the author's tone or attitude (serious, sarcastic, preachy, humorous, angry, insulting, etc.)?

6. What is the author's purpose (to share, inform, entertain, and/or persuade)?

7. Who is the author's intended audience?

8. What is the source of the author's detail (observation, personal experience, research, and/or reasoning)?

To be an active reader, you must do more than let the words sound in your ears. You must become actively involved by focusing on what you are reading and considering its significance. The following steps can help you do that.

Step 1: Survey

Survey the material for an idea of what to expect. What does the title suggest the reading will be about? Has your instructor said anything about the material that shapes your expectations? Check for headings, boldface, italics, lists, pictures, and captions. Quickly read the opening and closing paragraphs, along with the first sentence of several other paragraphs. What do all these suggest about the content of the material? Can you tell whether the author is expressing feelings, explaining something, or trying to convince you of something?

Step 2: Read without Interruption

Read the material quickly but attentively. If you encounter a word you do not understand, circle it to check later; if you do not understand a passage, place a question mark next to it. The important thing is to keep going, getting as much as you can without laboring over anything. As you read, try to determine the writer's thesis.

After this reading, answer as many of the active-reader questions as you can. Then look up every word you circled and write the meanings in the margin near the circled word. Pay particular attention to specialized vocabulary in text books. Now take a break if you need one.

Step 3: Read and Study

Pick up your pen and read again. This time, underline the thesis, if it is stated (textbook chapters may not have an overriding thesis) and the main ideas (often found in topic sentences). Avoid underlining too much—aim for the thesis and main points. Write your reactions to the material in the margins. Note strong agreement or disagreement ("True!" or "Absolutely not."); write a question mark next to anything you do not understand and an exclamation point next to anything you particularly like. In addition, write associations that occur to you ("learned this in history class" and "makes me think of the Iraq War"). Finally, look for the answers to the active reading questions that you still need. If you are unable to answer some of the questions or if you have other questions, write them down to ask in class. (For an example of a marked text, see pages 433–434.)

Step 4: Test Yourself

Close the book after your studied reading and write a brief summary of the material. Or recite a summary to yourself. This testing helps lock the main points in your memory.

A SAMPLE ACTIVE READING

The following essay has been marked the way an active reader might mark it. After the essay are the answers to the questions an active reader asks. Studying this material will help you appreciate how an active reader interacts with a text.

Students in Shock

John Kellmayer

Kellmayer explains that colleges are aware of the pressures students face, and they are trying to help students manage their stress. As you read, notice the active reading comments, think about how *you* would mark the text.

If you feel overwhelmed by your college experiences, you are not alone—many of today's college students are suffering from a form of shock. <u>Going to college has always had its ups and downs, but today the "downs" of the college experience are more numerous and difficult, a fact that the schools are responding to with increased support services.</u>

1

thesis

Lisa is a good example of a student in shock. She is an attractive, intelligent twenty-year-old college junior at a state university. Having been a straight-A student in high school and a member of the basketball and softball teams there, she remembers her high school days with fondness. Lisa was popular then and had a steady boyfriend for the last two years of school.

2

Now, only three years later, Lisa is miserable. She has changed her major four times already and is forced to hold down two part-time jobs in order to pay her tuition. She suffers from sleeping and eating disorders and believes she has no close friends. Sometimes she bursts out crying for no apparent reason. On more than one occasion, she has considered taking her life.

3

good, realistic examples

Dan, too, suffers from student shock. He is nineteen and a freshman at a local community college. He began college as an accounting major but hated that field. So he switched to computer programming because he heard the job prospects were excellent in that area. Unfortunately, he discovered that he had little aptitude for programming and changed majors again, this time to psychology. He likes psychology but has heard horror stories about the difficulty of finding a job in that field without a graduate degree. Now he's considering switching majors again. To help pay for school, Dan works nights and weekends as a sales clerk at Kmart. He doesn't get along with his boss, but since he needs the money, Dan feels he has no choice except to stay on the job. A few months ago, his girlfriend of a year and a half broke up with him.

4

Howie is like Dan.

Not surprisingly, Dan has started to suffer from depression and migraine headaches. He believes that in spite of all his hard work, he just isn't getting anywhere. He can't remember ever being this unhappy. A few times he considered talking to somebody in the college psychological counseling center. He rejected that idea, though, because he doesn't want people to think there's something wrong with him.

5

Common reaction to idea of counseling

Source: Reprinted with permission of Townsend Press.

A frightening statistic. How was it learned?

6   What is happening to Lisa and Dan happens to millions of college students each year. <u>As a result, roughly one-quarter of the student population at any time will suffer from symptoms of depression</u>. Of that group, almost half will experience depression intense enough to (warrant) professional help. At schools across the country, psychological counselors are booked up months in advance. Stress-related problems such as anxiety, migraine headaches, insomnia, (anorexia) and (bulimia) are epidemic on college campuses.

call for

an eating disorder involving starvation

an eating disorder involving binge eating followed by forced vomiting

7   Suicide rates and (self-inflicted) injuries among college students are higher now than at any other time in history. The suicide rate among college youth is fifty percent higher than among nonstudents of the same age. It is estimated that each year more than five hundred college students take their own lives.

caused by one's self

8   College health officials believe that these reported problems represent only the tip of the iceberg. They fear that most students, like Lisa and Dan, suffer in silence.

Why blame families for problems schools create?

9   There are three reasons today's college students are suffering more than in earlier generations. First is a weakening support structure. The transition from high school to college has been difficult, but in the past there was more family support to help get through it. Today, with divorce rates at a historical high and many parents experiencing their own psychological difficulties, the traditional family is not always available for guidance and support. And when students who do not find (stability) at home are bombarded with numerous new and stressful experiences, the results can be devastating.

permanence

I know several people who had to drop out because of lack of money.

10   Another problem college students face is financial pressure. In the last decade tuition costs have skyrocketed—up about sixty-six percent and ninety percent at private schools. For students living away from home, costs range from five thousand dollars to as much as twelve thousand a year and more. And at the same time that tuition costs have been rising dramatically, there has been a cutback in federal aid to students. College loans are now much harder to obtain and are available only at near-market interest rates. Consequently, most college students must work at least part-time. And for some students, the pressure to do well in school while holding down a job is too much to handle.

This school does a terrible job of advising on majors and careers.

11   A final cause of student shock is the large selection of majors available. Because of the magnitude and difficulty of choosing a major, college can prove a time of great indecision. Many students switch majors, some a number of times. As a result, it is becoming commonplace to take five or six years to get a degree. It can be depressing to students not only to have taken courses that don't count towards a degree but also to be faced with the added tuition costs. In some cases these costs become so high that they force students to drop out of college.

12   While there is no magic cure-all for student shock, colleges have begun to recognize the problem and are trying in a number of ways to help students cope with the pressures they face. First of all, many colleges are upgrading their psychological counseling centers to handle the greater demand for services. Additional staff is being hired, and experts are doing research to learn more about the psychological problems of college students. Some schools even advertise these services in student newspapers and on campus radio stations. Also, upperclassmen are being trained as peer counselors. These peer counselors may be able to act as a first line of defense in the battle for students' well-being by spotting and helping to solve problems before they become too big for students to handle.

This school could use better RAs in the dorms.

13   In addition, stress-management workshops have become common on college campuses. At these workshops, instructors teach students various techniques for dealing with stress, including (biofeedback,) meditation, and exercise.

Technique for monitoring & controlling body functions

14   Finally, many schools are improving their vocational counseling services. By giving students more relevant information about possible majors and career choices, colleges can lessen the anxiety and indecision often associated with choosing a major.

If you ever feel that you're in shock, remember that your experience is not unique. Try to put things in perspective. Certainly, the end of a romance or an exam is not an event to look forward to. But realize that rejection and failure happen to everyone sooner or later. And don't be reluctant to talk to somebody about your problems. The useful services available on campus won't help you if you don't take advantage of them.

15

What about unreasonable profs & difficult classes as causes of shock?

Answers to Active-Reader Questions

1. **What is the author's thesis?**

   "Going to college has always had its ups and downs, but today the 'downs' of the college experience are more numerous and difficult, a fact that the schools are responding to with increased support services."

2. **What main ideas support the thesis?**

   About a quarter of the student population will experience depression; half of that group will need professional help.

   Stress-related problems are epidemic. Suicide and self-inflicted injuries are at an all-time high.

   One cause of the student shock is decreased family support.

   A second cause is financial pressure as a result of higher tuition and less financial aid.

   A third cause is difficulty choosing a major.

   Colleges are addressing the problem of shock by upgrading counseling services, offering stress-management workshops, and improving vocational counseling.

3. **Is the support for the thesis adequate and convincing?**

   The opening examples are well detailed and convince me that shock is a problem, but I think the reasons given for the shock are sketchy and incomplete. Other causes exist, such as difficult classes, unreasonable professors, and unprepared students. I'd also like to know where the author got his information. That would make the piece more convincing.

4. **Is the author expressing facts, opinions, or both?**

   both

5. **What is the author's tone or attitude (serious, sarcastic, preachy, humorous, angry, insulting, etc.)?**

   The author seems serious, concerned, and objective.

6. **What is the author's purpose (to share, to inform, to entertain, and/or to persuade)?**

   The author wants to inform the reader about the problem of student shock and explain how the problem is being addressed. He seems to do this to help students who suffer from shock.

7. **Who is the author's intended audience?**

   The <u>you</u> in paragraph 15 indicates that the audience is students.

8. **What is the source of the author's detail (observation, personal experience, research, and/or reasoning)?**

   The author must have done some research to learn about the extent of the problem and what colleges are doing. It's hard to know if any personal experience or observation was involved.

READING TO IMPROVE WRITING

Through active reading, you can improve your writing. Pay attention to the characteristics of what you read. Note how other writers develop details, use words, write openings and closings, create transitions, and craft sentences. By reading and noticing what other writers do, you will become aware of strategies to try in your own writing. Each time you read a selection in this chapter—or anywhere else— try to pick up something to incorporate in your writing. For example, from one reading, you may learn a new word to use; from another reading, you might learn how to use questions as topic sentences; and from a third, you might learn how to use a bit of humor to make a point.

The rest of this chapter presents brief readings organized by the patterns you learned about in Part Two. After each reading, there is a set of study questions that will help you recognize writing strategies you can use to improve your writing.

NARRATION

Did I Save Lives or Engage in Racial Profiling?

Lori Hope

When the author, traveling on an airplane with her son, became suspicious of a man who appeared to be Middle Eastern, she wrestled with whether to report her suspicions or keep quiet. As you read this 2002 essay from *Newsweek*'s "My Turn" column, ask yourself what you would do in a similar situation—and why.

Like most narratives, "Did I Save Lives or Engage in Racial Profiling?" answers these questions: What happened? Who was involved? When did it happen? Where did it happen? Why did it happen? How did it happen? Pay attention to the answers to these questions and decide which ones are emphasized most.

You will notice that the thesis comes at the end of the essay, rather than the beginning. You will also notice that some paragraphs lack topic sentences. Often, topic sentences are not needed when the narration's time sequence provides a sufficient organizational framework.

Before reading the essay, review the following vocabulary:

racial profiling—singling out people because of their ethnicity; in the essay, racial profiling refers to identifying males who look Middle Eastern as possible terrorists

Richard Reid—called the "shoe bomber" because in 2001 on a flight from Paris to Miami, he tried to light an explosive devise hidden in his shoe

avowed—confirmed, publicly stated

reeled—to be in a whirl or go round and round

jettisoned—thrown off

Half a lifetime ago, I read a magazine essay that took deep root within me, and still sprouts whenever I find myself tempted to react to someone based on skin color. The author, an African-American, described what it was like to see people cross the street when he walked toward them on a sidewalk. 1

When racial profiling became an issue in the war against terrorism, I—an avowed liberal—found myself wondering what I would do if I saw someone who appeared to be of Middle Eastern descent behaving in a way that could be considered "suspicious." A few months ago I stopped wondering. 2

3   A plane my 16-year-old son and I were scheduled to board was swapped with another because of mechanical problems. Although I was relieved to know we were boarding an aircraft that checked out, I still felt uneasy about flying because of the "shoe bomber" incident three days earlier. I hadn't noticed security checking anyone's shoes.

4   Once settled into the aisle seat, with my son next to the window, I learned there could be another delay because of weather. Before opening my novel I noticed a man in the exit row two seats ahead, looking toward the rear of the plane. He was olive-skinned, black-haired and clean-shaven, with a blanket covering his legs and feet. I thought that was strange, because I felt so warm. No one else was using a blanket.

5   Nine-C, as I called him, sat motionless for 10 minutes, except for glancing nervously down the aisle every few minutes. Then his leg started to shake, and he seemed to be reaching for something under his blanket. He bent over. Adrenaline coursed through my body. I sensed something horrible. The plane was still on the ground, but I felt airsick.

6   "You're being ridiculous," I told myself. "Nine-C just wants to get home. He's cold; he has to use the bathroom. Just relax and keep your water bottle handy, in case he lights a match."

7   But he was very big, and the people sitting near him were not. And I wondered, "What if he goes to the bathroom to light his bomb?" Then I looked at my son—I thought of his potential, his brilliance as a musician and mathematician. How could I tell if 9-C was a terrorist? I couldn't.

8   I forced myself to walk to the rear of the plane. "What should a passenger do if she sees someone behaving in a way she considers odd?" I asked the flight attendant.

9   "Tell me about it."

10   "I'm probably just being paranoid," I started, and described what I'd seen. When I got back to my seat, I tried to forget my suspicions, having turned them over to an expert. A few minutes later, a flight attendant asked the passengers in row nine how they were doing. Another attendant came down the aisle, looking carefully at both sides.

11   "We need to de-ice the wings," announced the captain, apologizing for yet another delay. He emerged from the cockpit, walked back to 9-C's row and looked out to examine the wings. The other pilot did the same.

12   Soon afterward, we learned we were returning to the gate because of "another minor mechanical problem." Absorbed in my book, I hardly paid attention. When I looked up a chapter later, I saw that 9-C was gone. Was he in the bathroom?

13   We took off, and once at cruising altitude, I walked to the rear to see if he'd changed seats. But he was nowhere. I asked the flight attendant where he was. "We don't know what happens once security gets them. After the shoe-bomber, we're glad to get rid of anyone suspicious."

14   I felt awful. I didn't mean for 9-C to be taken away. I had probably ruined an innocent traveler's day, not to mention delaying an already late flight. And I hadn't even noticed he'd gone. I vowed not to scare my son; I'd keep the story to myself.

15   But I couldn't. The head flight attendant asked me to come to the front of the plane. My heart pounded and my cheeks burned; I felt ashamed and afraid. "Thank you for alerting us to that man," he said, smiling. "We all observed him, including our pilots. He seemed depressed, but also very nervous. Security did a background check and decided to question him. If he's OK, we'll compensate him. You did the right thing. Once we're in the air, it's too late."

16   We were moved to first class, and I wrote an incident report. Later, while waiting for our luggage, I reeled with questions: Had other passengers wondered about 9-C? Where was he now? Would I ever know whether he was a danger? Most important, had I become a racial profiler, bulldozing the roots of that powerful essay that had shaped me in my youth?

Perhaps I had. But I'm not sure I regret it. I can live with the guilt, grief and anger.   17
Even though I lost a part of myself and may have gotten an innocent man jettisoned
from the plane, it's not the same world it was half a lifetime ago.

Study Questions

1. The best statement of the thesis comes at the end of the essay. In your own
   words, write out that thesis. Why does it come at the end of the essay?

2. What purpose does the dialogue in paragraphs 6 and 7 serve? In paragraphs
   8–10, 11, 13, and 15?

3. Which of the who? what? when? where? why? how? questions does Hope
   answer in the most detail? Why does she use so much detail? Which does she
   answer in the least detail? Why does she use so little detail?

4. Which paragraphs open with transitions that show chronological order?

5. What strategy or vocabulary did you learn in this reading that you might try out
   in your own writing?

6. **Other Patterns** What description appears in paragraphs 4 and 5? What purpose does that description serve? How is cause-and-effect analysis part of the
   essay?

From Reading to Writing

1. Narrate an account of a time you were suspicious of someone. Explain what
   you did and whether you now believe you did the right thing.

2. Narrate an account of a time someone was suspicious of you. Explain what
   happened and why you think it happened.

3. Tell a story about something that caused you to wonder about what you should
   do. Tell what you decided to do and why.

4. Tell a story that reveals how you act when you do not feel safe.

5. Tell a story about a time you judged someone on the basis of that person's appearance. Alternatively, tell about a time someone judged you on the basis of your
   appearance.

6. Use your imagination and retell Hope's story from the point of view of the
   passenger in seat 9-C.

DESCRIPTION

A Link to the Living

Patsy Garlan

A visit to her daughter's human anatomy laboratory prompted Patsy Garlan to write this description, which first appeared in *The Atlantic Monthly* (2000). If you think the description will be ghoulish, you will be surprised by the author's respectful tone. Pay particular attention to the sensory details and specific word choice. Also notice that Garlan describes two subjects.

Before reading the essay, review the following vocabulary:

cavernous—vast; spacious

formaldehyde—a gas used as a disinfectant and preservative

Dante—in his epic poem, *The Inferno,* Dante acts as narrator, guided through Hell by the Roman poet Virgil

gurney—wheeled cart or stretcher

1   You can imagine how startling it was when my daughter the medical student inquired, "Would you like to see my cadaver?" A glance at her eager young face filled with cheerful expectancy made me soften the fervor of my denial to "Oh, no, darling, no—I don't think so. No. No."

2   But then I thought, How often does a person, a layperson, have an opportunity like this—to look inside the body of another human being? You'll be forever sorry if you pass up this chance. I glanced at her again. She was waiting for me to come round. As she always did—as kids do. "Well," I said, "what would it be like?"

3   So off we went, in the warm dusk of the New Hampshire evening. I found myself fighting off my apprehension and hoping I would be able to control my queasiness. As we descended the stairs heading deep into the cavernous basement of the medical-school building where the anatomy lab was housed, she began to prepare me. It will be cold, because—you know. And there will be a smell of formaldehyde—don't mind it; you get used to it.

4   We entered the dimly lit lab. I want to say, we crossed the threshold—"Abandon all hope, ye who enter here." I put my trust in her, like Dante following Virgil into the underworld. We wound our way among the sleek gurneys with their sheet-shrouded burdens. Not another soul breathed in that vast space. The smell of formaldehyde was an assault. The silence was thick, as if the bodies had absorbed all the sound, like flannel, like blankets, like snow.

Source: Copyright © 2000, as first published in *The Atlantic Monthly*.

She showed me first the trays of parts, stainless-steel basins of raw things—one 5 full of kidneys, another of livers—like offerings in a meat market. She spoke in hushed tones, as if we were in an intensive-care room or a nursery. We approached the gurney that bore the cadaver she had been dissecting. Slowly, gently, she turned back the cover from the thin white feet and legs. "We'll start here," she said. "The head is so very personal." I knew she was allowing me time to prepare for the intimacy of that encounter.

She pointed to a clipboard on a low wall, where the history of the cadaver was 6 detailed. He was an old man—and an old cadaver, having been in storage for many months. I don't remember why he died. She told me that in some medical-school labs the students make dark jokes and horse around, probably in an effort to handle their feelings. She was grateful that the attitude here was different.

She raised the sheet from the lower torso, which was laid open like a display pack- 7 age. I was astonished to see that our bodies' essential parts are all neatly organized, many in their own little membranes like plastic-wrapped leftovers in a well-maintained refrigerator. I had always assumed that the coils of intestines, the stomach, the liver, the spleen, would be jumbled up together. The tidy reality was strangely satisfying.

She had been working on a section of colon, I think it was. I watched in fascination 8 as she carefully removed the covering from the head. She said. "It is so important to us students to have this experience. And if people are willing to donate their bodies for us, we must, must give them due respect."

I gazed at the small face of an old man, an old man who somehow linked my 9 daughter and me and all human flesh together, in the semi-dark, in this timeless moment.

Outside, green, growing leaves were gleaming softly under a star-studded sky. Up 10 into the freshness of evening we came, full of a sense of the enduring connectedness of all living things, and of the child who becomes the parent and the parent the child.

Study Questions

1. Garlan describes two subjects. What are they?

2. What is the dominant impression of each subject that Garlan describes?

3. Cite an example of each of the following: sensory detail of smell, sensory detail of sound, and sensory detail of sight.

4. A **simile** is a comparison of two unlike items, using the word *like* or the word *as*. For example, in paragraph 7, Garlan says that body parts were "like plastic-wrapped leftovers in a well-maintained refrigerator." Cite another simile in the essay. Are the similes an effective descriptive strategy? Explain.

5. What strategy does Garlan use to conclude her essay? Does the conclusion provide a satisfying finish? Explain.

6. What strategy or vocabulary did you learn in this reading that you might try out in your own writing?

7. **Other Patterns** How does Garlan use narration in the essay?

From Reading to Writing

1. Like Garlan, describe a place that is very quiet. Alternatively, describe a place that is very noisy. Try to select a place that you can visit to select your sensory details.

2. Describe a friend or relative. Be sure to have a dominant impression, such as "trendy," "dainty," or "imposing."

3. Describe a laboratory or some other specialized classroom on campus. Remember to include a dominant impression.

4. Like Garlan, describe a place most people do not see, such as the kitchen of a local restaurant, the stockroom where you work, the basement of your house, or the broadcast booth of the campus radio station. Remember to include your dominant impression.

5. Write an editorial for your local or campus newspaper to encourage people to donate their bodies to medical schools' anatomy labs.

6. In the last paragraph, Garlan mentions "the child who becomes the parent and the parent the child." Tell about a time a parent and child reversed roles.

ILLUSTRATION

Words That Wound

Kathleen Vail

In this 1999 article from *American School Board Journal,* Kathleen Vail addresses the serious issue of bullying in our schools, using examples to illustrate both its devastating effects and our lack of an appropriate response. As you read, think about the fact that Vail's original audience was public school managers. Consider her purpose for writing and whether she achieves that purpose. Also, notice that Vail combines illustration with narration and cause-and-effect analysis in order to achieve her purpose for writing.

Before you read, review the following vocabulary:

Columbine High School—in 1999, two students killed thirteen people and wounded twenty-three others at this school in Colorado

crusader—a person who works for a cause

condoning—approving

battery—a beating

lobby—to try to influence a legislator to pass a law

Brian Head saw only one way out. On the final day of his life, during economics class, the 15-year-old stood up and pointed a semi-automatic handgun at himself. Before he pulled the trigger, he said his last words: "I can't take this anymore." 1

Brian's father, William Head, has no doubt why his only child chose to take his life in front of a classroom full of students five years ago. Brian wanted everyone to know the source of his pain, the suffering he could no longer endure. The Woodstock, Ga., teen, overweight with thick glasses, had been systematically abused by school bullies since elementary school. Death was the only relief he could imagine. "Children can't vote or organize, leave or run away," says Head. "They are trapped." 2

For many students, school is a torture chamber from which there is no escape. Every day, 160,000 children stay home from school because they are afraid of being bullied, according to the National Association of School Psychologists. In a study of junior high and high school students from small Midwestern towns, nearly 77 percent of the students reported they'd been victims of bullies at school—14 percent saying they'd experienced severe reactions to the abuse. "Bullying is a crime of violence," says June Arnette, associate director of the National School Safety Center. "It's an imbalance of power, sustained over a period of time." 3

4   Yet even in the face of this suffering, even after Brian Head's suicide five years ago, even after it was revealed this past spring that a culture of bullying might have played a part in the Columbine High School shootings, bullying remains for the most part unacknowledged, underreported, and minimized by schools. Adults are unaware of the extent and nature of the problem, says Nancy Mullin-Rindler, associate director of the Project on Teasing and Bullying in the Elementary Grades at Wellesley College Center for Research on Women. "They underestimate the import. They feel it's a normal part of growing up, that it's character-building."

5   After his son's death, William Head became a crusader against bullying, founding an effort called Kids Hope to prevent others from suffering as Brian had. Unfortunately, bullying claimed another victim in the small town of Woodstock: 13-year-old Josh Belluardo. Last November, on the bus ride home from school, Josh's neighbor, 15-year-old Jonathan Miller, taunted him and threw wads of paper at him. He followed Josh off the school bus, hit the younger boy in the back of the head, and kicked him in the stomach. Josh spent the last two days of his life in a coma before dying of his injuries. Miller, it turns out, had been suspended nearly 20 times for offenses such as pushing and taunting other students and cursing at a teacher. He's now serving a life sentence for felony murder while his case is on appeal.

6   Bullying doesn't have to result in death to be harmful. Bullying and harassment are major distractions from learning, according to the National School Safety Center. Victims' grades suffer, and fear can lead to chronic absenteeism, truancy, or dropping out. Bullies also affect children who aren't victimized: Bystanders feel guilty and helpless for not standing up to the bully. They feel unsafe, unable to take action. They also can be drawn into bullying behavior by peer pressure. "Any time there is a climate of fear, the learning process will be compromised," says Arnette.

7   A full 70 percent of children believe teachers handle episodes of bullying "poorly," according to a study by John Hoover at the University of North Dakota at Grand Forks. It's no wonder kids are reluctant to tell adults about bullying incidents. "Children feel no one will take them seriously," says Robin Kowalski, professor of psychology at Western Carolina University, Cullowhee, N.C., who's done research on teasing behavior.

8   Martha Rizzo, who lives in a suburb of Cincinnati, calls bullying the "dirty little secret" of her school district. Both her son and daughter were teased in school. Two boys in her son's sixth-grade class began taunting him because he wore sweatpants instead of jeans. They began to intimidate him during class. Once they knocked the pencil out of his hand during a spelling test when the teacher's back was turned. He failed the test. Rizzo made an appointment with the school counselor. The counselor told her he could do nothing about the behavior of the bullies and suggested she get counseling for her son instead. "Schools say they do something, but they don't, and it continues," says Rizzo. "We go in with the same problem over and over again."

9   Anna Billoit of Louisiana went to her son's middle school teachers when her son, who had asthma and was overweight, was being bullied by his classmates. Some of the teachers made the situation worse, she says. One male teacher suggested to her that the teasing would help her son mature. "His attitude was 'Suck it up, take it like a man,'" says Billoit.

10   Much bullying goes on in so-called transition areas where there is little or no adult supervision: hallways, locker rooms, restrooms, cafeterias, playgrounds, buses, and bus stops. When abuse happens away from adult eyes, it's hard to prove that the abuse occurred. Often, though, bullies harass their victims in the open, in full view of teachers and other adults. Some teachers will ignore the behavior, silently condoning it. But even when adults try to deal with the problem, they sometimes make things worse for the victim by not handling the situation properly. Confronting bullies in front of their peers

only enhances the bullies' prestige and power. And bullies often step up the abuse after being disciplined. "People know it happens, but there's no structured way to deal with it," says Mullin-Rindler. "There's lots of confusion about what to do and what is the best approach."

Societal expectations play a part in adult reactions to childhood bullying. Many teachers and administrators buy into a widespread belief that bullying is a normal part of childhood and that children are better off working out such problems on their own. But this belief sends a dangerous message to children, says Head. Telling victims they must protect themselves from bullies shows children that adults can't and won't protect them. And, he points out, it's an attitude adults would never tolerate themselves. "If you go to work and get slapped on the back of the head, you wouldn't expect your supervisor to say, 'It's your problem—you need to learn to deal with it yourself,'" says Head. "It's a human-rights issue."   11

Ignoring bullying is only part of the problem. Some teachers go further by blaming the victims for their abuse by letting their own dislike for the victimized child show. "There's a lot of secret admiration for the strong kids," says Eileen Faucette of Augusta, Ga. Her daughter was teased so badly in the classroom that she was afraid to go to the blackboard or raise her hand to answer a question. The abuse happened in front of her teacher, who did nothing to stop it.   12

Head also encountered a blame-the-victim attitude toward his son. Brian would get into trouble for fighting at school, but when Head and his wife investigated what happened, they usually found that Brian had been attacked by other students. The school, Head said, wanted to punish Brian along with his attackers. "The school calls it fighting," Head says. "But it's actually assault and battery."   13

And changes are coming. This past April, five months after Josh Belluardo's death, the Georgia State Legislature passed an anti-bullying law. The law defines bullying as "any willful attempt or threat to inflict injury on another person when accompanied by an apparent present ability to do so" or "any intentional display of force such as would give the victim reason to fear or expect immediate bodily harm." Schools are required to send students to an alternative school if they commit a third act of bullying in a school year. The law also requires school systems to adopt anti-bullying policies and to post the policies in middle and high schools.   14

Head was consulted by the state representatives who sponsored the bill, but he believes the measures don't go far enough. He urges schools to treat bullying behavior as a violation of the state criminal law against assault, stalking, and threatening, and to call the police when the law is broken.   15

He knows it's too late for Brian, too late for Josh, too late for the teens who died in Littleton. But he continues to work, to educate and lobby on the devastating effects of bullying so that his son's death will not have been in vain.   16

"We should come clean and say what we've done in the past is wrong," says Head. "Now we will guarantee we'll protect the rights of students."   17

Study Questions

1. In your own words, write out the thesis of "Words That Wound." Where in the essay is the thesis stated?

2. For what reason do you think Vail wrote "Words That Wound"? Do you think she achieves her purpose? Why or why not?

3. Which paragraphs include examples? How do the examples help Vail achieve her purpose for writing?

4. In the introduction, how does Vail stimulate readers' interest in her essay?

5. What strategy or vocabulary did you learn in this reading that you might try out in your own writing?

6. **Other Patterns** Which paragraphs include narration? How does that narration help Vail achieve her writing purpose? How does Vail use cause-and-effect analysis to achieve her purpose?

From Reading to Writing

1. Bullying is not the only problem that students face in elementary, middle, and high school. Identify another problem and use examples to illustrate it.

2. Identify a problem that college students face, and use examples to illustrate it.

3. Bullying also occurs outside of school—in the workplace and on the athletic field, for example. Give examples of bullying that occurs outside of school.

4. If you have witnessed or been the victim of bullying, give your own examples of it, being sure to mention the effects.

5. Pick a hurtful behavior besides bullying and use examples to illustrate it and its effects.

6. Give examples of ways students, teachers, and parents can prevent bullying.

Beauty and the Beef

Joey Green

One-time contributing editor to *The National Lampoon* and *Spy* magazine, Joey Green has written more than thirty books, including *Contrary to Popular Belief* (2005), *Rainy Day Magic* (2006), and *Joey Green's Fix-It Magic* (2008). He has also appeared on *The Tonight Show with Jay Leno* and *The View* and has been profiled in *People* magazine. In "Beauty and the Beef," which originally appeared in *Spy* magazine (1996), Green uses process analysis to explain why that fast-food hamburger looks so good on television. Be sure to notice how description and contrast help Green achieve his purpose.

Before reading the essay, review the following vocabulary:

Madison Avenue—a reference to the advertising industry

preternaturally—supernaturally

When was the last time you opened a carton in a fast-food restaurant to find a 1
hamburger as appetizing as the ones in the TV commercials? Did you ever look past the counter help to catch a glimpse of a juicy hamburger patty, handsomely branded by the grill, sizzling and crackling as it glides over the roaring flames, with tender juices sputtering into the fire? On television the burger is a magnificent slab of flame-broiled beef—majestically topped with crisp iceberg lettuce, succulent red tomatoes, tangy onions and plump pickles, all between two halves of a towering sesame-seed bun. But, of course, the real-life Whoppers don't quite measure up.

The ingredients of a TV Whopper are, unbelievably, the same as those used in real 2
Whoppers sold to average consumers. But like other screen personalities, the Whopper needs a little help from makeup.

When making a Burger King commercial, J. Walter Thompson, the company's 3
advertising agency, usually devotes at least a day to filming "beauty shots" of the food. Burger King supplies the agency with several large boxes of frozen beef patties. But before a patty is sent over the flame broiler, a professionally trained food stylist earning between $500 and $750 a day prepares it for the camera.

The crew typically arrives at 7:00 a.m. and spends two hours setting up lights that 4
will flatter the burger. Then the stylist, aided by two assistants, begins by burning "flame-broiling stripes" into the thawed hamburger patties with a special Madison Avenue branding iron. Because the tool doesn't always leave a rich, charcoal-black impression on the patty, the stylist uses a fine paintbrush to darken the singed crevices with a sauce

Source: From *Spy* magazine, 1996. Reprinted by permission of the author.

the color of motor oil. The stylist also sprinkles salt on the patty so when it passes over the flames, natural juices will be encouraged to rise to the meat's surface.

5   Thus branded, retouched and juiced, the patties are run back and forth over a conveyor-belt broiler while the director films the little spectacle from a variety of angles. Two dozen people watch from the wings: lighting assistants, prop people, camera assistants, gas specialists, the client and agency people—producers, writers, art directors. Of course, as the meat is broiled blood rises to the surface in small pools. Since, for the purpose of advertising, bubbling blood is not a desirable special effect, the stylist, like a prissy microsurgical nurse, continually dabs at the burger with a Q-Tip.

6   Before the patty passes over the flame a second time, the food stylist maneuvers a small electric heater an inch or so above the burger to heat up the natural fatty juices until they begin to steam and sizzle. Otherwise puddles of grease will cover the meat. Sometimes the patties are dried out on a bed of paper towels. Before they're sent over the flame broiler again, the stylist relubricates them with a drop of corn oil to guarantee picturesque crackling and sizzling.

7   If you examine any real Whopper at any Burger King closely, you'll discover flame-broiling stripes only on the top side of the beef patty. Hamburgers are sent through the flame broiler once; they're never flipped over. The commercials imply otherwise. On television a beef patty, fetchingly covered with flame-broiling stripes, travels over the broiler, indicating that the burger has been flipped to sear stripes into the other side.

8   In any case, the camera crew has just five or ten seconds in the life cycle of a TV Whopper to capture good, sizzling brown beef on film. After that the hamburger starts to shrink rapidly as the water and the grease are cooked from it. Filming lasts anywhere from three to eight hours, depending on the occurence of a variety of technical problems—heavy smoke, grease accumulating on the camera equipment, the gas specialist's failure to achieve a perfect, preternaturally orange glowing flame. Out of one day's work, and anywhere between 50 and 75 hamburgers, the agency hopes to get five seconds of usable footage. Most of the time the patties are either too raw, bloody, greasy or small.

9   Of course, the cooked hamburger patty depicted sitting on a sesame seed bun in the commercial is a different burger from those towel-dried, steak-sauce-dabbed, corn-oiled specimens that were filmed sliding over the flames. This presentation patty hasn't been flame-broiled at all. It's been branded with the phony flame-broiling marks, retouched with steak sauce—and then microwaved.

10   Truth in advertising, however, is maintained, sort of: when you're shown the final product—a completely built hamburger topped with sliced vegetables and condiments—you are seeing the actual quantities of ingredients found on the average real Whopper. On television, though, you're only seeing half of the hamburger—the front half. The lettuce, tomatoes, onions and pickles have all been shoved to the front of the burger. The stylist has carefully nudged and manicured the ingredients so that they sit just right. The red, ripe tomatoes are flown in fresh from California the morning of the shoot. You might find such tomatoes on your hamburger—if you ordered several hundred Whoppers early in the morning, in Fresno. The lettuce and tomatoes are cut, trimmed and then piled on top of a cold cooked hamburger patty, and the whole construction is sprayed with a fine mist of glycerine to glisten and shimmer seductively. Finally the hamburger is capped with a painstakingly hand-crafted sesame-seed bun. For at least an hour the stylist has been kneeling over the bun like a lens grinder, positioning each sesame seed. He dips a toothpick in Elmer's glue and, using a pair of tweezers, places as many as 300 seeds, one by one, onto a formerly bald bun.

11   When it's all over, the crew packs up the equipment, and 75 gorgeous-looking hamburgers are dumped in the garbage.

Study Questions

1. In which paragraph does the process analysis begin? What is the purpose of the paragraphs that come before the process analysis?

2. For what purpose do you think Joey Green wrote "Beauty and the Beef"?

3. In which paragraphs does Green explain how steps in the process are performed? In which paragraphs does he explain why steps are performed? How do these explanations help Green achieve his writing purpose?

4. What strategy does Green use for his conclusion?

5. What strategy or vocabulary did you learn in this reading that you might try out in your own writing?

6. **Other Patterns** How does the description in paragraphs 1, 9, 10 and elsewhere help Green achieve his writing purpose? How does the contrast in paragraphs 1, 7, 9, and 10 help him achieve his writing purpose?

From Reading To Writing

1. Explain a process related to buying, growing, preparing, or serving food, such as planting a garden, cooking the perfect omelet, decorating a cake, or setting a festive table.

2. Explain a process for making something seem more appealing than it really is.

3. Explain a process for displaying something attractively, such as staging a house for sale or arranging flowers in a centerpiece.

4. Explain a process for making something or someone look beautiful.

5. In paragraph 10, Green says this about advertising the Whopper: "Truth in advertising, however, is maintained, sort of." Do you think that when food stylists beautify products for television, truth in advertising is maintained? Explain your view.

6. Select a television or magazine advertisement and explain how it motivates consumers to buy the product or use the service that is advertised.

Supermodel?

Jenny Bradner

In this 2001 essay that first appeared in the newspaper supplement *Family Style,* Jenny Bradner objects to the popular definition of a supermodel and offers her own definition as a replacement. The essay refers to a fairy tale called "The Emperor's New Clothes," which is about an emperor who was approached by two swindlers who promised to make him the most beautiful suit of clothes in the world—and one that would appear invisible to anyone who was stupid or incompetent. The swindlers pretended to weave the clothes, and the people, including the emperor himself, were afraid to admit that they saw nothing.

Before reading the essay, review the following vocabulary:

accolades—honors; praise

emulation—imitation

paradox—contradiction

lemmings—small rodents known to migrate into the sea where many are drowned; a reference to following a trend or leader, even if doing so leads to disaster

Rothschild—a wealthy banking family

Michael Jordan—a famous basketball player

Claudia Schiffer and Carol Alt—supermodels

Gandhi—an Indian nationalist leader who believed in securing Indian independence through nonviolence

Mother Theresa—a Catholic missionary who worked with the poor in India

Cal Ripken—a famous baseball player

---

1   I'm scanning the pages of *Cosmopolitan* magazine and I'm offended. I'm offended that these airbrushed women—women of cosmetic surgery and eating disorders, women caked with cosmetics and enhanced by lights and wardrobe—are the members of a segment of society that we have deemed both super and models.

2   Maybe you're thinking I am some overweight, miserable housewife with nothing better to do than pick on the beautiful elite. Not so. I'm just frustrated by the accolades these magazine images receive when I am surrounded by examples of real people who truly are both super and models.

The dictionary describes *super* this way: "a generalized term of approval," and "being of a high grade or quality, very large or powerful, or exhibiting the characteristics of its type to an extreme or excessive degree." It defines *model* like this: "an example for imitation or emulation or one who is employed to display clothes." So, while I see how such a pairing of words does describe Cindy Crawford and her cohorts, I am also left to ponder the paradox of identifying this clique as both super and models.   3

I wonder if we have trouble calling a person either super or a model if he or she bears any resemblance to ourselves. That is, we don't believe that others would consider us to be super or models, and, thus, the term must only refer to those who bear no resemblance to us. And models certainly fit *that* bill. In general, they are taller and thinner, and have features more striking than many other individuals. But does that really make them supermodels? Or does it just make them freaks of nature?   4

Maybe you'll argue that the *super* in supermodel refers not to what they look like, but rather to their careers—to the unbelievable fees they command. And that *model* refers simply to the act of displaying clothes. Either way, the message is obscene: If you are tall, thin, and strangely attractive, and if you can make more money and last longer in the business than other models, then you are deemed a supermodel.   5

And truthfully, *model* no longer refers only to displaying clothes. It actually and quite frighteningly has come to mean *role model* in a truly shocking way: If during your career you inspire thousands of little girls to put stock in their beauty instead of their brains, and if your work helps lead them to self-destructive behaviors, including eating disorders and abusive relationships brought on by low self-esteem, then you have truly made it to the top. That's super? That's a model?   6

Do we really believe this, or have we fallen prey to the same thinking that got the emperor to walk naked through the streets and all of his people to exclaim and congratulate him on his fine new suit of clothes? Are we these lemmings? In some ways, sadly, yes.   7

But there is still hope. We know who our role models should be. We know that parents are super for reaching within and beyond themselves solely for the well-being of another human being. We know that teachers are super for working with children and adults to better their lives while getting little more than some personal satisfaction as compensation. Gandhi was super. Mother Theresa was super. People who commit their lives to improving the lives of others are super. *They* are models.   8

Cliché? Call it what you will. But if you ask me, we've got the wrong bunch up on pedestals. We know who our role models should be, but in our own reversion to our awkward middle-school days, we just can't bring ourselves to stand up and shout, "The Emperor's naked!" And until we can do that, supermodels will continue to reign as our super models, and teenagers will continue to develop eating disorders.   9

I use supermodels as the examples and not the rule only because the phrase fits so neatly. But they aren't the sole offenders. Professional athletes, actors, the painfully wealthy. None of these bear resemblance to the truest meaning of the term supermodel, but they have captured our love and admiration seemingly for no other reason than that they are bigger than life. They, too, contribute to making regular people feel like failures, causing children and adults alike to suffer in pursuit of the unattainable.   10

Let's roll out the red carpet to honor those who deserve honoring. And while we're at it, let's rein in the salaries of professional athletes and fashion models, and beef up those of teachers and social workers. Not possible? Well, let's at least remember to thank our parents and teachers and not covet Carol Alt's thighs or Cal Ripken's swing. Besides, who among us really wants to give up chocolate glazed donuts and lazy coffee dates with friends?   11

I can't be a Rothschild. I can't be Michael Jordan or Claudia Schiffer. I can, however, be honest and kind, intelligent and generous. Not very glamorous, I know. But far more valuable.   12

Study Questions

1. What is Bradner defining, and what is her assertion about the term she is defining?

2. Generally, definition paragraphs and essays should not include dictionary-style definitions. However, "Supermodel" includes two dictionary definitions in paragraph 3. Are those definitions a problem? Why or why not?

3. Bradner uses sentence fragments intentionally in paragraphs 9 and 12 in order to create a special effect. Identify the fragments. Why do you think she uses them? (If you want to use fragments for special effect, consult with your instructor.)

4. How does explaining what her term is *not* help the author achieve her purpose for writing?

5. For what purpose do you think Bradner wrote "Supermodel?"

6. What strategy or vocabulary did you learn in this reading that you might try out in your own writing?

7. **Other Patterns** How does the author use examples to develop her definition? How does she use contrast?

From Reading to Writing

1. Write a definition of *supermodel* that explains what most people think a supermodel is.

2. Bradner says in paragraph 8, "We know who our role models should be." Pick one person you think of as a role model. In a paragraph, tell why that person is a role model for you.

3. Explain how you respond to the models you see in a magazine. Why do you have that reaction?

4. Write a definition of *role model* or *hero*.

5. In paragraph 11, Bradner says that we should "rein in the salaries of professional athletes." Argue for or against Bradner's view.

6. Why do we look up to supermodels, athletes, actors, and rock stars?

They Shut My Grandmother's Room Door

Andrew Lam

Pacific News Service editor Andrew Lam is a short-story writer and journalist who lives in San Francisco. In the following essay, Lam draws on experiences in Vietnam and the United States to contrast the two cultures' views of death. Be sure to determine which culture's view he prefers.

Before reading the essay, review the following vocabulary:

convalescent home—nursing home

Tet—the Vietnamese new year

disjointed—disconnected

escrow—money held as part of a contract

filial piety—the respect of a son or daughter

wafting—floating through air

1   When someone dies in the convalescent home where my grandmother lives, the nurses rush to close all the patients' doors. Though as a policy death is not to be seen at the home, she can always tell when it visits. The series of doors being slammed shut remind her of the firecrackers during Tet.

2   The nurses' efforts to shield death are more comical to my grandmother than reassuring. "Those old ladies die so often," she quips in Vietnamese, "everyday's like new year."

3   Still, it is lonely to die in such a place. I imagine some wasted old body under a white sheet being carted silently through the empty corridor on its way to the morgue. While in America a person may be born surrounded by loved ones, in old age one is often left to take the last leg of life's journey alone.

4   Perhaps that is why my grandmother talks now mainly of her hometown, Bac-Lieu; its river and green rich rice fields. Having lost everything during the war, she can now offer me only her distant memories: life was not disjointed back home; one lived in a gentle rhythm with the land; people died in their homes surrounded by neighbors and relatives. And no one shut your door.

5   So it goes. The once gentle, connected world of the past is but the language of dreams. In this fast-paced society of disjointed lives, we are swept along and have little

time left for spiritual comfort. Instead of relying on neighbors and relatives, on the river and land, we deal with the language of materialism: overtime, escrow, stress, down payment, credit cards, tax shelter. Instead of going to the temple to pray for good health, we pay life and health insurance religiously.

6   My grandmother's children and grandchildren share a certain pang of guilt. After a stroke which paralyzed her, we could no longer keep her at home. And although we visit her regularly, we are not living up to the filial piety standard expected of us in the old country. My father silently grieves and my mother suffers from headaches. (Does she see herself in such a home in a decade or two?)

7   Once, a long time ago, living in Vietnam we used to stare death in the face. The war in many ways had heightened our sensibilities toward living and dying. I can still hear the wails of widows and grieving mothers. Though the fear of death and dying is a universal one, the Vietnamese did not hide from it. Instead we dwelt in its tragedy. Death pervaded our poems, novels, fairy tales, and songs.

8   But if agony and pain are part of Vietnamese culture, pleasure is at the center of America's culture. While Vietnamese holidays are based on death anniversaries, birthdays are celebrated here. American popular culture translates death with something like nauseating humor. People laugh and scream at blood and guts movies. The wealthy freeze their dead relatives in liquid nitrogen. Cemeteries are places of big business, complete with colorful brochures. I hear there are even drive-by funerals where you don't have to get out of your own car to pay your respects to the deceased.

9   That America relies upon the pleasure principle and happy endings in its entertainments does not, however, assist us in evading suffering. The reality of the suffering of old age is apparent in the convalescent home. There is an old man, once an accomplished concert pianist, now rendered helpless by arthritis. Every morning he sits staring at the piano. One feeble woman who outlived her children keeps repeating, "My son will take me home." Then there are those mindless, bedridden bodies kept alive, through a series of tubes and pulsating machines.

10   But despair is not newsworthy. Death itself must be embellished or satirized or deep-frozen in order to catch the public's attention.

11   Last week on her eighty-second birthday I went to see my grandmother. She smiled her sweet sad smile.

12   "Where will you end up in your old age?" she asked me, her mind as sharp as ever.

13   The memories of monsoon rain and tropical sun and relatives and friends came to mind. Not here, not here, I wanted to tell her. But the soft moaning of a patient next door and the smell of alcohol wafting from the sterile corridor brought me back to reality.

14   "Anywhere is fine," I told her instead, trying to keep up with her courageous spirit. "All I am asking for is that they don't shut my door."

Study Questions

1. What subjects is Lam contrasting?

2. For what purpose do you think Lam wrote "They Shut My Grandmother's Room Door"?

3. Explain the difference between the way Americans and Vietnamese view death. How does the closed door reflect the difference?

4. Lam uses both a point-by-point organization and a subject-by-subject organization. (See pages 110–111 for more on these organizational strategies.) Which paragraphs are organized with a subject-by-subject pattern? Which paragraphs are organized with a point-by-point pattern?

5. Lam concludes his essay by saying, " 'All I am asking for is that they don't shut my door,' " What does he mean? How does that statement bring the essay to a satisfying finish?

6. What strategy or vocabulary did you learn in this reading that you might try out in your own writing?

7. **Other Patterns** Which paragraph includes examples? How does illustration help Lam achieve his purpose for writing?

From Reading to Writing

1. In paragraphs 4 and 5, Lam contrasts the present time in the United States and an earlier time in Vietnam. Contrast some aspect of your life now with that aspect at an earlier time. For example, you can consider your attitude toward school, the way you view friendship, what you do to relax, or your idea of a good time.

2. If you have lived with or cared for an elderly relative, tell what the experience was like.

3. Lam accuses Americans of avoiding aging and death. Agree or disagree with him, citing examples to support your view.

4. Compare or contrast the rituals surrounding death in your culture or religion with those of some other culture or religion. To learn about the rituals of another culture or religion, interview one or more people.

5. Despite her age, her stroke, and her confinement to a nursing home, Lam's grandmother had a "courageous spirit" (paragraph 14). Tell about an elderly person you know or knew and explain the nature of that person's spirit. As an alternative, tell about the spirit of someone you know who lives with adversity.

6. In paragraph 8, Lam says that "pleasure is at the center of America's culture." Agree or disagree, using examples to support your view.

CAUSE-AND-EFFECT ANALYSIS

Sometimes Honesty Is the Worst Policy

Judy Mandell

Judy Mandell has experienced age discrimination. In this 2002 essay, which first appeared in *Newsweek*'s "My Turn" column, she discusses the effects of that discrimination as well as what causes some women to lie about their age. As you read, consider how the author uses contrast and examples to support her points.

Before reading the essay, review the following vocabulary:

fabricate—make up

naïve—inexperienced and lacking sophistication

prone—having a tendency toward something

1   For as long as I've known her, an elderly relative of mine has lied about how old she is. She lives in a retirement community in the South. She looks great for her age—but I can't tell you what it is. I'm sworn to secrecy. Her friends think she's three years younger. "What's a few years among friends?" I asked her. "No one wants to be with an old lady," she answered.

2   She takes lying about her age to the extreme. Several years ago, when she was the only survivor of an automobile accident, she had the presence of mind to fabricate her age to the emergency medical technicians as they wheeled her into the ambulance. She was nearly arrested by U.S. Immigration officers because she crossed off and changed her birth date on her passport. For her, tampering with official documents is a way of life; she recently made me promise not to put her true age in her obituary.

3   I, on the other hand, had never lied about my age. I was proud, in fact, even when I turned 50. Why should I lie? I was told I looked good, and I felt great. My kids were grown, my marriage was fine, and I had a great job. I loved it when people said, "Your kids are *that* old? I can't believe it!" I thought that people who wouldn't reveal their age suffered from low self-esteem. That is, until my boss, the new, thirtysomething school headmaster, found out how old I was.

4   I taught part time and did fund-raising for a small private school. I was the second oldest person on the faculty. I never imagined that it could matter until the morning I met with the headmaster in his office. We chatted about the school, the students and me. "How old are you?" he asked. When I answered 50, he seemed to stop breathing. He definitely stopped talking. There was a long, strange silence.

5   "Why are you asking?" I said.

Source: From *Newsweek*, October 21, 2002. All rights reserved. Reprinted by permission.

"Never mind," he answered.   6

I should have lied.   7

I was angry that my boss had asked that question, but I didn't want to rock the   8
boat, so I let it pass.

Several weeks later the headmaster informed me that the school was having finan-   9
cial difficulties. They "just couldn't afford me," he said. I was let go.

Sure, there were age-discrimination laws 10 years ago, but I had no proof that age   10
was the reason I was fired. I just took it on the chin, telling myself this guy was a jerk, I'd
have more time for my writing and, anyhow, I must look pretty good if he was so shocked
that I was 50.

My friend PJ, a book editor, never cared about who knew her age—until recently.   11
"I don't look my age, but that doesn't matter anymore," she told me. "When younger people know I'm in my mid-50s, they treat me differently. They realize I'm their parents' age."

Another friend, a mother of three, lies about her age or avoids the subject. When   12
her husband left her for a younger woman, she had a tummy tuck and a face-lift. She's
dating, but it's hard to find a man interested in a 45-year-old woman. She says she'll
tell her age if she finds someone she wants to settle down with. In the meantime, she's
keeping it a secret.

After I lost my job, I decided to keep quiet, too. I even requested that my date of   13
birth be dropped from the Library of Congress data on the copyright page of my books.

Then last month I accepted an invitation to have lunch with a New York book edi-   14
tor. We had had several phone conversations but never met in person. I knew she was
under 30, but of course I had never told her how old I am.

I worried, even obsessed, about how she would react when she saw me. But when   15
we finally met, I detected no disappointment. In fact, we had fun, chatting and laughing like a couple of teenagers. After a while, I told her my age and asked her how she
viewed women over 50.

Her answer surprised me. She confided that women over 50 made her nervous   16
because she was afraid that they would perceive her as young. And to her, being young
meant being naïve and prone to errors. She viewed older women as worldly, seasoned,
deserving of respect. Although I envied her age, she seemed to envy mine.

Since that lunch, I've felt a lot better about my age. Sure, there are things about   17
getting older that aren't terrific, like memory lapses and sagging skin, but in many ways,
being mature is an advantage.

Not everyone agrees, so I still avoid the subject. But the next time I'm nervous or   18
self-conscious about telling a younger person my age, I'll try to remember that she may
be questioning how she will measure up to me.

Study Questions

1. According to the essay, what are the effects of being perceived as old?

2. What caused the author to change her mind about telling people her true age?

3. Explain the significance of the title. Do you think the title is a good one? Why
   or why not?

4. Give the transition that opens each of the following paragraphs, and state what
   relationship the transitions signal:

   a. paragraph 3

   b. paragraph 12

   c. paragraph 14

5. What strategy or vocabulary did you learn in this reading that you might try out in your own writing?

6. **Other Patterns** How does Mandell use comparison-contrast to help make her point? How does she use illustration?

From Reading to Writing

1. Using cause-and-effect analysis, explain why we value youth more than age.

2. Mandell focuses on the effects of age discrimination on women. Explain the effects on men.

3. Discuss the effects of being the age that you are.

4. Explain how age affects the way you perceive and react to people.

5. Explain how some aspect of the media, such as movies, television, advertising, or magazines affects the way we perceive age.

6. Tell about another time when honesty is not always the best policy.

What Are Friends For?

Marion Winik

A creative writing instructor and commentator for National Public Radio, Marion Winik has written *First Comes Love* (1997), a candid memoir about her marriage to a gay man who died of AIDS; *The Lunchbox Chronicles* (1999), voted *Child* magazine's book of the year; and *Above Us Only Sky* (2005). "What Are Friends For?" is from her memoir *Telling* (1995). As you read the essay, notice the humor and ask yourself what it adds to the piece.

Before reading the essay, review the following vocabulary:

accentuate—emphasize

inopportune—inconvenient

spectrum—scale

1   I was thinking about how everybody can't be everything to each other, but some people can be something to each other, thank God, from the ones whose shoulder you cry on to the ones whose half-slips you borrow to the nameless ones you chat with in the grocery line.

2   Buddies, for example, are the workhorses of the friendship world, the people out there on the front lines, defending you from loneliness and boredom. They call you up, they listen to your complaints, they celebrate your successes and curse your misfortunes, and you do the same for them in return. They hold out through innumerable crises before concluding that the person you're dating is no good, and even then understand if you ignore their good counsel. They accompany you to a movie with subtitles or to see the diving pig at Aquarena Springs. They feed your cat when you are out of town and pick you up from the airport when you get back. They come over to help you decide what to wear on a date. Even if it is with that creep.

3   What about family members? Most of them are people you just got stuck with, and though you love them, you may not have very much in common. But there is that rare exception, the Relative Friend. It is your cousin, your brother, maybe even your aunt. The two of you share the same views of the other family members. Meg never should have divorced Martin. He was the best thing that ever happened to her. You can confirm each other's memories of things that happened a long time ago. Don't you remember when Uncle Hank and Daddy had that awful fight in the middle of Thanksgiving dinner? Grandma always hated Grandpa's stamp collection; she probably left the window open during the hurricane on purpose.

4   While so many family relationships are tinged with guilt and obligation, a relationship with a Relative Friend is relatively worry-free. You don't even have to hide your vices from

this delightful person. When you slip out Aunt Joan's back door for a cigarette, she is already there.

5   Then there is that special guy at work. Like all the other people at the job site, at first he's just part of the scenery. But gradually he starts to stand out from the crowd. Your friendship is cemented by jokes about co-workers and thoughtful favors around the office. Did you see Ryan's hair? Want half my bagel? Soon you know the names of his turtles, what he did last Friday night, exactly which model CD player he wants for his birthday. His handwriting is as familiar to you as your own.

6   Though you invite each other to parties, you somehow don't quite fit into each other's outside lives. For this reason, the friendship may not survive a job change. Company gossip, once an infallible source of entertainment, soon awkwardly accentuates the distance between you. But wait. Like School Friends, Work Friends share certain memories which acquire a nostalgic glow after about a decade.

7   A Faraway Friend is someone you grew up with or went to school with or lived in the same town as until one of you moved away. Without a Faraway Friend, you would never get any mail addressed in handwriting. A Faraway Friend calls late at night, invites you to her wedding, always says she is coming to visit but rarely shows up. An actual visit from a Faraway Friend is a cause for celebration and binges of all kinds. Cigarettes, Chips Ahoy, bottles of tequila.

8   Faraway Friends go through phases of intense communication, then may be out of touch for many months. Either way, the connection is always there. A conversation with your Faraway Friend always helps to put your life in perspective: when you feel you've hit a dead end, come to a confusing fork in the road, or gotten lost in some crackerbox subdivision of your life, the advice of the Faraway Friend—who has the big picture, who is so well acquainted with the route that brought you to this place—is indispensable.

9   Another useful function of the Faraway Friend is to help you remember things from a long time ago, like the name of your seventh-grade history teacher, what was in that really good stir-fry, or exactly what happened that night on the boat with the guys from Florida.

10   Ah, the Former Friend. A sad thing. At best a wistful memory, at worst a dangerous enemy who is in possession of many of your deepest secrets. But what was it that drove you apart? A misunderstanding, a betrayed confidence, an unrepaid loan, an ill-conceived flirtation. A poor choice of spouse can do in a friendship just like that. Going into business together can be a serious mistake. Time, money, distance, cult religions: all noted friendship killers. . . .

11   And lest we forget, there are the Friends You Love to Hate. They call at inopportune times. They say stupid things. They butt in, they boss you around, they embarrass you in public. They invite themselves over. They take advantage. You've done the best you can, but they need professional help. On top of all this, they love you to death and are convinced they're your best friend on the planet.

12   So why do you continue to be involved with these people? Why do you tolerate them? On the contrary, the real question is, What would you do without them? Without Friends You Love to Hate, there would be nothing to talk about with your other friends. Their problems and their irritating stunts provide a reliable source of conversation for everyone they know. What's more, Friends You Love to Hate make you feel good about yourself, since you are obviously in so much better shape than they are. No matter what these people do, you will never get rid of them. As much as they need you, you need them too.

13   At the other end of the spectrum are Hero Friends. These people are better than the rest of us, that's all there is to it. Their career is something you wanted to be when you

grew up—painter, forest ranger, tireless doer of good. They have beautiful homes filled with special handmade things presented to them by villagers in the remote areas they have visited in their extensive travels. Yet they are modest. They never gossip. They are always helping others, especially those who have suffered a death in the family or an illness. You would think people like this would just make you sick, but somehow they don't.

A New Friend is a tonic unlike any other. Say you meet her at a party. In your bowling league. At a Japanese conversation class, perhaps. Wherever, whenever, there's that spark of recognition. The first time you talk, you can't believe how much you have in common. Suddenly, your life story is interesting again, your insights fresh, your opinion valued. Your various short-comings are as yet completely invisible.

14

It's almost like falling in love.

15

Study Questions

1. For what purpose do you think Winik wrote "What Are Friends For?"

2. Is each of Winik's eight groups of friends developed in approximately the same amount of detail? Is each developed in enough detail? Explain.

3. What is the principle of classification? *Hint:* Consider the title. (See page 131 on principle of classification.)

4. Winik presents each of her groups in a topic sentence. What are those topic sentences?

5. Cite two examples of humor in the essay. How does that humor help Winik achieve her writing purpose?

6. What strategy or vocabulary did you learn in this reading that you might try out in your own writing?

7. **Other Patterns** How does Winik use illustration to develop her classification of friends? Is that illustration important? Explain.

From Reading To Writing

1. Write your own classification of friends, using either different categories than Winik or different characteristics for some of the same categories. You do not have to use eight categories.

2. Write a classification of annoying people.

3. Write a classification of kinds of people you work with or kinds of students in one of your classes.

4. How important are friends in our lives? Explain their role and what they bring to our lives.

5. Select one kind of friend, such as the Buddy, Relative Friend, or Former Friend, and write a definition of that kind of friend.

6. What makes a best friend? In an essay, write a definition.

Thirsty? Try the Tap

Andrew D. Brunhart

Retired from the Navy after thirty years of service and currently the Deputy Director of the United States Mint, Andrew D. Brunhart was the general manager of the Washington Suburban Sanitary Commissions when he wrote "Thirsty? Try the Tap" for the *Washington Post* in 2007. (The Washington Suburban Sanitary District is the water and sewer agency for Montgomery and Prince George's County.) In the article, Brunhart argues that tap water is better than bottled water. When you are through reading, determine whether Brunhart convinces you.

Before reading the essay, review the following vocabulary:

agua—water

rampant—widespread or out of control

1   Pop quiz. You are running out the door but want to grab a drink. You know that drinking water is good for you, so you reach in the fridge for some agua. Do you grab (a) one of your store-bought bottles of drinking water that can cost over $1 or (b) your reusable sports bottle filled with drinking water from your tap that costs a fraction of a penny?

2   We at the Washington Suburban Sanitary Commission (WSSC) want the 1.8 million people we serve every day (and everyone else) to know why water straight from the tap is good for you, good for your pocketbook and good for the environment.

3   "But the quality is different," you say. "Bottled water is tastier and healthier." Not so. Water from the tap repeatedly wins taste tests across the country. And tap water includes fluoride, an essential additive to help children develop strong teeth.

4   According to a recent study from the Centers for Disease Control and Prevention, a growing number of young children are getting more cavities. A leading suspect is bottled water. Why? Most bottled brands do not contain fluoride.

5   "But bottled water is convenient," you say. "I can just grab one and go." Let me ask you another question. What's more convenient? Turning on the tap, filling a sports bottle and putting it in the refrigerator, or getting in the car, driving to your store, loading water into your cart, standing in the supermarket checkout line, putting the water in your car, driving it home and loading it into your fridge?

6   There isn't any question that using tap water is also better for your pocketbook. It simply costs less. A *lot* less. One dollar of WSSC water will fill more than 2,000 20-ounce plastic bottles, just like the one you buy at the store or get from a machine for $1.25. It's easy to see the better value.

7   "But is our tap water safe?" you ask. According to the Environmental Protection Agency, the United States has one of the safest water systems in the world. The WSSC tests the drinking water hundreds of thousands of times a year. In our 89 years of

providing tap water to Montgomery and Prince George's counties, our water quality has always met or surpassed EPA standards.

Finally, there is the environmental impact of drinking from a bottle instead of from the tap. Every plastic bottle of water requires the use of oil for making the bottle and transporting it to stores. Every day, an estimated 60 million plastic water bottles are thrown away. Most are not recycled. Millions end up in our local landfills. 8

In June the U.S. Conference of Mayors recognized the problems created by the rampant use of bottled water. It passed a resolution promoting the use of tap water and called for greater scrutiny of the impact of discarded bottles on landfills. 9

The WSSC is taking action as well. For years we have used small bottles of water with our name on them as a promotional tool. They have been a popular giveaway at community events, and we get many more requests than we can accommodate. But we will end that practice. We will still gladly come to community events and bring educational materials. But when our current supply of bottled water runs out, we will purchase no more. 10

So those are the facts. Tap water is safe. Tap water is healthy. Tap water is less expensive than bottled water, and it is better for the environment. Fill up that reusable sports bottle today. 11

Study Questions

1. For what purpose do you think Brunhart wrote "Thirsty? Try the Tap"?

2. Which sentence is the thesis of the essay?

3. What reasons does Brunhart give to support his position? (See page 143 on reasons and evidence.)

4. What evidence does he give to back up each reason?

5. Does Brunhart write a convincing argument? Explain.

6. What strategy or vocabulary did you learn in this reading that you might try out in your own writing?

7. **Other Patterns** How does Brunhart use contrast to help achieve his purpose for writing?

From Reading To Writing

1. Argue for a change on your campus that will help the environment or save energy, a change such as switching campus vehicles to hybrids, eliminating water bottles in all campus stores and restaurants, or switching to solar power.

2. Argue for or against mandatory recycling on your campus or in your town.

3. Write an argument to persuade students to do something that is good for them, such as stop drinking, become a vegetarian, eat organic produce, or give up soda.

4. Write a plan for helping people become less dependent on the automobile, and try to convince people to adopt your plan.

5. What can students do to save energy and improve the environment? Write a plan and try to convince students to adopt it.

6. Define "earth-friendly" or "environmentalist."

SUCCEEDING IN COLLEGE

Use Active Reading When You Read Your Textbooks

Use the active reading strategies you learned in this chapter when you read your textbooks, keeping the following points in mind.

- You may not be able to locate a thesis in textbook material, so concentrate on underlining or highlighting main ideas and important examples—the ones you want to be sure to learn for your examinations.

- Be careful not to underline or highlight too much, or you will end up memorizing most of the textbook when you study for your exams.

- Make sure you fully understand everything you underline or highlight. If you have any questions, write them down to ask in class.

- Pay particular attention to boldface terms; they are probably important vocabulary words you should learn.

- Carefully read summaries at the ends of chapters, and be sure you can answer any end-of-chapter questions.

Write about It

Select a textbook chapter you must know for one of your classes and read it with the active reading strategies. Then write up an explanation of how well you think the procedure worked for you, noting why you think the way you do.

CHAPTER 27
Writing Summaries and Essay Examination Answers

As a college student, you will often write summaries and essay examination answers to demonstrate that you have read and comprehended assigned materials. In this chapter, you will learn how to handle these important writing tasks.

WRITING A SUMMARY

A **summary** is a restatement—*in your own words*—of an author's most important ideas. When you summarize, you record an author's central point and major supporting details using your own wording and style.

You may be asked to summarize readings or chapters in textbooks so an instructor can check whether you understand reading assignments. In addition, you may have to include summarized material in research papers.

The Characteristics of a Summary

To write a successful summary, keep the following points in mind:

1. *Include only the author's central point (the thesis) and major supporting details.* Do not include minor details, examples, or explanations unless these are necessary for clarification.

2. *Include only the author's ideas.* Do not comment on something the author has said, because a summary focuses exclusively on what the author said.

3. *Keep the summary significantly shorter than the original.* Because you are including only the most important ideas, your summary is bound to be shorter than the original.

4. *Preserve the author's meaning.* Do not alter the author's meaning in any way. Here are two examples:

original:	Some states still have not enacted legislation mandating barrier-free structures.
unacceptable restatement:	No laws require barrier-free buildings in many states.

explanation:	*Many* in the restatement changes the meaning of the original because the author said *some*.
acceptable restatement:	In a number of states no laws require barrier-free buildings.
explanation:	Use of *a number of* does not alter the author's meaning.
original:	States that did not raise the drinking age to twenty-one would lose their federal highway funds.
unacceptable restatement:	States were being pressured to make twenty-one the legal age to drink.
explanation:	The restatement alters meaning by omitting important information: the fact that states that did not raise the drinking age would lose federal highway funds.
acceptable restatement:	Failure to make twenty-one the legal drinking age would cost states their federal highway funds.
explanation:	All the important information is in the restatement.

5. *Use your own wording and sentence style.* You must preserve the author's meaning, but you should restate the author's ideas in your own way. Here is an example:

original:	The trouble with Little League is that the coaches have emphasized winning at the expense of skill acquisition and having fun.
restatement:	Little League coaches stress winning rather than enjoyment and learning, thus creating problems.

Do not merely substitute **synonyms** (words with similar meaning) for the original words. Substituting synonyms is *not* restating in your own style because sentence structure is not altered. Here is an example:

original:	The trouble with Little League is that the coaches have emphasized winning at the expense of skill acquisition and having fun.
unacceptable restatement:	The problem (synonym) with Little League is that the managers (synonym) have stressed (synonym) beating the opponent (synonym) at the cost of (synonym) acquiring skills (synonym) and having a good time (synonym).
explanation:	The preceding restatement is unacceptable because sentence structure has not been changed. Instead, synonyms have been substituted for words in the original.

6. *Use some of the author's words when there is no acceptable substitute, or when you particularly like the author's phrasing.* In the Little League example, a restatement may include the words *Little League* because no other words will do. However,

if you use original words that are not part of your normal vocabulary or that are part of the author's distinctive phrasing, use quotation marks around the words. Here is an example:

original:	The trouble with Little League is that the coaches have emphasized winning at the expense of skill acquisition and having fun.
restatement:	Little League coaches stress winning but do not stress "skill acquisition" and the enjoyment of the game.
explanation:	"Little League," "coaches," and "winning" are used without quotation marks because there is no substitute and the words are part of most people's vocabulary. "Skill acquisition" appears with quotation marks because the phrase is part of the author's distinctive phrasing.

Use quotations when necessary, but do not overuse them. Most of the summary should be in your own words.

7. *Open with the author's name, the title of the material being summarized, and the author's topic, purpose, and/or thesis*. Here are sample openings for a summary of "Students in Shock" on pages 433–435.

> author's name, title, and topic presented: In "Students in Shock," John Kellmayer warns students about the stress associated with college and advises them to cope with the stress by taking advantage of certain campus resources.
> author's name, title, and thesis presented: John Kellmayer's "Students in Shock" explains that colleges are doing more to help students who are having problems.
> author's name, purpose, and thesis presented: To make college students aware of some of the challenges they might face and how to deal with them, John Kellmayer discusses common student problems and campus resources for solving those problems.

Notice that in each example, the verb that functions with the author's name or essay title is in the present tense. Even though the work was written in the past, use the present tense:

> John Kellmayer *warns* . . .
> "Students in Shock" *explains* . . .
> John Kellmayer *discusses* . . .

8. *To achieve coherence, repeat the author's name with a present tense verb*. Use phrases like these:

> Kellmayer also explains . . .
> Kellmayer continues by describing . . .
> Kellmayer goes on to show . . .

How to Write a Summary

Step 1   Read the material as many times as necessary to understand everything. Look up unfamiliar words.

Step 2   Underline the thesis, topic sentences, and major supporting details.

Step 3   On a separate sheet, write the underlined ideas in your own words.

Step 4   Write a first draft, opening with a sentence that includes the author, title, and the author's thesis, topic, and/or purpose. Use a present tense verb with the author's name. Then go to your list of restatements and write these in the same order the ideas appear in the original.

Step 5   Review the summary to be sure you can answer *yes* to the questions in the checklist that follows.

Step 6   Edit your summary carefully for mistakes.

✓ Checklist for a Summary

Before submitting your summary, be sure to work through this checklist.

☐ 1. I have opened with the author, title, and/or thesis, topic, or purpose.

☐ 2. I have included only the thesis and major supporting details.

☐ 3. I have altered the author's sentence structure and wording.

☐ 4. I have done more than substitute synonyms.

☐ 5. I have preserved the original meaning.

☐ 6. I have used quotation marks around words that are part of the author's special phrasing.

☐ 7. I have not added meaning.

☐ 8. I have referred to the author and the essay in the present tense.

☐ 9. I have written a summary that is shorter than the original.

☐ 10. I have edited carefully to find and correct mistakes.

☐ 11. I have proofread carefully after copying or typing the summary into its final form.

A Sample Summary

In the next essay, "How Bingeing Became the New College Sport," the main ideas and major supporting details have been underlined to mark them for inclusion in the summary that follows the essay.

Read through the essay, paying particular attention to the underlined material. Then read the summary that follows the essay. Notes in the margin of the summary call your attention to important features.

How Bingeing Became the New College Sport

Barrett Seaman

In this 2005 *Time* magazine article, Barrett Seaman discusses the college practice of drinking large amounts of alcohol in a short period of time. He has also written *Binge: What Your College Student Won't Tell You* (2005). As you read this essay, think about the amount of drinking that occurs on your campus.

In the coming weeks, millions of students will begin their fall semester of college, with all the attendant rituals of campus life: freshman orientation, registering for classes, rushing by fraternities and sororities and, in a more recent nocturnal college tradition, "pregaming" in their rooms. 1

Pregaming is probably unfamiliar to people who went to college before the 1990s. But it is now a common practice among 18-, 19- and 20-year-old students who cannot legally buy or consume alcohol. It usually involves sitting in a dorm room or an off-campus apartment and drinking as much hard liquor as possible before heading out for the evening's parties. While reporting for my book *Binge*, I witnessed the hospitalization of several students for acute alcohol poisoning. Among them was a Hamilton College freshman who had consumed 22 shots of vodka while sitting in a dorm room with her friends. Such hospitalizations are routine on campuses across the nation. By the Thanksgiving break of the year I visited Harvard, the university's health center had admitted nearly 70 students for alcohol poisoning. 2

When students are hospitalized—or worse yet, die from alcohol poisoning, which happens about 300 times each year—college presidents tend to react by declaring their campuses dry or shutting down fraternity houses. But tighter enforcement of the minimum drinking age of 21 is not the solution. It's part of the problem. 3

Over the past 40 years, the U.S. has taken a confusing approach to the age-appropriateness of various rights, privileges and behaviors. It used to be that 21 was the age that legally defined adulthood. On the heels of the student revolution of the late '60s, however, came sweeping changes: the voting age was reduced to 18; privacy laws were enacted that protected college students' academic, health and disciplinary records from outsiders, including parents; and the drinking age, which had varied from state to state, was lowered to 18. 4

Then, thanks in large measure to intense lobbying by Mothers Against Drunk Driving, Congress in 1984 effectively blackmailed states into hiking the minimum drinking age to 21 by passing a law that tied compliance to the distribution of federal-aid highway funds—an amount that will average $690 million per state this year. There is no 5

469

doubt that the law, which achieved full 50-state compliance in 1988, saved lives, but it had the unintended consequence of creating a covert culture around alcohol as the young adult's forbidden fruit.

6   Drinking has been an aspect of college life since the first Western universities in the 14th century. My friends and I drank in college in the 1960s—sometimes a lot but not so much that we had to be hospitalized. Veteran college administrators cite a sea change in campus culture that began, not without coincidence, in the 1990s. It was marked by a shift from beer to hard liquor, consumed not in large social settings, since that is now illegal, but furtively and dangerously in students' residences.

7   In my reporting at colleges around the country, I did not meet any presidents or deans who felt that the 21-year age minimum helps their efforts to curb the abuse of alcohol on their campuses. Quite the opposite. They thought the law impeded their efforts since it takes away the ability to monitor and supervise drinking activity.

8   What would happen if the drinking age was rolled back to 18 or 19? Initially, there would be a surge in binge drinking as young adults savored their newfound freedom. But over time, I predict, U.S. college students would settle into the saner approach to alcohol I saw on the one campus I visited where the legal drinking age is 18: Montreal's McGill University, which enrolls about 2,000 American undergraduates a year. Many, when they first arrive, go over board, exploiting their ability to drink legally. But by midterms, when McGill's demanding academic standards must be met, the vast majority have put drinking into its practical place among their priorities.

9   A culture like that is achievable at U.S. colleges if Congress can muster the fortitude to reverse a bad policy. If lawmakers want to reduce drunk driving, they should do what the Norwegians do: throw the book at offenders no matter what their age. Meanwhile, we should let the pregamers come out of their dorm rooms so that they can learn to handle alcohol like the adults we hope and expect them to be.

Summary of "How Bingeing Became the New College Sport"

[1]In "How Bingeing Became the New College Sport," Barrett Seaman argues that lowering the legal drinking age to 18 or 19 will reduce the amount of binge drinking that occurs on college campuses. [2]The author notes that currently 18-, 19-, and 20-year-old college students who are not old enough to drink legally engage in a practice called [3]"pregaming," which [3]"involves sitting in a dorm room or an off-campus apartment and drinking as much hard liquor as possible before heading out for the evening's parties."

[4]Seaman, who researched college drinking for his book *Binge,* says that students are being hospitalized for alcohol poisoning because of their drinking habits. Some students even die. He goes on to say that colleges tend to respond by trying to enforce the legal drinking age law by making their campuses dry or by eliminating fraternity houses. However, Seaman maintains that this approach is [3]"part of the problem."

[5]Seaman gives the history of the drinking age. He says that after the late 1960s, the legal drinking age was lowered from 21 to 18, but in 1984 Congress tied federal highway funds to a 21-year-old drinking age. As a consequence, students began switching from beer drunk in public to hard liquor drunk secretly in dorms and apartments. The college presidents and deans that the author spoke to believe that the higher drinking age is part of the problem because it inhibits their [6]"ability to monitor and supervise drinking activity." If the drinking age were 18 or 19, Seaman believes that an initial increase in binge drinking would be followed by a [6]"saner approach to alcohol."

[1]The opening sentence includes the author, title, thesis, and present tense verb, *argues.*

[2]"The author" is used as transition. Note the present tense verb and restatement of the first important idea.

[3]Quotation marks appear around the author's exact words.

[4]The author's name and "he goes on to say" are used for transition; note the present tense and restatement of important ideas.

[5]This paragraph combines Seaman's points about the history of the drinking age with points about the solution to the problem. Notice the use of the author's name for transition and the present tense verbs.

[6]The quotation marks are used because the phrase is the author's distinctive style.

Summarize paragraphs 6 and 7 of "Words That Wound" on page 443. Be sure to use the checklist on page 468 to guide your work.

WRITING ESSAY EXAMINATION ANSWERS

Essay examinations require you to write answers that are paragraph length or longer. Because these examinations are an important part of college, you should learn to deal with them effectively.

How to Take an Essay Examination

Remembering information is not enough when you are taking an essay examination. You must also present that information in a clear, well-written answer. The following steps can help you.

Step 1   Read the directions before doing anything. The directions may tell you how many questions to answer and how long your answers should be, like this:

> Answer three of the five questions. Each of your answers should be at least a page.

Step 2   Read all the questions before you begin. Part of your brain can work on question 2 while you are answering question 1. Also, you may find clues to answers for later questions while you are working through the exam.

Step 3   Decide how to budget your time. If you must answer four questions in 60 minutes, then you know you can devote 15 minutes to each answer. However, pay attention to how many points each question is worth. If you must answer three questions in 60 minutes and one question is worth 50 points and the other two are worth 25 points, you should spend 30 minutes on the 50-point question and 15 minutes on each 25-point question.

Step 4   Check the question for direction words. Words like these direct the form your answer should take:

> **analyze**—Break something down into its parts and discuss each part.
>
> *Example:* Analyze the impact of U.S. isolationism after World War I.
>
> **classify**—Group things according to their characteristics.
>
> *Example:* Classify the most frequently occurring defense mechanisms.
>
> **compare**—Technically, this means "show the similarities," but often *compare* is used to mean "show the similarities *and* differences."
>
> *Example:* Compare the symbolism in the poetry of Maxine Kumin and Margaret Atwood.
>
> **contrast**—Show the differences.
>
> *Example:* Contrast the foreign policies of Presidents George W. Bush and Bill Clinton.
>
> **define**—Give the meaning of a term and include some information (often examples) to show you understand it.

Example: Define manifest destiny.

describe—Give the significant features or tell how something works.

Example: Describe how plants convert carbon dioxide into oxygen.

discuss—Mention all the important points about a topic.

Example: Discuss the reasons for the creation of the League of Nations.

evaluate—Give your view about the worth of something, being sure to support your opinions with detail.

Example: Evaluate proficiency testing as a way to ensure that students learn basic skills.

explain—Give the reasons for an occurrence.

Example: Explain the main causes of the Great Depression.

illustrate—Provide examples.

Example: Illustrate the use of intermittent positive reinforcement to control behavior.

show—Explain or demonstrate something.

Example: Show how hypnosis can improve the quality of daily life.

summarize—Briefly give the major points.

Example: Summarize Jackson's reasons for opposing the Bank of the United States.

support—Give reasons in favor of something.

Example: Support the plan to institute twelve-month school years in grades kindergarten through twelve.

Step 5   Plan your answer. Jot down the points you will cover (on the back of or in the margin of your test sheet), and then number the points in the order you will write them. This planning will help you write a well-organized answer. Also, if you list your points, you need not worry about forgetting something you intended to say. Organize simply— do not write introductions or conclusions; just give the information needed in the answer.

Step 6   Begin your answer with a sentence that reflects the question. For example, if the question is "Contrast the psychoanalytic views of Freud and Jung," you could begin with something like this: "The psychoanalytic views of Freud and Jung differ in several important ways."

Step 7   Revise and edit quickly. Pay special attention to clarity and completeness, but also look for serious mistakes in grammar and usage. Make changes directly on the original—you do not have time to recopy.

Test-Taking Strategies

The most important test-taking strategy is studying beforehand. When you sit down to take your test, the following strategies can be helpful.

- If you do not understand the directions or a question, ask your instructor for clarification. You may not get help, but there is no harm in trying.

- Wear a watch to keep track of the time and know when to move on to the next question.

- Leave generous margins and write on every other line so you have space in case you must add something when you revise.

- Skip the questions you are unsure about and return to them after answering the ones you are more confident about. In the course of answering other questions, you may think of the answers to a question you skipped.

- If you do not know an answer, guess. You may get partial credit.

- Do not write more than you are asked for. You will not get extra credit, and you are taking time away from answers that *will* give you credit.

- Never pad your answers with unrelated information to hide that you do not know the information requested. Your instructor will recognize the padding.

FAQ
Q: What if I run out of time before I've answered all the questions?

A: List the points you would include if you had more time. Although the answer is not in essay form, you may get partial credit.

Two Answers to Study

To understand the traits of an effective essay examination answer, study the two answers that follow. They were written in response to this question:

> Explain and illustrate the way language affects perception.

The first answer is acceptable, but the second is not. Study the marginal notes that call your attention to the traits of each answer.

acceptable answer:

> Language affects perception because it determines what we know about the world and how we think. By emphasizing certain aspects of reality, language calls them to our attention; by deemphasizing other aspects, it causes us not to notice them. Thus, language structures our perception. For example, the Hopi Indians focus on the validity of information more than when actions occur, but English speakers are more interested in time than validity. This distinction is partly a result of the fact that Hopi verb conjugations indicate whether information is being reported directly, whether it is a belief, or whether it is a generalization. English verb conjugations, however, communicate when an event occurs.

The answer opens with words that reflect the question. Every sentence contributes accurate information to the answer. There is no padding and no unrelated information. Transitions help the answer flow well. There is no introduction or conclusion.

unacceptable answer:

> [1]No one will deny that language is very important in many areas. [2]Language is so important that linguistics is a vital area of scholarship. [3]One thing that we know is that language is very important to perception. [4]In fact, it affects perception dramatically in many ways. [5]Most important is the fact that language affects our view of reality. [6]This can be seen by the way Hopi Indians conjugate verbs to show that validity is important. [7]For us, tense is important because our reality is related to time. [8]Everyone should understand that the perception of reality is based upon language. [9]We should, therefore, appreciate language far more than we do. [10]I know that I plan to take as many linguistics courses as I can, which should also help me learn more about reality.

The first two sentences stall. They contribute nothing, and they do not reflect the question. The third and fourth sentences begin to acknowledge the question, but they are wordy. Sentence 5 addresses the question directly, but it is the only one that does, so the answer is incomplete. Sentences 6 and 7 relate to the question, but they are unclear. The next sentence is repetitious, and the last two are padding.

Practice 27.2

Answering the following essay questions will give you valuable practice and help you become more skilled.

1. Based on "Thirsty? Try the Tap" (pages 462–463). Why does Andrew Brunhart believe that tap water is better than bottled water? Do you think states should place an extra tax on bottled water to discourage people from buying it? Why or why not?

2. Based on "How Bingeing Became the New College Sport" (pages 469–470). Barrett Seaman makes a recommendation for solving the problem of binge drinking on campus. What is that recommendation and why does he think it will work? Do you agree with him? Explain why or why not.

3. Based on "Students in Shock" (pages 433–435). Summarize the causes of shock among college students and what schools are doing to help students deal with that shock. Mention at least one other action schools can take to help students deal with shock.

SUCCEEDING IN COLLEGE

Prepare for Examinations

One way to prepare for an exam is to form a study group with some classmates. Each of you can develop two or three essay questions, and you can answer each other's questions. The person who wrote the question must determine whether all the necessary points were included in each answer.

Another way to prepare is to summarize parts of textbook chapters to be sure you understand the material. You can review your summaries as a study aid.

If you think you need to improve your test-taking skills, visit your campus study skills center to learn helpful strategies.

Write about It

Are you good at taking essay examinations? Explain why or why not.

For more practice with summaries and essay examinations, go to www.mywriting lab.com.

Editing Workshop

The exercises in this appendix will help you practice your editing skills. In the first ten exercises, you will edit to correct one kind of error at a time; in the remaining exercises, you will edit to correct multiple kinds of errors.

EDITING FOR ONE KIND OF ERROR

Practice A.1: Sentence Fragments

Edit to eliminate the fragments.

[1]Many animals got their names in surprising ways. [2]Consider the gorilla, for example. [3]When he was sailing along the west coast of Africa around the fifth or sixth century B.C. [4]A navigator named Hanno reported seeing something rather odd. [5]Later writing about his travels. [6]Hanno reported seeing "a tribe of hairy women." [7]He further reporting that his African guides called these women "gorillai." [8]Centuries later, historians decided that Hanno was observing from a distance, and he really saw gorillas.

[9]More than 2,000 years after Hanno navigated the coast of Africa. [10]American missionary and naturalist T. S. Savage discovered great apes in the wild. [11]Writing of his discovery in a natural history journal, Savage remembered Hanno's reference to the large, hairy women. [12]And called these creatures "gorillas."

Practice A.2: Run-On Sentences and Comma Splices

Edit to eliminate the run-on sentences and comma splices.

[1]If you are a baseball fan, you may have wondered about the origin of the "bullpen," which is the place where relief pitchers warm up. [2]There actually is a game called bull pen perhaps you think the name comes from that. [3]However, the term actually comes from newspaper reporters, they would write that a pitcher whose ball was hit particularly hard was "slaughtered." [4]Eventually, this led to comparing pitchers with bulls and the game with a bullfight. [5]When a pitcher was taken

out of the game and another sent in, the reporters wrote, "Another bull was led to slaughter." [6]In bullfighting, a pen is kept near the arena this pen is called the "bullpen." [7]Thus, the place where relief pitchers warm up and wait to be called into the game was dubbed the bullpen.

Practice A.3: Verb Forms

Find and correct the verb form errors.

[1]Every once in a while, newspapers print "stupid criminal" stories. [2]This one run in the Tallahassee *Democrat*. [3]A police officer in Tallahassee, Florida, been on routine patrol when he heard music blaring from a car parked at a convenience store. [4]He pulled in to tell the driver to turn the volume down. [5]Then he noticed the car be parked in a handicapped space. [6]The officer told the driver to move, but the man said he only need a minute. [7]Of course, before approaching the car, the officer has began a license check, and about this time it came back: The man had stole the car. [8]The police officer arrested the man on charges of grand theft auto, drug possession, and parking in a handicapped spot. [9]Clearly, this man had forgot that he was not a criminal mastermind.

Practice A.4: Subject-Verb Agreement

Cross out the incorrect verbs and write the correct forms above them.

[1]Animals that produce poison uses it for self-defense or to attack prey. [2]The poisons come in different toxicities. [3]Some does not kill. [4]A few of the animals produces just enough poison to stun the enemy long enough to escape. [5]For example, frogs with poisonous skin tastes unpleasant, so the predators release them. [6]One of the South American frogs have poison under the skin. [7]Indian hunters use this poison to tip their arrows. [8]For this reason, this variety of frogs are called "arrow-poison frogs."

[9]Not all poisonous animals are seriously harmful to humans. [10]However, there are a variety of ants that can give people a nasty sting. [11]The North American harvester ants are one of those animals that harms humans. [12]Living in desert regions, they feeds on grass seeds, but if they encounter people, they will bite. [13]Some kinds of scorpion has a sting so powerful that it can kill humans. [14]In addition, box jellies, which lives off the coast of Australia, is the most dangerous jellyfish. [15]Their sting kills a person in less than three minutes. [16]Anyone swimming near these sea creatures are in grave danger. [17]Perhaps the most poisonous of all spiders are the

American black widow. [18]The female of the species is more dangerous than the male. [19]Its bite, which is extremely painful, sometimes causes death. [20]There is also the stonefish, which live in warm seas. [21]It lies hidden on coral reefs. [22]If one of its spines are touched, it gives out a poison that can kill a person in a few hours.

Practice A.5: Pronoun-Antecedent Agreement

Cross out the incorrect pronouns and write the correct forms above them.

[1]We are accustomed to seeing women wearing earrings in their ears, and it's not unusual for a man to pierce one or both of their ears. [2]Both a man and a woman will pierce his or her ears for the same reason: decoration. [3]Pirates, however, wore earrings for a different reason. [4]Believe it or not, some people theorize that a pirate pierced their ears for health reasons.

[5]According to acupuncturists, a person has pressure points just above their earlobe which help to improve eyesight, increase energy, and reduce appetite. [6]Obviously, everybody on a long sea voyage would want his or her eyesight and energy bolstered and appetite suppressed. [7]Some of the pirates also had waxy lumps dangling from the bottom of his earrings. [8]Each of these waxy lumps had their specific purpose—to protect the pirates' hearing. [9]During exchanges of cannon fire, the pirates used the wax as their earplugs.

Practice A.6: Subject, Object, and Possessive Pronouns

Cross out the incorrect pronouns and write the correct forms above them.

[1]I have always been fascinated by the people who developed computers and computer applications. [2]They are capable of considerably more abstract thinking than me. [3]For example, consider something as small as the computer mouse. [4]We computer users may not realize that the computer mouse was invented by Douglas Engelbart, who was a leader of Stanford Research Institute's oNLine System project. [5]Interestingly, other researchers and him thought the mouse would increase the intellect of we humans.

[6]The first mouse was a wooden box with one button. [7]People whom wanted to use it had to tilt it so that one wheel was in the air. [8]Engelbart's rather clunky wooden mouse has evolved over the years to the sleek machine that you and me now use. [9]However, the evolution continues. [10]Researchers have developed prototypes that

are easier for you and me to use. [11]For example, one invention is a glove that allows users to click and move the cursor by waving their hands.

Practice A.7: Modifiers

Eliminate the problems with modifiers.

[1]Because Julius Caesar wrote so extensive, historians know much about the life of a Roman soldier on the march in 60 B.C. [2]A soldier was awakened at dawn by bugles on the march. [3]His breakfast consisted of wheatcake made from grain and wine ground by the soldier himself. [4]He ate the breakfast very fastly and then took down his tent, which he shared with other soldiers. [5]He also took down the camp wall, which was made of the most sharp stakes available.

[6]Marching along in armor, the soldier's possessions were carried for a distance of about twenty-three miles. [7]Around midday, the soldiers stopped and ate their lunch (another wheatcake) very quick. [8]The soldier spent the afternoon building a new camp. [9]To make the camp, soldiers dug into the earth about six feet and piled up the dirt to make a wall inside the trench. [10]They stuck their stakes into the top of the wall and lashed them together good. [11]With the wall made, the soldiers could set up their own tents and eat supper (more wheatcakes and watered-down wine). [12]After eating supper, recreation was allowed. [13]However, it got dark soon after supper, so there was little the soldiers could do except sit around the fire, exchange stories, and play dice. [14]Of course, the men had to take turns standing a four-hour watch as sentries.

Practice A.8: Commas

Add the missing commas, and cross out the ones that do not belong.

[1]Peterborough New Hampshire high school student Colin Rizzio was taking the SAT exam in October, 1997. [2]He noticed something unusual about an algebra problem. [3]He copied the problem down, and showed it to his math teacher the next week. [4]As Rizzio suspected the teacher confirmed that there was a flaw in the problem, and he advised Rizzo to report it to the Educational Testing Service which is the organization that develops and administers the test. [5]Five months later Rizzio found out he was right and history was made. [6]He had found the first defective question on the SAT in fourteen years.

[7]As a result of Rizzio's discovery the scores of more than 45,000 students were increased. [8]Most were increased by ten points but some were increased by twenty or thirty points. [9]Rizzio was interviewed for many newspapers and appeared on *Good Morning America, CBS Morning News* and *Today.* [10] "I'm glad I did it" Rizzo said. [11] "I didn't think it would be this big."

Practice A.9 Semicolons

Add the missing semicolons, and cross out the ones that do not belong. If appropriate, replace incorrect semicolons with commas, and replace incorrect commas with semicolons.

[1]The now extinct mammoth roamed the earth until as recently as 10,000 years ago. [2]The mammoth was 12 feet high, it could weigh as much as 14,450 pounds. [3]Slightly larger than today's elephants, but with far longer tusks—up to 16 feet long—mammoths survived Arctic temperatures thanks to extra fat stores and hairy coats. [4]Although you might guess otherwise because of their size; mammoths were plant-eaters. [5]Their teeth became well-worn from chewing stringy plants; in fact, mammoths' teeth were almost identical to those of today's elephants. [6]Mammoths living farthest north had a more difficult time finding plants to feed on; primarily because of the frozen ground of the Arctic region. [7]Their fat, which was especially thick around the shoulders, was used as an emergency store of food.

[8]Because of the enormous size of the full-grown mammoth; only the most fearless creatures attacked it; and that included saber-toothed tigers and humans. [9]Saber-toothed tigers primarily attacked mammoth young however, humans hunted full-grown mammoths with spears and axes, putting the carcasses to a variety of uses. [10]First they would use the flesh, which was a good food source, then they would use the hide which made excellent clothing, finally they would use the bones and tusks, which were building materials for huts.

Practice A.10: Apostrophes

Correct the sentences by doing the following, as needed: Add an apostrophe, add an apostrophe and an *s,* eliminate incorrect apostrophes, or move incorrectly placed apostrophes.

[1]When the people of Texas severed ties with Mexico, the Mexican government sent in 4,000 troops under General Santa Anas direction. [2]As the Mexican army approached, 150 men who were determined to defend the city of San Antonio

retreated to the Alamo, one of Spains missions built in the previous century. [3]They were joined by fifty other men, but they werent any match for the superior numbers. [4]After a thirteen-day siege, all the Texans died.

[5]When General Sam Houston assembled his forces', he set out to face the Mexican army to secure independence. [6]Houstons' rallying cry—indeed, Texans rallying cry—in the war for independence from Mexico was "Remember the Alamo." [7]The Mexican's defeat at Houston's hands was quick and decisive. [8]Texas gained its independence.

[9]From 1846 to 1848, Mexico and the United States fought a war over the Texas boundary. [10]The war ended with the Senates ratification of the Treaty of Guadalupe Hidalgo, and Mexicos loss of half of it's territory. [11]Thats how New Mexico and California fell within this countrys borders.

EDITING FOR MULTIPLE KINDS OF ERRORS

Practice A.11: Sentence Fragments, Run-On Sentences, and Comma Splices

Edit to eliminate four sentence fragments, one run-on sentence, and two comma splices.

[1]In the 1920s and 1930s, psychologists from Harvard University studied the effects of lighting on worker performance at the Western Electric Hawthorne plant in Cicero, Illinois. [2]Wanting to determine the effects of different lighting. [3]The researchers varied the amount of light in the factory over time. [4]Sometimes they increased it, sometimes they decreased it. [5]The researchers were surprised by the outcome. [6]Productivity improved no matter what they did. [7]Even when the light was lowered to the level of moonlight. [8]Worker productivity did not decline. [9]As it turned out, the researcher realized that an interesting phenomenon was occurring. [10]Workers knew they were being observed therefore, they wanted to impress the researchers. [11]This phenomenon came to be called the "Hawthorne Effect." [12]The Hawthorne Effect being something researchers now try to guard against. [13]If participants figure out what researchers are looking for. [14]They may try to behave accordingly. [15]One way to minimize the Hawthorne Effect is for researchers to conceal themselves, that way, participants do not know they are being watched. [16]Many researchers conceal themselves by using one-way mirrors. [17]However, researchers cannot always prevent the Hawthorne Effect.

Practice A.12: Subject-Verb Agreement, Tense Shifts, and Verb Forms

The following paragraph has six subject-verb agreement errors, four tense shifts, and one incorrect verb form. Cross out the incorrect verbs and write the correct ones above the line.

[1]Either elaborate rituals or simple copulation mark the courtship of spiders. [2]Some crab spiders, for example, showed almost no courtship behaviors other than actual copulation. [3]Others wrap the female in silk threads. [4]The threads does not immobilize the female but communicate the intentions of the male. [5]Then there is wolf spiders. [6]When a female wolf spider passes a male, the male begins a series of exhausting courtship behaviors. [7]These included crouching, foreleg extension and waving, drumming, and abdominal vibrations. [8]Similarly, jumping male spiders used visual signals to communicate with females. [9]Although some lifts a leg or two, others perform a complex dance to attract the female. [10]If one of the females are receptive, she assumes a crouching posture. [11]The male then extends his forelegs, touches the female, and climbs on her back to begin copulation. [12]Because the webs of a spider is used for prey capture, it is essential that males who are courting web spinners vibrate the female's web in a way that is distinct from the vibrations of a trapped insect. [13]One group of male spiders approaches the female only after she has eaten and thus is unlikely to gobble up a suitor. [14]Despite his best efforts, however, the male spider often be in big trouble. [15]In certain species, the females, which are commonly larger than the males, kill and eat the male after mating. [16]Although this fate is not always what occurred, most males live only long enough to mate once or twice before they die.

Practice A.13: Subject-Verb Agreement and Pronoun-Antecedent Agreement

The following paragraph has six errors with subject-verb agreement and four errors with pronoun-antecedent agreement. Cross out the incorrect verbs and pronouns and write the correct forms above them.

[1]Sand tiger sharks has the five senses that humans has—with some interesting twists. [2]A sand tiger shark senses the slightest odors underwater. [3]In one experiment, they could smell a drop of fish extract diluted a million times. [4]As for touch and taste, each of the sand sharks have a particularly interesting mechanism. [5]Jelly-filled sensory pores in a long pointed snout are linked to nerves that let the shark detect even weak electrical signals produced by a fish's movements. [6]That is why members of the shark family is able to pinpoint a stingray buried in the sand and

make a meal of them. [7]The eyes, ears, and teeth of a sand tiger shark are equally amazing. [8]Sharks have panoramic vision, so they see very wide views of their world. [9]The back of each of their eyes have their own set of cells to act like a mirror and increase the light, giving sharks night vision. [10]The hearing of sharks is so good that they can detect the splashing of a wounded fish a mile away. [11]Additionally, the teeth of a shark are always growing. [12]A row of new teeth move forward to replace rows of broken teeth in less than two days. [13]Clearly, anyone who encounters a shark better watch themselves.

Practice A.14: Tense Shift and Person Shift

The following paragraph has four inappropriate tense shifts and four person shifts. Cross out the incorrect verbs and pronouns and write the corrections above the line.

[1]The productivity of the land of medieval Europe was limited by inadequate technology. [2]The farmers of this land were so poorly equipped that you cannot efficiently cultivate and harvest your crops. [3]Almost all agricultural tools were made of wood, a weak and impractical material for use on the thick European soil. [4]These tools were so limiting that much work is invariably accomplished with bare hands, a technique that caused the soil to lose fertility. [5]As a result, you have to rest large portions of land for entire growing seasons, a fact that decreased the output of your farm. [6]The lack of technology and equipment allowed the unpredictable weather to wreak havoc on farm productivity. [7]Without advanced drainage systems, fields are flooded during an excessively wet season. [8]Similarly, without irrigation technology, fields were dried up by droughts. [9]Because of the lack of advanced technology, medieval Europe often suffered severe food shortages.

Practice A.15: Forms of Adjectives, Adverbs, and Dangling Modifiers

The following paragraph contains seven errors with forms of adjectives and adverbs, and two with dangling modifiers. Cross out the errors and make corrections above them.

[1]Some people are just natural funny. [2]They manage to find humor in even the most commonest situations. [3]My friend Peggy, for example, is one of the most funniest people I know. [4]In fact, she has been funny for as long as I have known her good. [5]I remember all the way back to junior high school when Peggy got up to sharpen her pencil. [6]Wearing her pencil down in math class, the pencil sharpener located in the closet on the wall was needed. [7]Peggy walked to the closet, and some perverse impulse must have taken over because she entered the closet, closed the

door behind her, and stayed there for the rest of class. [8]Wondering if she was missed, the door was cracked from time to time and she peeked out. [9]No one, apparently, noticed but me. [10]It was all I could do to keep from falling on the floor laughing hysterical. [11]When the bell sounded, Peggy just walked out of the closet casual and headed for her next class, sharpened pencil in hand. [12]Of all of the stunts Peggy has pulled, that is one of the memorablest.

Practice A.16: Range of Errors

The following paragraph contains:

1 incorrect verb form	1 run-on sentence
2 errors in subject-verb agreement	1 comma splice
1 error in pronoun-antecedent agreement	4 comma errors
1 sentence fragment	1 dangling modifier
2 errors in parallelism	2 errors in capitalization

Edit directly on the page to correct the errors. In some cases, more than one correction is possible.

[1]Thunderstorms be most likely to happen in the spring and summer months and during the afternoon and evening hours, however, they can occur year-round and at all hours. [2]Along the gulf coast and across the southeastern and western United States, most thunderstorms occuring during the afternoon. [3]In the Plains states, thunderstorms frequently occurs in the late afternoon and at night. [4]Occasionally thunder and lightning accompanies snow or freezing rain. [5]For example lightning resulted in power outages near Washington D.C. during the blizzard of 1993. [6]A person should never take a thunderstorm lightly, for they are at risk from lightning, flooding, and tornadoes can pose a threat. [7]People who are outdoors, in or on water, and people on or near hilltops are at risk from lightning associated with thunderstorms. [8]During heavy thunderstorms, people in cars are at risk from flash flooding also people in mobile homes are at risk from tornadoes. [9]When learning of an approaching thunderstorm, reasonable caution should be exercised.

Practice A.17: Range of Errors

The following passage contains:

1 spelling error	1 unstated antecedent
1 semicolon error	1 frequently confused word

4 comma errors

3 errors with apostrophes

1 tense shift

1 incorrect noun form

1 sentence fragment

1 incorrect modifier form

1 comma splice

5 errors in capitalization

Editing directly on the page, correct the errors. In some cases, more than one correction is possible.

[1]Susan B. Anthony who was born in 1820 and died in 1906 was an american pioneer of womens rights. [2]The daughter of a quaker abolitionist she became a teacher after being educated in New York. [3]Disatisfaction with it caused her to except the position of assistant manager of the family farm in upstate New York. [4]Here she being exposed to the strong held views of such men as William Lloyd Garrison and Frederick Douglass. [5]As a result, she becomes an advocate of reform. [6]Her early efforts in this area failed, she was not taken seriously because she was a women. [7]Eventually, she teamed up with Elizabeth Cady Stanton and together they founded the American equal rights association to work for womens' suffrage. [8]For the remainder of her life; she was devoted to this cause. [9]As a result of her tireless work and ceaseless travel, womens' suffrage became a recognized cause in both America and Europe.

Answers to Pretests

PAGE 193—IDENTIFYING SUBJECTS AND VERBS

Subjects	*Verbs*
1. mother	packed
2. Tuition	is
3. Marcos	has eaten
4. Mother	returned, studied
5. people	do know
6. Joan, her brothers	bought
7. carton	is
8. Jacques	has been studying
9. keys	are
10. excuse	will be
11. (you)	answer
12. holidays; all of us	are; can relax, recover
13. students	are making
14. accidents	can be
15. my parents, I	will move, buy

PAGE 210—USING COORDINATION AND SUBORDINATION

1. S	5. S	9. C
2. C	6. S	10. C
3. S	7. C	
4. C	8. C	

PAGE 237—AVOIDING SENTENCE FRAGMENTS

1. F	5. F	9. F
2. F	6. F	10. F
3. F	7. F	
4. S	8. S	

PAGE 251—AVOIDING RUN-ON SENTENCES AND COMMA SPLICES

1. CS	5. RO	9. RO
2. RO	6. CS	10. C
3. RO	7. C	
4. C	8. C	

PAGE 261—WRITING SENTENCES WITH VARIETY AND PARALLELISM

1. a. no

   b. yes

   c. yes

   d. no

2. a. Better sentence: The twins are energetic, talented, and personable.

   b. Better sentence: Cal's blood test showed that both his cholesterol and triglyceride levels were high.

   c. Better sentence: The new house is not only beautiful but energy efficient.

   d. Better sentence: Either Hank will spend his savings on a trip to Europe, or he will use the money to buy a car.

PAGE 280—CHOOSING WORDS CAREFULLY

1. b	4. b
2. b	5. a
3. a	

PAGE 295—USING VERBS CORRECTLY

A. 1. C	5. I	9. C
2. I	6. I	10. I
3. C	7. C	
4. I	8. I	

B. 1. means	5. practices	9. work
2. visits	6. decides	10. sleeps
3. plan	7. are	
4. likes	8. wants	

C. 1. C	3. TS	5. C
2. C	4. TS	

PAGE 327—USING PRONOUNS CORRECTLY

1. I	5. their	9. me
2. they	6. its	10. its
3. me	7. its	
4. her	8. whom	

PAGE 353—USING MODIFIERS CORRECTLY

1. no	5. no	9. yes
2. yes	6. no	10. no
3. no	7. yes	
4. yes	8. no	

PAGE 367—USING CAPITAL LETTERS AND PUNCTUATION CORRECTLY

A.
1. no	3. yes	5. no
2. no	4. yes	

B.
6. .	8. .	10. .
7. !	9. ?	

C.
11. no	15. no	19. no
12. no	16. no	20. no
13. yes	17. yes	
14. yes	18. no	

D.
21. yes	23. yes	25. no
22. no	24. yes	

E.
26. yes	28. yes	30. yes
27. no	29. yes	

F.
31. no	34. yes	37. yes
32. yes	35. yes	38. yes
33. no	36. yes	

PAGE 401—ELIMINATING PROBLEMS WITH FREQUENTLY CONFUSED WORDS AND SPELLING

1. no	5. yes	9. no
2. no	6. no	10. yes
3. yes	7. yes	
4. yes	8. no	

Credits

TEXT CREDITS

Courtland L. Bovée and John V. Thill, *Business in Action,* 4th ed. Copyright © 2008. Reproduced by permission of Pearson Education, Inc.

Jennifer Block Bradner, "Supermodel?" Copyright © 2001.

Andew D. Brunhart, "Thirsty? Try the Tap." From *The Washington Post,* October 14, 2007, Copyright © 2007 The Washington Post. All rights reserved. Used by permission.

Neil A. Campbell, Jane Reece, Martha Taylor, Eric Simon, and Jean Dickey, *Biology: Concepts and Connections* 6th ed. Copyright © 2009. Reproduced by permission of Pearson Education, Inc.

George C. Edwards III, Martin P. Wattenberg, and Robert L. Lineberry, *Government in America: People, Politics and Policy,* brief 9th ed. Copyright © 2008. Reproduced by permission of Pearson Education, Inc.

Patsy Garlan, "A Link to the Living." Copyright © 2000, as first published in *The Atlantic Monthly*.

Joey Green, "Beauty and the Beef" from *Spy* magazine, 1996. Reprinted by permission of the author.

Lori Hope, "Did I Save Lives or Engage in Racial Profiling?" from *Newsweek,* April 1, 2003. All Rights Reserved. Reprinted by permission.

Jacqueline Jones, Peter H. Wood, Thomas Borstelmann, Elaine Tyler May, and Vicki L. Ruiz, *Created Equal: A History of the United States,* Volume 2, 3rd ed. Copyright © 2009. Reproduced by permission of Pearson Education, Inc.

John Kellmayer, "Students in Shock." Reprinted with permission of Townsend Press.

Michael Kimmel and Amy Aronson, *Sociology Now*. Copyright © 2009. Reproduced by permission of Pearson Education, Inc.

Andrew Lam, "They Shut My Grandmother's Room Door." Copyright © by Andrew Lam. Andrew Lam is the author of "Perfume Dreams: Reflections on the Vietnamese Diaspora."

Judy Mandell, "Sometimes Honesty Is the Worst Policy." From *Newsweek,* October 21, 2002, © 2002 Newsweek, Inc. All rights reserved. Used by permission.

Frank Schmalleger, *Criminal Justice: A Brief Introduction,* 7th ed. Copyright © 2008. Reproduced by permission of Pearson Education, Inc.

Barrett Seaman, "How Bingeing Became the New College Sport" Copyright © 2001 TIME Inc. Reprinted by permission.

Janice Thompson and Melinda Manore, *Nutrition: An Applied Approach* 2e. Copyright © 2009. Reproduced by permission of Pearson Education, Inc.

Kathleen Vail, "Words That Wound." Reprinted with permission from *American School Board Journal,* September 1999. Copyright © 1999 National School Boards Association. All rights reserved.

Marion Winik, "What Are Friends For?" from *Telling*. Copyright © 1994 by Marion Winik. Used by permission of Villard Books, a division of Random House, Inc.

Richard T. Wright, *Environmental Science,* 10th ed. Copyright © 2008. Reproduced by permission of Pearson Education, Inc.

PHOTO CREDITS

20: Shoe-New Business MacNelly. Distributed by King Features Syndicate; 35: © Corbis; 61: B. Bird/zefa/Corbis RF; 70: Creatas/Jupiter Images; 78: Blasius Erlinger/zefa/Corbis; 88: The Advertising Archive; 97: Scott Lilienfeld et al., *Psychology: From Inquiry to Understanding,* ©2009, figure 3.17; 105: 4-17-04 ©2004 DILBERT: ©Scott Adams/Dist. by United Features Syndicate, Inc., www.dilbert.com scottadams@aol.com; 116: ©2008 Dave Coverly; 127: Carlos Osorio/AP Images; 139: Rusty Kennedy/AP Images; 151: Philip Morris Company; 173: Photonica/Getty Images; 192: Photodisc/Photolibrary.